SEGREGATING
SOUND

REFIGURING
AMERICAN MUSIC   A series edited by Ronald Radano and Josh Kun
Charles McGovern, contributing editor

Inventing Folk and Pop Music

in the Age of Jim Crow

SEGREGATING
SOUND

KARL HAGSTROM MILLER

Duke University Press

Durham and London

2010

© 2010 Duke University Press

All rights reserved

Printed in the United States of America on
acid-free paper ∞

Designed by Heather Hensley

Typeset in Minion Pro by Keystone Typesetting, Inc.

Library of Congress Cataloging-in-Publication
Data appear on the last printed page of this book.

Chapter 5 is reproduced with permission of
Palgrave Macmillan. It was originally published
as "Talking Machine World: Selling the Local in
the Global Music Industry, 1900–1920," in A. G.
Hopkins, ed., *The Universal and the Local in Global
History* (Hampshire: Palgrave, 2006), 160–90.

CONTENTS

ACKNOWLEDGMENTS

This book grew out of my doctoral dissertation but the seeds of the work began to germinate long before I entered the graduate school classroom. Growing up, I imagined myself as a working guitarist. Much that I know about music and money, I absorbed from hanging out with those that were making my dream their reality. I thank them for their patience, wit, and excitement: from Dow Daggett, my childhood guitar teacher in San Antonio, whose fleet-fingered lessons veered between the Carter Family and the Jazz Messengers to the pianist who deadpanned, "Son, you want to be a professional musician? Don't play for free." My parents gave me constant encouragement to follow my interests in music and history (even when they heard me play). Without their love and example I never could have begun this project, let alone finish it. I also thank the late Oliver Williams, Mike Weatherly, and everyone in the Lafayette Inspiration Ensemble. At a crucial point of grad school despair they took me in and reminded me of the power and beauty of song.

Many scholars and friends lent a hand as I worked on this project. I thank them all for their criticism and encouragement. Robin Kelley and Daniel Walkowitz wrestled over early drafts and helped push the dissertation toward its final form. Ellen Noonan graciously read multiple drafts of every chapter and never failed to tell me they were good despite her list of incisive criticisms. I thank her and John Spencer for their friendship and fellowship from day one. I also thank David Suisman for the endless talk about history and music. Others critiqued portions of the dissertation or helped me work out particular problems while lingering over coffee. The work is better for the efforts of Thomas Bender and the staff and fellows at the International Center for Advanced Studies, Tricia Rose, Walter Johnson, Liz Cohen, Pete Daniel, Lawrence Levine, Judith Jackson Fossett, David Nasaw, John Troutman, Norman Kelley, Hal Barton, Molly Mitchell, David Voorhees, Martin Miller, and Sonja Miller.

Crucial financial support was provided by New York University, the University of Texas, the Smithsonian Institution, the International Center for Advanced Studies at NYU, the Humanities Institute at the University of Texas, and several Fortune 500 companies whose managers didn't notice their temp was spending most of his time reading Stuart Hall. Seth Kaufman and the folks at barnesandnoble.com actually paid me money while teaching me how to write, and Tom Wilcox, friend, muse, and evolutionary biologist, came through in the final stretch. Thanks for having faith in a historian's skills as a lab tech and extending my conception of the longue durée.

My friends and colleagues at the University of Texas have been very supportive. I could not have finished the book without their help, encouragement, and criticism. David Oshinsky and Michael Stoff have provided advice and encouragement throughout my time here. Many others have offered helpful comments on all or portions of the manuscript, including Julia Mickenberg, Shirley Thompson, Dan Birkholtz, Cole Hutchinson, Tracie Matysik, Erika Bsumek, Robin Moore, Jim Sidbury, Carolyn Eastman and the Wednesday night crew—it's hard to complain about the quality of free pizza. I especially thank Evan Carton and the participants in the Humanities Institute Faculty Fellowship Program, as well as Tony Hopkins and the contributors to the history and globalization workshops that culminated with the publication of *The Universal and the Local in Global History*. They provided the intense, smart, and loving intellectual communities that I imagined joining back when I was filling out grad school applications. I also have to give it up to Howard Miller and Alan Tully, supporters from day one, who by their examples have taught me more about teaching politics and the politics of teaching than I ever imagined possible.

My deep thanks go to Emily and Norm Rosenberg, the dyamic duo whose dazzling lectures transformed me into an undergrad history major, for pitching Duke University Press and introducing me to my editor Valerie Millholland. Valerie and the team at Duke have improved the book each step of the way. Thanks go to Valerie, Miriam Angress, Ken Wissoker, Neal

McTighe, Amanda Sharp, Lynn Walterick, the outside readers, and everyone else who lent a hand.

A special nod goes to Ronald Radano and Charlie McGovern. Friends and inspirations long before they began work on this series, their support and informed critiques delivered in myriad conversations helped make the book better—and much more fun to write.

Finally, Amy Hagstrom Miller provided more encouragement, inspiration, criticism, and financial help than everyone else combined. I thank her for her love and her life. This book is for Amy and our beautiful boys Lucas and Henry.

INTRODUCTION

Ralph Peer shook his head. A scout for the Victor Talking Machine Company in the 1920s, he could not believe the number of white southern singers who dug commercial popular music. "They would come in to me, people that could play a guitar very well and sing very well, and I'd test them. 'What other music have you got?' Well, they'd sing some song that was popular on record, some pop song," he recalled. "So I never bothered with them. They never got a chance."[1]

Dorothy Scarborough shared Peer's impatience. After collecting African American folk songs throughout the South in the early 1920s, the white scholar lamented, "How often have I been tricked into enthusiasm over the promise of folk-songs only to hear age-worn phonograph records,—but perhaps so changed and worked upon by usage that they could possibly claim to be folk-songs after all!—or Broadway echoes, or conventional songs by white authors!"[2]

The black Mississippi guitarist Robert Johnson knew lots of songs by white authors. He played them whenever he could. "Robert didn't just perform his own songs," his friend Johnny Shines insisted. "He did anything that he heard over the radio. ANYTHING that he heard. When I say anything, I mean ANYTHING—popular songs, ballads, blues, anything. It didn't make him no difference what it was. If he liked it, he did it."[3]

Southern musicians performed a staggering variety of music in the early twentieth century. Black and white artists played blues, ballads, ragtime, and string band music, as well as the plethora of styles popular throughout the nation: sentimental ballads, minstrel songs, Tin Pan Alley tunes, and Broadway hits. They embraced pop music. Many performed any music they could, regardless of their racial or regional identities. Such variety could appear in the same set as a performer eased from one song to the next. Observers agreed that rural southerners loved all sorts of music. Yet they fought about whether that was a good thing. Scarborough and Peer were not pleased to discover Broadway in the back-woods. A southerner singing pop music was the last thing they wanted to hear.

This book explores the transformation in the meaning and symbolic power of southern music between the 1880s and the 1920s. Through a process I call segregating sound, a variety of people—scholars and artists, industrial-ists and consumers—came to compartmentalize southern music according to race. A fluid complex of sounds and styles in practice, southern music was reduced to a series of distinct genres associated with particular racial and ethnic identities. Music developed a color line. The blues were African American. Rural white southerners played what came to be called country music. And much of the rest of the music performed and heard in the region was left out. By the 1920s, these depictions were touted in folk song collec-tions as well as the catalogues of "race" and "hillbilly" records promoted by the phonograph industry. Such simple links among race, region, and music were new. They did not reflect how generations of southern people had understood and enjoyed music. Johnny Shines emphasized Robert Johnson's broad repertoire in a repetitive cadence designed to overcome doubters. His apparent need to be emphatic suggests how thoroughly the logic of segre-gated sound had become common sense—even while most observers ac-knowledged that it failed to reflect the music actually played and heard by southern people.

Three innovations of the late nineteenth century form the basis of my story. Southern states began passing segregation legislation in the 1880s, limiting black access to public spaces and the electoral ballot. In 1896, the Supreme Court endorsed southern segregation, ruling in *Plessy v. Ferguson* that "separate but equal" facilities for the races were constitutional. Southern states passed a flood of new segregation laws following the ruling as white southerners enforced Jim Crow through violence, intimidation, and lynch-ing. White residents constructed a massive legal and extralegal regime that denied black citizenship and humanity while writing white fantasies of black inferiority and isolation across the southern landscape.[4] Second, the Ameri-can Folklore Society formed in 1888 out of a strategic alliance between anthropologists and literary studies scholars interested in promoting folklore as a legitimate field within the modernizing university. Folklorists provided authoritative new ways to talk about racial and cultural authenticity. In an age when social standing, cultural continuity, and economic stability were up for grabs, folklore offered a portrait of fixed and distinguishable racial cultures deeply rooted in history. Finally, two revolutions in the commercial music industry transformed how people made and heard music. In the 1880s and 1890s, New York sheet music publishers perfected the mass-production of popular songs and their distribution throughout the nation. In the same era, the talking machine, invented by Thomas Edison in 1877, changed the way people conceived sound. The metaphysical marvel separated the voice from the body and enabled music to travel independently of musicians. It came to dominate the music industry by the early twentieth century.

Academic folklore and the music industry are rarely discussed in histories of segregation, yet they helped to orchestrate a sonic demarcation that corresponded to the corporeal distinctions emerging under Jim Crow.[5] Both institutions became enamored with the South and developed their own definitions of southern music. Folklorists identified southern music as a compendium of distinct and ancient traditions, the collection of which could help explain the long histories of race, literature, and civilization. The music industry viewed the South dually as a land of potential consumers and an object of northern fantasy—the exotic, pastoral region depicted in countless popular songs. Neither of these interpretations made room for the perspective of southern musicians, who often identified everything they heard as southern music. Hymns, ballads, minstrel numbers, blues, fiddle tunes, and songs from New York touring shows: they were all sounds of the southern experience. They could all be used to convince local listeners to part with their money. These incompatible interpretations of southern music repeatedly collided as these groups came into increasing contact between the 1880s and the 1920s.

Two conclusions that began to coalesce out of these encounters formed the basis of the musical color line. The first was that commercial popular music was foreign to southern culture. Pop music was an import and an imposition, not a critical component of southern experience or identity. Dorothy Scarborough and Ralph Peer lamented hearing popular songs precisely because they were trying to collect distinctive southern music. Broadway hits did not count. Southern music thus came to be understood as a subset of the music performed and enjoyed by southerners. Mass-produced pop constituted a huge body of music embraced by black and white residents alike. Its exclusion from portrayals of southern culture exaggerated both regional and racial differences.

The second conclusion determined that there existed a firm correlation between racialized music and racialized bodies: black people performed black music and white people performed white music. Never complete or uncontested, this conclusion took far longer to coalesce than the first. It nevertheless marked a transformation in conceptions of both southern and American popular music. At the beginning of my story black and white performers regularly *employed* racialized sounds. By the end, most listeners expected artists to *embody* them. This change closed off significant swaths of music to both black and white performers. When black Mississippi Delta audiences derided the African American musician Tom Dumas for playing "white folks' music," for example, his sense of betrayal caused him to put away his violin for good. "This fiddle is been in the family for four generations. My daddy's granddaddy had it," he later said in his own defense.[6] At the same time, the new correlation between sound and race represented a triumph for African American artists intent on challenging blackface minstrelsy, the nineteenth-century juggernaut founded on the premise that white artists could perform black music—that racialized sounds were not restricted to racialized bodies.

Minstrelsy emerged in the 1830s out of northern working-class immigrant theaters to become the most popular and profitable form of entertainment in the country by the mid-nineteenth century. It involved the performance of supposedly African American song and dance by white actors under blackface masks of burnt cork. From the common use of dialect or malapropisms to represent black speech to the ubiquitous exaggerations of black physical deviation from white norms (often sliding into comparisons with the animal kingdom), minstrelsy traded on images of African American difference and inferiority. Minstrel shows depicted southern slaves happy in their bondage and free African Americans unfit for citizenship. Just as often as they imagined Zip Coon failing in his sartorial or linguistic appropriations of white urban culture, minstrels rendered former slaves—always migrating but rarely arriving—sadly longing for the safety, security, and interracial harmony of the old plantation. Minstrelsy did all this within the irreducible context of the blackface mask—a prop that performed racial distance under the auspice of racial passing.[7]

Minstrelsy was a primary medium through which nineteenth-century Americans came to understand musical authenticity. From the start, white minstrels claimed an almost ethnographic authority in their portrayals of black characters. Performers touted themselves "students of the negro" and assured audiences that they were enjoying authentic renditions of black song.[8] The pitch worked. Many early minstrel audiences made little distinction between blackface and black music.[9] Minstrelsy taught some white Americans all they knew about black culture. Prior to its ascendance, many associated black soundings not with music but with noise. They could not grasp what they heard. Minstrelsy identified its music as something originally possessed by black people. It provided a rhetorical framework that enabled white Americans literally to hear black music for the first time, a way to identify "negro melodies" as a comprehendible category even as it presented demeaning caricatures as the real thing.[10]

Minstrelsy taught that authenticity was performative. Genuine black music emerged from white bodies. The thin veneer of burnt cork announced that truth claims were inextricably bound with deceptions, authority with masquerade. This is not to deny minstrelsy's dire political power. It is to suggest that audiences had to play along. Minstrel authenticity was not rooted in history, heritage, or collective memory. It was founded on consensus. Like visitors to P. T. Barnum's museum, minstrel fans decided to embrace the blackface humbug. It was real to the extent that those present were willing to call it so. The fact that minstrel audiences chose to spend hard-won free time fantasizing about black inferiority and black expressivity can tell us a great deal about their desires. It can also teach an important lesson about a conception of authentic music that, I will argue, reached far beyond the minstrel stage. The performative authenticity born from blackface informed depictions and interpretations of a variety of "genuine" music well into the twentieth century.

The musical color line emerged as the new notions of authenticity developing in folklore studies collided with the one that had long been proffered by minstrelsy. Folkloric authenticity maintained that truthful music came from outside the marketplace. Music primarily was a form of expression, not only of individual feelings or collective culture but also of essential racial characteristics, capacities, and stages of evolution. Folklore located authenticity in isolation from modern life and modern media. Minstrelsy, on the other hand, suggested that musical authenticity was a product of racial contact and interaction through the market. Music was not primarily a form of self-expression but a method of play-acting. If minstrel authenticity maintained the mutability of racial identity, folkloric authenticity posited its fixity. It was a fresh and powerful cultural paradigm calibrated to the new realities of the segregated South.

Folklore, at least in name, so thoroughly trounced minstrelsy that historians rarely discuss the process of its ascendance. The folkloric paradigm is the air that we breathe. It provides the basis for most of our music histories and analyses, even many of those that are critical of folkloric authenticity. Yet this study finds that neither model of authenticity emerged from the era intact. The folkloric paradigm ascended, in part, by inheriting and perpetuating some of the qualities of minstrel authenticity: folklorists invested minstrel and hillbilly stereotypes with scientific authority; the African American performer Bob Cole pitched his act as "Genuine Negro Songs by a Genuine Negro Minstrel"; Texas singer Vernon Dalhart claimed his "negro dialect" marked him a bona fide white southerner. I will show how performers and thinkers combined the two notions of authenticity into a series of mongrels that often tendered authentic minstrel deceits as authentic folkloric truths. The blues and country records of the 1920s were but two of the results. The messy and incomplete intersection of minstrelsy and folklore has left several generations of listeners and scholars frustrated with commercial pop fakery and dubious about genuine folk music.

Music, History, and Difference

My tale diverges from the stock narratives of blues and country music. The blues, the familiar story goes, had deep roots in African and African American musical practices and forms, from the call and response of work songs to the solo improvisations of field hollers and the communal singing and consciousness forged through the spirituals. Country music likewise arose out of a combination of British ballads and Irish fiddle tunes, songs from the Appalachian mines and the cattle range. Outside musical influences were present but they usually functioned as seasoning rather than main ingredients. The stories we have inherited often remain indebted to the folkloric paradigm developed in the early twentieth century. I do not doubt the veracity of such tales, but I think they have mistaken a part for the whole. This approach yields narratives that lead from social isolation to contact, from pure musical styles to compounds, from music made outside the commercial market to music that is deeply integrated into it. They imply that what is most important about these genres are their respective roots in African American and rural white folk cultures. They suggest that continuities within these traditions are more significant than transformations, the origins of a style more revelatory than the changing ways in which a variety of people may have used it. Standard approaches assume that the commodification of music is a problem that must be investigated, that music bought is somehow less true than music made.

I take a different approach. I begin from the premise that people's music worlds were less defined by who they were—in terms of racial, class, or regional identity—than by what music they had the opportunity to hear. From this perspective, the mass-produced music that flooded the South in the last decades of the nineteenth century did not necessarily cause crises of identity or disrupt long-honored musical folkways. I do not assert that southerners made no stark distinctions between the music offered by the commercial industry and that of their own making. I simply do not assume that they did. I then ask how some of the songs they enjoyed came to be identified with their core racial identities and others dismissed as less fundamental. Most observers agree that black and white southerners sang mass-produced pop songs. The fact that this music has not played a prominent role in histories of southern music, it seems, can be explained in one of two ways. Either southern people repudiated it, refused to contaminate their regional music with its presence, or chroniclers of southern music dismissed commercial pop as immaterial to southern culture. Evidence supports the latter conclusion. Crass, clichéd, formulaic, mass-produced pop: there was rarely a time in southern history that most people knew about this music and rejected it. This simple fact can tell us a great deal about the history of music, race, and region. It also can provide insight into historians' commitment to narratives of difference.

The cultural component of segregation, typified by the musical color line, was in some ways more successful than its legal counterpart, its narrative of discrete racial and regional cultures remaining ensconced long after the doctrine of separate but equal ceased to be the law of the land. In 1966, the year after Congress passed the Voting Rights Act, the eminent historian

David Potter famously dictated that southern historians "should focus their analysis at points where the conditions of the Southern region differ from those of other regions and should concentrate their attention upon historical developments which are relevant to these differences." Southern historians James Cobb and Edward Ayers each begin recent explorations of southern identity by acknowledging the influence Potter's decree had and continues to have on the field. Through the dogged pursuit of difference, southern identity was described as the antonym of an equally mythical northern character of American culture. Such distinctions could have profound effects on interpretations of southern music, causing catholic artists to fall into the crack between Mason and Dixon—of what is or is not "southern"—or to find their expansive repertoires reduced in order to establish an imagined regional distinctiveness.[11] A history attuned to continuities across regions stands a better chance of accurately chronicling the development of American popular music and, in fact, subtle regional differences. My story is centered in the South, but it charts the traffic of people, ideas, and products across the nation and the globe. I find that the very idea of southern musical distinctiveness was born out of the movements of southern migrants and northern touring shows, the actions of northern scholars and southern informants, and visions of racial and cultural differences culled from New York and Atlanta, China and Mexico.

Folklore provided much of the methodology and rationale for defining southern cultural distinctiveness in the age of Jim Crow. I pull on a significant body of literature bent on historicizing the folkloric project of the late nineteenth and early twentieth centuries. Concepts of folklore and the folk, of course, stretch back much farther, yet the process of professionalization during this period solidified folkloric theory in new ways and provided an institutional base that was quite unique in its ability to police admission and propagate scholars' work.[12] Throughout the book I approach folklore as an intellectual project, a set of ideas and frameworks for interpreting culture and history that developed largely within the academy. Thus I do not understand the term "folk music" to refer to a kind of music or a kind of music culture that exists out in the field prior to its discovery. Rather, I think that the preponderance of commercial music in the South before, during, and after the great wave of southern song collecting by folklorists suggests that "folk music" was a framework placed on an existing, complex musical culture, a model that did little to describe the musical complexity on the ground. Folklore was something that happened to certain sounds and styles at particular times as part of larger political projects of reclamation, differentiation, and control, including Jim Crow segregation.[13]

This new folkloric paradigm changed music making and meaning throughout the South and the nation. The identification of some southern music as folk music presented a variety of opportunities and obstacles to musicians, thinkers, and ordinary citizens. Some embraced the designation wholeheartedly or rejected it out of hand, while still others twisted it to suit their own needs. Folklore, for example, opened new avenues for the consumption of ideas about primitivism and exoticism that could function as a salve for the alienation of urban, industrial life.[14] At the same time, the folkloric paradigm provided new tools to coalesce racial, class, and regional identities into a cohesive whole and bring new constituencies into being. Folklore provided a framework for marginalized groups to forge collective identities out of a shared culture and memory rather than a shared oppression.[15]

I am guided by a growing collection of scholarship that has questioned the historical and functional split between folk and mass-produced music. Some have demonstrated that twentieth-century consumers used commercial music in the same ways earlier writers thought they only used folk music. Despite pop music's distant corporate origins, it helped people to craft unique individual and group identities, preserve collective memory, and maintain living traditions.[16] Others have emphasized that supposed folk cultures have rarely been as isolated from outside influences or market forces as they have been imagined to be. Depictions of pure folk cultures— in commercial culture as well as in scholarship—often have been elaborate, if well-intentioned, exaggerations that have obscured the very contact and commercial transactions that brought them into being.[17] Blues and country music, I will argue, are a case in point. Often sold as the uncut sounds of modern primitives, they emerged out of artists' long and learned engagement with a variety of popular styles from Tin Pan Alley and Broadway to the minstrel stage.

Minstrelsy was absolutely crucial to almost every musical development I explore, from the folklore and popular music of the 1890s through the rise of the race and old-time trade in the 1920s. Throughout most of this period, minstrelsy provided the foundation for important struggles between black and white Americans over both the meaning of black music and access to the commercial stage. Folklorists largely were absent from these contests for the simple fact that they remained unwilling to take commercial culture seriously. While they parsed the difference between pure folk song and mass-produced fare, others were in the trenches battling over the very commercial tunes to which so many people were listening. It was in the marketplace that the most electric and enduring debates about music, race, and meaning were occurring, and minstrelsy was the lingua franca. I try to chart some of the dramatic and subtle changes that minstrelsy underwent between the 1880s and the 1920s. It weathered a series of challenges from both white and black performers and thinkers, yet some of its pernicious tropes about black difference and inferiority simply reemerged in new guises. Indeed, blackface began to collapse only when these very same debates came to be waged in the language of folklore.[18]

Charting the interplay between minstrel and folkloric authenticity leads me to an interpretation of blackface's legacy that is markedly different from that of previous scholars. Eric Lott, in his landmark study of nineteenth-century minstrelsy, turns to the words of the scholar John Szwed to characterize the slow fade of blackface in American culture by the 1920s. "The fact that, say, a Mick Jagger can today perform in the same tradition without blackface simply marks the detachment of culture from race and the almost full absorption of a black tradition into white culture," notes Szwed.[19] It is a powerful argument, yet it is based upon some of the assumptions about culture and chronology that I want to call into question. Szwed, working within the folkloric paradigm, imagines that an identifiable and distinct black tradition existed prior to white appropriation through an emergent minstrelsy and that minstrelsy primarily involved the white performance and usurpation of this tradition. In the pages that follow, I will argue the exact opposite.

I proceed from the premise that minstrelsy emerged before the folkloric paradigm. Legions of Americans were intimately familiar with the conventions and racial politics of minstrelsy long before American folklore scholarship even got off the ground. Folklore, a new paradigm that rooted cultural and racial difference in the deep historical past, challenged the primary minstrel assertion that blackface performers sang black music. The 1920s witnessed the ascendance of folklore and the separation of minstrelsy—always more about white fantasy than black reality—from attempts at representing blackness. African American artists discredited white delineators by claiming the artistic, economic, and moral authority to perform authentic black music. Southern white artists responded by scrubbing off their burnt cork. They stopped identifying their acts as racial masquerade and simply claimed that this was how white southerners sang. The process—though incomplete and contested—involved not a severing of race from culture but a new attachment of race to culture through folklore. Mick Jagger, in this reading, does not represent the "almost full absorption of a black tradition into white culture." He illustrates the extent to which imitating black performance remained a constituent component of white identity. He is noteworthy and appeared transgressive because he represents the survival of the performative authenticity born from minstrelsy in the age of the folkloric paradigm.

I remain wary of the pitfall of inscribing contemporary racial demarcations onto the past. If historians have pursued regional and cultural disparities, they have emphasized racial difference as well. As the historian Nell Irvin Painter suggests, this is the legacy not only of the white historians who wrote black people out of the story of the South but also of black historians and their allies who tried to redress this imbalance by uncovering the history of an autonomous black cultural world. The politics of segregation and civil rights, white supremacy and black freedom, often encouraged scholars to produce stories of racial difference, separation, or autonomy.[20]

An emphasis on racial distinctiveness has been particularly prevalent in music history because of the questions that writers have attempted to answer. A significant body of music scholarship traces the genealogy of individual modern genres. Authors following this approach have provided essential knowledge about the histories and sounds of American vernacular music, and I draw heavily on their insights throughout the book.[21] However, it is difficult to remain attuned to interracial continuities—let alone differences—in a book singularly dedicated to the blues or country music. Genre studies have a tendency to reinscribe those folkloric narratives that lead from social isolation to contact, from pure musical styles to hybrids. In other words, they often replicate the image of a distinct and demarcated folk culture that then moves into the commercial realm. I find it odd that while the scholarship on segregation chronicles white southerners' obsessive parsing of racial difference and policing of racial distance (the creation of a segregated South), there is little corresponding music literature that moves from racial interaction to separation. Racialized genres often beget racially specific histories.[22]

A number of authors have complicated the notion of distinct racial musical traditions. From the age of slavery into the twentieth century, musicians copied, stole, and collaborated across the racial divide. This resulted in a large interracial repertoire, what the music historian Tony Russell has called a "common stock" of songs from which singers, both black and white, could draw.[23] While demonstrating that the color line did not characterize southern music before Jim Crow, studies dedicated to chronicling black and white musical interaction often have remained enamored with the regional distinctiveness of southern music and less interested in the impact of commercial pop on southern lives. The best of this literature nevertheless identifies interracial musical commonalities while remaining attuned to the history of white supremacy. An interracial musical culture had nothing to do with interracial harmony or equality. As Jenny Proctor, a former slave, reminded about interracial celebrations in antebellum Alabama, "We had some co'n shuckin' sometimes but de white folks gits de fun and de nigger gits de work."[24] When black and white southerners danced to the same rhythm, white southerners were almost always calling the tune.

Other scholars have critiqued the notion of distinct racial musical traditions by emphasizing the ways in which ideas about racial identity and difference have changed over time. Racial meaning, like musical meaning, is made material in the everyday actions of particular people at specific times. Each may best be understood as process rather than fact, verb rather than noun. This does not mean that identity does not have very real effects. It reminds that specific connections between race and music have been entangled in larger cultural and political struggles for power. Racialized definitions of cultural production have laid the foundation for important communities of association and action. In other cases they have severely constrained particular artists and communities whose culture did not fit within the prevailing categories.[25]

One can see the fluctuating connections between racial meaning, music, and power in the history of scholarship on African American music. The study of black music has tended to produce stories of racial difference because of the high political stakes involved in writing African American cultural history. Chroniclers of African American creativity have confronted continuous assertions that black culture does not exist. Early white observers dubbed slave music noise.[26] Later writers labeled the spirituals unsophisticated imitations of white hymns,[27] jazz a byproduct of black primitivism,[28] and even hip-hop as outside the definition of music.[29] Within this context, it is easy to see recent scholarship depicting race as a mythical social construction as the same old song. It is a postmodern twist on the notion that "the Negro," in the infamous words of Nathan Glazer and Daniel Patrick Moynihan in 1963, "is only an American and nothing else. He has no cultural values to guard and protect."[30] While continually deflating such claims, writers on black music have done far more. They have chronicled a deep and abiding African American music tradition that regularly builds on musical precedents and fosters collective memories of African and African American culture while accommodating new experiences, conditions, and dreams. While some have asserted essentialist concepts of race in order to accomplish this, many authors have penned nuanced histories that subtly balance the changing politics of race with the continuities of African American cultural memory.[31]

Indebted to this scholarship, I think music accomplishes far more than driving collective memory. Focusing on a core black culture inevitably pushes to the periphery sounds and interpretations that do not sufficiently preserve collective memory but may nevertheless be meaningful sources of pleasure, pay, and political power. Black Americans were never limited to a cultural life that drew on only the traditions and folkways signifying communalism, however rich these traditions were and continue to be. Instead, I think that attention to the music that does not fit within distinct racial traditions, what Christopher Waterman dubs the "excluded middle" of American music, can give us new insights into the multiple ways people crafted complex identities—how they fought to celebrate collective memory and communal identities while refusing to be defined by them.[32]

Listening, Performance, and Repertoire

This study puts the music shared by black and white citizens at its center and then examines the struggles over the shifting location of the color line. I acknowledge that black and white southerners developed a number of songs and styles that were rarely known or embraced by their counterparts. I give relatively little attention to this music, assured that previous studies have done far more than I could to chart its histories and analyze its meanings. There is little here about African precedents, spirituals, ragtime, or jazz. There is not much about the ways in which African Americans used sound and lyrics to forge a common sense of black identity, preserve collective memory, or carve out autonomous cultural spaces. I do not need to provide further proof that African Americans did all of these things. I likewise do not detail the ways in which European musical traditions shaped the sounds of the white South from Appalachia to Texas. Nor do I adequately demonstrate that black and white southerners developed a variety of unique regional or local styles of fiddling, blues guitar picking, and falsetto singing. Scholars who have examined these styles can testify to the profound diversity of southern music and its deep roots in a number of different national and diasporic histories. I can only hope that interested readers will turn to many of the excellent books, cited throughout *Segregating Sound*, that tell these parts of the story.

I likewise give relatively little attention to differences in black and white performance styles. I instead emphasize repertoires—what songs musicians played rather than how musicians played them. This emphasis runs somewhat counter to that of recent folklore scholarship. Performance practices and theory have assumed a central place within contemporary academic folklore. In the 1970s, Richard Bauman, Américo Paredes, Roger Abrahams, and others challenged one of the central assumptions of the founding generations of folkloristics by arguing that performance, rather than the text, is the thing. Scholars have done a wonderful job identifying the distinguishing characteristics of many musical cultures, challenging the romanticism of their predecessors, and demonstrating how music cultures remain living and changing entities.[33] Students of African American music have similarly emphasized performance—from call and response, improvisation, and additive rhythms to music's functional role within everyday life—as they have defined the essential qualities of the black music tradition.[34] I was bred on this literature and think it is fundamental to understanding aspects of American music history and culture. Yet the search for common stylistic elements of a music culture poses multiple risks. It can define music cultures according to abstract musical elements rather than lived experience. It can exclude practitioners who maintain social, cultural, and political ties to the culture in question but whose music does not exhibit the essential qualities. At the same time, it can assume difference rather than similarities across racial lines, suggesting that core performance characteristics are unique performance characteristics. While a focus on performance might be best for identifying a core musical vocabulary or group identity formation, I hope *Segregating Sound*'s emphasis on repertoire helps to identify interracial and transregional conversations.

I focus on repertoires to avoid the potential dangers of overstating the differences between black and white performance styles. I am reminded of the critique launched against evolutionary anthropology's quest to discern ultimate racial difference by comparing cranial measurements during the late nineteenth century. To paraphrase, the differences within African American or white music cultures were more extreme than the differences between black and white music cultures. In terms of training, song structures, arrangements, and vocal timbre and delivery, African American singers such as Mamie Smith and Ethel Waters shared more in common with white vaudevillians like Marie Cahill and Marion Harris than they did with fellow African American artists such as Elizabeth Cotten or Mississippi John Hurt. One can hear commonalities in Smith's and Cotten's delivery—their worried approach to the beat or their use of pendular thirds, for example— that suggest the contours of a black music tradition. Yet to focus on these aspects of the performances at the expense of the overwhelming similarities between the music of Smith and Harris risks reinscribing the very logic of racial separation and distance I am attempting to historicize in this book. The historical concept that black people sang one way and white people sang in a fundamentally different way emerged out of the shift from minstrel authenticity to folkloric authenticity that defined the musical color line. The sonic evidence suggests a much more complicated story. This is not to equate Mamie Smith and Marion Harris. Smith daily experienced racism and exclusion at the hands of both white society and the music industry, each of which granted easy access to Marion Harris due to her white privilege. It is rather to suggest that regimes of white supremacy and segregation, particularly at the beginning of my story, more systematically targeted racialized bodies than racialized sound. The emergent musical color line eventually brought the logic of segregation into the realm of sound and style, linking sonic signifiers of race to the corporeal bodies and physical landscapes that Jim Crow already had been trying to contain for several decades. Ultimately, I am less interested that listeners attributed racial meaning to musical performance than *how* they did it, whether they were operating through the minstrel or folkloric paradigm. In the passages where I do talk about musical performance and stylistic characteristics I thus use the language of my sources rather than reading contemporary terms back into the historical past.

Finally and perhaps most importantly, an emphasis on repertoire, I believe, helps to get at the experience of hearing music in the pre-phonograph South. This was a time when all performance was necessarily live performance. Consider a simple example: A local musician—black or white —performs the Tin Pan Alley smash "After the Ball" on Decatur Street in Atlanta in the late 1890s. What do passersby take from the performance? A stylistic analysis—if we could access the performance in the first place— might suggest that listeners would hear a southern reinvention of a northern commercial song, possibly an indigenization of what was considered a foreign genre. It admittedly might sound little like the same tune sung from the New York stage. *Segregating Sound* maintains the importance of this interpretation but focuses on a different set of possibilities. Encountering "After the Ball" on Decatur Street, I contend, local listeners would not have been wowed primarily by its southern inflection. Indeed, in the world of live performance, almost everything that they heard shared the same southern inflection. I think their ears would have perked to the qualities of the composition and all that it represented. Broadway tunes infiltrated the South. But they largely did so through southern singers. When southerners heard "After the Ball" prior to the spread of the phonograph, they did not marvel at the ways in which southern artists brought it into the realm of regional performance styles. They instead celebrated it as evidence of their own connections to the music—and by extension the culture and society— of the Midwest, New York City, and the nation at large. This may have been particularly true of segments of the southern population aggrieved by segregation, sharecropping, millwork, or other southern forms of exploitation, those who imagined the North not as a foe to be repelled but as a potential promised land. An emphasis on repertoire over performance style helps to get at such feelings.

I am guided by the ethnomusicologist Steven Feld's description of music listening as a "feelingful activity." Listeners derive pleasure not by comprehending any singular or essential meaning in a piece of music, he argues, but through experiencing a flood of intersecting ideas and associations over the course of a performance. Music evokes multiple metaphors. Engaged listeners continually compare the music that they are hearing to their vast collection of past experiences, determining whether the sounds are like or unlike music that they already know. They revel in the dialectic interplay of familiarity and strangeness as expectations are repeatedly fulfilled and up-ended through the course of the music. It is through grappling with all the possibilities, privileging some associations while diminishing others, that listeners distinguish themselves from each other. Musical identification oc-curs less through *what* one hears than through *how* one hears—how one crafts a sense of oneself through the process of attributing meaning to sound.[35]

Feld's notion of "feelingful" listening discourages privileging some mu-sic and some metaphorical meanings over others. Everything a person hears helps build imaginary and social worlds of association. Every song likewise provides fodder for numerous listeners. One cannot easily divide the flood of ideas that music evokes in a given listener into those that are essential to identity formation and those that are not. Many white northerners, for example, loved listening to southern African Americans sing the blues. Some aspects of this music were soothingly familiar and others were con-fusing or exciting for their strangeness. As they reveled in the tumble of sound and meanings, they built a sense of who they were through their reactions. If Feld is correct (and I think he is), notions of co-optation, crossover, or exoticism utterly fail to capture the complexities of such phe-nomena. These terms suggest that listeners are wrong. They implicitly priv-ilege the musical meanings assumed to be most closely associated with the creator's social identity and suggest that alternate meanings are somehow less real, important, or revelatory. I disagree.

Listeners construct individual and collective musical worlds out of sounds that they make themselves and sounds that they do not. This study attempts to demonstrate that a variety of listeners embraced and used music often assumed to be outside of their core culture. I will argue, for example, that southern African Americans' attraction to Tin Pan Alley tunes—even as they sang the blues, spirituals, and square dance calls—is significant to understanding their worldviews. This does not deny the importance of spirituals or blues to African American music culture. Nor does it suggest that nineteenth-century listeners did not hear and understand music to be signifying racial meaning and memory. It rather contends that black south-erners at the turn of the twentieth century did not listen or organize their lives through the folkloric paradigm. By delving into what they may have heard when listening to Tin Pan Alley and how they may have claimed mass-produced music as part of their own culture, I hope to reveal that people understood themselves in complex, often contradictory, ways.

Southerners found in music a wide variety of meanings that had little to do with the cultural categories we have inherited to talk about them. Music may have signified change, offering sounds that did not painfully remind one of the suffering of the past. It may have symbolized urban sophistication, high culture, or distant exotic lands—each expanding a listener's gaze beyond local conditions and promising that a different, perhaps better, world existed. It may have meant the expansion of one's possible audience, opening an artist to a wider scope of professional opportunities. Performance of music could be a claim to ownership or to legitimate participation in a society that in other ways denied access. Musical styles and songs could have been desired because they were beautiful, challenging, or just a whole lot of fun. In the following pages, we will see that music could be an opiate and a weapon, a means to tell the truth and to lie, a testimony about the obstacles in one's path and a way to get over. Quite often, it was all of these at the same time.

I have designed each chapter of *Segregating Sound* to address a particular historical or theoretical problem suggested by the historiography on southern and American music. They necessarily overlap chronologically, examining the same period of time from different perspectives or outlining relatively distinct processes and distant conversations that converge as the book progresses.

The first two chapters concern musical life in the South during the late nineteenth and early twentieth centuries, a time largely before the musical color line had come to dominate depictions of southern music. I begin with the southern embrace of pop music. While observers such as Ralph Peer and Dorothy Scarborough interpreted this music as a problem, chapter 1 places mass-produced pop at the center of an interracial music culture in the South. It charts the systematic distribution of commercial songs throughout the region and then explores the southern reaction to two of the most popular genres of the age: sentimental ballads and what were known as coon songs. Many southerners integrated these foreign products into their musical lives. Mass-produced ditties sat beside songs from a variety of regional and traditional genres even as they helped both black and white southerners negotiate the Jim Crow regime white residents were constructing throughout the region.

Chapter 2 shifts focus from southern audiences to southern musicians. Local and regional artists developed sophisticated markets for their music long before they caught the ears of academic and corporate collectors. Local music economies encouraged musicians to play anything and everything that could attract a paying audience, rewarding diverse repertoires and the ability to perform for multiple audiences. Versatile musicians stood a better chance of coaxing coins from listeners' pockets in southern cafes, streets, and touring shows. The black singer Samuel Chatman put it bluntly: "You take a fellow that can play anything, he can get a job more or less anywhere."[36] Several of the musicians I examine eventually were heralded as the embodiments of distinct racial folk music traditions, yet they spent years prior to their "discovery" playing around and across the musical color line they would later help to define.

I next examine the development and popularization of the new paradigm of authenticity coming out of academic folklore. The first half of chapter 3 charts the foundational debates about race and culture within the American Folklore Society. The organization established a common theoretical ground among its members by combining different conceptions of folk isolation coming out of philology, literary studies, and anthropology. The society determined to collect and interpret artifacts that were isolated from modern American culture by race, time, evolution, or exposure to media. These interlaced concepts of folk isolation drove early collecting projects and, I argue, established that trained scholars were better equipped than the folk themselves to determine the value and importance of folk songs. I then explore a number of ways in which academic ideas about folk culture intersected with American popular ideas about race, music, and commerce. Folklore acquired academic authority, but it remained deeply entangled with the commercial culture scholars explicitly excoriated. Many early collectors simply substantiated the stereotypes of race and region spilling from minstrel and vaudeville stages. At the same time, their work helped to create a consumer demand for authentic folk music. Performers got cash on the barrelhead when they advertised their products as traditional alternatives to mass-produced fare.

Chapter 4 tells the story of the generation of southern musicians who moved to New York City to participate in the national music industry between about 1899 and 1920. Musicians such as Bob Cole, Vernon Dalhart, and Marion Harris are often overlooked in histories of southern music.

They left the region and became national celebrities more concerned with making money than remaining true to local southern styles. Yet these musicians played a crucial role in opening the New York music industry to southern musicians and paving the way for the race and old-time trade of the 1920s. Confronting an urban music scene overrun with songs about an exotic South, they claimed to be more authentic representations of stereotypical blackface minstrels and white hillbillies. I chart the tangled web of negotiations and affiliations that occurred as folkloric visions of authenticity began to replace minstrel authenticity and southern migrants began to convince northern audiences that they were uniquely qualified to sing southern songs.

Chapter 5 looks at the history of the phonograph industry and asks a simple question: Why did the race and old-time trade begin in the early 1920s? After decades of denying African American artists access to the recording studio and showing almost no interest in rural white musicians, the industry produced droves of records by these groups in a few short years. I discover that efforts to create a sustainable market for the talking machine in the opening years of the century had locked the industry into a dualistic vision of American music. Companies celebrated uplifting art music and denigrated everything else as mere novelty. This dualism left the industry unable to comprehend distinct regional, racial, or ethnic markets within the United States. At the same time, companies' international departments were developing thriving markets for their wares throughout Asia, Europe, and Latin America. Desperate to achieve a foothold in these new markets, industry giants developed marketing strategies that combined geographic expansion with the recording of local music, often defined in racial or ethnic terms. When the First World War temporarily suspended international trade, companies turned to immigrant consumers within the United States, bringing their models of racial and ethnic marketing home.

Chapters 6 and 7 tell how the race and old-time records of the 1920s emerged out of the twin processes described in the two preceding chapters. The racial genres, on one hand, were an extension of the phonograph industry's international campaigns. By 1920, the successes they had achieved internationally and with U.S. immigrant consumers enabled them to see African American and southern white consumers as separate niche markets. This approach encouraged companies to record distinct music by these groups. It also persuaded them to disregard the extent to which southern artists and audiences had already embraced national popular music. On the other hand, the genres emerged out of the intersection between minstrelsy and folklore. They were the culmination of the struggle of southern musicians to control representations of the region and the shift in expectations, examined throughout the book, that musicians should embody musical genres rather than simply employ them—that racial bodies performed racial music.

The final chapter charts the tentative triumph of the folkloric paradigm through an examination of folklore collections from the 1920s and early 1930s. Folklore came to surpass minstrelsy to become the primary framework through which scholars, performers, and audiences debated the meaning of race, music, and the market. Folklorists accomplished this by subtly changing their definitions of folk songs to include certain styles of mass-produced song.

The result was a fundamental rewriting of the meaning and sounds of southern music—the formation of a musical color line that stretched from the library shelf to the record catalogue, the tent show to the concert hall. Scholars' and capitalists' power to control public imagery and shape (or reinforce particular versions of) public perception was far more profound than the power of often-marginalized musicians to counter such claims. Moving from live to recorded performance, from local to national audiences, many southern artists jettisoned the broad repertoires that had won them local success. They instead found favor by actively personifying the racial musical categories the academy and the phonograph industry associated with a southern culture defined through its primitivism, exoticism, and supposed distance from modern urban culture.

Artists responded to this conundrum in different ways. Some contested the images created around them, attempting to break their expressive culture out of the confines of commercial and scientific classifications. Others, however, embraced the role of premodern primitive. It expressed some of their own misgivings about a modernism based upon their exploitation. Many who came to represent traditional culture, in fact, were not premodern but those who had experienced modernization at its most brutal: sharecroppers, factory workers, and prison laborers. Playing the role of the premodern offered them both a voice with which to challenge their conditions and a possible ticket out. Many, however, remained aware that they were entering into a bargain that denied their human and artistic freedom.

They stopped singing many of the songs that brought them joy. They pretended their lives could be contained by the categories that confronted them, knowing all along that they owned a world much larger than the one they portrayed. Unearthing their stories can lead us to visualize musical and cultural categories as points of contention rather than assumed points of departure, vibrant subjects for historical research rather than ways in which to limit one's scope of inquiry. It also can help explain the joyful defiance of singers like Robert Johnson, who gleefully performed anything. And when I say anything, I mean ANYTHING.

TIN PAN ALLEY ON TOUR

The Southern Embrace of Commercial Music

Some of the earliest written examples of African American blues lyrics come to us from a white man named Charles Peabody. An archaeologist with Harvard's Peabody Museum, he supervised an excavation of Native American burial mounds in the Mississippi Delta during the summers of 1901 and 1902. Peabody was fascinated by the music sung by the local African American laborers he employed on the dig. In 1903, he published a description of what he had heard in the *Journal of American Folklore*.

> They had me arrested for murder
> And I never harmed a man.

Peabody transcribed a number of his workers' lyrics, " 'hard luck' tales" that closely resembled blues stanzas later recorded throughout the South. Contemporary scholars have found Peabody's observations very useful in their attempts to chart the early history of the blues. He discovered that a new style of music—the blues or a close relative—was being sung in the early-twentieth-century South.[1]

Peabody was less thrilled to hear his workers sing commercial popular hits, mass-produced songs sold throughout the country. "Undoubtedly picked up from passing theatrical troupes, the 'ragtime' sung for us quite inverted the supposed theory of its origin," he reported. He felt cheated when his requests for a recital resulted in " 'Goo-Goo Eyes' with any number of encores, and 'Nigger Bully' and others quite as original probably with Miss May Irwin as with them."[2] "Goo-Goo Eyes" was most likely "Just Because She Made

Dem Goo Goo Eyes," a song about a blackface minstrel's failure to find love, written in 1900 by professional composers Hughie Cannon and John Queen. It was featured in at least six major touring shows soon after its publication. "The Bully Song," first published in 1895, was perhaps the biggest hit ever enjoyed by the white singer May Irwin, one of the most recognized entertainers of the day. Peabody found the songs mundane, hardly worth comment. He was not interested in hearing music that was equally familiar to Harvard archaeologists and black workers in rural Mississippi.[3]

Yet commercial popular songs constituted a significant portion of the music heard in the early-twentieth-century South. If scholars have seized upon Peabody's collection of indigenous southern lyrics, they have paid far less attention to his revelations about pop music's penetration into the region. Peabody's brief article shows that Mississippians were aware of songs just recently published in distant New York City. It demonstrates that they liked these songs enough to learn them, remember them, and sing them with their peers. And it shows that some of the same people who sang the blues also sang imported commercial pop tunes. Collectors such as Ralph Peer and Dorothy Scarborough, who scoured the region in the following decades, came to similar conclusions.[4] Lamentations aside, these observers got it right. Southern people *were* busy listening to the products of the commercial music industry.

Acknowledging the prevalence of mass-marketed music in the South necessarily complicates our understanding of the relationship between race and music in the age of segregation. Charles Peabody was primarily interested in identifying the "sharp contrast" between black and white music, and he belittled evidence to the contrary.[5] He was far from alone. Defining racial difference was one of the great intellectual and political enterprises of the day, visible from scholars' theories about separate racial cultures and cranial capacities to legislators' construction of "separate but equal" segregation regimes. The history of mass-produced music in the region reveals that these projects of racial separation were incomplete in their execution and inaccurate as descriptions of southern lives. Black and white southerners sang many of the same songs, tunes they often had learned by hearing the same touring musicians while attending the same performances. These shared songs did not result in shared perspectives or mutual understanding between black and white, however. Indeed, Peabody's two examples were coon songs, tunes that traded on derogatory stereotypes of African Americans. Racial commonalities had nothing to do with racial harmony. Rather, commercial pop functioned as a common ground upon which black and white southerners negotiated some of the meanings and effects of the new racial regime that white residents were imposing on the South.

The Spread of Commercial Music in the South

In the late nineteenth century, three processes converged to bring northern commercial music to southern ears. An expansion of railroad lines made it possible to deliver a wealth of new consumer products into even previously remote areas of the South. Sheet music publishers, concentrated in Manhattan along what came to be known as "Tin Pan Alley," perfected the mass production and distribution of popular songs. And a changing theater economy pushed successful northern shows and songs into cities and small towns across the region. As a result, mass-marketed songs flooded the South. They found willing buyers.

Railroad expansion provided the stimulus. United States train companies completed approximately 100,000 miles of rail between 1869 and 1900, the pace in the South exceeding that of any other region. By 1890, an estimated 90 percent of southerners lived in counties served by railroads. Residents of relatively isolated rural climes found themselves connected to each other and points beyond through the expanding web of steel. The railroad helped fuel southern urbanization. Villages cropped up at a remarkable rate, many of them around new railroad depots. Larger cities across the region experienced population booms that doubled the national average, spurred by their growing importance as regional centers of trade. The railroad also fueled southern industrialization. In the 1880s, southern extractive industries such as sawmills, mining, and turpentine manufacturing blossomed. Textile manufacturers, encouraged by the region's cheap labor and new connection to national transportation networks, created mills employing almost 100,000 workers by 1900, an increase of almost one thousand percent over 1870 figures. The railroad boom inaugurated a revolution in the southern consumption of mass-produced fare. From soap, clothing, and canned goods to beauty aids, tools, and musical instruments: mail order catalogues from New York and Chicago firms opened a new world of consumer goods. The number of southern general stores skyrocketed in the late nineteenth century, averaging 144 merchants per county in 1900. General stores tantalized with their eclectic array of items available for cash or credit. New access to goods helped many southerners feel a part of national trends in fashion, literature, and music.[6]

Among the goods stuffing southern general stores was sheet music, the product of an industry that was reaching a new level of consolidation and sophistication. Beginning with the founding of the T. B. Harms publishing house in 1881, New York became the center of popular music publishing in the United States. By the turn of the century almost every major publishing house in the country was located on or near Manhattan's 28th Street, later dubbed Tin Pan Alley. The city's publishers perfected the mass production of songs. Earlier publishers had been comparatively unorganized, featuring a diffused list of various styles, surviving off loopholes in copyright law, or signing individual compositions in a business model akin to today's book publishing industry. Tin Pan Alley changed the game. Firms specializing in popular songs developed compositional and lyrical formulas based on past hits. Most paid a flat rate of ten to twenty-five dollars per song to staff or freelance composers to write specifically for the company. They thus often owned the tune before it was even written. Tin Pan Alley publishers issued thousands of titles in the hopes that a few would score with the nation's public.[7]

Tin Pan Alley firms also systematized the process of promoting songs through popular stage performers and musical comedy actors. "The way to popularize a ballad is to have it first sung by a well known artist, after which all the other singers will eagerly fall in line," insisted the composer and publisher Charles K. Harris. Stage singers could introduce the song to their audiences and encourage listeners to purchase the musical score for themselves. Firms did not leave much to chance. "Song pluggers, from early morning until late at night, stood in front of their respective publishing houses waiting for singers to come along, when they would grab them by the arm and hoist them into the music studios. There was no escape," Harris explained. "Once the singers entered the block, they left it with a dozen promises ringing in the pluggers' ears,—promises to sing the newly acquired compositions." As the evening wore on, pluggers descended on theaters, hotels, and vaudeville stages to continue whispering their songs in singers' ears. If words failed, publishers showered coveted singers with gifts ranging from cigars and drinks to fur coats and expensive stage scenery. The system worked.[8]

Charles Harris, for example, worked diligently to convince singers to perform his 1892 ballad "After the Ball." He unsuccessfully courted singers in the Howard Burlesque Company and the Primrose and West Minstrels, before he persuaded prima donna Annie Whitney of Clark's Burlesquers to give the song a try. May Irwin heard Whitney sing it and added it to her own act. The song began to catch on. Unaware of Irwin's support, Harris bribed the popular balladeer James Aldrich Libby to sing "After the Ball" on tour. He reportedly offered the singer positive newspaper reviews, five hundred dollars, and a percentage of sheet music profits. Libby was happy to comply. Sales of "After the Ball" grew, and the song began getting picked up by other singers, including William Windom, a featured performer with the Primrose and West Minstrels, one of the very companies that had initially passed on the song. "After the Ball" became one of the biggest songs of the 1890s. Such twisted paths to success were common as Tin Pan Alley scored hit after hit. "There was no system, no set rules, no combination of publishers, no music publishers' association; simply, do as you please, everybody for himself, and the devil take the hindmost," Harris concluded.[9]

A revolution in American theater production and booking helped to funnel Tin Pan Alley songs into towns across the nation. Prior to the 1860s, legitimate theater outside of a few major cities depended on local stock companies, relatively stable and self-contained troupes of actors, musicians, and producers that developed a repertoire of plays they could perform throughout a year. In the 1840s and 1850s, stock company managers began importing traveling New York stars to perform the lead roles in their local productions. The star system proved the death knell for the stock company. Audiences began expecting extravagant stars whose expensive paychecks cut into the salaries of stock actors. The quality and reliability of stock troupes declined along with their wages. Star actors, in reaction, began bringing supporting actors and musicians on the road with them in order to assure a quality production. By 1890, the process had culminated in the practical replacement of local stock theater by touring companies and the emergence of New York as the national center of theater production.[10]

The availability and cost of railroad travel forced touring shows into quite small towns across the country. The success of a touring company depended upon the creation of a good route. Two qualities characterized the ideal route. First, it put troupes in well-known theaters in major cities when wallets were full and competing shows were absent. Second, it provided enough one-night stands between major cities that railroad transportation costs would not overwhelm profits. Tour managers obsessed about limiting the length of "jumps" from one performance to the next and kept a running list of small towns along a route that would be good for a pit stop. The need for stops between major cities, the *New York Dramatic Mirror* reported in 1882, meant that each town with two thousand residents got performances of two to three plays a week.[11]

In a meaningful sense, theater from New York became American theater. Just as southern consumers bought Velvet Skin Soap and Ayer's Hair Vigor at their general stores, they lined up for New York theater productions featuring Tin Pan Alley songs. Theater companies did whatever they could to associate themselves with the city. Average productions made their profits on the road. Mounting a show in New York was expensive, audiences were fickle, and most companies ended their stay in debt. Yet a production that could boast a stint on Broadway could make up for hometown losses by taking New York to the hinterland. Even if troupes never played the city, they were better off pretending that they had. Manager John Golden surveyed the national theater business in 1925, years after the emergence of New York as a successful brand. "I found second-rate New York productions advertising all-star New York casts that had never been nearer New York than Xenia, Ohio," he wrote. "I found plays billed as New York successes, of which I, a fairly well-informed New York manager, had never even heard. I saw displayed in more than one of the theatres, photographs of players who were supposed to be in the cast but who, I knew, were actually playing in New York."[12] Southern audiences actively sought New York theater, and entertainers willingly complied. Southern tours were the lifeblood of many troupes, the only way they could fill seats and make payroll during the slow winter months.

New York became the center of a national theater-booking network just as it was emerging as the home of the song publishing and theater industries. Each summer representatives of theaters from across the country would descend on the city to find attractions that could fill their houses over the coming season. Negotiations were tense and contracts untrustworthy as approximately 5,000 theaters in 3,500 cities and towns attempted to secure the talents of about 250 touring companies in the early 1880s. Beginning in the 1870s, small town theaters banded together into circuits. Negotiating performance contracts as a group enabled them to book top attractions by insisting that a production appear in all or none of the circuit's theaters.

Centralized booking agencies emerged in the 1880s and 1890s. Serving as middlemen between attractions and individual theaters or circuits, booking firms brought a new level of organization and centralization to national theater tours. They took a bite out of the profits for each show, the remainder being split between the house and the attraction according to percentages negotiated through the agency. Yet they offered predictability: a full season for theaters and a full tour for troupes.[13]

One of the largest booking agencies in the country specialized in the South. Formed by Marc Klaw and Abraham Erlanger in 1887, the partnership gained control of a modest booking agency serving Texas theaters. The pair identified the South as a region ripe for theater centralization. In 1888, they announced, "We have made a close study of this territory, KNOW EVERY INCH OF GROUND WORTH PLAYING; EVERY THEATRE IN THAT SECTION FIT TO PLAY IN."[14] The firm offered their information free to any troupe interested in touring the region. Klaw and Erlanger controlled bookings in two hundred theaters across the South by 1895. The following year, it joined with two other major booking agencies to form the Theatrical Syndicate, an organization that virtually monopolized theater bookings throughout the country for the next fifteen years. The Syndicate came to dominate national bookings by insisting on exclusive contracts with theaters and attractions. Once in the fold, a touring company could play only Syndicate houses on tours planned by the agency. Likewise, member theaters relinquished all control over their season to the Syndicate, taking virtually whatever attractions the agency was sending through the region.[15]

Once the Syndicate controlled premiere venues, other theaters scurried to join for fear of being denied access to established eastern attractions. "We would like to know if you have any shows that you could give us for the coming season," the manager of the Idle Hour Theatre Company in Marianna, Arkansas, wrote to Klaw and Erlanger in 1910. "We have a town of 6000 people with Opera House with good stage, Seating capacity of between 400 & 500 if you have anything that you think would suit us for size of Town Opera house &, etc. let us hear from you."[16] Other small town theaters made similar requests, their letterheads festooned with statistics advertising their facilities and potential audience. "Alexandria Population 11,000; Pineville across the Bridge 1,000; Run Excursions and Draw from 40,000," boosted the letterhead for the New Rapides Theatre in Alexandria, Louisiana. It then listed the city's distance from nine other towns, its seven railroad lines, five newspapers, and three major hotels before describing its "strictly modern," steam-heated building.[17] "We are bigger than you think," it implied, even before anyone typed a word on the page.

Southern theater operators who failed to join the Syndicate could turn to other theatrical conglomerates that could bring profitable second-tier companies to their stages. The American Theatrical Exchange, founded in Galveston, Texas (with offices in New York), booked a significant number of theaters in Louisiana, Arkansas, Kansas, Oklahoma, and Texas, as well as a few in Georgia, South Carolina, Tennessee, and Missouri. In 1912, the firm boasted 123 theaters in Texas alone, most of them in smaller towns from Ansop and Baird to Wolf City and Yoakum.[18] The Harrison Brothers, a nationally known African American minstrel company, traveled through Texas in late 1900 on a circuit that would become part of the American Theatrical Exchange. They staged sixteen engagements in seventeen nights. Their itinerary, typical of many contemporary outfits, included both significant cities and smaller towns: West, Waco, Calvert, Bryan, Navasota, Houston, Beaumont, and La Grange.[19] Even towns without a proper theater tried to get in on the act. "Crops in Southern Kansas have been so good this year that every farmer has plenty of money," the trade magazine *Billboard* reported in 1900. "In order to enjoy the use of some of it, the agriculturists have decided to import vaudeville into their midst, as it were, and to save themselves the trouble of riding fifty miles to the nearest large towns, they have fitted up the schoolhouses in several towns, so that entertainments may be given properly." The author dubbed the new group of rural schoolhouses the "potatobug circuit," reporting that at least fifteen performances would be arranged at each school.[20] Small communities actively courted traveling theater companies.

Through touring shows, southerners came into contact with the songs and styles of the commercial theater popular throughout the nation. Successful plays and melodramas often interpolated new songs into their performances, a practice pushed by song publishers hoping to create a hit.[21] Vaudeville revues, musical farces, blackface minstrel shows, African American minstrel companies, and operatic divas regularly stopped in small towns to avoid large jumps between paying gigs. Ticket prices to opera house concerts ran as low as twenty-five cents for balcony seats, even as the choice orchestra seats went for much more. These prices excluded a significant portion of the southern working class, yet tickets remained obtainable by large segments of the population. Even more southerners heard the music featured in commercial minstrel shows. Traveling troupes regularly conducted public parades to drum up business for their evening performances. Usually taking place in the late afternoon, the parade featured selections of the music from the official concert. It was often followed by a free outdoor performance leading into the theater. According to W. C. Handy, who toured with Mahara's Colored Minstrels in the 1890s, parades featured a plethora of musical styles, from John Philip Sousa marches and classical overtures to Stephen Foster medleys, British ballads, and the latest Tin Pan Alley hits of the day. Some residents were impressed enough by the afternoon teasers to purchase tickets to the evening show; many more caught the free music then went about their business with the songs of the out-of-town musicians lodged in their heads.[22]

Publicly attended touring productions were one place that southerners enacted and experienced Jim Crow segregation. At a time when some New York theaters were banning African American customers, many smaller southern venues were continuing to encourage their attendance. Most southern states did not pass laws regarding the segregation of public performance spaces. Instead, policy regarding the admission of African Americans was left to the manager of individual theaters. Many of them did admit black customers, though often segregating their ticket windows, entrances, and seating. Mixed-race audiences were common for concerts by both black and white touring companies. The *Baptist Pioneer* reported in 1890 that even as minstrel companies touring the South advertised themselves as "all white" in order to conform with local racial regimes, "numbers of Afro-Americans go to hear those minstrel troupes belittle them in the most degrading and obscene manner." Black attendees, the paper reported, were relegated to "a little pen 'for colored people only.'" In 1889, the African American vocalist Madame Selika made headlines around the country when she refused to perform in southern houses that admitted black patrons but would not sell them first-class tickets. African Americans thus did attend the variety of shows that toured through the South. Walking into the theater involved an unmistakable enactment of local racial hierarchies as well as a participation in the commercial music and drama that was at the very same time weaving a common musical culture among Americans across the country.[23]

African American touring artists encountered regular and sometimes violent protests from white southerners intent on enforcing Jim Crow. Theater managers billed Madame Selika as a Cherokee rather than as an African American performer in order to defuse any possible opposition to a black performing star. "The fact of the matter is they will all sing when the receipts justify it. Neither do they draw the color line on those who wish to hear them," charged the *Indianapolis Freeman*. In 1894, a black production of *Uncle Tom's Cabin* arrived in Charlottesville, Virginia, to find their playbills painted black and vandalized with the letters "S. V. C." for Sons of Confederate Veterans.[24] "The towns in most of the southern states were very rough to us because the Civil War was still pretty fresh in their minds," noted the African American performer Tom Fletcher. Touring the region with an African American minstrel troupe around the turn of the century, Fletcher regularly played in predominantly white small towns that harassed African American strangers. "Usually they had signs prominently displayed which read 'Nigger, Read and Run.' And sometimes there would be added 'and if you can't read, run anyhow,'" Fletcher recalled. "In our minds most of these people did everything the savages did except eat humans." Fletcher's company devised a strategy to avoid attacks. They would parade in full regalia while playing "Dixie" in order to move between their train and the concert hall without assault. Once the evening concert was over they would parade back to the train and leave town immediately. "Some of the towns were so small that we had to start at one end of the town for the entire show to be seen," Fletcher noted.[25]

W. C. Handy, touring in the 1890s with the African American company Mahara's Minstrels, found his life endangered numerous times. In one Texas town, a white mob hurled rocks at the company as they were parading through town. On another occasion, Texas Rangers foiled a gang's attempt to infiltrate the theater and break up the show. Each time the troupe was scheduled to pass through Orange, Texas, near the Louisiana border, a mob would wait and hurl bullets at the passing train. Handy and his company learned to douse the lights and lie low. In Austin, Texas, a mob led by a local doctor threatened to lynch the entire company when one was diagnosed with smallpox. Handy recalled the fate of a fellow performer named Louis Wright, who had left Mahara's to work with the Georgia Minstrels. Wright was walking with a female companion through a Missouri town when a group of white people pelted the duo with snowballs. Wright cursed at them and returned to the theater. Later that night a mob descended backstage to lynch the young man. Police arrived and arrested the entire company. After flogging several people while in custody, they finally identified Wright. "The law gave him to the mob," Handy recalled, "and in almost less time than it takes to tell it they had done their work. He was lynched, his tongue cut out and his body shipped to his mother in Chicago in a pine box." The threat of white violence against touring black musicians was constant and palpable to Handy, who carried a cache of handguns with him on the road.[26]

The New York theater and song-publishing industries helped each other dominate the American music business. Exact numbers are notoriously difficult to come by, but the assessments we have suggest that the fortunes of song publishers and touring attractions rose and fell together. The music bibliographer D. W. Krummel estimates that there was an average of 12,000 songs published each year in the United States during the 1870s, before the rise of Tin Pan Alley. Annual averages rose to 20,000 songs in the 1890s and peaked at an average 25,000 in the first decade of the century. They then began a relatively steady decline over the following several decades.[27] The number of touring shows in the United States followed the same arc. The theater historian Alfred L. Bernheim estimates that there were approximately 250 legitimate companies touring at any given time during the 1880 season. The number rose with the organization of circuits and booking agencies, peaking with an approximate average of 339 simultaneous touring outfits in 1900. While falling slightly in subsequent years, the number stayed relatively steady through the first decade of the century, after which it declined dramatically. According to Bernheim's estimates, there were never more than ninety-seven simultaneous touring shows between 1915 and 1928, a period that saw an average of only sixty-nine shows on the road at any given time.

There are a variety of possible causes for the decline of the road show after 1910, a time when new theater productions in New York continued to increase. Some blamed the Syndicate's stranglehold; some lambasted the declining quality of touring shows; others cited the rise of alternate amusements, including motion pictures, phonographs, automobiles, and less centrally organized forms of live theater such as vaudeville and tent shows. Not the least of the problems was the intense competition that had developed between the Syndicate and a competing firm run by J. J. and Lee Shubert. The two brothers started with a few theaters in 1900. By 1905, they had developed a plan to challenge the Syndicate across the country. One result of the Shuberts' expansion was that many smaller towns that struggled to support one theater suddenly had two. Ticket sales faltered, and in many cases both theaters failed. By the second decade of the twentieth century, touring shows were left with far fewer places to perform in the hinterlands.[28] The golden age of Tin Pan Alley, the 1890s and the 1900s, was also the peak era of touring shows in the United States. Together they brought manufactured songs to almost every corner of the nation.

The Sentimental Ballad and the Coon Song: Minstrelsy's Separated Twins

Two kinds of songs became particularly popular with southern audiences during the ascendance of Tin Pan Alley and the Theatrical Syndicate: sentimental ballads and what were known as coon songs. Later folklorists and commercial record scouts encountered them regularly while traveling through the South, and many of these early Tin Pan Alley hits made their way into race and hillbilly record catalogues and folk song collections in the 1920s. Each offered a new twist on the minstrel tunes that had propelled collaborations between touring companies and song publishers before the Civil War.[29] Beginning in the 1830s, early blackface minstrelsy had thrived on raucous tunes such as "Jim Crow" or "Zip Coon" that parodied African American dancing and celebration. By the 1850s, minstrel show composers had turned toward depicting romantic nostalgia for an idealized southern past expressed through burnt-cork caricatures of black southerners. Stephen Foster's "Old Folks at Home" (1851) featured a fugitive slave "longing for de old plantation." The ubiquitous "Dixie" (ca. 1859) waxed for the "land of cotton" where "old times are not forgotten." Classic minstrel tunes offered a lost pastoral in which family and home were isolated from the ravages of political and economic strife and African Americans pined for the comforts of slavery. It proved to be a potent combination for white southerners interested in defending slavery during the sectional crises of the 1850s. Songs such as Will Hays's "Little Log Cabin in the Lane" (1871), C. A. White's "The Old Home Ain't What It Used to Be" (1874), and James Bland's "Carry Me Back to Old Virginny" (1878) continued the tradition into the post–Civil War era by lamenting the passing of the mythical Old South. In the 1890s, sentimental ballads and coon songs essentially split the twin sentiments that had propelled classic minstrelsy. They severed expressions of nostalgia from depictions of black inferiority, enabling each to be conveyed unencumbered by the other. While minstrelsy had traded on a fantasy of interracial intimacy under slavery, the combination of sentimental ballads and coon songs spoke a language of racial separation in the era of segregation.

The classic Tin Pan Alley ballads of the 1890s were maudlin tearjerkers, narrative tales of lost love or dead mothers in waltz time. Charles K. Harris's "After the Ball" (1892) was one of the early hits of the genre and alerted the industry to its sales potential. Originally composed for an amateur minstrel production, Harris's song was a tragic story of a man who left his sweetheart on the dance floor to get a drink of water. Upon returning to find her kissing another, he dropped his glass and ran away to nurse his broken heart, only to discover too late that the mysterious suitor was the young lady's brother. The entire story was presented in flashback, an uncle explaining his life of loneliness to the young niece sitting on his knee.[30]

"After the Ball" and other sentimental ballads helped expand the language of nostalgia and loss available to southern audiences. It was devoid of the explicit romance for the antebellum South that characterized minstrel tunes such as "Old Folks at Home," trading the old plantation and the interracial family for the genteel ball and Victorian decorum. The song remained, however, one of longing for what once was, lost love substituting for the Lost Cause. The expression of a generic, supposedly depoliticized nostalgia was one of the major features of the Tin Pan Alley ballad. "I find that sentiment plays a large part in our lives," the composer Charles Harris explained. "The most hardened character or the most cynical individual will succumb to sentiment sometime or other."[31] If minstrel composers provoked sentimentality for slavery, Tin Pan Alley writers evoked sentimentality for an idealized vision of romantic love. Tin Pan Alley ballads' focus on gendered rather than racialized nostalgia expanded their potential consumer base while continuing to enable listeners to use manufactured songs to pine for a more virtuous idealized past.

The work of Gussie L. Davis demonstrates how effortlessly Tin Pan Alley writers shifted their emphasis from the Old South to the new age. The African American songwriter wrote many of his early compositions for the minstrel stage. In 1894, he penned "Sing Again That Sweet Refrain, or Far From the Old Folks at Home," a tribute to Stephen Foster's classic that was promoted by the white singer Rees Prosser of the A. G. Field Minstrels. "Sweet Refrain" painted the scene of a crowded minstrel show in which a blackface performer sings Foster's hit "about his old plantation home down upon the Swanee River far away." A "grey-haired darkey" rose from the audience and begged the performer to "sing again that sweet refrain," because "it takes me back to slav'ry days fore I was sold away." Davis's "Sweet Refrain" was a simple reiteration of the themes and imagery of Foster's midcentury minstrel hit. The song mimicked Foster's idealization of the Old South as a place not of racial violence but of familial love, evoking the "mem'ry of a mother long ago."[32]

Davis also penned two of the most popular sentimental ballads of the era. In 1893, he wrote "The Fatal Wedding" with the lyricist and minstrel performer William Windom. (A testament to the convoluted racial politics of the 1890s stage, Windom was an African American who passed for white so he could don blackface as a featured singer with the all-white Primrose and West Minstrels, with whom he first sang "After the Ball.") Following directly in the heels of Harris's hit, "The Fatal Wedding" was a slow waltz that told the gut-wrenching tale of a woman who interrupts a wedding to announce "the bridegroom is my husband, sir, and this our little child." The infant suddenly dies; the groom commits suicide; and the two are buried in adjoining graves. The bride's mother, however, offers to care for the young stranger because she saved her child from the bigamist. In 1896, Davis composed what would become his most successful song, "In the Baggage Coach Ahead." It was another classic example of the Tin Pan Alley sentimental ballad. The song takes place in the sleeping car of a train, where an inconsolable baby cries in its father's arms. Other passengers demand silence, complaining that they cannot sleep. One woman then suggests the father take the baby to its mother, a request that sets up the song's kicker. "I wish I could," the father replies, "but she's dead in the coach ahead." All the "mothers and wives" on the train rise to help, and soon the babe is sleeping in peace.[33]

The shift from the old plantation to the modern railroad car removed much of the racial context that minstrelsy used to link familial love with white supremacy and slavery. Yet, as the African American Davis was probably aware, "In the Baggage Coach Ahead" carried a racial subtext. Davis wrote the song the same year the Supreme Court's *Plessy v. Ferguson* established the "separate but equal" justification for segregation when ruling on a case about removing an African American man from a first-class train car. Sleeping berths were reserved for white passengers in the segregated South, and Jim Crow accommodations often doubled as baggage cars. If the characters in Davis's drama were black southerners, it was becoming increasingly likely that the babe would be crying beside its mother's coffin rather than in a car once removed. "Baggage Coach" revealed none of this. Indeed, one African American newspaper commented in 1895, "Few of the many millions of people who have sung or otherwise enjoyed 'The Fatal Wedding,' 'The Light House by the Sea,' and 'The Maple on the Hill,' and numerous other popular songs are aware that Gussie L. Davis, the man who composed them, is a negro."[34] The sentimental ballad left the realities of segregation unstated just as its minstrel predecessors usually failed to acknowledge slavery's brutality. Both served up a romantic nostalgia defined through a mother's unerring love.

At the same time, sentimental ballads could help southerners grapple with the changes wrought by the commercial revolution they were experiencing. "After the Ball" was simultaneously about public amusements and the private home. It offered two narratives: one depicted a dance full of strangers whose actions could be misinterpreted; the other portrayed the intimacy of story time in the family rocking chair. Davis made a similar move as he ended each of his songs: "The story has been often told by firesides warm and bright / Of bride and groom, of outcast and the fatal wedding night" in one case, and "every one had a story to tell in their home of the baggage coach ahead" in the other. Each assured that public tragedy would convert to private morality lessons when witnesses shared the story with their loved ones back home. Each likewise found mothers ameliorating the tragedy by offering maternal care to those in need. Integrating these two supposedly antithetical worlds into one seamless narrative, such songs helped listeners negotiate the distance between public and private allegiances. These were the very fissures that national touring companies and song publishers—along with the entire commercial revolution of the era— were helping to exacerbate. Embracing "After the Ball" and its kin meant not having to choose. Tin Pan Alley ballads offered commercial leisure that celebrated domesticity. Listeners could identify with both by singing along with the odes to private virtue echoing from the public stage.

The sentimental ballad's celebration of domesticity also helped publishers appeal to young upper- and middle-class women, the targeted consumers of sheet music. Piano manufacturers in the late nineteenth century built on long held associations between their instrument and female gentility and domesticity. They marketed training in the piano as an essential part of young women's education, as well as a symbol of their manners, breeding, and self-control.[35] Etiquette books concurred. "Music has an influence peculiar to itself," advised *The Ladies' Book of Etiquette and Manual of Politeness* in 1879. "It can allay the irritation of the mind; it cements families, and makes a home, which might sometimes be monotonous, a scene of pleasant excitement. Pursued as a recreation, it is gentle, rational, lady-like."[36] Teachers encouraged young ladies to learn European music, Italian art songs being seen as particularly suited for the discriminating—if not overly gifted—young pianist.[37] Established music publishers scoffed at such a limited repertoire. European music lacked copyright protection in the United States and could not provide the basis for a publishing business. The sentimental ballad offered a solution. "The day of the Negro and jubiliee [*sic*] song is over," Gussie Davis explained in 1888. "Women are the supporters of the music dealers. A man goes to the theater, hears a song, likes it, but is content to gain snatches of it, and whistling suffices him. A woman buys it and sings it at home. She can not sing a minstrel or Negro song in the parlor, and refined people would not allow it in the house."[38] By creating songs of unquestionable morality and domesticity, publishers could get white female consumers to shift from unprotected classics to copyrighted new compositions.

Tin Pan Alley song publishers accomplished their goal. Sentimental ballads were big sellers. Tellingly, their sales corresponded quite closely to the sale of pianos in the United States. The piano trade expanded significantly between 1890 and 1910. Between 1870 and 1890 the number of pianos grew 1.6 times as fast as the nation's population. But it increased 5.6 times as quickly as the population in the 1890s and 6.2 times as fast in the first decade of the new century. Piano production hit a high mark in 1909 with the introduction of 364,545 new instruments.[39] It is difficult to know to what extent piano sales drove the consumption of sheet music or popular songs encouraged the purchase of pianos. It is clear, however, that touring attractions, song publishing, and piano sales each rose in the 1890s and reached their peak around 1910. The three industries were intimately intertwined.

The connection among the piano, music publishing, and touring industries had two significant effects. First, it brought the ideology and symbolism of the private home to the public stage. Sentimental songs transformed music hall shows precisely because the performance was no longer an end in itself but a means to advertising songs supposedly suitable for the home.

While critics decried the corrupting influence that commercial music was having on the nation, the marketing of sentimental songs from the stage in fact brought celebrations of virtue and domesticity to the public theater. Davis's "Sweet Refrain" offers a case in point. Unlike Foster's original ode, the song was about the theater's power to evoke domestic longings: a man interrupts a performance because it makes him miss his mother. Visions of Victorian domestic propriety and sentimental love made their way from the parlor to the nation's stages as publishers plugged their sentimental songs into stage acts to advertise them to largely amateur female piano players.

Second, it brought the freedom and danger associated with the public stage into the private home. Popular sheet music expanded young women's opportunities for sensual expression even as it explicitly depicted feminine restraint. "There are many young women, who, when they sit down to the piano to sing, twist themselves into so many contortions, and writhe their bodies and faces about into such actions and grimaces, as would almost incline one to believe that they are suffering great bodily torture," lamented the etiquette guru Richard A. Wells in 1894. "Their bosoms heave, their shoulders shrug, their heads swing to the right and left, their lips quiver, their eyes roll; they sigh, they pant, they seem ready to expire!" Young pianists embraced the sensuality of music making, free expression that was emphasized on the musical stage but discouraged of young ladies at home. Wells understood a direct correlation between female exuberance and stage performance. "What they call *expression in singing*, at the rate they would show it, is only fit to be exhibited on the stage, when the character of the song intends to portray the utmost ecstasy of passion to a sighing swain," he insisted. Tin Pan Alley enabled young women to revel in the freedom associated with public popular culture. They could, for the time of their performance, be as sensual and free as the performer who made the song famous. Playing Tin Pan Alley songs had the added benefit of mild rebellion. Pedagogues who preferred that their students perform Italian art songs largely dismissed publishers' sentimental ditties as "poor music, feeble, ephemeral compositions" not worthy of their students' time. Performing them—with the emotional intensity reserved for the stage and their private fantasies—enabled young women to use their hard-won musical skills for their own purposes and to declare that their worlds were much larger than their sequestered drawing rooms.[40]

Alice Person discovered that the titillation of playing popular songs remained connected to minstrelsy's tradition of racial masquerade in the minds of white southerners. Born in 1840 in Petersburg, Virginia, Person made the unique transition from parlor pianist to independent music publisher. She was raised the daughter of a bank employee and enjoyed all "the elegancies and refinements of life" typical of a white family of means in the antebellum South. Trained on the family piano, the young woman enjoyed "playing principally bright lively pieces, and the old plantation melodies so dear to the Southern heart." Person's fortunes left her in 1863. She found herself with a disabled husband, a failing farm, and an expanding brood. Suddenly forced to provide for her family, she began pitching a patent medicine remedy for which she became known across the region. She also built a reputation as a pianist by performing regularly in music stores, state exhibitions, and her own medicine shows. In 1889, she published *A Collection of Popular Aires as Arranged and Played Only by Mrs. Joe Person at the Southern Expositions*. The book contained fifteen piano arrangements, many of which were well-known minstrel songs from the mid-nineteenth century, including Stephen Foster's "Camptown Races" and "Nelly Bly," James Bland's "Carry Me Back to Old Virginny," and Dan Emmett's ubiquitous "Dixie." These were old-style minstrel tunes designed to set the feet in motion as they waxed nostalgic about the Old South.[41]

By the time of its publication, Person's book was something of a nostalgia piece itself. Southern audiences were already becoming familiar with the new songs and styles arriving from the New York music industry. Person elicited both glee and fear from the southern society women to whom she tried to sell her book in the 1890s. She remembered making a call on one southern woman to demonstrate some of her arrangements. She noticed the woman tapping her foot and asked the prospect if she liked what she heard. "Like it? Why I like it better than any music I ever heard in my life!" was the reported reply. Yet the dancing woman declined to purchase the collection. "*I-learn-those-pieces*? No Madam, I wouldn't have that music in my house for anything in this world . . . I like it too well; it made me pat my foot, and I am *afraid of it*." Despite such remonstrative protests (or perhaps because of them), Person found that significant numbers of southern women bought her collection. There remained a market for classic minstrel tunes, yet the meaning of the songs had changed since Person played them as a young girl and found them "so dear to the Southern heart." These black dialect songs, once celebrated as sentimental paeans to a pastoral South, were heard as dangerous and transgressive by her customers in the 1890s. Person's prospects may have interpreted her old minstrel tunes through the lens of the coon song, the new musical means of black derision and white racial passing.[42]

Coon songs of the 1890s jettisoned the nostalgia essential to the classic minstrel song and expanded upon early minstrelsy's uses of black stereotypes. The raucous, comic songs usually depicted an African American world devoid of white presence beyond the police or other authorities. Minstrelsy's assumed interracial love between master and slaves was nowhere to be found. Lyrics conformed to thick though dubious black dialect, and the music often featured syncopation suggesting ragtime rhythms. At their most potent, coon songs traded in racist stereotypes of chicken thieves and watermelons, razor fighting ruffians and Zip Coon–inspired urban dandies, to portray African Americans as often-violent simpletons unequipped for either citizenship or domestic love. The genre emerged in the 1880s but took off after the African American composer and performer Ernest Hogan's "All Coons Look Alike to Me" became a big hit in 1896. According to one estimate, there were over six hundred coon songs published during the 1890s and the coon song craze lasted well into the next decade. Coon songs were written by both white and black composers and performed in a variety of touring productions, including black and white minstrel shows, vaudeville revues, and musical comedies. Coon songs were contradictory to their core, and the controversy surrounding them was a source of both their power and their popularity. A more sustained exploration of the coon song craze appears in chapter 4. Here I am interested in how southerners received these mass-marketed songs. Southerners from across the color line sang them, yet black and white southerners also vigorously denounced the genre.[43]

Coon songs allowed white southerners an opportunity to revel in the physical and expressive freedom they associated with African American culture while enacting white supremacy. The black protagonists in coon songs drank and ate too much, they gambled and stole, and they regularly evaded authority. White fans could commit all these sins through song while simultaneously identifying them as racial traits that proved African American inferiority. In addition, white performers and audiences could act out the violent assault and murder of African Americans through coon songs. Coon songs traded on the entertainment value of black dismemberment and murder. "De Coon Dat Had De Razor," written in 1885 by the African American performer Sam Lucas, depicted a black dance to which "Horace Jinks" brought the coon song weapon of choice.

> He carved poor Johny's coat tail off, Den cut him to de fat;
> He cut his ear clear off his head, Den cut his beaver hat.
> Aunt Hannah said "for gracious sake you'll kill poor Johny Frazier."
> But de coon he didn't notice her, But slashed on wid de razor.

The song concluded with a policeman refusing to apprehend Jinks for fear of getting cut.[44] "The Bully Song," overheard by Charles Peabody in 1903, featured similarly graphic depictions of violence against a black man. "The Bully Song" was a first-person tale told from the perspective of a "Tennessee nigger," who is looking for "the bully da'ts just come to town." Over the first several verses, the narrator imagines the violence he will reap when he finds his target: "Took along my trusty blade to carve dat nigger's bones / Just a lookin' for dat bully, to hear him groans." The search ends in murder, as the narrator declares, "When I got through with bully, a doctor and a nurse / Wan't no good to dat nigger, so they put him in a hearse."[45] The protagonists' murder of an African American man again meets no reprisal or conviction.

Southern white violence against African Americans reached epic proportions in the years of the coon song craze. Between 1889 and 1909, white southerners lynched an estimated 1,700 black victims. In the 1890s, a lynching occurred on average once every two and a half days. Countless more African Americans were assaulted, maimed, or murdered at the hands of white southerners intent on terrorizing the black population and enforcing Jim Crow. The frequency of lynching tended to be higher in areas where local whites encountered black southerners whom they did not know, people on the move. It thus corresponded in some ways to the geography of the commercial revolution that brought rail travel, industry, and touring shows into the region. In the new century, the lynchings of African Americans became public spectacles, events advertised in advance and drawing thousands of onlookers. The ritualized murder of black citizens became entertainment for white southerners.[46] Commercial coon songs provided the musical equivalent of the southern culture of racial violence, complete with the law's refusal to punish the killers of black victims. They could serve as both a fantasy enactment and a rhetorical justification of white attacks on black southerners. Legions of white southerners could vicariously attack black bodies by attending coon song performances or by singing the songs in the privacy of their own homes. They could acquit themselves of the responsibility for their actions by invoking the always-incomplete racial masquerade of the genre, hiding their violent fantasies behind the mask of the savage black brute.

At the same time, coon song violence helped normalize and dismiss the actual violence perpetrated against black southerners. Coon songs were supposedly comedy numbers, their victims' missing ears and knife wounds played for laughs. Yet the African American journalist R. H. Harbert of San Antonio, Texas, understood how coon imagery helped perpetuate lynching. Harbert published an editorial in 1893 denouncing both the spate of lynching and white newspapers' use of the words "coon" and "nigger" when reporting on African American activities. "Any man or medium which daubs you with 'coon', does it with a view of degrading you and bringing you into contempt," he wrote. Harbert blamed these papers for inciting white violence. "They inflame the dormant feelings of their people into a frenzy by prejudice and magnified pictures of the acts or intended acts of the Negroes, when in truth no such intentions ever had a lodging in their brain," he insisted. The *San Antonio Light*, a major white newspaper, reprinted Harbert's editorial only to deflate it with stereotypes. Harbert "is squealing and kicking at himself, and everything in sight," the *Light*'s introduction ran. "He must have struck a bad lot of watermelons, and is full of 'bile.'"[47] Coon song imagery thus provided a way of making light of black victimization and belittling the black activists who spoke out against it.

While many white southerners embraced the coon song, others lambasted the genre for what they believed it said about race, commerce, and southern history. Coon songs ignited intergenerational conflicts between white southerners raised on the myths of racial harmony under slavery proffered by classic minstrelsy and those coming of age in the era of segregation and northern commercial song. The African American writer Charles Chestnutt attempted to portray these overlapping conflicts in *The Colonel's Dream* (1905), his fictional meditation on southern white identity. In one passage of the novel, the titular Confederate veteran's evening is disturbed when a gaggle of young people "launched into the grotesque words of the latest New York 'coon song'" at the parlor piano. The colonel winces at the "first discordant note," and he pines to hear his own generation's stereotype of black music. "A plantation song of the olden time, as he remembered it, borne upon the evening air, when sung by the tired slaves at the end of their day of toil, would have been pleasing, with its simple melody, its plaintive minor strains, its notes of vague longing; but to the colonel's senses there was to-night no music in this hackneyed popular favourite." Chestnutt wrote. "In a metropolitan music hall, gaudily bedecked and brilliantly lighted, it would have been tolerable from the lips of a black-face comedian. But in this quiet place, upon this quiet night, and in the colonel's mood! it seemed like profanation."[48] Chestnutt's colonel abhorred the coon song because it was a product of the northern commercial stage and, he believed, a tin-eared rendition of black southern song. To add insult to injury, the coon song was the sound of the younger generation slipping from the grasp of their southern elders. Singing these clangorous songs, they were rejecting his fantasies of southern history, southern distinctiveness, and the familial love between master and slave for which he had fought. The coon song disrupted and contradicted the myths of the Old South and the Lost Cause.

White southern critics of the coon song concurred: northern commercial composers attempting to portray the black South got it wrong. In 1901, a *Baltimore Sun* columnist wailed, "There is about as much difference between 'coon song' and negro melody as there is between last summer's straw hat and a Thanksgiving turkey stuffed with oysters."[49] When it was announced that "plantation melodies" would represent the United States at a Berlin music festival in 1902, a newspaper writer in Galveston, Texas, opined, "Lovers of Southern music should take pride in seeing that a revival of the plaintive and pleasing plantation tunes of the old South should dispel the idea that the modern 'coon song' is typical and genuine Southern music."[50] White southerners rejected the coon song, while asserting their authority to judge black southern authenticity.

All these colliding interpretations of the coon song are apparent in an incident reported by the *Atlanta Constitution* in 1906. A local white boarding house resident named Will Crim allegedly accosted four fellow boarders because he was disturbed by the young men's boisterous singing of a coon song called "Rastus Johnson Brown." The song was most likely "What You Goin' to Do When the Rent Comes 'Round? (Rufus Rastus Johnson Brown)," published by the songwriting veteran Harry von Tilzer in 1905.

The quartet was returning from a night at the theater where they had heard a comedian sing the song. "They could not help, they said, from singing a few bars of the stirring coon song before they slept." Crim burst from his room, hurling curses as he threatened the boys with a knife. The boys ran and later had Crim arrested. At his arraignment, Crim admitted he had been drunk. "But," he said, "that singing was something terrible. It was enough to have made any man wish 'Rastus Johnson Brown' strung up and skinned alive."[51] Intergenerational conflict, the juvenile embrace of commercial theater, and a song's power to make a white southerner imagine lynching a black man: the incident reveals that, despite protestations, mass-produced music had become a means of articulating and negotiating white southern identity.

African Americans also forged the coon song into an expression of their own needs and desires. Many black writers denounced coon songs as demeaning and dangerous. Echoing black southern voices such as R. H. Harbert, the composer Samuel Coleridge Taylor dismissed them as the "worst sort of rot," lacking any "real Negro character." W. E. B. Du Bois insisted that coon songs belonged to "a mass of music in which the novice may easily lose himself and never find the real Negro melodies." On the other hand, several elements of the genre enabled black listeners to hear very different meanings in the songs. First, the coon song craze marked a significant new level of black participation and visibility in the national music business. Ernest Hogan, Bob Cole, Will Marion Cook, Bert Williams, and George Walker: some of the most sophisticated and successful black composers and performers of the age were at the center of the craze and used the popularity of the genre to break into Broadway, publishing, and touring markets. The coon song was the sound of black triumph over segregation. Second, contrary to Taylor's complaint, coon songs often incorporated important aspects of black creativity that enabled listeners to hear the genre as a new benchmark in black authenticity. The coon song craze corresponded to the rise of ragtime, a distinctive style developed by southern and midwestern African American artists that traded on syncopation and polyrhythmic display. Many popular coon songs incorporated elements of ragtime, thus enabling them to be heard as distinctly African American products. Finally, as the historian Karen Sotiropoulos has demonstrated brilliantly, black performers and composers used the genre to talk about African American politics and culture with black patrons without disturbing the expectations of white audiences. Such political content literally and figuratively went "over the heads" of white patrons interested in confirming their own prejudices to reach black listeners in the segregated balcony.[52]

If "The Bully Song" allowed the vicarious thrill of assaulting a black victim, it also could be heard as a tale of the heroic protection of an African American community. The bully, the song tells us, had been seen "round among de niggers a layin' their bodies down." The protagonist is bent on ending this indiscriminant violence against the black population. After killing the bully, the narrator promises, "You don't hear 'bout dat nigger dat treated folks so free; Go down upon the levee, and his face you'll never see." "The Bully Song" in this reading joins a long list of tales about heroic black bad men in the tradition of Staggolee, or Railroad Bill. African Americans, the historian John Roberts has shown, greeted such black badmen with ambivalence. The characters helped negotiate the tensions between two unacceptable extremes: lawlessness within the black community and the oppressive hand of white law enforcement. Even when his vigilante violence is designed to maintain order or rebalance the scales of justice under Jim Crow, his actions run the risk of bringing white police into black neighborhoods.[53] At the same time, the narrator of "The Bully" offers an individual solution to the problem of institutional racism. He thus creates a second interpretive tension: are his actions the result of rare, clear-headed courage or a mental snap, the insanity of imagining one person can force systemic change? The answer ultimately is moot as the narrator ends the song by boasting of his own power:

> My madness keeps a risin', and I'se not gwine to get left,
> I'm gettin' so bad dat I'm askeer'd of myself.
> I was lookin' for dat bully, now he's on the shelf.[54]

African Americans listening to "The Bully Song" could imagine a successful triumph over oppression even as they acknowledged the risks of going it alone. This interpretation helps explain the popularity of the song with black listeners and performers before it was ever published. W. C. Handy recalled hearing the tune from black St. Louis roustabouts. The sportswriter Charles Trevathan reportedly heard the song performed by an African American singer at Babe Conner's cabaret in the same city before introducing it to May Irwin.[55]

"I Got Mine" (1901) by the white composers John Queen and Charlie

Cartwell offers another example of the ways in which African American southerners interpreted coon songs. The song became very popular with both white and black southerners and enjoyed a long life in the region. Folklorists collected numerous versions during the decade 1910–20, and it was performed in the 1920s by southern black artists Frank Stokes and Pink Anderson as well as by white string band musicians Fiddlin' John Carson and the Skillet Lickers. The original song relates three vignettes typical of the genre: a crap game, a chicken dinner, and a frustrated courtship. The song begins:

> I went out to a nigger crap game, it was against my will
> The coons took all my money except one greenback dollar bill
> There was a hundred dollar bet upon the table, the niggers point was nine
> Just then the coppers stepped through the door but I got mine.
> *Chorus*
> I got mine, boys, I got mine.
> I grabbed that hundred dollar bill thro' the window I did climb
> Ever since then I've worn good clothes living on chicken and wine.
> I'm the leader of society since I got mine.

At one level, "I Got Mine" replicates many of the standard stereotypes of the coon song genre. In addition to its language and imagery, the song portrays its black protagonist as greedy and dishonest, taking whatever he can get for himself. The final verse twists the title phrase as the protagonist gets his comeuppance. When he is shot after confronting a man sitting with his sweetheart, the phrase "I got mine" suddenly suggests punishment rather than entitlement. White audiences could laugh at the antics of the first verses while resting assured that the black thief ultimately pays for his crimes.

African American listeners, on the other hand, could hear "I Got Mine" as a story of survival within a racist society. The protagonist escapes a police raid of a black party and finds a way to acquire the signs of material success he could not afford otherwise. "I got mine" could become a declaration of self-asserted autonomy—the seizing of reparations, back pay or other rewards earned but denied. The folklorist Newman White reported five different versions of "I Got Mine" collected from black Alabamans around 1915. Most hewed quite closely to the original lyrics, but they often avoided the original's use of racial epithets. A few versions did retain the theme of punishment, finding the protagonist in jail: "But the ball and chain went round my leg, since I got mine." Most, however, did not include the turn toward punishment in the final verse. They rather expanded on the original's theme of self-protection and self-interest. One version from Lowndes County, Alabama, for example, finds the singer shooting his antagonist rather than getting shot himself: "A coon reached for his forty-four / but he didn't reach for it in time; For I reached up on the mantelpiece, An' I got mine." Another version sung by a road crew in northern Alabama follows the police raid with the lines "Some of the boys got six months, some got ninety-nine. I didn't get no months at all, but I got mine." Black folk sources emphasized the song's theme of triumphing over unjust authority while diminishing its use of black stereotype. Frank Stokes's commercial recording in 1928 offered the most explicit rendering of the social injustice theme, ending each verse with "I belong to the knock-down society, but I got mine." Tellingly, the recorded version by the white string band the Skillet Lickers largely maintained the racial epithets from the original lyrics while landing the protagonist in jail following the crap game.[56]

The different versions of "I Got Mine" offer insight into the southern embrace of coon songs and northern commercial music. First, it appears that many black and white southerners were exposed to commercial coon songs and accepted them as part of their musical world. Touring shows and sheet music publishers found willing southern audiences who used the products of the commercial marketplace to form cultures of their own. Second, coon songs, like music in general, were open to multiple interpretations. The various versions of "I Got Mine" offer a glimpse into the process of selective hearing and interpretation at the heart of the listening experience. The original version contained themes of both black inferiority and the challenge to authority. Different artists emphasized divergent meanings that were already present. Listeners went through the same process of discrimination and interpretation as they heard the coon song on the southern stage. As the flood of contradictory meanings in the music washed over them, southerners often did not reject the genre because they found some of its possible meanings offensive. They rather emphasized other meanings that were more to their liking. The process baffled the white sociologist Howard Odum. In 1911, he wrote about the popularity of coon songs and other commercial hits among black southerners. "Young negroes pride themselves on the number of such songs they can sing, at the same time that they resent a request to sing the older melodies," he explained. "Very small boys and girls sing the difficult airs of the new songs with surprising skill, until one wonders when and how they learned so many words and tunes."[57]

In the late nineteenth century, black and white touring artists performed much of the same material. Audiences and stage productions were segregated, but the music, claimed by black and white alike, was not. Jim Crow involved labeling and segregating racialized bodies, yet it was far less effective at attributing clear racial identities to music. A southern theater experience involved a black or a white singer projecting a popular song—associated with minstrelsy or vaudeville, the old plantation or the Victorian parlor, Italian opera or black spirituals—across a racially divided hall. White listeners took comfort when the racial hierarchy written across the concert hall's seating was echoed in the minstrel's lament for the passing of slavery, and they could hear the beauty of Verdi's *Il Trovatore* as sung by Madame Flowers, Sisteretta Jones, or other African American divas as evidence that segregation was just: Jim Crow kept the majority of inferior black people in their place without hindering the respectable, diligent or talented. Black patrons often heard the same sounds as challenges to the very status quo their white counterparts believed was being maintained. The embrace of northern entertainment—from Flowers and Jones to vaudeville and high drama—offered a small way of transcending the color line that defined their relationship to southern white society. And the spectacle of white southerners dropping their cash to see African American performers—professionals whose talent declared black inferiority a lie and whose movements could not be contained by local ordinance—proved thrilling entertainment and a moral victory of its own. When the African American prima donna Flora Batson Bergen toured the South in 1889, an older black gentleman in Memphis explained to a reporter, "She sings the devil right out of the white folks, and when you get the devil out of the white people they are just as good as colored people."[58]

As Charles Peabody's comments in the *Journal of American Folklore* in 1903 reveal, white supremacy did not prevent black and white southerners from embracing the same mass-produced music. Rather, it influenced the ways in which different southerners would interpret, invoke, or deny music that straddled the color line. Tin Pan Alley songs became an integral part of southern culture. In 1894, the Junior Brass Band of Fort Smith, Arkansas, marked their trip to the nearby town of Van Buren with an afternoon parade—a tactic probably copped from shows that toured on a much grander scale. The African American youth orchestra pulled locals into their evening concert, along with many Fort Smith residents who caught the train to Van Buren for the show. The featured song of the night was "After the Ball."[59] It was a telling choice of material. Only two years after its publication, the stage hit was the feature of an African American brass band in Arkansas, a familiar crowd pleaser designed to put over the Fort Smith youth with their Van Buren brethren. Two small southern communities expressed their commonality through a commercially published and marketed song. The national music industry was doing its job very well.

MAKING MONEY MAKING MUSIC 2

The Education of Southern Musicians in Local Markets

Around 1927, Texas native Henry Thomas recorded "Railroadin' Some" for Vocalion Records. The song was most likely autobiographical. The African American singer, born in 1874, had spent a good part of his life traveling the rails, and "Railroadin' Some" depicted a man on the move. Over a monotonous, chugging guitar chord punctuated by quill blasts and whistles—the unmistakable sound of a moving train—Thomas did not sing as much as bark in the cadence of a conductor.

> I leave Fort Worth, Texas, and go to Texarkana,
> And double back to Fort Worth,
> Come on down to Dallas,
> Change cars on the Katy
> Coming through the territory to Kansas City
> And Kansas City to Saint Louis,
> And Saint Louis to Chicago
> I'm on my way, but I don't know where.
> Change cars on the T.P.,
> Leaving Fort Worth, Texas,
> Going through Dallas,
> Hello, Terrell,
> Grand Saline,
> Silver Lake,
> Mineola,
> Tyler,

Longview,
Jefferson,
Marshall,
Little Sandy,
Big Sandy,
Texarkana,
And double back to Fort Worth.
Change cars on the Katy,
Leaving Dallas, Texas,
Coming through Rockwell,
Hello, Greenville,
Celeste,
Denison,
South McAlester,
Territory,
Muskogee,
Wagner,
Parsons, Kansas,
Kansas City,
Sedalia,
And I change cars and jump in St. Louis.
Hello Springfield,
I'm on my way, Chicago.
Bloomington,
Joliet,
Can the Highball pass on through?
Highball on through, Sir.
Grand Crossing,
Thirty-first Street Depot,
Polk Street Depot,
Chicago.[1]

"Railroadin' Some" is full of restless energy. Thomas's breathless incantation implied that the only thing that mattered about each town or city was that another would follow it. The singer subtly relaxed his phrasing when he sang the last "Chicago," indicating that the song might be a tale of a serpentine but successful migration to the destination city of so many black southerners. Yet he had already left Chicago once in the first stanza, and there was little to suggest he would not do so again. "Railroadin' Some" sounds like a list of way stations rather than destinations. In either case, it showed that Thomas endorsed an important African American tactic for evading the harsh realities of Jim Crow and sharecropping. Confronted with this twin curse, many black southerners chose to get up and leave. African Americans had long prized mobility as an expression and enactment of their freedom, one almost as difficult under sharecropping contracts as it had been under slavery. Taking to the rails, moving from town to town or lighting out for Kansas, Chicago, or New York, was an escape not only from southern racism but also from the drudgery and debt of farm labor. Henry Thomas must have known this. The son of slaves turned sharecroppers, Thomas worked the soil beside his eight siblings until he was old enough to get out. From what is known about him, the singer spent a good part of his life traveling just as he depicted in "Railroadin' Some." When he began his long journey, he joined legions of itinerant black southerners who were often uncertain about where they were headed but sure of what they were leaving behind.[2]

On the other hand, "Railroadin' Some" can be heard as the calculated itinerary of a working musician. Thomas was known to ride the railroad circuit around Texas and Louisiana. He played music as he went and became a recognized presence in many of the small-town depots mentioned in his song. The lyrics' circuitous route betrays the telltale logic of the traveling musician: perform in each location often enough to build a reputation but rarely enough to find audiences thankful for catching you. Indeed, "Railroadin' Some" charts a schedule remarkably like the routes followed by countless established acts as they moved through the South on tours booked by the Theatrical Syndicate. In this hearing, Thomas's charged vocal cadence is the sound of a professional not acknowledged as such. He proves an intimate knowledge of the regional geography. He demonstrates a persistent work ethic. Then he demands respect. As he hits the name of each city on the highest note of each phrase and insistently pushes from one to another, it is as if he is declaring, "I know what I am doing. I have thought this out. This is my job."

Little separates these two interpretations of "Railroadin' Some." There existed no stark dividing line between amateur and professional musicians, vagabonds and touring artists, in the early-twentieth-century South. Performers worked along a continuum between these two extremes, their relative positions often more a result of their social and economic conditions than their desires, their self-conceptions, or the work that they did as musicians. What distinguished musicians like Thomas from their peers in the Theatrical Syndicate—who enjoyed advanced bookings, access to theaters, purchased train tickets, and reserved accommodations (if they were lucky)—was less their artistic philosophies or attitudes toward commerce than their access to capital and institutional support.[3] Many southern working-class musicians understood their art as a career, an alternative to more difficult and confining forms of labor. They took their craft seriously, and they developed a wide set of skills and attitudes, both musical and social, to eke a living out of their music. As I will demonstrate, two of the most significant aspects of their self-fashioned careers were the abilities to play fast and loose with musical styles and to show a conscious disregard for the color line that was coming to characterize the Jim Crow South. These skills marked them as professionals, even if our current conceptions of music and markets might fail to identify them as such.

A body of thought about the relationship between music and work has hindered our ability to see musicians such as Henry Thomas as working professionals. The first arose out of the distinction between civilized art music and primitive folk music developed by academic and popular writers during the late nineteenth century. Pundits celebrated civilized music for the hard work it required, yet they valorized primitive music precisely because it apparently required no work at all. At that time, musical training was considered an important part of middle-class women's education and socialization. Etiquette books insisted upon the cultivation of musical skills so that young women could infuse the home with both social grace and morally uplifting culture. From midcentury, piano instructors in the United States had increasingly insisted that proper practice should be hard work. Many teachers subjected students to the Klavier Schule of Siegmund Lebert and Ludwig Stark, whose *Method* dominated private piano curriculum in the United States. *Method*, first published in 1858 and in its seventeenth printing by 1884, emphasized a virtuosic dexterity and finger strength only achievable through hours of intense and painful exercises. As young students cramped their digits running repetitive scales up and down the keyboard, teachers heeded pedagogues' advice that "five finger exercises are the things which most pupils dislike and shirk, and only the severest discipline on the part of the teacher will *make* the pupil take the daily dose of them which he requires." Intense practice regimes conformed to a larger Victorian ideology that discouraged idleness and suggested that hard work—like art—cleansed the spirit and inculcated virtue.[4]

This understanding of music as work for the civilized middle class stood in stark contrast to contemporaneous depictions of music in primitive or folk cultures. Primitive people were naturally musical, scholars insisted. Primitive music did not require work. It simply occurred. Depictions of primitive people's natural musical abilities were ubiquitous during the late nineteenth century. They were central to both the communal theories of folk song composition popular in American scholarship and the cultural evolutionary paradigm driving anthropological theory. Exactly *because* it was not a conscious act, scholars maintained, primitive music contained some fundamental human truths that the civilized person could no longer access. The training, practice, and hard work deemed necessary for the budding civilized musician was therefore a hindrance to the primitive musician. It diminished the power of the music by replacing unconscious expression with conscious contrivance, authenticity with artifice. Scholars largely viewed working-class musicians such as Henry Thomas, who lacked access to formal music education and did not perform art music repertoires, through the lens of primitivism rather than civilization.

We have largely abandoned the rhetoric of primitivism and civilization so popular at the turn of the twentieth century, but sediments of it remain in the distinction between functional and contemplative art that continue to fuel writing about music. At its most basic, this distinction revolves around the value of contextual or extramusical material in determining music's meaning. Does music stand alone or can it only be understood within a cultural context? Western art music's perceived lack of functionality—it is art for art's sake—remains a dominant if besieged concept in academic music curricula, while scholars of African and African American music exhibit a tenacious attachment to musical functionality and what it implies about the holistic integration of music into everyday life.[5] Like the rhetoric of civilization and primitivism, the dichotomy between contemplative and functional music subtly has hindered investigations of the latter as hard work. Art music, when valued for its contemplative or transcendent qualities, encourages technical analysis focused on the work required to compose and perform it. Non-art music, when valued for its functional role within a particular society, encourages cultural analysis that is less about how it is technically made than what it means. Further, an ethnographic focus on functionalism has tended to valorize musical amateurism—demonstrating how whole communities participated in music making and how their music was a result of widely held community traditions, needs, and attitudes toward performance. Through this framework, one is more likely to see Henry Thomas's travels and music as outgrowths of a generalized southern African American culture and predicament than as the actions of a conscious and committed professional musician.

This tendency can be seen in a final literature concentrating on music and work: folklore collections of occupational groups. Since the publication of John Lomax's *Cowboy Songs* in 1910, occupational categories have been one of the most popular ways in which to catalogue folk music, perhaps second only to racial and ethnic groupings. In this paradigm, work songs were a component of the labor process. They were thus deeply connected to people's everyday lives and explicitly functional. Songs sung during work served a number of purposes, from regulating the pace of labor or communicating across the worksite, to building collective identity among workers or lodging protests about work conditions. Collections of songs of the lumberjack, the miner, the field hand, the railroad worker, the levee camp, or the maritime trades offered unique insights into the cultures of particular work sites and particular sets of workers. They also encouraged readers to appreciate music as a by-product of these various kinds of labor rather than as a form of labor in its own right.[6]

Yet many working-class musicians, far from seeing their music as an extension of their labor, described their music as an alternative to it. "I *always* felt like I could beat plowin' mules, choppin' cotton, and drawin' water," the black artist Muddy Waters recalled. "I did all that, and I never did like none of it. Sometimes they'd want us to work Saturday, but they'd look for me, and I'd be *gone*, playin' in some little town or some juke joint."[7] Other musicians told similar stories. The African American musician Samuel Chatman explained why his brother Lonnie played music. "All of 'em farming but one," he stated. "Lonnie didn't like to work. He always stayed on the road somewhere, him and Walter Johnson. That's the reason Walter was playing with us cause he didn't want to work and Lonnie didn't want to work and they'd stay gone, playing music."[8] The black singer and guitarist

Walter Vinson simply stated that he played music because he "got tired of smellin' mule farts."[9] Bill Broonzÿ noted that when white listeners discovered his musical skill, "We would be playing and sitting under screen porches while the other Negroes had to work in the hot sun."[10] The African American youngster Deford Bailey was a domestic worker until his wealthy white boss learned that he could play parlor songs on his harmonica. "From then on, she had me stand in the corner of the room and play my harp for her company," he recalled. "Before she found out I could play, I had to work like the rest of the help. From then on, I just fooled around . . . I never did no more good work. My work was playing the harp."[11] Finally, the poet Langston Hughes recalled a conversation with Bessie Smith, the African American blues singer, in which "her only comment on the art of the Blues was that they had put her 'in de money.' "[12] For these black artists, music was a way out. As an alternative means of employment, it could register subtle protest against the structural racism of the southern economy. As it did for Henry Thomas, music offered an escape, a freedom—however tenuous—of the economic as well as the physical and cultural kind.

White working-class artists told similar stories about using music to escape from work. Jimmie Rodgers, a white singer from Meridian, Mississippi, joined his father working for the railroad as soon as he was old enough. As he honed his skills singing blues and common stock tunes, Rodgers found a receptive audience among the black railroad employees with whom he labored in the years leading up to 1920 . The dangerous and difficult work took its toll on his tubercular body, and he had to quit several times when the strain proved too much to bear. Rodgers eventually formed a band to play in the resorts of nearby Lauderdale Springs. His group specialized in the Tin Pan Alley songs that were popular with the resort patrons, including "I'll See You in My Dreams" and "How Come You Do Me Like You Do." He was able to leave railroad work behind, even as he sometimes evoked it in his songs.[13] Dave Macon, the white singer born in 1870 on the Cumberland Plateau in Tennessee, established a small freight hauling business around 1900. He spent the next couple of decades pushing his mule wagon between Murfreesboro and Woodbury. Reflecting on his eventual transition to a music career, Macon compared himself to a racehorse "that for fourteen long weary years was harnassed [sic] to pull a heavy dray wagon." The new job was akin to trading his regular load for a light buggy.

"It is not known whether it was the lightness of the buggy compared with her daily task or the rush of the talent to become free. Anyway it was like a bird gaining its freedom from the clasp of a cruel boy," he explained.[14]

Like Henry Thomas, these black and white artists forged their music as a response to their working-class experiences. However, their music did not conform to our common understanding of work songs. Music was not a way to pace work, to make labor their own, or even to comment on it and the meaning it held for them. Music was a way to stop working—or at least to work at a task over which they had much more control. Their vision of music presents a challenge to both the separation of art from life held as the art music ideal and the alternative vision that roots musical power and authenticity in the functional ties between music and workaday life. These musicians often understood their music as functional: it served particular purposes and was performed within contexts that gave the music meaning. Yet they refused to limit their music to that which represented their current conditions or the work they despised. Instead, they used music to imagine new opportunities and alternatives for themselves and to bring these futures into being. They may have created music that did not sound like what we might expect from domestic workers and farm laborers, but that was pre-cisely the point. Instead of creating music that spoke of their labors, they played music that transformed them. They used music to forge new identi-ties for themselves as skilled professionals and grassroots musical entrepre-neurs. This was only possible after they had worked hard to develop their craft and learned how to get paid for their efforts. What follows is an attempt to describe the process by which such southern musicians learned these skills. It was a schooling often more rigorous than that received in the nation's premiere conservatories, if only because the stakes were so high.

Learning How to Play

Not everybody with a bad job could use music as an escape. Playing music required skill, and skill came from practice. When artists approached music as a job, they educated themselves in the specific skills necessary to making music. Contrary to the myth of natural musical ability, musicians spent hours and years practicing their craft and perfecting their delivery. The African American pianist Roosevelt Sykes, for example, insisted that it took skill to play the blues: "Because there's a thousand of people worried to death, and house done burned down and everything, husband lost his family, he can't sing a tune. If that's the case that worried people play the blues, you'd be surprised at how many people could sing the blues. That's not the case. Blues is a talent."[15] Like any talent, music took time and energy to develop. The black guitarist Ashley Thompson, born in 1896 nearRipley, Mississippi, explained, "You got to make your own blues, you got to take your time and study, and fix your words where they'll all . . . fit and match . . . You intend to put em on record or anything like that, sing em out in public, you got to get your words where they'll fit in."[16] This process took time and technical skill. Jack Owens, a black farmer and singer from Mississippi, explained how he transformed improvised work songs into set compositions. "See, you just be out in the fields. Sometimes you strike a little tune, something like that, and it come to you," he explained. "Then you come back and strike your box [i.e. Guitar] and start to hum it on your box. When you know anything, you got a little tune."[17] Hobart Smith, a white singer born in 1897 in Smyth County, Virginia, related a very similar process of composition.

> You've first got to get the tune on your mind and then find it with your fingers—keep on till you find what you want on the neck. But keep that tune in your mind just like you can hear it a playin.' I've been to the cornfield many of a time when I was a farmer and I'd hear a good fiddle tune or a good banjer piece and I'd commence whistlin' it. And I'd whistle that till my mouth got so tired, and I'd go home keepin' it on my mind. I'd go pretty fast and I'd whistle all the way into the holler on the mountain and my banjer would be hangin' on the wall . . . I'd keep that tune right on my mind and I'd find that tune on the string before I'd quit.[18]

Converting the music in one's head into one's fingers took practice. "It's kind of hard to do, I'll tell you, but I does it," asserted Owens.

In addition to practicing their instruments, some musicians learned to read sheet music in order to increase the number of songs in their repertoire. Even those who could not read musical notation still found sheet music useful. Huddie Ledbetter recalled, "I used to look at the sheet music and learn the words of a few of the popular songs like *Aggravatin' Papa*."[19] Ashley Thompson recalled learning Tin Pan Alley tunes from a white woman who lived nearby during the 1920s. He could not read music, but he bought sheet music for the woman to teach him. Over the course of their relationship, the two learned several published blues and Tin Pan Alley compositions, including "Wang Wang Blues" (1921) and "Baby Face" (1925) by the Tin Pan Alley scribes Benny Davis and Harry Akst.[20] Mississippian Lonnie Chatmon turned to his brother-in-law to teach him how to read music. All of Chatmon's study and practice paid off, recalled fellow musician Walter Vinson. "He didn't make no mistakes; he didn't play no discords," Vinson declared. "He was a violin *player*."[21]

Aspiring musicians such as Chatmon sought out lessons and advice from those who could already play. Musical apprenticeships could occur across the color line. Ashley Thompson explained, "I got interested in music after I got 15 years old. A white fellow stayed right there next to me, he played all the time and I stayed over there and he learnt me what I knew and I just kept on."[22] The white singer Gene Austin, born in 1900 and raised by an itinerate blacksmith around Yellow Pine, Louisiana, learned through a similar process. "There was a little colored gal, used to come around and do some work for us when we could afford it," he recalled. "I knew she used to sneak into the colored church on weekdays and play the little organ they had out there. So one day I told her I'd give her two bits if she'd show me how to play a song called 'Hard Times.' She did it, and that's the first piece of music I ever learned."[23] Hobart Smith likewise recalled learning his fiddle style from Jim Spencer, an older black violinist who lived nearby. "He played 'Jinny Put the Kettle On' and all those old tunes like that, you know," Smith recalled. "And he would come up to our house and he'd play one night for us, and he'd go over to my uncle's and play one night for them, and then go down to my aunt's in the other holler—we lived in three different hollers in the mountains, you know. He'd make a round." "Jinny Put the Kettle On" was a tune long popular with American fiddlers. Its history reached back into eighteenth-century Scotland, yet it had traveled throughout the United States well before Smith or Spencer ever heard it. While Spencer was playing at the white houses in the area, young Smith was taking mental notes. "I'd hear old-timey fiddlers in different places and I'd just get it in my head and work it out with my fingers," Smith admitted. Smith's recollections divulge a dual process of racial appropriation and accommodation. Black musicians learned the tunes and styles that could impress local white audiences. White listeners in turn picked up playing styles and pointers from African American artists. Smith also recalled learning his guitar style from Blind Lemon Jefferson when he heard Jefferson play for black workers at a nearby railroad camp around 1912. "I think that right about there I started on the gittar," he explained. "I liked his type of playing. I just watched his fingers and got the music in my head and then I'd thumb around till I found what I was wantin' on the strings."[24]

Jefferson often turned his performances into impromptu lessons for musicians in the large crowds that gathered to hear him. The black musician "Lightnin'" Hopkins recalled joining the elder guitarist at a church picnic in 1920 until Jefferson dissented, "Boy, you've got to play that right."[25] "Knocky" Parker, the white pianist for Texas swing innovators The Light Crust Doughboys, recalled learning his style while sitting at Jefferson's side. Parker sat in with Jefferson at Dallas's Lone Star Saloon during the early twenties. "He'd play and I'd play the same thing on the piano; my piano playing is very much like a stringed instrument . . . now I played then exactly the same thing I play now and they taught me this. They'd play on the guitars and I learned from this and all those other little instruments too." Parker's comments suggest the occurrence of a number of translations: from blues to western swing, from guitar to piano, and from black to white. Yet Parker played down these translations, insisting that there was not much of a communication gap to overcome. "Down there in the southwest, country music and the black music came from the same roots," Parker explained. "We all had guitars and we always had the Spanish influence. The Spanish motif is stronger in the Southwest and this comes over to the blacks a whole lot. The blacks played nice pretty little Spanish folk tunes but I can't remember which ones . . . But we kind of understood that this was international culture."[26]

While Parker's invocation of interracial musical culture may appear to be a romantic ode to racial harmony, more likely the interracial musical culture was founded on the desire to make money. Money remained a central, often primary, concern for these musicians. According to several probably apocryphal stories about Lemon Jefferson, the blind guitarist had ears sensitive enough to identify a coin by the sound it made dropping into his tin cup and the denomination of a bill by its feel in his hands. He would send pennies back to the donor and admonish audiences, "Don't play me cheap."[27] The guitarist liberally and graciously shared his knowledge and skills with other musicians, but these lessons were conducted from the bandstand or the street corner while in the process of getting paid for his efforts.

The Places and Prices of Performance

Indeed, once technical skills were developed, musicians could begin to seek compensation for their talents. This brought another set of skills into play, as artists began forging relationships with various audiences within shifting, and often unpredictable, performance contexts. Many southern working-class musicians did not have access to the most fruitful gigs in urban theaters, opera houses, and nationally touring shows. They nevertheless created opportunities to get paid wherever they could.

Sometimes musicians tapped into an informal barter economy. As one anonymous white singer explained his train travel through Arizona, "Some people pay as they go. I play as I go."[28] Huddie Ledbetter and Blind Lemon Jefferson similarly played music in exchange for free train travel around the Dallas area in the years after 1910. Ledbetter recalled, "We didn't have to pay no money in them times. We get on the train, the driver takes us anywhere we want to go. Well, we just get on and the conductor say 'Boys, sit down. You going to play music?' We tell him, 'Yes.' "[29] Bill Broonzy found as a young boy that his performances at white houses brought him food, old clothing, and his first manufactured violin—a replacement for the home-made instrument with which he began his studies.[30] In each of these cases musicians were able to reap important benefits from their music. These informal, everyday opportunities constituted significant, if often hidden, markets for music. Those skilled not only in music but also in the art of the deal could alchemize their tunes into material goods, even when cash remained difficult to come by.

The white singer Dock Boggs, on the other hand, became adept at converting his music into hard currency. In an interview in 1969, the Virginia native born in 1898 recalled riding through the mountains in a friend's Model A Ford when the pair had no money to fill their gas tank. They approached a group of men sitting on a park bench, who soon recognized Boggs and asked him to play. Boggs responded, "Banjer is plumb sick. And that there car, gas tank's about empty. My stomach's about empty." His pitch worked. "They give me about three or four dollars 'fore I even started up on my banjo," he smiled. Boggs fetched his instrument out of the car and took up another collection before hitting a note. "I played about an hour, hour and a half, and I had plenty money to fill up the gas tank plenty money to eat dinner on, plenty money to buy extra oil and get to the top of the mountain," he concluded.[31] Boggs's tale reveals that his talents extended beyond his banjo picking. His ability to turn music into money rested on his skill at transforming a few folks on a park bench into a paying audience.

Other musicians formalized Boggs's approach, strategizing about what location would give them the best exposure to passing crowds with pocket change and time to linger. Close proximity to a popular place of business, especially one that also served as a community social center, offered better possibilities for making some money. The Mexican-born singer Lydia Mendoza described her family's process of finding locations to play in south Texas. "We would arrive at a place and ask permission to sing, and, sometimes, they wouldn't give it to us, and we would have to move on and find another spot. If we were given permission, however, and if it was a store or a barbershop, we would set up and play outside. They would put out some chairs for us, and we would play and sing out in front of the place for whatever the people cared to give us."[32] At times such arrangements could be reciprocal. Using the storefront as a stage, musicians could attract an audience of possible customers for the business.

Some musicians transformed their street performances into regular appearances, the predictability of which would attract paying crowds. The white guitarist Riley Puckett, born in 1894 outside Atlanta, was known for his regular street performances in that city. *Talking Machine World* noted, "On Sunday afternoons, from April to November, he can be found stationed at one of the busy crossroads, with motorists by the hundreds gathered to hear him. He charges no fee, but those who are entertained pay him liberally."[33] If his later recording output is any indication, Puckett appealed to his transient audience by drawing on a vast repertoire of songs and styles including blues, minstrel songs, rags, and a large number of popular songs from the late nineteenth and early twentieth centuries.[34] Blind Lemon Jefferson routinely performed on the streets of Wortham, Texas, in the years 1910–20. Quince Cox, a Wortham native, would go down to listen and give coins to the guitarist. "He used to play at Jake Lee's barbershop every Saturday, and people from all over came to hear him play," Cox noted. "Then he'd get on this road at ten or eleven o'clock, and he'd walk to Kirvin, seven or eight miles." By 1917, Jefferson had established a regular appearance in the Deep Ellum district of Dallas. The African American guitarist Mance Lipscomb recalled, "When we got to Dallas, we hung around where we could hear Blind Lemon sing and play . . . He hung out 'round the track, Deep Ellum. And people started coming in there, from 9:30 until 6:00 that evening, then he would go home because it was getting dark and someone carried him home."[35]

Like Dallas's Central Track in which Jefferson plied his trade, other urban areas became central entertainment districts due to a combination of zoning laws, segregation, tourism, and the development of nightlife. These districts became regular places in which musicians could perform on the streets for money. Decatur Street in Atlanta, Beale Street in Memphis, and Storyville in New Orleans became centers for black nightlife that attracted both black and white customers.[36] San Antonio's Market Square, a popular tourist site among Mexican, Tejano, and white visitors, attracted many performers. Lydia Mendoza recalled the competition among street singers at Market Square.

> There were . . . more than ten groups there all spread out throughout the open area of the Plaza. And they'd just be hanging around there playing dice at the tables; waiting for someone to turn up . . . As soon as a car would enter, everybody, all the musicians, would run and crowd around to see.
>
> "Can I sing for you? Me? Can I sing for you? Do you want to hear 'La Adelita'? Can I sing 'Rancho grande' for you?"
>
> Well, times were hard and those musicians all made their living the same way we did: just from what people would give them. Everybody was chasing after the *centavos* in those days.

While they made very little money in Market Square, Mendoza reminded, it was far more than the family had collected as migrant farm workers. "And, you know, believe it or not, we used to make enough money there to pay the rent and buy clothing and food and everything."[37]

Working at house parties and dances offered a step up from street performances, because the gigs usually offered a significant audience and the probability of getting paid. Sam McGee was born in 1894 in Williamson County, south of Nashville, Tennessee. In his late teens and early twenties, the white guitar and banjo player performed for white square dances that could last until daybreak. The dances would take place at someone's house, where the furniture would be pushed back and sawdust or cornmeal spread on the floor to facilitate sliding feet. "They'd have us up on a platform in a corner, and that dust would come up—your eyes would look like two burnt holes in a blanket," McGee recalled. "We were paid—three figures would be called a set and they'd charge them, have a man go around and take up money from all of them, 10 [cents] a set. Well . . . these callers would call a set so long; maybe they'd dance twenty minutes on one figure, and it would take three of them." McGee received free food in addition to his pay. "They'd treat you like you were a king," he remembered. "About 12 o'clock they'd always have a lot of stuff cooked up and you could go in and eat or drink anything you wanted to, and the first thing you know, they were lined up and going again."[38]

Bukka White, born in 1909, performed at similar African American functions around his native Huston, Mississippi, when he was a young child. The events, held in someone's house or in a large common building on a plantation, were called "frolics" or "suppers," depending on how much food was for sale. "You see, they had square dancin'—what they call now. But now you see at the suppers then they would dance, and . . . at the end of the set everybody would carry their partner to the table and treat 'em," White explained. "That's the way they made their money. Which sardine was a nickel, you know, and two apples for a nickel and they were payin' me fifteen cents a night and two apples and a box of sardines." This was a lot of money for a child performer. "It appeared to me in them days that I was gettin' a hundred dollars 'cause I didn't know what to do with the fifteen cents if you want to hear the truth," he admitted while noting that his carefree attitude was a result of his youth.[39]

Some black musicians found that they could make more money playing for white audiences than they could for black patrons. Black groups such as Cannon's Jug Stompers from Memphis and the Dallas String Band played in streets for white and black audiences, received extra tips for serenading, and often played instrumental songs for white dances. The economic disparity between black and white southerners deeply affected the terrain upon which such interracial musical interaction took place. Sam Chatman explained that musicians would usually receive about two dollars for playing at a black house party. Out of this income they would have to buy their own food and drink. White parties, on the other hand, could bring in an average of five dollars per musician as well as a plate of food. In addition, the white parties Chatman remembered usually wound down before midnight, while the black functions could go well into the morning hours. For struggling musicians like Chatman and his brothers, the early end to a party could mean a precious few extra hours of sleep before having to wake for their day jobs the next morning.[40]

Some black musicians noted that it was safer to play at white functions. Ashley Thompson insisted, "We run into some of those colored cafes and do pretty good and some of them would be so rough, you couldn't stay in em, make no music."[41] The impression that white functions were safer for black musicians than African American parties may have been influenced by two factors. White southerners were more accepting of black musicians than they were of African American people in general. Nathaniel D. Williams, the African American newspaper writer and DJ in Memphis, explained, "First place, he could go into the white man's home and entertain playing music. Second, he could go to his most exclusive places and in playing music later on, and as he saw a whole lot more, and he talked to a lot of these people. And there was a difference in their approach that the white listeners would use to the Negro musicians than they did the other Negro."[42] White southerners treated African Americans better as musicians than they did when encountering them on the street, in the fields, or any other arena of interracial contact in the Jim Crow South. Thus black musicians could find white dances comparatively free from white violence, exploitation, or condescension. The discrepancy became clear as soon as they left the white dance at which they were performing. Musicians remember police officers harassing African Americans simply for being in white neighborhoods. Sam Chatman recalled that the police in Jackson, Mississippi, regularly stopped black musicians on the streets as they walked home from their gigs and tried to make arrests for public drunkenness. Chatman escaped such charges because he did not drink, but some of his friends were not so lucky. Musicians "done made $6 and got about 15 [in fines] the next day," he complained.[43]

The unequal enforcement of the law in the Jim Crow South contributed to some musicians' assumptions that black parties were more dangerous than white ones. Southern police regularly raided black parties and nightspots. Raids officially were used to enforce gambling or liquor regulations, but police largely used them to discourage the congregation of large crowds of African Americans, intimidate black citizens, and disrupt the operation of black-owned businesses. When such raids occurred, anyone present— including musicians—could be the subject of police harassment, violence, or arrest. On the other hand, southern police often did little to investigate and prosecute black-on-black crime. Arthur Crudup was born in 1905 in Scott County, Mississippi. The African American singer maintained that Jim Crow operated by a series of unspoken rules. "It was three things that a black person didn't do," Crudup noted. "Don't touch a white woman, a white face cow, and a bale of cotton and you could get along." He explained that many plantation owners protected workers from the law as long as workers did not commit one of these taboo offenses. They preferred to keep their laborers in the field rather than losing them for committing a crime against an African American victim. They thus refused to allow police onto the farm to respond to disturbances, and they proved willing to pay some fines incurred by their black workers (and count it against future pay). This kept the workers on the job. It also made workers beholden to the plantation owner and less likely to complain about harsh treatment from them. "Any time that you go to jail for killing a colored person, why most any white man would go your bond and if it's any way, if you had just a little bitty proof that you killed him in self defense, he could nearly bout get you out and if the jury did give you any time why you wouldn't be there long before they'd have you out on parole. But now if you killed a white man you can just get ready to run from now on because it ain't no possible chance regardless of what he's done," Crudup noted.[44]

Such realities helped to make African American parties potentially violent in a way that their white equivalents were not. The vast majority of black parties were perfectly peaceful, Crudup insisted, but such unequal law enforcement made African American parties a good place for people interested in creating a disturbance or settling a dispute. Sam Chatman recalled, "Now some people will get a grudge against another one and wait til they get at a party to show it. Got all week to do it but they got to come to your house to do it. See, they'll meet you out in the field and won't do nothing, wait til you get to a party, one night you going to bring it up, start shooting the lights out." Without official intervention, black revelers usually took care of most disputes themselves. "Anything happen we just didn't let it happen cause all the doctors had to come on horse and buggies," he explained.[45]

We can hear in the recollections of these African American musicians several of the circumstances that shaped artists' attempts to forge professional musical careers in the Jim Crow South. First, making money required far more than musical skills. Musicians had to become students of southern culture in all its complexity as well as know regional geography, build alliances with local businesses, develop marketing strategies and word-of-mouth networks to secure gigs, and understand both the letter of the law and its de facto enforcement in different cities and towns. Second, musical interaction across the color line was a product of segregation. Black and white southerners listened to many of the same songs and styles, often performed by the same artists. Yet this reality, far from reflecting similar sensibilities or attitudes of interracial commonality, emerged out of the logic of Jim Crow and the economic exploitation of black labor at its core. Black musicians determined to escape sharecropping discovered that their prospects were better if they learned to perform for white audiences. White southerners commanded more disposable income, their dances were less likely to be disrupted by the law, and they proved more willing to pay black musicians than they were other African American workers, especially if musicians were able to conform to white expectations of black performance gleaned from the minstrel stage.

This final reality can be seen in musicians' experience in traveling medicine shows. Musicians who had honed their skills performing on the street and freelancing at parties could graduate to the semiregular employment of the medicine show. The peak of patent medicine shows in the South occurred between 1880 and 1906, when the Pure Food and Drug Law restricted the trade, but medicine shows continued in the South well into the twentieth century.[46] Sometimes patent medicine "doctors" were little more than traveling street performers themselves, setting up a box on a corner and employing one or two actors or musicians to help draw a crowd. "Doctors" with more ambition and capital launched elaborate productions in tents and theaters that rivaled the larger vaudeville companies of the day. N. T. Oliver, a patent medicine salesman, experienced this full range of patent medicine productions as he crisscrossed the nation in the final decades of the nineteenth century. He launched everything from impromptu street performances to touring companies of "seventy persons and twenty-eight head of horses," often within the same year as his fortunes waxed and waned.[47]

Medicine shows could offer local musicians entry into the world of organized, paid performance. Oliver often entered a town and quickly corralled street musicians to perform in his shows. In Jackson, Tennessee, a rival doctor named Jim Lighthall set up on a nearby street corner. "Two buskers, both first rate artists, had come to town that day, playing the saloons," Oliver recalled. "I added them to our show and opened on a good corner a block below Lighthall." The rival's one-man operation could not compete, and he quickly skipped town. On another occasion in Louisville, Kentucky, Oliver hired an eight-piece African American brass band, paying the group seventy-five dollars a week to join his large traveling entourage.[48] Such opportunities could lead to even better gigs on the vaudeville and musical theater stage. N. T. Oliver himself received offers to perform in "legitimate" theater following his famed medicine shows. His memoir is filled with artists and entrepreneurs fluidly moving among national vaudeville, minstrel show, and medicine show circuits.[49]

Medicine show performers acquired a vast repertoire of songs and comedy skits. "Master of no act, perhaps, he is the jack of many; versatility is his greatest asset. He is the stand-by of the street show which demands an endless change of bill," Oliver explained. One performer "did twelve specialties, and did them well, besides carrying more than a hundred colored acts in his memory." Well-known songs and skits were the stock and trade of medicine show performers, black and white. They enabled performers to quickly create a full-length show even when they had just joined an ensemble, and knowledge of the stock repertoire often was requested specifically in job advertisements in trade papers such as *Billboard*. Many were borrowed from the nineteenth-century minstrel stage, making the blackface performer a ubiquitous presence on the medicine show stage.[50]

Blackface characters played a contradictory role in relation to the patent medicine "doctor," granting him prestige through both association and distance. On one hand, performing minstrel songs established the credibility of the medicine show by forging links to more "legitimate" and popular forms of theater. Most audiences were intimately familiar with the tropes and songs of the minstrel stage, having learned them from traveling shows, national media, and sheet music. Blackface performers supplied the comic and sentimental songs of the day.[51] Their presence marked the medicine show as standard entertainment and, in turn, normalized the exotic, fantastic claims of the offered remedies. On the other hand, the patent medicine "doctor" established his authority by lording over blackface performers, who often played the comic buffoon.

Arthur Jackson knew both sides of the blackface dialectic. The African American performer, born near Jonesville, North Carolina, in 1911, traveled with medicine shows for several decades. He sang a wide variety of British ballads, black spirituals, common stock folk songs, and harmonica features. In addition, Jackson performed a large number of set minstrel bits.[52] In one example, Jackson, who had lost his leg while attempting to jump a train and adopted the stage persona of "Peg Leg Sam," appeared alone on stage and began a practiced and oft-repeated routine:

PEG: Anybody want anything? See me. *I'm* the boss around here.

CHIEF: What'd you say, Sam?

PEG: I say, *here come* the boss around here.[53]

Such routines established the credibility and authority of the man hawking the medicine by placing it in stark contrast to the illegitimate authority of the blackface performer. This dialectic proved difficult for many African American performers hired to play the blackface fool. The black instrumentalist Gus Cannon recalled that he had to have a stiff drink before taking the stage with Dr. Stokey out of Clarksdale, Mississippi. "Had all that cork on our face . . . made us look even blacker . . . shit," he recalled, "painted our mouths white . . . made 'em look big . . . I had to have a shot of liquor before the show. If I didn't it seemed like I couldn't be funny in front of all them people. When I had one it seemed like them people was one and I would throw up the banjo in the air and really put on a show."[54]

Other performers turned the humbug of the show to their own ends. Joe Williams, a black musician born in Tennessee in 1903, joined a medicine show when he was nine years old because he "didn't want to plow, didn't want to chop cotton." After winning a dance contest sponsored by a traveling medicine show, the youngster went on the road with the troupe. Like those of N. T. Oliver, Williams's show traveled a yearly circuit, taking the young boy as far north as Pittsburgh before hitting Texas for the winter months. He worked with the show for six or seven years. Williams explained, "I learned everything to be done about that show. I even drive trucks, done everything. They had a stage—reckon about ten feet, and we'd run down when we'd do our acts, go out and sell medicine all through the streets. It was just a crooked show; they'd sell water, everything, just get it bottled up."[55] Williams had to proffer his own scam in order to make a profit as a medicine show performer. "There's no money to be made in a show, I can tell you that part," Williams explained. "You supposed to make a dollar and a half a night. The only way you could get your money, you had to be slick like the show. What you do, if you supposed to sell twenty-five bottles, you take you forty bottles and them other dollars goes in your pocket. That's the only way you get your money. All of us do it just so we can get something. *You'd* have done it."[56]

In the turn-of-the-century South, many musicians played where they could. Caught between the unsavory options of debt-ridden sharecropping and performing to audience expectations on the stage, many chose the latter. They consciously cultivated their musical skills and donned professional identities that stood in stark contrast to their experiences as laborers in field and factory. They emphasized the importance of compensation for their art, understood their music as an alternative to other forms of labor, and they consciously commodified it. Musicians were often as commercial as their options. The places and prices of performance they developed existed upon a continuum from the spontaneous dealings of the barter economy to the semiregular working of the medicine show. At each step, southern musicians displayed a savvy understanding that making money with their music required not only musical skill but a deep understanding of how to respond to audience needs and desires.

Sizing Up the Audience: Getting Paid for Forging Common Feeling

When Henry Thomas finally recorded for Vocalion at the age of fifty-two, his twenty-three selections revealed a consummate and eclectic artist, one adept at performing a wide variety of songs and styles popular with black and white southerners around the turn of the century. "John Henry" was an established common stock tune. "Old Country Stomp" featured the straight four-four rhythm and square-dance calls demanded by black and white audiences in the late nineteenth century. "Arkansas" was a mildly disguised version of the popular 1898 coon song "Let Me Bring My Clothes Back Home" by the African American songwriting stalwart Irving Jones and collected by the sociologist Howard Odum from southern black informants around 1911. "Bob McKinney" was a medley of a number of popular songs, including the ubiquitous blues "Make Me out a Pallet on Your Floor," and "The Bully Song" was made popular by the vaudevillian May Irwin and sung by the black laborers overheard by the archeologist Charles Peabody in Mississippi around 1902. "Shanty Blues" shared a melody with the white Georgian Fiddlin' John Carson's "The Smoke Goes out the Chimney Just the Same" but added the bottleneck slide guitar associated with African American blues guitarists of the Mississippi Delta by the time he recorded it. Thomas's eclecticism—his employment of a variety of songs and styles enjoyed across the color line—was not unique. It was shared by many of his southern peers who considered themselves professional musicians in the early twentieth century.[57]

The economics of live music performance encouraged musicians to command large repertoires. "You take a fellow that can play anything, he can get a job more or less anywhere. It's what he can do with it," explained Samuel Chatman.[58] A diverse repertoire enabled musicians to appeal to a broad selection of different audiences across the South. Musicians who could overcome differences of race, class, or region stood in the best position to get paid. At the same time, broad repertoires appealed to individual listeners, both black and white. Different songs and styles helped them to express various emotions and aspects of their complex identities, to voice their conflicting desires, and to show off their assorted dance moves. Those musicians who could supply all of a listener's needs fared the best. As the historian Charles Wolfe has noted, "When most people bragged about their community fiddler, they usually bragged about the large number of tunes he played, not especially about his technical skill or inventiveness."[59] This would change as phonograph records and radio came to replace live performers as the source of everyday music. Recorded sound, as we will see, gave rise to new arguments about musical authenticity that encouraged listeners to expect artists' identities to correspond to the style of music that they played. Consumers could salve their needs for musical variety simply by purchasing records by different performers. This was not yet the case in the early-twentieth-century South. When audiences pined for blues, ballads, or minstrel songs, old favorites or contemporary Tin Pan Alley hits, they turned to local musicians, the only game in town. Multifaceted people rewarded multifaceted artists with cash on the barrelhead.

Many southern working-class musicians thus developed repertoires that were as broad as possible. Roosevelt Sykes became adept at pulling on his broad repertoire to accommodate different audiences. "Well by me associating with different musicians and by me being a traveler and folks [giving me music] in all parts of the country," he explained, "I done play a little like the Memphians, little like the Chicagoians, play a little like the Vicksburg, Mississippians, play a little bit like the Texans, a little western stuff, just whatsoever, well, do a little jazz of the New Orleans style. See, I had a variety which I do have now, you know."[60] By first playing in the style that an audience wanted to hear, Sykes found he could slowly introduce his personal material and make the performance his own. The differences between regional styles did not operate as a barrier between Sykes and the different audiences he encountered in his travels. Sykes instead used these differences as a bridge to connect himself with multiple audiences, as well as a way to add variety to his everyday performances. Ashley Thompson's ability to play a wide variety of tunes meant that he could coax more money out of patrons' pockets. "Sometimes we'd run in some fellow ask you to come in a place, somebody there know us, he want me to play and I sit down and play him a piece," he explained. "Well, then along come a white fellow, he want me to play, ask me could I play this piece, and I'll tell him, yeah, and I'd go to playing that for him and next time I know anything, they'd have a big crowd there." Thompson could sometimes bring in as much as twenty to twenty-five dollars during an evening in a cafe.[61] Musical versatility—being able to answer any request a listener might have—increased the ability to get paid.

These examples suggest a need to rethink what we have come to understand about the connections between musicians, repertoires, and audiences. Students of African American music have developed flexible models of the relationship between audiences and artists by focusing on the poetics of live performance. Christopher Small, in his monumental *Music of the Common Tongue*, states this approach more forcefully than most. Music of the African diaspora, Small claims, is distinguished by its fluid attitude toward performance. The process of making music—"musicking" in Small's parlance—involves living relationships among participants, rather than the creation of an authoritative, finished text. In the process of "musicking" the barriers between performer and audience, participant and observer, are nonexistent. "The African musician," Small explains, "thinks of music primarily as action, as process, in which all are able to participate."[62] Other scholars have come to similar conclusions about the blurred division between performer and observer within African American culture. Hazel Carby finds the power of African American music in the complex interweaving of the single performer and the general audience: the singer's "I" becomes the audience's "we" in the process of making music together.[63] Likewise, the blues scholar William Barlow identifies the fluid interplay between artist and audience as a major characteristic of the genre. Borrowing the words of the folklorist John Work, Barlow insists, "The blues singer translated every happening into his own intimate inconvenience."[64] The audience's "we" becomes the singer's "I". Carby and Barlow use the professed intimacy of African American artists and audiences to extrapolate the attitudes and concerns of the larger body from the words of the individual musician.

While these authors demonstrate the valuable lens music can offer into shared beliefs and attitudes, the assumed collective nature of black music can conceal more complex relationships between artists and audiences. First, the collective paradigm obscures possible conflicts between artists and the audiences with whom they supposedly share so much. It cannot account for bad singers—artists who ultimately fail to communicate much about the collective condition of their audience or their community. It leaves little room for audiences who walk out on an unsatisfactory performance or boo a singer back into the woodshed. As such, it fails to acknowledge *good* singers, having no vocabulary to distinguish individual motivations, talents or desires.[65] It thus has a tendency to trap individuals within a racial collectivity, naturalizing music as an outgrowth of one's life rather than a cultivated talent and obscuring the meaning and uses of art that falls outside of racially defined cultural borders.[66]

This trap of collectivity has caught black artists within a double bind. First, as Ralph Ellison forcefully argued in 1963, a focus on the "condition arising from collective experience" "leaves no room for the individual writer's unique existence . . . The individual Negro writer must create out of his own special needs and through his own sensibilities, and these alone. Otherwise, all those who suffer in anonymity would be creators."[67] Second, and perhaps most fundamentally, a strict focus on audience reception does not explore the possibilities of multiple audiences feeling represented by the same artist. Thomas, Chatman, and Sykes consciously shaped their art to appeal to a variety of audiences within a number of performance contexts. They prided themselves on their ability to perform for both white and black audiences. There is no indication that they maintained a hierarchy of authenticity—finding some artist/audience connections to hold the key to essential racial or class cultures while dismissing others as somehow less fundamental. They and other artists built local and national careers by appealing to multiple audiences, constantly shaping and shifting their presentation and image in order to touch listeners from a variety of subject positions.[68]

Indeed, this ability was a central part of their identities as professional musicians. Professionalism involved focusing attention on what music best suited a particular audience rather than one's individual tastes or desires. "You know, sometimes I won't be in the mood for them," lamented the African American singer Bukka White about audience requests. "But they pay me, and when I'm playing out like that, I'm playing what the people want. Cause when I play what I want while sitting here at home . . . I get my guitar and play what I want but then I'm working for you I play for what the people like if I can play it. I ain't gonna say I can do something I can't but if I say I can, I can!"[69] The white singer and guitarist Cliff Carlisle admitted, "Actually to put a song over, or to make a good rendition of a song, especially one you write yourself—and I hope you won't get the wrong impression . . . you have got to be more or less an actor, and you act it in your own mind."[70] Roosevelt Sykes claimed that the ability to separate one's own needs from those of an audience was central to the profession. "Blues is like a doctor," he explained. "Doctor studies medicine; course he ain't sick, but he studies to help them people. A blues player ain't got no blues, but he plays for the worried people. He don't really have no blues when he play em but he has the talent to give to the worried people. See they enjoy it. Like the doctor works from the outside of the body to the inside of the body. But the blues works . . . on the insides of the inside, see."[71]

Sykes's analogy to the medical profession was an apt one. The musician, like the doctor, drew on a reserve of knowledge to "treat" an audience according to a perceived need. The ability to separate one's own desires from the music that one played—to consciously act a part, to play the role one deemed necessary for the occasion—often was central to the musician's artistic and economic success.[72] On successful occasions there may have appeared to be little conflict or negotiations between artists and audiences. This was true only when musicians consciously acted to make it so. Each performance was an opportunity for the artist to build a bridge of common feeling and common culture. There thus was something at stake in every performance. The working musician developed the skills to forge these cultural connections, to bring "intimately desired relationships . . . into existence for the duration of the performance," and with the help of a gathered audience transform "I" into "we" night after night.[73]

The black fiddler Howard Armstrong, for example, recalled the ways in which his string band would have to adjust their playing for the variety of dance audiences he found in eastern Tennessee around 1920. His recollections reveal that musicians were adept at sizing up the class as well as the racial identity of their audiences. "We had to learn to play the pop songs like 'I'm Looking Over a Four-leaf Clover' and 'Brown Eyes Why You Blue.' You couldn't play blues for whites then. If you came out there playing some low-down blues, either they'd pack up and leave or you'd have to pack up and run," Armstrong recalled. "And when we played for the black people, it would all depend on what element we played for. Because there were the upper class, or elite, black people. We would call them 'siddity' which is blackchat for highfalutin, high-strung or elite . . . and you couldn't play no low-down funky blues for them neither. We'd have to play basically what we had to play for highbrow white people." While the upper classes of both races tended to demand the same music, there was also significant overlap among black and white working-class audiences. "If we played for the country white people, the common class, well, we'd play square-dance music like 'Old Joe Clark' and 'Ida Red,'" explained Armstrong. "Now, the regular black people you could play blues for. That's what they'd want to hear. They'd also have square dances, and you'd be surprised to know how close they were to the white square dances."[74]

Armstrong's comments are rare for their detail and deserve closer inspection. First, Armstrong described the overlapping preferences of his Tennessee audiences with the ease of a seasoned professional. While a study of the separate genres or audiences Armstrong discussed might miss the common denominators, Armstrong's own ability to perform across the caste and color lines reveals that stylistic difference did not necessarily come from separate sources. Armstrong noted musical differences yet he employed them all, stepping on stage and performing whatever any particular audience wanted to hear.

Second, it should be noted that his observations describe a time in which black and white dance practices were becoming more distinct than they had been a few decades earlier. By 1920, the blues had been circulating through southern black communities for about twenty years and had been a national commercial fad for approximately eight. The blues had become established as a favored style for many African American dancers during this process. Sam Chatman, born in 1899, was a bit more explicit about the change in black dance fashions. "In the olden times, back when I was a real young boy everybody square-danced," he explained. Yet in the 1920s, "they come up with the shimmy she waba and black bottom and Charleston, all that, one-step, two-step and waltz." When playing for African American parties, "you had to pick slow blues so they could slow-drag. Now white folks, they'd have their parties, when we played for them, we'd have to play fox-trot."[75] African American dancers' preference for the blues was more prominent in the Mississippi Delta than in many other regions. Raised in the hills of Mis-

sissippi, the black fiddler Tom Dumas was popular with black square dancers at the turn of the century. When he moved to the Delta, he was surprised
when African American residents complained that he played "white folks'
music." He soon stopped playing altogether. "This fiddle is been in the
family for four generations. My daddy's granddaddy had it," he lamented. "I
used to play for dances way yonder when I was quite a boy, fifteen or sixteen
years old. I just took it up. But these here Delta folks, they don't like
fiddling."[76] The thirst for blues soon spread out of the Delta, and not all
black southerners were happy about the changing dance styles. "The blues
done ruined the country," complained Mississippian Lucius Smith. "It just
make 'em go off at random, I'd say, frolicking, random, you see." Smith
preferred the older styles. "Now such as 'Walking in the Parlor' and all them
other old pieces, that's dancing on a set . . . calling figures, promenade,
swing your right partner, all that, you know . . . But the 'Memphis Blues' and
all that, it done brought about a whole lots of it, you know, I'd say, trouble."
Smith, born in 1885, associated the new sound of the blues with the drink-
ing, cacophony, and chaotic movements of young revelers. Musicians such
as Howard Armstrong had to learn to navigate such regional and generational—as well as class and racial—differences within their audiences.[77]

Nevertheless, it is important to note Armstrong's description of the
tastes of the "regular black folk." They were multiple. Armstrong insisted
that black audiences requested blues at the same time that they enjoyed
square dances similar to those at white functions. Less a fundamental rejection of these older, more racially nebulous, styles, Armstrong suggested a
calculated and conscious cohabitation of the two on the African American
dance floor. Black audiences enjoyed them both, perhaps finding each feeding a different aspect of their identity or feelings, fueling a slightly different
set of desires or memories. His comments were not unlike those of the
stride pianist James P. Johnson, who played for African American basement
parties in New York in 1913. Johnson insisted that there was one style that
would always bring screams of glee from the black southern migrants on the
floor. "These Charleston people and the other Southerners had just come to
New York. They were country people and they felt homesick," Johnson
explained. "When they got tired of two-steps and schottisches (which they
danced with a lot of spieling), they'd yell: 'Let's go back home!' . . . 'Let's do a
set!' . . . or, 'Now, put us in the alley!' I did my Mule Walk or Gut Stomp for
these country dances." Johnson's Harlem dancers enjoyed "going home"

only after—and perhaps because—they already had enjoyed songs that spoke to their new homes, urbane sophistication, or any number of other feelings or aspirations. Johnson, like Armstrong, was able to deliver.[78]

White audiences displayed a similar mix of musical desires. They requested square dances and fiddle tunes, as well as a wide variety of popular songs and hits of the day. By the early 1920s, if not earlier, white audiences also regularly requested that performers—black and white—treat them to the blues. White interest in the early blues is an important and underexplored aspect of southern music cultures in the early twentieth century and needs a little investigation. Armstrong claimed that if he played blues for white dancers "either they'd pack up and leave or you'd have to pack up and run." He remained aware of the possible implications of playing a song for the wrong audience. At the same time that some black musicians chose not to sing the blues at white dances, however, there is a lot of evidence to suggest that white listeners sought out the music. As we will see in a later chapter, the African American bandleader and composer W. C. Handy, whose early blues publications garnered him the name "Father of the Blues," was first introduced to the power of the music in 1903 when white patrons requested it at a high society dance he was playing in Clarksdale, Mississippi. Handy's brass band, versed in the popular hits of Broadway and Tin Pan Alley, was unable to deliver, but a local black trio soon took the stage and gave the white dancers what they wanted.[79] When African American artists began making blues records in the 1920s, white southerners bought them in large numbers. Store ledgers from rural white neighborhoods reveal that blues records by the likes of Blind Lemon Jefferson sold just as well as those by white fiddlers and hillbilly singers.[80] The blues queen Bessie Smith played to segregated audiences when she toured the South in 1923, yet white as well as black audiences gobbled up all the tickets they could find to her sold-out concerts.[81] A closer examination of the multiple reasons different white southerners may have been interested in hearing the blues can suggest not only the ways in which music helped constitute identity in overlapping, often contradictory, ways. It also illustrates the difficult job artists had sizing up their audiences.

Let's begin with Armstrong's implicit assertion that playing blues for white audiences could be dangerous. This may have been true for a couple of reasons. Blues lyrics could contain overt protests against southern racism. They also could display sexual content, either explicitly or, more often, through innuendo. In a South dominated by Jim Crow and lynch law, songs of protest or sexuality could be incredibly dangerous for African Americans to share with white listeners. As several blues scholars have theorized, this resulted in blues artists developing separate repertoires to perform for black and white patrons, saving the explicit blues for the former and censoring their lyrics or using double entendres for the latter.[82]

Yet white audiences enjoyed sexual blues for the very mix of eroticism, transgression, and humor that made them popular with black performers and audiences. The sexual double entendres that drove so many blues lyrics did not hide the blue content from white ears. The folk song collector Guy Johnson admitted in 1927, "It is doubtful if any group ever has carried its ordinary vulgarities over into respectable song life so completely and successfully as the American Negro. And the ease with which the Negro has put this thing over leads one to suspect that the white man, too, enjoys seeing 'the other meaning.' " When a blues singer announced "you got a good little car, you know too many mens under your steering wheel," white listeners got it.[83] Thinly veiled lyrics enabled attentive white listeners to imagine themselves in on the joke, to take part in the social transgression of talking about sex in public. Laughing at blues innuendo enabled them to collude vicariously with the black performer whose "I" momentarily became the white audience's "we." In this context, the apparent blackness of the blues was not a put-off for many southern white people. It could be an additional turn-on, fitting smoothly into white audiences' long history of reveling in supposedly authentic black music and black bodies on the minstrel stage. Indeed, white singers from Marion Harris to Bob Clifford used the blues both to update their minstrelsy with the modern sounds of black authenticity and to express sexual dreams and desires they remained uncomfortable conveying in supposedly more respectable musical forms.[84]

Black blues of protest and pain also found willing audiences among some white southerners. Some white listeners prized such songs for their authenticity and sought them out in order to feel the thrill of peaking behind the veil of the color line, sharing in a critique of segregation while remaining safely ensconced in their white skin. One wonders how often black musicians confronted questions like those the white folklorist John Lomax posed to Georgia native Blind Willie McTell in 1940.

LOMAX: Any complaining songs, complaining about the hard times and sometimes mistreatment of the whites. Have you got any songs that talk about that?

MCTELL: No sir. I haven't. Not at the present time, because the whites is mighty good to the southern people as far as I know.

LOMAX: You don't know any complaining songs at all?

MCTELL: Well . . .

LOMAX: "Ain't it Hard to be a Nigger, Nigger." Do you know that one?

MCTELL: No. That's not in our time. Now as for spiritual down here, it's a mean world to live in but that still don't have reference to the hard time.

LOMAX: It's just because of the white it's a mean world to live in?

MCTELL: No, it's not all together. It has reference to everybody.

LOMAX: It's as mean for the whites as it is for the blacks. Is that it?

MCTELL: That's the idea.

LOMAX: You keep moving around like you're uncomfortable. What's the matter, Willie?

MCTELL: Well, I was in an automobile accident last night and still shuck up.[85]

Tension is palpable in this exchange. The ballad hunter was thirsty, but the singer ducked each query, refusing to acknowledge the presence of southern racism or African American resistance to it. If the passage offers a window into the contested relationship between folklorist and informant, it also reveals black strategies for dodging white interrogation in the Jim Crow South. Black musicians had to remain wary of such queries, carefully assessing the intentions of the white inquisitor, for more often white southerners made such requests to gauge black acceptance of Jim Crow and ensure that they were willing to play by its rules. The wrong answer could result in reprimand or violence. Thus even as Lomax hungered to hear songs of protest, McTell could not be sure of his intentions and appeared ready to take Howard Armstrong's advice to get up and run.

Indeed, it appears that at least some white listeners enjoyed hearing such songs simply because they took pleasure in black pain. On a collecting trip through northern Mississippi in 1942, John's son Alan Lomax recorded Sid Hemphill, an African American musician born in 1876. Hemphill's composition "The Strayhorn Mob" tells the tale of a local lynching that had occurred many years before. According to Hemphill's song, a lynch mob from Strayhorn went to the jail in Senatobia and demanded an African American prisoner be released to them. When the jailer refused, they shot at him, breached the jail, and took the victim back to Strayhorn where they lynched him. At trial, the song concludes, all members of the mob were acquitted. Hemphill's harrowing tale of white vigilantism and murder is all the more powerful because his lyrics identify members of the lynch mob by name: Will Springfield, Mister Hunter, Sam House, and Norman Clayton. When Lomax asked him about the song, Hemphill explained that he wrote it at the request of one of the members of the mob. "One of the men that was in it writ it all down and give it to me and my buddy and told us to make up a song . . . a one Mister Sam House," he said. "Did you ever play the song for him," Lomax asked. "Many times," he replied. "He liked it, huh?" "*Too good*," emphasized Hemphill before adding, "You know Mister Norman Clayton? Well, he was in it. He pitched me fifty cents, give me fifty cents and go on tell me to play. And by the time I play four or five verses he be gone and laugh and go on and leave. His daughter was the same way."[86] I know of no other instance in which white southerners so brazenly commissioned a black musician to pen an ode to their masochism.

Yet "The Strayhorn Mob" stands as an important example of the complexities of the interracial music culture that characterized the early-twentieth-century South. Born out of African American creativity and white cash, Hemphill's song was an expertly designed double entendre, a testimony and an accusation masked as a simple narrative. Black and white residents alike, albeit for drastically different reasons, celebrated the song. It kept alive the memory of white terrorism within the local black community at the same time that it enabled white supremacists to celebrate their own power over African American citizens. Its presence suggests that some white southerners may have heard similar songs of dispossession, racism, and death by African American singers as welcome proof that Jim Crow and white supremacy were working.

At the same time, some white working-class listeners found that the blues spoke to their own sense of marginalization and loss. John Jacob Niles recalled hearing a white blues singer named Jack Spicer near Pikeville, Kentucky, in 1908. "When he did his usual sixteen-measure mountain songs —the things all mountain musicians have inherited from the English folklorists of long ago—he sang in the voice of a mountain-man singer," Niles reported. "But the three-line, twelve measure [blues] songs were apparently intended for . . . getting over dejection."[87] His observation suggests how quickly blues became integrated into the common stock of songs and styles shared by working-class southerners across the color line. The white singer Roscoe Holcomb used very personal terms to describe his reaction to hearing Blind Lemon Jefferson for the first time. He recalled, "Up 'til then the blues were only inside me; Blind Lemon was the first to 'let out' the blues."[88] Hobart Smith and "Knocky" Parker, as we have seen, likewise turned to Jefferson to learn how to play. The guitarist's music and message hit a common chord in these white listeners who appear to have been genuinely touched and inspired to create music of their own.

Common work experiences could foster this kind of interracial musical exchange. Levee and lumber camps, railroad projects, textile mills, mines, and large farms often found black and white workers in close proximity even when jobs and living spaces were segregated. White and black workers traded music to a significant extent considering the violent politics of race in the New South. The coal mining camps of Logan County, Virginia, offer but one example. According to the white fiddler Sherman Lawson, the railroad came to Logan County around 1905, opening the mines to a surge of migrants in search of work, including many African American hopefuls. Bill Hunt was one of them, settling in the county sometime between 1907 and 1909. The black guitarist, in his mid-fifties by the time of his arrival, suffered an unknown physical malady that kept him out of the mines. Instead, he performed music for tips as he traveled from camp to camp. Hunt played the guitar with a bottleneck slide, a blues style then beginning to sweep the Deep South but less familiar in coal country. His music nevertheless proved popular among black and white mineworkers. Hunt maintained a regular gig on the steps of a company store and, according to Lawson, often made more money than the clerk working inside. Lawson regularly dropped by with his friend and musical partner Frank Hutchison, a white mineworker born in the mid-1890s. Hutchison soon became hooked. He would spend four or five hours a day sitting beside the elder guitarist, studying his style, and ultimately trying his own hand at the blues tunes Hunt carefully taught him. Hunt eventually left town and lost contact with Logan County. Lawson did not know where he went but remembered Hunt fondly as a skilled musician and a generous teacher. Hutchison had learned his lesson well. He excelled at Hunt's bottleneck guitar technique, and his rhythmically sophisticated vocal delivery found him adroitly anticipating or delaying the beat and swooping across bar lines in a manner common among African American blues singers. Yet even as he was becoming one of the era's most accomplished white students of the blues, the singer exercised his racial privilege by occasionally donning a minstrel mask for kicks. Hutchison's blackened face serves as a stark reminder that the interracial music culture of the early-twentieth-century South did not develop outside or despite the racism of the Jim Crow regime. It was forged out of—and could help perpetuate—segregation's potent formula of racial contact governed by white control.[89]

African American musicians intent on providing each audience with what it wanted understood that their task required more than matching musical style to the dancers' race and class. They also had to assess the extant desire for the transgression or maintenance of the emerging musical color line. Black artists had to determine how safe each environment was—how well they had forged a common feeling with their white audience—in order to determine whether to perform the blues. It was a complex calculus that combined issues of repertoire and the color line, authenticity and sexuality, social transgression and the desire and danger of implying too close an association between the black singer's "I" and the white audience's "we." In most cases, they made the safe and sane decision to play something else. Other times they opted to perform the blues, believing they had established a commonality with their audiences that held the possibility of being transformative. It was just one of many calculations they would make as they plied their trade night after night.

Frank Hutchison recorded a number of the songs that Bill Hunt had taught him after he began working for the Okeh label in 1926. One of the most powerful was "Miner's Blues." The song was at once a lament about the trials of mine work and a release from them. On his 1928 recording, Hutchison picked a guitar counterpoint in a slow drag, his rhythmic hesitations and worried notes establishing a haunting tension reminiscent of Blind Lemon Jefferson. Over the twelve-bar tune, he wailed, "If you don't believe I'm sinking, look what a hole I'm in." It was an apt metaphor for the trap of mine work, yet he defiantly refused to get sucked down. The song declared,

> Ain't gonna work on no tipple, ain't gonna lay no track
> Ain't gonna work on no tipple, ain't gonna lay no track
> Gonna hang around my shanty, do the ball and jack.

White and black Logan County residents could relate to the themes in "Miner's Blues." The song spoke to suffering and redemption that crossed the color line. Miners could gather around the company store after a long day in the depths to hear Bill Hunt, or eventually Frank Hutchison, acknowledge their agony then invite them to revel, if just for a moment, in their wildest dreams: quitting the massive tipple machinery that sorted coal into railroad cars, living a life of leisure, and dancing the ball and jack. Yet it is important to recall that "Miner's Blues" was not mere fantasy for the singers themselves. Bill Hunt never worked in the mines, and Hutchison used his music to pull himself out of them. Lawson and Hutchison performed regularly around Logan and surrounding counties, playing everywhere from dances and theaters to corn-shuckings. Lawson soon had to stop because it interfered with his day job, but Hutchison quit the mines as soon as he could. He "didn't like to work," recalled Lawson. "He made money without working!" Yet the guitarist simply had his eyes on another job. While his friend went back to his regular post, Hutchison spent his days practicing, adding common stock and popular tunes to his songbag, and railroading around the region to promote upcoming shows. Hutchison, like so many working-class musicians in the New South, used his music to forge an alternative to hard labor. By singing "Ain't gonna work on no tipple," he made the declaration true.

ISOLATING FOLK, ISOLATING SONGS 3

Reimagining Southern Music as Folklore

When the Harvard-trained folklorist John Lomax published a collection of cowboy songs in 1910, Theodore Roosevelt heartily endorsed the project. *Cowboy Songs and Other Frontier Ballads* opened with an enthusiastic letter from the president to the ballad hunter. "You have done a work emphatically worth doing and one which should appeal to the people of all our country," Roosevelt wrote. Justifying the value of the project, the former Rough Rider turned to visions of a European past. "There is something very curious in the reproduction here on this new continent of essentially the conditions of ballad-growth which obtained in mediaeval England; including, by the way, sympathy for the outlaw, Jesse James taking the place of Robin Hood," he enthused. Roosevelt found that the "crude home-spun ballads" that cropped up in "the back country and the frontier" offered spiritual nourishment that the "ill-smelling," clever "music hall songs" heard in most of the nation could not provide. Barrett Wendell, a Harvard English instructor, continued this theme in his introduction to the volume. "In the ballads of the old world, it is not historical or philological considerations which most readers care for," Wendell explained. "It is the sense, derived one can hardly explain how, that here is expression straight from the heart of humanity; that here is something like the sturdy root from which the finer, though not always more lovely, flowers of polite literature have sprung." Roosevelt and Wendell believed that Lomax had uncovered evidence of the past living in the present. Cowboys on the shrinking frontier, isolated from the ubiquitous, self-conscious music of the modern marketplace, had preserved the ancient art of ballad making. Their physical and social isolation had enabled them to create music that spoke to a deep, fundamental "human rhythm" and truth.[1]

The informants whose handwritten transcripts Lomax used to forge parts of *Cowboy Songs* often had a more complicated story to tell about their musical lives. They heartily fought social isolation, attempting to remain connected to the larger cultural currents of the nation while riding the desolate plains. One Texan wrote to Lomax in 1910, "About the first thing I recolect [sic] at about 5 years of age was sitting in the saddle and riding around the cows (and sorts of other livestock)[.] And our music outside of a Jews harp or a violin for an old time dance was all vocal[,] and we picked up all the comic and sentimental songs we could hear and learn and would some times attempt to rhyme songs ourselves."[2] The comic and sentimental songs popularly available through sheet music and touring shows con- stituted a hearty portion of the music sung by cattle drivers. Cowboys, it appears, thirsted for such material and got it any way they could. In fact, after the publication of *Cowboy Songs*, Lomax received numerous requests from drivers asking for copies of the book.[3] When they received it in the mail, cattle drivers may have been surprised to read that their experiences resembled "mediaeval England" more than the time and place in which they lived.

Yet *Cowboy Songs* was not designed to be an accurate depiction of the complex lives of contemporary cattle drivers. Rather, Lomax attempted to portray an image of a separate world, one that shared very little with turn- of-the-century American politics and popular culture. "But are you really in earnest in claiming that the songs you send me are real range songs, un- touched by any emendation of yours?" Lomax wrote to an informant in 1911. "I am after the untutored and unedited expressions of the original plainsmen. I am frank to confess that what you send me savors of the conventional popular song."[4]

What was going on here? Why did Lomax reject the popular songs his informants shared with him? What did he believe was at stake in the por- trayal of cowboys isolated on the American plains? And why did Lomax think he was better qualified than cattle drivers to assess the qualities of cowboy culture? This chapter attempts to answer these questions by tracing the intellectual roots of Lomax's study. The first part of the chapter looks at the development of the concept of isolation within the academic discipline of folklore. In the decades preceding *Cowboy Songs*, folklore provided ammunition for a wide variety of scholars interested in divining the origins of contemporary literature, charting the evolutionary history of the human races, or reinventing the modern university. Identifying isolated cultures such as that of Lomax's cowboys was a crucial aspect of each of these projects. The chapter then examines a series of ways in which scholars' ideas about isolation shaped—and were shaped by—popular attitudes toward folklore around the turn of the twentieth century.

Academic and popular writers helped shape a powerful new image of southern music as folk music. The folk designation maintained an assumption of isolation, the idea that the southern folk were ignorant of the very music we saw them embracing in the previous chapters. Calling something folk music separated it from its surroundings and asked it to answer questions posed elsewhere. Yet the mythology erected around folk music dramatically altered the opportunities available to southern musicians even as it provided the context in which many Americans first encountered the songs of the South. The perceived sound and meaning of southern music— its beauty and breadth, its racial and class connotations, and even its very existence—were intimately intertwined with the politics of folklore at the turn of the century. Therefore it is important to examine the development of writers' ideas about folklore—what they believed they were doing, what they understood when they spoke of isolated cultures, and why they were aghast to hear pop music on the plains yet so excited to find medieval knights on American soil.

The Meanings of Isolation

When founders established the American Folklore Society in 1888, they imagined the new organization could accomplish two goals. It could professionalize folklore studies by distinguishing serious scholars from untrained collectors, and it could define an interdisciplinary common ground between its anthropology and literary studies members. The inaugural issue of the Society's *Journal of American Folklore* attempted to establish disciplinary standards of a "scientific character." Guidelines insisted that journal submissions conform to "the spirit of modern scholarship." They "should be limited to a particular theme, should be free from controversial reference, treated solely with a view to the elucidation of the theme in hand, and should follow the narrow path of historical criticism, rather than diverge into the broad fields of philosophical speculation." By these means, the Society attempted to distance their endeavor from the venerations of folk and medieval culture popular among amateur enthusiasts and mass audiences.[5]

The campaign for professionalization involved articulating the means of studying folklore so that it could provide evidence for scholars' disputes about race, evolution, art, and the foundations of human culture. Was the human story one of progress or of decline? Was racial difference a fundamental result of evolutionary development or were different races equal in their capacity and potential? Had modern people lost the connection to nature that was central to their ancestors' survival? A key to unlocking these mysteries, scholars believed, was finding groups that they could study in isolation. The pursuit and study of isolated peoples and lore became the common thread that held the diverse membership together over the coming divisive decades. Even as scholars debated the meaning of race, culture, and evolution, they agreed upon both the necessity and the possibility of studying cultures in isolation from each other.[6]

William Wells Newell, the journal's first editor, helped articulate this common ground when he began the inaugural issue with a description of the organization's purpose, titled "On the Field and Work of a Journal of American Folk-Lore." His essay implicitly suggested four major ways in which contributors would conceive isolation. First, Newell identified folk isolation in racial or national terms. He called for the collection of folklore within four separate areas: "Old English Folk-lore," the "Lore of Negroes," "Lore of the Indian Tribes," and a catch-all category consisting of "Lore of French Canada, Mexico, etc." Second, Newell alluded to the separation of savagery from civilization. Discussing Native American lore, Newell called for the collection of "a complete representation of the savage mind in its rudeness as well as its intelligence, its licentiousness as well as its fidelity" before Native Americans were "allowed" to acquire "civilization." Newell's third suggestion of folk isolation placed authentic folk culture in the historical past. Newell did not call for the collection of all English lore but "Relics of Old English Folk-Lore." Finally, Newell defined folk culture through its isolation from modern commercial culture and the printing press, its distance from the "inferior rhymes of literary origin, diffused by means of broadsides and songbooks." Newell's list may appear gangly and idiosyncratic, full of overlaps and ellipses. Yet what he attempted—and largely achieved—was an integration of the languages of isolation popular within anthropology and literary studies.[7]

Each of these concepts of isolation grew out of previous debates about the relationships among language, history, and race. Until about the last quarter of the nineteenth century, these questions had been the province of philology, a broad science that combined etymology and grammar with history, geography, and philosophy. Philologists mounted a romantic quest for the origins of civilization, the discovery of the pure roots—understood as both the chronological beginning and the vital essence—of contemporary culture. In practice, they tended to focus very specifically on the history and structure of the written word. Poring over Greek and Latin texts, philologists parsed their structure, word choice, and grammar in order to "recover the remoter history of man, through the fragments of dead languages," in the words of one textbook in 1839. Philologists were less interested in literary texts for their content or context. They believed that close attention to grammar and etymology could reveal fundamental truths about the spiritual and poetic power of a people. The best philologists, in the words of Harvard's George Lyman Kittredge, "looked through the form and strove to comprehend the spirit."[8]

Classical philologists paid scant attention to English and other vernacular languages throughout most of the nineteenth century, preferring the earlier and supposedly more pure languages of Greek and Latin. In the 1840s, however, language professors campaigned to bring English literature into the classroom. Their strategy was to out-philologize the classical philologists. They argued that the study of English could be just as exacting and demanding as the interpretation of Greek and Latin had become. Folklore, or oral literature, assumed a prominent place in this transition. English ballads and folk tales took the place of Homeric epics for modern philologists interested in the etymological and structural origins of the written English language. They signified "the sturdy root from which the finer, though not always more lovely, flowers of polite literature have sprung," to borrow Barrett Wendell's characterization of *Cowboy Songs*.[9]

Philological interpretations of language were intimately intertwined with nineteenth-century theories of race. During the early nineteenth century, ethnological attempts at racial classification regularly used linguistic commonalities as proof of racial kinship, and philologists believed that the origins and comparative sophistication of the separate races were evident in the very structures of the written text. Philologists promised they could establish the fact of a pure European race by scientifically isolating Europe's cultural and linguistic history. By the 1830s, the concept of a historical Indo-European language system had largely transformed into the idea of a distinct Indo-European—or Aryan—race.[10] Modern English philology expanded upon the relationship between language and race. It borrowed increasingly from social Darwinism, drawing links between linguistic study and the theories of racial and cultural evolution then being promoted within anthropology and the social sciences. A literature textbook explained in 1896, "As literature is a reflection and a reproduction of the life of the peoples speaking the language in which it is written, this literature is likely to be strong and great in proportion as the peoples who speak the language are strong and great. English literature is therefore likely to grow, as it is the record of the life of the English speaking race and as this race is steadily spreading abroad over the globe."[11]

The wedding of philology with modern literature proved a potent if ambiguous partnership. On the one hand, it democratized and expanded the university curriculum. Students long had clamored for the inclusion of English in their studies, establishing off-campus societies to discuss contemporary literature and listen to writers such as Ralph Waldo Emerson declare the classical college education "a system of despair" that drowned students in "the deadness of its details." Emerson was one of the most popular speakers on the college literary society circuit in the 1840s and 1850s. It was among audiences of disgruntled college students that his celebration of the common man—"working in the fields or swapping stories in the barn, men wholly uneducated, but whose words had roots in their own experience," as F. O. Matthiessen described it—took shape and had its most immediate effect. "I ask not for the great, the remote, the romantic; what is doing in Italy or Arabia; what is Greek art or Provençal minstrelsy," Emerson wrote. "I embrace the common, I explore and sit at the feet of the familiar, the low. Give me insight into to-day, and you may have the antique and future worlds." Such rhetoric resonated with college students drowning in the details of their philology classes. Bringing English literature into the classroom promised to invigorate a college education increasingly seen as a patrician luxury when not dismissed as a soul-crushing bore.[12]

On the other hand, modern philology contended that the significance of

English literature was not apparent to the average reader. Its mysteries and magic were only available to professionally trained scholars. This apparent contradiction would not go away for it provided part of the rationale for including English as a discipline within the modern university. Only somewhat impenetrable subjects qualified as the focus for academic careers based on research and specialization. This trade-off would have profound effects on developing ideas about folklore, vernacular culture, and southern music. Its very logic maintained that quality folk culture was isolated in the past far from current concerns, that scientific inquiry into literature revealed essential racial difference rather than commonality, and that the value of folk songs could not be imagined by average people, let alone the singers who performed for them.

The work of Francis James Child reveals both the promise and the peril of this trade-off. When the Harvard professor became the first president of the American Folklore Society he had already begun to publish his five-volume *The English and Scottish Popular Ballads*. The definitive collection—scholars and performers still refer to old English ballads by their "Child number"—featured the words to over three hundred narrative songs. Most entries included a significant number of variations of the same ballad gleaned from manuscripts and oral recitations in a number of different languages. Showing his own roots in the philological method, Child painstakingly compared and contrasted each version for narrative, meter, word choice, antiquity, and provenance while saying very little about the ballads' meaning or historical context. *Popular Ballads* was wildly influential among future folklorists and ballad hunters. The scholar's unparalleled attention to detail demonstrated how English literature could be the subject of scientific inquiry, proved the existence and quality of an English ballad tradition, and provided a benchmark for future folk song scholarship.[13]

Interlaced concepts of isolation played prominently in Child's understanding of English balladry. First, he saw the ballad as a premodern product, a thing of the past whose ranks were "sealed and dried up forever."[14] Education and literacy, he contended, had brought an end to the oral traditions that produced the ballads. The printed word forced an end to oral texts and introduced self-consciousness and artistic pretenses that made ballads "extremely difficult to imitate by the highly-civilized modern man." Yet Child imagined that extant ballads might still survive among people isolated from "book culture." "The less book education," he maintained, "the more hope, with persons of native intelligence, of a memory well stored with traditional treasures."[15] Second, Child maintained that manuscripts and informants could not be trusted. "In no field of literature have the forger and the manipulator worked with greater vigor and success," explained George Lyman Kittredge in his introduction to *English Ballads*. Child, through a "constant association with the spirit of the folk," possessed a particular "instinct" for sussing out forgery or modern addendums to the ancient songs.[16] Such "improvements are more to be feared than the mischances of a thousand years," explained Child himself. "The professional ballad-singer or minstrel, whose sole object is to please the audience before him, will alter, omit, or add, without scruple, and nothing is more common than to find different ballads blended together."[17] It was a telling comment for it placed the trained, expert scholar in direct competition with professional performers and the audiences they served. The job of the scholar was painstakingly to salvage songs from singers.

Child's lack of attention to the origins of the ballads left the door open for future scholars to build on his work. Two competing camps developed rather quickly. One, championed by William Wells Newell, maintained that Child's ballads were the products of skilled, literary minds. In an influential article in 1899, Newell argued that the ballads had been preserved, rather than created, by unlettered folk. Incapable of poetic artistry themselves, the folk merely remembered ballads from a previous era when "the best minds had so occupied themselves" with their composition. "The popular ballad, left to the mercy of the less educated and thoughtful part of the community, became a survival instead of a living art," he maintained. It was a short step from this conclusion to the search for extant ballads in contemporary isolated communities. Newell's theory, the folkloric equivalent of diamond mining, suggested that ancient treasures could be unearthed amid the cultural detritus of contemporary marginalized groups.[18] His influential article encouraged several important collectors—including Louise Pound, E. C. Perrow, W. Roy Mackenzie, and Alphonso Smith—to turn their attention to the isolated regions of the United States and beyond in search of long-buried musical gems.[19]

The second camp argued that Child's ballads were the products of communal composition by the unlettered folk. Communalists were a notoriously contentious group, yet they shared one important assertion that separated them from the likes of Newell; they insisted that the folk created the ballads. It was a dramatic, potentially democratic claim for it granted the folk their own creativity and established the roots of modern literature among the masses rather than the elite. The communal theory of composition shattered Child's notion that ballads were the products of a previous age, their ranks "sealed and dried up forever." It implied that existing isolated groups might invent new folk songs in similar ways to the ancients. It also suggested that contemporary examples could prove the communal creation of the Child ballads. This was exactly what the belabored equations between Lomax's cowboys and medieval knights were all about.[20] The possibility of discovering folk ballads in the process of their birth, even more than Newell's hope of finding musical diamonds in the rough, sent collectors scurrying into the rural climes of the nation.

Francis Gummere was perhaps the most passionate and articulate of the communalists. He asserted that ballads arose out of the social dance of an isolated people. "Opposed to that memorial and prophetic dreamer on the peak, there is seen, in the primitive stages of poetry, and in certain survivals, a throng of people without skill to read or write, without ability to project themselves into the future, or to compare themselves with the past, or even to range their experience with the experience of other communities, gathered in festal mood, and, by loud song, perfect rhythm, and energetic dance, expressing their feelings over an event of quite local origin, present appeal, and common interest," he contended.[21] Gummere acknowledged folk ownership of the ballads only by systematically denying the folk the education, consciousness, and self-awareness that marked civilized people. In their more extreme declarations, communalists argued that ballads lacked individual origin. "The folksong composes itself," maintained the Grimm brothers, through the spontaneous creativity of the folk.[22] Others insisted that folk song composition involved individuals acting as undistinguished mediums for the folk. The music critic H. E. Krehbiel explained, "The creator of the folksong is an unindividualized representative of his people, himself a folk-product . . . His potentiality is racial or national, not personal."[23]

In order to make their case for this generalized folk author, communalists drew on the anthropological theories of the day. Krehbiel employed the work of the anthropology pioneer Herbert Spencer and used biological metaphors to describe the process of communal composition. Folk songs— "echoes of the heart-beats of the vast folk"—resulted from "involuntary" muscular movements of the folk.[24] Gummere similarly evoked Spencer and approached the history of English literature from a hierarchical model of progress indebted to theories of cultural evolution. It is a testament to the common theoretical ground emerging within folklore studies that communalists' "primitive stage of poetry" easily blurred into anthropologists' "primitive mind."[25]

Anthropologists at the time were undergoing their own process of professionalization and theoretical development. Extracting themselves from broad philosophical disciplines such as philology, many within the discipline employed the "comparative method" of ethnology pioneered by the nineteenth-century evolutionists E. B. Tylor and Lewis Henry Morgan. The comparative method, an extension of Darwinism into the realm of culture, was based on the assumption that all human cultures developed along a similar evolutionary continuum from savagery to civilization. Proponents attempted to reconstruct the history of civilized cultures by comparing them with those of contemporary races that occupied different stages of evolutionary development. The comparative method rooted human cultural difference in biology. Tylor claimed that the varying attainment of civilization by Europeans and Africans was mirrored in differing biological structures of the brain—differences that could help identify universal scientific laws of cultural and biological development. Cultural difference was an indicator of biological difference. The connection between cultural and biological development implied cultural change that was only possible on the slow Darwinian evolutionary clock: for the present, savage races were doomed to lower level mental activity and excluded from the ranks of the civilized.[26]

Isolation was central to theories of cultural evolution. Daniel Brinton, the founder of the department of ethnology at the University of Pennsylvania, was one of the most vociferous proponents of cultural evolution. In 1895, eight years after he became a founding board member of the American Folklore Society, Brinton published an address titled "The Aims of Anthropology" that demonstrates the way in which cultural evolutionists combined Newell's different meanings of isolation. Brinton identified an urgent task for the "new science": "to discover the human laws of growth" by exploring "man's mental or psychical nature." Brinton understood cultural evolution in racial as well as temporal terms. "When we find a living nation of low culture, we are safe in taking its modes of thought and feeling as analogous to those of extinct tribes whose remains show them to have been in about the same stage of culture," he explained. Culture—the "outward expression of the inward faculties"—reflected racial biological difference. Brinton thus insisted that ethnology must separate humanity into "subspecies" or "races" in order to chart the civilizing process.[27] Brinton found that folklore provided fresh ammunition for his task. The "various customs, institutions, thoughts, etc., of different peoples," he believed, could identify the "separate ethos that inform the development and achievements of the race[s]." "The patient and thorough investigations of these peculiarities is, therefore, one of the most apposite aims of modern ethnology." Physical isolation affected culture in similar ways to racial isolation, Brinton maintained. Each marked one's distance from civilization. As civilization progressed, remnants of the previous culture persisted in those least affected by the change. The history of previous epochs thus could be gleaned from the study of not only "primitive" peoples but those on the margins of contemporary society. Folklore, Brinton explained, "investigates the stories, the superstitions, the beliefs and customs which prevail among the unlettered, the isolated and the young; for these are nothing less than survivals of the mythologies, the legal usage and the sacred rites of earlier generations." Folklore, the product of savage races, also represented bits of precivilized culture persisting within civilized society.[28]

Brinton's essay reveals a number of important characteristics and rhetorical moves common to the cultural evolutionist paradigm that dominated anthropological theory in the late nineteenth century. First, it must be stressed, Brinton's goal was a deeper understanding of civilization, not primitivism. He turned to "lower culture" in order to better understand the history of a progressing civilization. Second, Brinton's search for old lore at the margins of contemporary society echoed the folklore concept of his literary peers, marking a growing common ground between the two fields as a cohesive agenda for folklore studies took shape. Finally, Brinton affected a subtle slippage among these modes of isolation. He drew implicit parallels between less civilized "races," children, and those who lack education or exposure to contemporary culture. These slippages would have dire consequences when the biological determinism central to the evolutionary paradigm was thrown into the mix, for it would enable Brinton and other evolutionists to identify the culture born from an education denied as a biological trait—ignorance as a racial destiny.

In 1896, the anthropologist Franz Boas, another founding board member of the American Folklore Society, launched a vicious attack on the evolutionary paradigm. In an article titled "The Limitations of the Comparative Method," Boas refused the assumption that similarities between cultures separated by time and space arose out of a common process of mental development. "We must also consider all the ingenious attempts at constructions of a grand system of the evolution of society as of very doubtful value, unless at the same time proof is given that the same phenomena could not develop by any other method," he wrote. "Until this is done, the presumption is always in favor of a variety of courses which historical growth may have taken." This possibility, Boas found, dismantled the comparative method, and the cultural evolutionary paradigm at its core. It suggested that culture, rather than reflecting a fundamental biological difference among the races, could account for difference by itself. Individual cultures developed under their own internal logic rather than in a single, progressive evolution toward civilization. Cultures stood in relative rather than hierarchical relations to each other.[29]

Boas, like his adversaries, could only prove his theory by studying groups in isolation. His argument required limiting the scope of studies to societies with knowable boundaries. "Its application is based, first of all, on a well-defined, small geographical territory, and its comparisons are not extended beyond the limits of the cultural area that forms the basis of the study," he explained. Boas acknowledged that identifying a pure local culture was difficult because "intercourse between neighboring tribes has always existed and has extended over enormous areas." It was therefore necessary to trace the historical record back to a time prior to contact in order to understand a group's unique contributions to its cultural development. "There has been a time of isolation during which the principal traits of diverse cultures developed according to the character and environment of the tribes," he asserted. "But the stages of culture representing this period have been covered with so much that is new and that is due to contact with foreign tribes that they cannot be discovered without the most painstaking isolation of foreign elements." It was only once this has been done, however, that Boas believed useful comparison could be done. "When we have cleared up the history of a single culture and understand the effects of environment and the psychological conditions that are reflected in it we have made a step forward, as we can then investigate in how far the same causes or other causes were at work in the development of other cultures," he insisted.[30]

"The most painstaking isolation of foreign elements": Despite all of its apparent differences, the Boasian project hewed very closely to that of Francis James Child and his literary studies peers. Each located a people's essence in a distant historical past in which a pure, isolated culture was unsullied by outside influences. It was the job of the learned scholar to separate the essential components of a culture from its superfluous contemporary elements. At the turn of the twentieth century, literary and anthropological folklorists remained deeply indebted to their philological forefathers.

Isolation proved a very flexible concept. The four definitions of isolation highlighted by Newell often overlapped and reinforced each other as scholars used evidence of one type of isolation to prove another. Lack of "book culture" suggested a premodern temperament. Historical texts were interpreted through the lens of progressive evolution. Primitive poetry evoked primitive minds. While debates raged within the new discipline, the core assumptions remained: the racial, temporal, evolutionary, and premodern isolation of the folk from the world of the folklorist. The folk were a people apart, and—be it because of biology or history, lack of education or lack of self-awareness—by definition they were feeble stewards of their own cultural possessions. Scholars were doubly committed to this conclusion: by defining their subjects they defined themselves as serious professionals with a mandate to salvage important cultural artifacts before they disappeared forever. The American Folklore Society began with the twin goals of identifying a disciplinary common ground between anthropologists and literary scholars and distinguishing its professional membership from armchair enthusiasts. The organization accomplished the former through its commitment to isolation. Its success in achieving the latter was far more questionable.

The Uses of Isolation

In the summer of 1895, a writer for the *New York Times* tried to enter a plantation cabin in Brooklyn's Ambrose Park. A young boy blocked his path.

> "Hi, dar! you brack rascal, git out'n de gennmen's way. Doan you see he wanter git inter der cabin tu see yer ol daddy, wat's wukin foah deah life?"
>
> The infantile black Georgian, failing to obey his mammy's word of command, was summarily removed from the doorway, and the reporter entered the cabin, and found old Joe hard at work mending a dilapidated pair of trousers that he had brought with him from the outskirts of Atlanta.[31]

The reporter was attending a preview of *Black America*, an extravagant theater production created by Billy McClain, an African American minstrel show and circus veteran. Before settling down for a concert in a large amphitheater, patrons could wander around a vast recreation of a southern plantation featuring an acre plot of cotton and 150 cabins in which the cast of 500 African American southerners lived for the duration of the run. The show drew 200,000 visitors over the summer before a scaled-down version traveled to Boston, Philadelphia, Baltimore, Washington, D.C., and London.[32] While racial tensions wracked the city outside its gates, *Black America* featured supposedly genuine black southerners who did not demand citizenship or equality, jobs or decent housing.[33] Attendees could experience a black "mammy" showing them deference and actually witness "old Joe" working for dear life. Despite bringing blackface fantasies to life, *Black America* was not an "open air minstrel show," insisted the *Brooklyn Daily Eagle*. "It is an ethnological exhibit."[34]

For all of academic folklorists' attempts at professionalization, their theories of folk isolation and primitivism were deeply intertwined with the popular culture and politics of the late nineteenth century. Never simply a story of one influencing the other, the convoluted relationship that developed between academic theories and popular culture became exactly what many founders of the American Folklore Society explicitly had dreaded. On the one hand, folklorists imbibed the common stereotypes about black and white southern culture that were circulating throughout the nation. When integrated into their scholarship, these stereotypes assumed the guise of scientific knowledge and the power of academic authority. On the other hand, academic folklorists fed a growing popular appetite for works that could locate a positive American identity and culture in the nation's supposedly uncorrupted, and racially unequivocal, past. It was a hunger that minstrelsy had been feeding for some time.

Black America signaled an early and incomplete injection of folkloric authenticity into the minstrel tradition. Promoters and reviewers adopted the emergent languages of folklore and anthropology to insist that the show's stock minstrel characters were no masquerade. Minstrelsy had always traded on its supposed authenticity. From its start, white delineators advertised that they had learned their acts directly from black performers. Promoters of *Black America* replaced these claims of individual pedigree with a rhetoric implying that the show as a whole had been designed to systematically preserve and present natural, unadorned black culture. Mc-Clain dispensed with many of the basic tropes of the minstrel stage. His actors wore no blackface makeup. Vocal quartets performed comic minstrel and coon songs, but they also sang spirituals and other religious material that provided a much more diverse portrait of African American music than contemporaneous shows. Advertisements promised the presentation of the "folk lore" and "home life" of "Southern Colored People," "showing the Afro-American in all his phases from the simplicity of the Southern field hand to his evolution as the Northern aspirant for professional honors."[35] Reviews largely agreed. "We see the negro himself, the American citizen and the colored voter, in the process of evolution," one writer explained. "We get glimpses of the working of his mind, learn what appeals will move him and in what lines he is most likely to make progress, and we see this none the less clearly that the exhibit is put in the guise of entertainment and not of instruction."[36] In *Black America*, actors performed the fantasy narrative of cultural evolution while the rhetoric of ethnography assured visitors they were encountering the real thing. "Mammy" and "old Joe" were marketed as subjects for anthropological contemplation rather than mere objects of love and theft.

Black America drew on a tradition of what the literary scholar Bernth Lindfors has called "ethnological show business." From the London stage depiction in 1810 of a San woman named Saarjie Baartman as the "Hottentot Venus" to the supposedly authentic Dahomeyan Village on the Midway at the Chicago World's Columbian Exposition of 1893, impresarios presented Africans on stage as both titillating entertainment and objects of scientific inquiry. London papers and patrons made a spectacle of Baartman's large rump, while the noted naturalist Baron Georges Cuvier eventually dissected her, saved specimens for posterity, and penned an essay on the scientific import of her bottom and genitalia.[37] In Chicago, the head of Harvard's Peabody Museum of American Archaeology and Ethnology, Frederic Ward Putnam, attested to the anthropological value of the Dahomeyan Village sideshow at the same time an Exposition guidebook declared, "The habits of these people are repulsive; they eat like animals and have all the characteristics of the very lowest order of the human family." In each case, sensationalized depictions of Africans' biological or cultural difference from white viewers promised the thrill of an encounter with fundamental racial difference while assuring customers that they were purchasing an edifying educational experience backed by the latest scientific knowledge. Indeed, leading anthropologists such as Putnam, Otis T. Mason, Alice Fletcher, and Franz Boas were directly involved in the Chicago Exposition. Official anthropological exhibits were designed to educate fairgoers in cultural evolutionary theory that located contemporary races along a continuum from primitivism to civilization. Xavier Pené, the impresario of the Dahomeyan Village, was only more cavalier in his portrayal of the same theory of white superiority. When Mason declared, "It would not be too much to say that the World's Columbian Exposition was one vast anthropological revelation," he made no distinction between the official fairground and the Midway because they communicated similar messages.[38]

Black America extended the strategies of ethnological show business's depictions of Africans to the portrayals of black southerners. Promotional material insisted that southern African American performers were better equipped to provide these new folkloric depictions than were their northern counterparts. "Real Blacks from the Southern Plantation. Not a lot of Northern Negroes," announced newspaper advertisements for the show. Nate Salsbury, *Black America*'s white promoter who had previously wowed New York audiences by producing *Buffalo Bill's Wild West Show*, explained that his southern performers were superior because they lacked the artifice of the commercial stage. "They are not show people, but are the genuinely southern negro in all his types," he insisted.[39] Newspaper reports picked up the theme that the show offered "a picture of the negro as he is in his Southern haunts, uncontaminated by Northern enterprise and Northern ways."[40] One review insisted, "Minstrels have never succeeded in doing what these uneducated darkies accomplish naturally."[41] Southern black renditions of plantation songs, explained another, were unique for their "naturalness," a trait believed missing from previous depictions of slaves on northern stages. "The North went wild over the production of 'Uncle Tom's Cabin' yet it was produced by counterfeit representatives of the characters portrayed," the review continued. *Black America*, by contrast, offered the "genuine article" that "cannot be imitated even by the blacks of the North, much less by the negro dilineators [*sic*] of modern minstrelsy."[42]

These reviewers did not conceive of *Black America* as an alterative to the stereotypes of minstrelsy. They insisted that African American southerners were superior performers of minstrel stereotypes. They beat black and white minstrels at their own game specifically because they were southerners whose act was no act at all. Indeed, reviews largely collapsed the distinctions between minstrelsy and folklore, on the one hand, and between the antebellum slave and the contemporary black southerner, on the other. In *Black America*, "we see him as the whole race was less than a quarter of a century ago and as a good part of it still is," noted the *Daily Eagle* reviewer.[43] Within the anthropological rhetoric of the show, slaves and black southerners were one and the same. Patrons could step into the southern past, according to one review, and partake in the "easy-going methods of enjoying life that prior to the war, under kind masters, it was the fortune of slaves to enjoy."[44]

Black America's romantic portrayal of a southern past helped it tap into a growing market for depictions of folkloric isolation among an urban middle class increasingly ill at ease with what civilization had wrought. The journalist Henry Childs Merwin gave voice to these shared concerns in 1897 in an *Atlantic Monthly* article titled "On Being Civilized Too Much."[45] Merwin believed that contemporary society had created "over-sophisticated and effete" individuals who had lost touch with nature. Their emotional core and necessary human instincts had been "dulled and weakened by civilization," he cried. Conscious reflection, necessary for the larger developments of national greatness and civilization, threatened civilized people's very existence for it stymied their primitive, animalistic instinct for survival. It was a constant trade-off: "every step in civilization is made at the expense of some savage strength or virtue." The arts and crafts movement, adventure literature, organized sports, game hunting: each enjoyed popularity as those "civilized too much" attempted to reassert their more primitive instincts. Yet Merwin suggested those sick with civilization turn to those who had not yet caught the disease. "Consult the teamster, the farmer, the wood-chopper, the shepherd, or the drover," he insisted. "You will find him as healthy in mind, as free from fads, as strong in natural impulses, as he was in Shakespeare's time and is in Shakespeare's plays. From his loins, and not from those of the dilettante, will spring the man of the future." Merwin's prescription echoed Ralph Waldo Emerson's earlier valorization of the "common man" as an antidote to the deadness of a college education.[46] By the turn of the twentieth century, these ideas were gaining new resonance and urgency as upper- and middle-class white Americans were finding civilized society not all it was cracked up to be.

A chorus of literary and journalistic depictions of an isolated, exotic

South—made possible by the growing availability of railroad travel to the region—provided readers afraid of being civilized too much with just the kind of examples Merwin suggested. In 1873, Will Wallace Harney, a physician, published a portrait of the Cumberland Mountains in *Lippincott's Magazine* that set a template for the local color portrayals of the region that would follow. His title, "A Strange Land and a Peculiar People," explicitly celebrated his subjects for their difference from the world of the magazine's readers. The article swerved from quasi-scientific descriptions of "marked peculiarities" in mountain residents' anatomy to sentimental portraits of their everyday lives. Out of the multifaceted culture he encountered, Harney chose to feature only those aspects of the mountains that could portray the population's internal homogeneity and ultimate difference from people elsewhere.[47] Over the next decades, authors such as Mary Noailles Murfree, James Lane Allen, and John Fox Jr. echoed Harney's claim to expertise based on direct—if sometimes very brief—observations of mountain life. Together they helped establish a popular image of the mountains sprawling over seven states as a distinct region called Appalachia. Appalachians, this literature implied, were Anglo-Saxon, close to the soil, and loyal to family, democracy, and tradition. On the other hand, Appalachians could be backward, primitive, quick to violence, and happy in their poverty. What wed these discrepant characteristics was Appalachia's isolation from modern civilization—its distance from the readers of local color literature. Appalachia was an ambiguous symbol. It connoted a racial commonality between subject and reader, yet inscribed a geographic, class, cultural, and temporal distance. Mountain whites, these writers implied, were "our contemporary ancestors" maintaining the Anglo-Saxon culture of a previous era.[48]

These popular visions of Appalachia shaped early depictions of the region in the *Journal of American Folklore*. In 1889, James Mooney published "Folk-Lore of the Carolina Mountains," the first examination of the region in the journal. Mooney quickly established the theme of mountain "isolation" leading to a "peculiar" population familiar to local color readers. He began, "The mountaineer of Western North Carolina belongs to a peculiar type which has been developed by environment and isolation into something distinctively American, and yet unlike anything to be found outside of the southern Alleghanies." He characterized mountain residents' isolation by telling a common joke about a rural Georgian who attempted to visit Augusta for the first time though he lived only twenty miles from the city

After three days of walking, he gave up and returned home only to declare, "Well, if the world's as big the other way as it is from here to 'Gusty, it's a darned big thing!"[49] In 1891, Adelene Moffat peppered her long descriptions of the mountain landscape and scenery, a local color staple, with humorous quotes from the locals emphasizing their isolation, lack of education, and incomprehension of their own history. "A dweller in one of these gulches, or 'coves,' as he would call them, being invited to give his opinion as to whether this tract of land had ever been at the bottom of the sea, answered that, 'Ef it twar so, twar before his pappy's or his granpappy's time,'" Moffat wrote. The line closely echoed standard jokes from "The Arkansas Traveler," the humorous sketch about an outsider encountering a squatter that was ubiquitous on the nation's stages during the late nineteenth century.[50] Other early reports to the *Journal* followed a similar mold. "I wish at this point to have it clearly understood, once and for all, that this paper was not undertaken in any spirit of condenscension [*sic*] or ridicule; it has a higher purpose," the collector Haywood Parker argued in his portrait of North Carolina mountaineers. "It is no disgrace to these people, isolated as they have been, that they have preserved the traditions and beliefs of their Anglo-Saxon ancestors of two hundred years ago," he continued. "A study of their folk-lore is specially interesting, as it gives us a glimpse of our ancestors— indeed, these mountaineers have been aptly called 'our contemporary ancestors.'"[51] Far from lifting the study of folklore to a new professional and scientific standard, early coverage in the *Journal of American Folklore* replicated the stereotypes, assumptions, and even the humor of the mountain images developed by amateur enthusiasts and local color writers. Their presence in the *Journal* enforced stereotypes of regional isolation and difference by granting them a patina of scientific and academic authority.

This academic authority could be used to assert mountain isolation even when informants explicitly denied it. After Louise Rand Bascom described the process of orally transmitting songs "in true ballad style" that she discovered in the mountains of western North Carolina, she admitted, "The mountaineers object to having it thought that the songs are in any way connected with oral tradition. One woman, for example, made this remark: 'You kin git 'em all in a book we've got that's got 'Nellie Grey,' 'Mollie Darling,' an' all them old songs in hit.'" Bascom was quick to refute such a challenge to her concept of folk isolation. "The book was not forthcoming upon request, and as the woman who ventured this remark belongs to the lowest class of mountaineers and cannot read, it is probable that she has never possessed such a book," Bascom parried. "Other illiterate mountaineers delight in talking of the 'ref'rence books in their trunks.' They certainly own no trunks, and probably the daily papers pasted on the walls to keep out the cold are the nearest things they own to 'ref'rence books,' and these, of course, have been given them."[52]

Once established by the folklorist, concepts of mountain isolation could be expanded to account for a more generalized isolated South. E. C. Perrow published one of the first substantial collections of southern folk songs in the *Journal of American Folklore*. "Songs and Rhymes from the South" contained 270 texts published serially between 1912 and 1915. The collection betrayed a significant debt to the images of the region developed in local color literature. Perrow framed his collection with an essay describing the cultural cohesion and geographical and temporal isolation of the Appalachian Mountains. "The relative inaccessibility of the country, as compared with the surrounding territory, has until very recently kept back the tide of progress, which, sweeping around this region, has shut up there a strange survival of a civilization of three hundred years ago," he explained. Isolation, Perrow argued, caused residents to "preserve primitive ideals" and dialect that "mark them as belonging to another age."[53] The mountain whites were an ideal population for the folk song collector. The region's residents supposedly preserved Gummere's ballad-making throng even as they maintained the small, cohesive culture favored by Franz Boas. "As a matter of fact, many of the traditional ballads have been found among them still alive; and yet other songs, apparently the very material out of which the popular ballad is made, may be picked up there to-day," Perrow explained.[54]

Yet the mountain culture that impressed Perrow had more to do with the popular portrayals of the region than it did with the songs he collected or the expansive claims he made about them. First, Perrow's depiction of Appalachian isolation was less fact than fantasy by the time he proposed it. The region had been in the midst of the same rapid commercial and industrial transformation that swept across the South in the last decades of the nineteenth century. Northeastern entrepreneurs built expansive textile, coal, and lumber industries in the mountains, resulting in a rapid expansion of land prices, wage labor, union organizing, and railroad lines deep into the recesses of the region. Mail-ordered goods—from tools and crockery to banjos and pump organs—transformed the ways residents cooked, dressed, and made music. And northeastern educators and settlement house workers encouraged mountain residents to take up northern, middle-class domestic sciences, gender roles, and political values, as well as the very English folk songs sought by collectors.[55] Perrow did note recent transformations in the region as summer resorts and railroads brought "quality" urban vacationers to the region. Yet he insisted "such visitors leave no impression on the people" other than encouraging a few locals to take up "the custom of wearing collars instead of the standard red handkerchief."[56]

Second, most of the songs in Perrow's collection were not from the mountains. Out of 270 entries, only ninety-eight (about 36 percent) were found among the white mountain population that occupied his introduction. The author associated the remainder with white and black communities throughout several southern states, including Virginia, Alabama, Mississippi, and South Carolina, as well as Missouri, Indiana, and Pennsylvania. Perrow received the texts from over fifty informants and collectors, including students from around the South and as far away as Harvard University. The focus on mountain isolation in the introduction, however, suggested that all the texts in the collection be understood as "of another age" and implied that the cultural isolation of the mountains characterized the South as a whole. It was a subtle but important categorical slip. The implicit equation between the mountains and the South marked the entire region as a place apart from the rest of the nation. It suggested that the South maintained a homogenous musical culture defined by its antiquity, its primitive ideals, and its ignorance of northern styles. A poor description of Perrow's own collection, it was an even more questionable characterization of southern song. Yet it fit well with the concepts of isolation promoted by academic scholars and the images of Appalachia spilling from the popular press. Perrow went in search of the scholar's ideal isolated community, and found it in the fantastic literary representations of an exotic South.

Scholarly and popular depictions of African American culture influenced each other in similar ways. Racial stereotypes of the popular stage were identified as racial characteristics in scientific studies. Minstrel imagery was already evident in *Slave Songs of the United States*, the first major collection of spirituals, published in 1867. The authors declared that the "negro melodies" that became popular with the rise of minstrelsy serve as a "tribute to the musical genius of the race." They proceeded to celebrate the spirituals while noting that the "civilized" qualities of black music probably result from close association with white people, that the "barbaric" tendencies are African in origin, and that the book is full of "some very comical specimens" of black mispronunciations of "half-understood" words.[57] The fluid equation of minstrel stereotypes with authentic folklore can also be seen in the work of the popular writer Joel Chandler Harris. The white *Atlanta Constitution* editor became well known for his depictions of southern black culture following the publication of his collection *Uncle Remus: His Songs and His Sayings* in 1880. The fictional character Remus was an elderly slave who shared folk tales and songs with his owner's young son. Harris portrayed Remus through a written dialect that supposedly reproduced the pronunciation and inflection of black southern speech. As the young child rested his head on the old man's arm, Uncle Remus related the adventures of Brer Rabbit, a wily trickster who regularly used his wit to escape the clutches of more powerful foes—or as Uncle Remus put it, "Brer Fox bin doin' all dat he could fer ter ketch Brer Rabbit, en Brer Rabbit bein doin' all he could fer ter keep 'im fum it." *Uncle Remus* met with rave reviews upon its release, and Harris's stories were syndicated in newspapers across the nation.[58]

Uncle Remus met success in part because it straddled the line between minstrelsy and ethnography, popular fancies and serious scholarship. Harris imagined his work a "sympathetic" portrayal of "a new and by no means unattractive phase of negro character" far removed from "the intolerable misrepresentations of the minstrel stage." Little in *Uncle Remus* directly confronted minstrel stereotypes, however. Fans of the genre could enjoy the humor of Harris's "old darkey" dialect and stories without rethinking their assumptions about black inferiority.[59] The stories likewise perpetuated minstrelsy's romantic portrayal of racial harmony in the Old South, invoking the comforting nostalgia "every Southern family" had for the cadence of black speech and tapping into a growing market for sentimental portrayals of slavery among white readers throughout the nation. Yet Harris's collection also appealed to those interested in authentic black folklore. Indeed, Brer Rabbit was a ubiquitous character within antebellum slave culture, his adventures shared for their entertainment value as well as their lessons about survival and resistance under slavery. Harris argued that his collection preserved this important African American lore, and the noted Smithsonian anthropologist J. W. Powell acknowledged the historical significance of his work.[60]

Harris thus perpetuated minstrel stereotypes while preserving authentic black folk culture. It was a slippery approach that he shared with many early contributors to the *Journal of American Folklore*. The first several journal entries to examine African American or Afro-Caribbean folklore focused on black superstition, "voodoo," and cannibalism. William Wells Newell contributed his "Myths of Voodoo Worship and Child Sacrifice in Hayti" to the inaugural issue of the journal in 1888.[61] The essay launched a scathing critique of recent reports of cannibalism in the country. It was a model of the American Folklore Society's mandate to use serious scientific methodology to dismantle amateur depictions of folk cultures. Later contributors were not as exacting. They combined reports of religious customs with stereotypes of black exoticism, difference, and depictions of slaves happy in their bondage.[62] Alcée Fortier, to offer just one example, provided an important description of slave music in 1888 in the article "Customs and Superstitions in Louisiana." New Year's Day celebrations on the antebellum plantation, Fortier wrote, were accompanied by music made on a "barrel with one end covered with an ox-hide,—this was the drum; then two sticks and the jawbone of a mule, with the teeth still on it,—this was the violin." He then detailed the multiple ways musicians made use of these instruments. Fortier framed such descriptions, however, within an apology for slavery ripped straight from the antebellum stage. Slaves "were, as a rule, well treated by their masters, and, in spite of their slavery, they were contented and happy." The music created by the "childlike slaves" was "strange and savage" but "not disagreeable as the negroes have a very good ear for music." Fortier concluded, "Very different is this scene from those described in 'Uncle Tom's Cabin,' for the slaves were certainly not unhappy on the plantations. The proof of this is, that, although our equals politically and citizens of the United States, they often refer to the time of slavery, and speak willingly of those bygone days."[63]

Of all the popular black stereotypes perpetuated by contributors to the *Journal of American Folklore*, none was more ubiquitous than that of the passive, nurturing, and contented mammy. "The old negro 'mauma' of the plantation life of the South is fast becoming a thing of the past. Once she was a familiar figure and a person of great importance," wrote John Hawkins in 1896. "Second in authority only to the white mistress, skilled in all domestic duties, full of superstition, the minstrel of family history and tradition, energetic and accustomed to rule, she was at once the comfort of master and mistress, the terror of idle servants, and the delight of the children of the household." Hawkins deemed himself fortunate to have had such a "mauma" care for him as a boy. His article describes a series of southern black customs and beliefs he discovered through an interview with his aging "maum' Sue," who was "ready as ever to tell of the old days of bondage, the passing of which she laments as much as the most unreconstructed slaveholder," according to the writer.[64]

One might imagine that the perpetuation of minstrel stereotypes as folklore was the work of the very amateur collectors the American Folklore Society designed to discredit, but prominent, distinguished white scholars regularly got in on the act.[65] Daniel Brinton, for example, embraced minstrel stereotypes in the 1890s, investing statements such as "The true negroes are passionately fond of music, singing, and dancing" with a patina of scientific truth culled from his stature as a celebrated scholar.[66] Otis T. Mason of the Smithsonian Institution was quick to evoke the stock mammy character in his defense of cultural evolution. "The assertion that there is no evidence of the introduction of uncivilized culture into countries already in possession of a higher culture is too sweeping," he complained in a review of George Laurence Gomme's *Ethnology in Folklore* in 1892. "Every white child that ever grew up in Virginia knows better, having had his youthful imagination crowded with fancies and peopled with lore furnished by 'ole mammy' and 'uncle Tom,' just as soon as he could crawl about."[67]

Scholars' embrace of minstrel stereotypes helped to legitimate black song as a signifier of *white* American identity. White writers framed black music within the context of white memory. Johann Tonsor, most likely the pseudonym of the collector Mildred Hill, filtered her 1892 presentation of "Negro Music" through a nostalgic mist of Old South imagery that would have found an easy home on the minstrel stage. "When he hears one of these quaint old airs, he needs but to close his eyes and the potent spell of the music revivifies the past," Tonsor wrote. "Old memories, that he had deemed forgotten, rise as if obedient to the voice of enchantment. He is again a child in the cradle, and his faithful old 'mammy,' as she rocks him, bends over him in the firelight and croons."[68] The sounds of blackness supposedly sent white readers into a communal reverie for a harmonious interracial past most vibrantly illustrated by white children suckling at the breast of a black nursemaid. It was imagery borrowed broadcloth from minstrelsy's sentimental odes to the old plantation, yet it was imbued with a highbrow legitimacy that could only come with a scientific pedigree. Tonsor and other white collectors helped make black song a safe, moving talisman for white national identity.

It is within the context of white response to black folk song that the Bohemian composer Antonín Dvořák called for the use of black song as the basis for an American school of composition. In 1893, early in his tenure at New York's National Conservatory, the esteemed composer famously declared, "I am now satisfied that the future music of this country must be founded upon what are called negro melodies."[69] Anglo-Saxonism ran deep among proponents of musical nationalism. They equated American identity with white racial purity and heard Dvořák's comments as the forfeiture of their birthright if not the delusions of a drinker.[70] Yet when Dvořák suggested that "negro melodies" could provide fodder for an American school of composition, he was talking—at least in part—about the music of the blackface minstrel. In his May 1893 interview, well before he arranged a Stephen Foster minstrel ditty for the concert stage, Dvořák identified these melodies as "folk songs" whose varied themes and moods could help an American composer express the "common humanity of his country." Then Dvořák unambiguously stated, "When the negro minstrels are here again I intend to take my young composers with me and have them comment on the melodies."[71] Evidence suggests that Dvořák was influenced by Tonsor's article on "Negro Music," and he apparently inherited the writer's approach to its subject.[72]

Like many white Americans, Dvořák did not distinguish between minstrelsy and African American folk music. Each genre drew on a similar set of symbols that subtly fused white fantasies about black marginalization and romantic nostalgia for the Old South. This potent combination made them the most American sounds many citizens had ever heard. "It is a proper question to ask, what songs, then, belong to the American and appeal more strongly to him than any other?" Dvořák wrote in 1895. "What melody could stop him on the street if he were in a strange land and make the home feeling well up within him, no matter how hardened he might be or how wretchedly the tune was played?" His conclusion: "the so-called plantation melodies and slave songs." The composer then apparently responded to critics of his equation between African American folk music and minstrelsy. "The point has been urged that many of these touching songs, like those of Foster, have not been composed by the Negroes themselves, but are the work of white men, while others did not originate on the plantation, but were imported from Africa," he reported. "It seems to me that this matters but little."[73] Dvořák could dismiss the charge because it was largely white nostalgia rather than black ownership that made "negro melodies" meaningful and useful to him.

If black folklore collections helped articulate a white American identity, they could also work to sever black folk music from the contemporary African American population. Just as Francis James Child extracted English ballads from untrustworthy singers and Franz Boas painstakingly isolated useful lore from "foreign elements," collectors of African American folk songs sought music that their informants were no longer interested in singing and then held up these outdated ditties as representative of racial culture and consciousness. Nowhere is this clearer than in the white vogue for the slave spirituals in the late nineteenth and early twentieth centuries. As Jon Cruz has convincingly chronicled, the first significant white celebration of the spirituals occurred within the context of the abolition movement. Spirituals—the songs of the contemporary slave population—offered moving testimony to black humanity under the cruel yoke of slavery. By the late nineteenth century, the spirituals had undergone a profound shift, in Cruz's terms, from testimony to artifact. No longer venerated as evidence of the current oppression of African Americans, spirituals were valued as echoes from the past. They provided beautiful proof of black creativity and pathos yet fostered nostalgia rather than political action. Much like minstrelsy, slave spirituals intimately linked African American culture with the past, with the South, and with slavery. They could enable white listeners to celebrate African American culture—and their own romantic memories of the South—without addressing contemporary segregation and violence against black citizens.[74]

Indeed, some scholars used their conclusions about African American folklore to lobby for Jim Crow laws, insisting there was a biological basis to African American's supposed inability to assume the responsibilities of citizenship. Daniel Brinton saw himself as part of this popular discussion of segregation, publishing "The Aims of Anthropology" in *Popular Science Monthly* not long after it appeared in an academic journal.[75] Anthropology's ability to chart the "racial mind, or the temperament of a people, with as much propriety and accuracy as we can of any of the physical traits," he maintained, "offers a positive basis for legislation, politics and education, as applied to a given ethnic group."

> These peculiarities, as ascertained by objective investigation, supply the only sure foundation for legislation; not *a priori* notions of the rights of man, nor abstract theories of what should constitute a perfect state, as was the fashion with older philosophies, and still is with the modern social reformers. The aim of the anthropologist in this practical field is to ascertain in all their details, such as religious, language, social life, notions of right and wrong, etc., wherein lie the idiosyncrasies of a given group, and frame its laws accordingly.[76]

Social isolation, enforced through Jim Crow legislation, was justified by the biological and cultural distance black people resided from civilized society, Brinton argued. As Lee Baker amply illustrates, it was this ability of evolutionary anthropology to reinforce racist stereotype that was crucial to the funding of early anthropological research and institution building.

The new century witnessed a veritable cacophony of similar pronouncements from white academics supporting Jim Crow legislation. Sociologists and historians joined evolutionary anthropologists in their attempts to define black inferiority as a racial trait that could only be overcome through a slow process of evolutionary change and to identify racial separation as the natural order of things. Most understood continued interracial contact as a threat to white purity and civilization. Without segregation, the writer Robert Shufeldt insisted, "the blacks will gradually be absorbed and all the evil effects resulting from such an amalgamation will have passed beyond the reach of any remedy."[77] Others argued that integrating African Americans into civilized society too quickly would prove harmful to them. "It is really the great tragedy of civilization," wrote the sociologist William Graham Sumner, "that the contact of lower and higher is disastrous to the former, no matter what may be the point of contact, or how little the civilized may desire to do harm." Sumner's influential work insisted that the desire for racial separation ran deep within both black and white folkways. Like Brinton, he believed that any attempt to reshape society by appealing to abstract principles or ethics was doomed to failure if it contradicted society's unspoken preference for racial separation. "Legislation cannot make mores," he asserted.[78] Similar conclusions were being reached within the historical profession. The Columbia historian William Dunning, through his own work and that of his students, launched a devastating reappraisal of Reconstruction as an era in which "all the forces [in the South] that made for civilization were dominated by a mass of barbarous freedmen." Only when white northerners realized their error and reconciled with their white compatriots in the South was order restored. "This may be fine romance, but it is not science," W. E. B. Du Bois later wrote. "And beyond this it is dangerous. It is not only part foundation of our present lawlessness and loss of democratic ideals; it has, more than that, led the world to embrace and worship the color bar as social salvation."[79] In an era of public lynching, segregation, and political disenfranchisement of African Americans, such scholarship granted scientific support to the status quo. It wrote contemporary white desires for racial difference and distance backward into historical record, claiming recent trends were rooted in long-standing cultural and biological truths.[80]

Two major strategies developed to combat these views. The first was pioneered by the African American writer James Monroe Trotter in his landmark book *Music and Some Highly Musical People* (1878).[81] Trotter chronicled the lives of numerous black artists, most of whom performed European classical music. He insisted that it was racism, rather than any fundamental racial difference, that necessitated his focus on "the musical celebrities of a single race." "The haze of complexional prejudice has so much obscured the vision of many persons, that they cannot see (at least, there are many who affect not to see) that musical faculties, and power for their *artistic* development, are not in the exclusive possession of the fairer-skinned race, but are alike the beneficent gifts of the Creator to all his children," he wrote. Trotter promoted a musical hierarchy that placed the European classical tradition as the ultimate musical expression. Black artists could match the highest attainments of European art house composers, thus disproving claims of black inferiority. He repeatedly cast his subject in the light of current debates about race, believing his book would perform "a much-needed service, not so much, perhaps, to the cause of music itself, as to some of the noblest devotees and the race to which the latter belong."[82] By emphasizing African American artists' command of classical performance and composition, Trotter hoped to challenge arguments about black inferiority. Several proponents repeated Trotter's strategic critique of the cultural evolutionary paradigm within the world of music in the coming years. It shaped the work of the *Negro Music Journal* through its fifteen month run in 1902 and 1903. It also shared a great deal with the promotion of black classical artists by African American newspapers such as the Chicago *Defender* and later by Black Swan Records in the 1920s. Each found the best way to defend against claims of black cultural inferiority was to promote the better classes of music among black consumers and performers.[83]

If Trotter turned toward the world of classical music, Franz Boas believed that a study of African American folklore could reveal the injustice of Jim Crow. In accordance with his theoretical interest in historically isolated cultures, Boas insisted that the history of African industry and arts suggested that the negative characteristics attributed to African Americans were a result of their oppression in the United States rather than their mental capacity. "There is nothing to prove that licentiousness, shiftless laziness, lack of initiative, are fundamental characteristics of the race," he concluded. "Everything points out that these qualities are the result of social conditions rather than hereditary traits."[84] In a commencement address at Atlanta University in 1906, Boas argued that the history of African arts should be a point of pride for African Americans. "If, therefore, it is claimed that your race is doomed to economic inferiority, you may confidently look to the home of your ancestors and say that you have set out to recover for the colored people the strength that was their own before they set foot on the shores of this continent," Boas concluded. Like his insistence on cultural relativism, the veneration of a civilized African past was a dramatic declaration. W. E. B. Du Bois remembered hearing the Atlanta University address: "I was too astonished to speak. All of this I had never heard and I came then and afterwards to realize how the silence and neglect of science can let truth utterly disappear or even be unconsciously distorted."[85]

Locating a positive image of black culture in the historical past was a double-edged sword. As Du Bois's comment suggests, evidence of ancient African industry provided positive imagery of black culture at a time when the mass media and white discourse equated conditions arising from economic and social oppression with biological inferiority. When attention shifted toward African American folklore, however, it could locate black authenticity outside of contemporary "high art," reifying the distinction between black culture and civilization. This paradox can be seen in the work of the Hampton Folk-Lore Society. The society was founded in the 1890s by Alice Mabel Bacon, a white faculty member at Virginia's Hampton Institute, a black college founded on the vocational education model championed by

Booker T. Washington. Interested in promoting the collection of black folklore, Boas and William Wells Newell encouraged Bacon and her students to publish in the *Journal of American Folklore* and supplied the Hampton society with equipment such as a gramophone for collecting African American folk songs.[86]

Bacon's vision of the Hampton Folk-Lore Society suggests the complicated interplay among black southerners, traditional culture, and the scientific study of folklore. In an address at the American Folklore Society conference in 1897, Bacon set education and civilization in opposition to folklore and illiteracy, identifying the consciousness of "common" black people with the latter. Bacon defined black folklore by its difference from white culture, stating the society was interested in collecting the "little things peculiar to their own race." She was discouraged that most students were uninterested in these unique aspects of black culture. Bacon found "old stories and superstitions and customs of their own race are only too apt to be looked down upon as all bad, and to be forgotten as quickly as possible." Bacon believed that education itself caused the problem: "Folk-lore has no greater enemy than the common school, and more than one half of the negro children of the country are now enrolled in the public schools." Bacon thus set up a dichotomy between the culture prized by the black students with which she worked and the "peculiarities" of black folklore. She then insisted that the folklore her students found embarrassing held the key to the consciousness of the black folk. Folklore enabled one "to enter more deeply into the daily life of the common people, and to understand more thoroughly their ideas and motives."[87]

Bacon's dichotomy between black education and black authenticity can be seen in the society's collection of black music. Bacon believed that Hampton's previous attempts to salvage black folk music had suffered from too much "civilizing" influence. The Hampton Institute, home of a jubilee choir, had "already done much work in the line of collecting, arranging for our system of musical notation, and publishing the negro spirituals, but that is not the kind of work that our Society wishes to do," she explained. An authentic representation of black religious song should not prepare it "to be sung as a regular four-part song by a choir or congregation, either white or black." Rather, Bacon hoped to "find the place and the history of each song" that the society collected. The songs and history that particularly interested Bacon were those of the isolated black community.

We hear again and again of some one who has recently come into the school with such beautiful new plantation songs; and then they are taken down by the music teacher, and the choir is drilled in the rendering of them and the whole school in time follows the choir's interpretation of them; and in a short time that song, with time and tune and spirit altered becomes a totally different thing from the weird melody chanted at baptism, or "settin' up," or revival meeting in the log cabins, or by the riverside, or in the meeting-house of some little negro settlement.[88]

Bacon's comments reveal the trade-off faced by scholars who promoted black folk culture as a corrective to popular images of black inferiority. Bacon understood the dramatic effect that notation and European art arrangements could have on the sound of the spirituals. Yet she associated these aural differences with different segments of the black population and degrees of authentic black culture. Bacon equated the "weird melody" of the "common people" with a song's "history," finding performances untouched by Western music standards to represent earlier incarnations of the song. The Hampton Folklore Society, Bacon hoped, would help overcome the educational divide between black southerners by introducing black folk culture and heritage to the students of the university. Like Boas's veneration of an African past, the study of the black folklore encouraged racial pride among the students. Yet Bacon's project left little room for the "common people" to do anything but represent this folk past. In her formulation, the black folk could receive a Hampton education or maintain their authentic culture. They could not do both.

W. E. B. Du Bois attempted to transcend this conundrum in his landmark collection of essays *The Souls of Black Folk* (1903). He identified the spirituals as a common and powerful heritage while refusing to limit his vision of black culture to this tradition. Music, of course, held a prominent place in the book. Du Bois began each chapter with a brief melodic quote from a traditional spiritual, and the book culminated in a chapter about these sorrow songs. The essay performed a number of balancing acts. Du Bois was steeped in the communalist theory of folklore, yet he fundamentally rejected the cultural evolutionary paradigm that equated black culture with primitivism. He was also writing in the shadow of minstrelsy. His essay excoriated blackface distortions of the "real Negro melodies" while maintaining, even celebrating, the market value of black song. He accomplished this balancing act through two novel strategies. First, he repeatedly located the creation of the spirituals in the historical past. "They that walked in darkness sang songs in the olden days—Sorrow Songs—for they were weary at heart," he began. Through "these weird old songs"—"the voices of the past"—"the soul of the black slave spoke to men." By repeatedly emphasizing the historical nature of the spirituals, Du Bois relieved the contemporary African American population from the burden of embodying the folk tradition. "True Negro folk-song still lives in the hearts of those who have heard them truly sung and in the hearts of the Negro people," he explained. The songs were the product of black memory rather than the result of black capacity or cultural isolation as was so often proposed by other scholars.[89]

Second, Du Bois repeatedly implied the materiality of the spirituals. They were "gifts," possessions that could be carried, shared, and sold. He summarized the history of the Fisk Jubilee Singers, the choral group from his alma mater that had arranged spirituals in standard European harmony in the 1870s and launched a successful fundraising tour for their university. Du Bois celebrated the tour as a cultural triumph. "The Fisk Jubilee Singers sang the slave songs so deeply into the world's heart that it can never wholly forget them again." Yet he also understood the tour as a financial success: "Seven years they sang, and brought back a hundred and fifty thousand dollars to found Fisk University." This combination of culture and capital was key to Du Bois for it established the spirituals as a living, contemporary asset even as they remained echoes of the slave past. After walking around Fisk, he wrote, "I saw the great temple builded of these songs towering over the pale city. To me Jubilee Hall seemed ever made of the songs themselves, and its bricks were red with the blood and dust of toil." The product of laboring slaves, the songs built Fisk both figuratively and literally. They were a financial as well as a cultural inheritance. Casting the spirituals as material possessions enabled Du Bois to celebrate the songs as important sources of black memory and black capital simultaneously. He could thus reject the division between folk song and the market promoted by academic folklorists and overcome the divide between education and authenticity that had plagued Alice Bacon.[90]

Yet Du Bois was not content to limit his portrait of African American culture to the black folk tradition. In the other significant passage about music in *The Souls of Black Folk*, the author imagined John, a young southern black man, encountering the music of Richard Wagner in a New York opera house. "The infinite beauty of the wail lingered and swept through every muscle of his frame, and put it all a-tune," he wrote. "A deep longing swelled in all his heart to rise with that clear music out of the dirt and dust of that low life that held him prisoned and befouled." The scene, as those who have read the book know, does not end well. John is expelled from the theater after an anonymous complaint from his white childhood friend who happened to be sitting nearby. Braced by the beauty of Wagner's music and the inability to escape southern racism, he determines to return home to "help settle the Negro problems there." The story ends with the harrowing sound of an approaching lynch mob. John's encounter with the European canon ends tragically, but Du Bois's admirable condemnation of the Jim Crow South should not blind us to his message that the complex musical souls of black folk were not limited by black desire as much as by white racism. It was a lesson American folklorists would be slow to acknowledge.

John Lomax's *Cowboy Songs* garnered significant comment in both academic and popular circles when it was published in 1910. Lomax's genius was his ability to create a popular book that maintained academic authority, a work that spoke to both camps simultaneously. On the one hand, the book contributed to the debates within American folk song scholarship. *Cowboy Songs* helped many collectors realize that it was possible to find extant American folk songs. Within five years, seven states formed folklore societies to collect southern folk song. The book also contributed to conversations about the Child ballads by drawing explicit parallels between the composition of American cowboy songs and the Old English ballads. Barrett Wendell, in his introduction to the book, enthused that the frontier ballads "should go far to prove, or disprove, many of the theories advanced concerning the laws of literature as evinced in the ballads of the Old World." It is clear that Lomax hoped to add evidence to the theory of communal composition. He was trained at Harvard under the communalist George Lyman Kittredge, and his communalist leanings revealed themselves throughout his book. The cowboy songs "seem to have sprung up as quietly and mysteriously as does the grass on the plains," he explained.[91] The folklorist Louise Pound, however, took exception to Lomax's communalist conclusions. After a detailed analysis of the poetic characteristics of Lomax's songs, Pound found them better evidence for the degenerationist position. "Working from both subject-matter and style," she concluded, "it would seem that among the cowboys of the Southwest are reproduced not the conditions which created the English and Scottish popular ballads but rather, it may be, some of the conditions which preserved them."[92] *Cowboy Songs* thus was taken as a serious contribution to the field even as its conclusions were debated.

It would take a number of years before scholars would begin criticizing the book for its unscientific treatment of its source material. The author was aware that this criticism might arise and attempted a preemptive strike. "As for the songs of this collection," he warned, "I have violated the ethics of ballad-gatherers, in a few instances, by selecting and putting together what seems to be the best lines from different versions, all telling the same story." After acknowledging the academic standards professed by his peers, Lomax washed his hands of them, concluding, "Frankly, the volume is meant to be popular."[93]

Indeed, *Cowboy Songs* won praise from the popular press, in part because of its presentation as a piece of serious scholarship. Unlike much adventure and local color literature, Lomax's work—a sober study propped up by a Harvard professor and a letter from the president of the United States—smacked more of primitives' actual lives than of civilized longings. One reviewer claimed the mundane character of the book's contents established its authenticity. "A most conspicuous quality, and perhaps the most emphatic stamp of genuine primitiveness, is the predominance of the pathetic and the utter absence of that neurotic worship of savagery which is so familiar a symptom of modern civilized art," the reviewer wrote. "The really strong and primordial man, living close to nature and the beasts, bays doglike to the mournful moon or wails feline lamentations for his absent loves; it is the epicene by-product of civilization who twitters of glorious passions and abysmal brutalities, and with manicured hand strokes the swelling muscles of the gladiator."[94] *Cowboy Songs* filled a void in polite literature by providing authentic evidence of uncivilized lives.

Lomax was far from alone in viewing American music through the lens of the founding debates of folklore studies. Many would follow, defining the scope of their inquiry by the imaginary lines drawn between racial cultures, savagery and civilization, and the past and the present. In coming years, folklorists would find their quest for isolated racial groups aided by the growing presence of Jim Crow throughout the South. Their work became less about nostalgia for a dying culture than the cultural justification of a current regime. Folklorists became intimately involved in the rhetorical preservation and explanation of segregation as they read very recent physical separation of the races back into the cultural past. They helped to naturalize segregation by insisting that the important aspects of African American or white folk culture were those that showed no sign of cultural miscegenation.

Folklorists asked the "folk" to conform to an image of cultural isolation that did not reflect their everyday lives. People whose voices were already marginalized within national political and economic debates due to their racial or class identities found themselves further constrained as scholars held them up as the "folk," who by very definition were national outsiders. John Lomax clearly explained this bargain to the frontier "knights" whose culture he tried to record. While gathering texts for a second edition of his cowboy ballad collection, the folklorist chided one informant. "You do not tell me if you founded the song you sent me on the poetry of Walt Whitman," he wrote in a letter to a man submitting a potential folk song. "I am really interested on this point, and would be glad to have you tell me definitely if you are acquainted with the work of this great American poet . . . If you know of the words of any *real* cowboy songs,—I mean the songs they sing around the camp fire on the range—I shall be very grateful for them."[95] "Folks" who longed to attend the national drama found playing the isolated or the primitive of the scholar's dream could be the price of the ticket. They knew they were performing a charade.

Reminiscing about *Black America* years later, the African American vaudevillian Tom Fletcher never mentioned the show's emphasis on southern authenticity or folk music. He understood *Black America* as a production designed to create jobs. "McClain was always looking for ways to put more and more people in show business," he insisted. "Free-born and possessing a formal education, he was a smooth talker and had plenty of nerve and through the years his activities were directly responsible for the employment of thousands of colored people in show business." Evidence suggests that at least some—I suspect a significant number—of the show's bit players were local residents, no more "southern" than the legion of migrants who had recently made New York home.[96] *Black America* succeeded, from Fletcher's perspective, precisely because it featured local celebrity performers who were already favorites with New York audiences. "Since the spectacle was to be put on in the summer time he had a chance at all of the top show people of the period: names like Madam Flowers, Fred Piper, Charley

Johnson, May Bohee, Madam Cordelia McClain, Jube Johnson, Ed Harris, Billy Farrell, Doc Sales. He was also able to get the most beautiful girls, singers, and dancers," he explained.[97] The *New York Clipper*, an entertainment industry paper, conformed to Fletcher's interpretation. While it mentioned that the show featured "real living scenes in the life of the real Southern negro," most of its coverage emphasized the shifting cavalcade of stars headlining on the Ambrose Park stage.[98] Nevertheless, McClain's insistence that southern artists could portray minstrel stereotypes with anthropological accuracy helped open New York theaters to southern performers. Many were poised to assume center stage.

SOUTHERN MUSICIANS AND THE LURE OF NEW YORK CITY 4

Representing the South from
Coon Songs to the Blues

In 1907, as the folklorist John Lomax collected material for *Cowboy Songs and Other Frontier Ballads*, a young white Texas singer picked up stakes and moved fifteen hundred miles to New York City. Vernon Dalhart, born Marion Try Slaughter in 1883, grew up in a rancher's family in and around Jefferson, Texas. As a young child, Dalhart had learned to ride horses and tend cattle on his uncle's five-hundred-acre ranch. In his teens he held a summer job as a cowhand, the cowboy songs loved by Lomax echoing through the youngster's head. These were not the only tunes occupying Dalhart, however. After his family moved to Dallas following the death of his father, the teen studied at the Dallas Conservatory of Music and hired himself out as a soloist to local churches and funeral homes. "It wasn't long before my ambitions outgrew Dallas," he later recalled. "I wanted to sing opera. That meant going to New York City and here I came." He took the names of two Texas towns to create his stage name.[1]

Dalhart struggled to make a living after his arrival in New York. "For a number of years I spent the daylight hours pushing pianos around as a shipping clerk in a piano store," he remembered. "At night I took voice lessons and on my way to and from work I studied opera. I learned four Italian operas *in Italian* hanging to a strap on the subway. Those weren't easy years."[2] In 1911, he finally landed a minor role in a touring production of Puccini's *Girl of the Golden West*, but his big break came in 1914 when he scored a lead role in Gilbert and Sullivan's *H. M. S. Pinafore* at the famed Hippodrome. Dalhart was closer to his dream of a successful music career than he had been back in Dallas. He was beginning to garner a reputation and enjoy positive reviews as a light opera tenor. Yet as he struggled to support his family on his intermittent stage work, he began imagining ways to trade on his southern identity in order to secure regular employment.[3]

Dalhart's journey to New York suggests an important counternarrative to the well-known tale of northern scholars descending into the South to discover traditional folk music. As John Lomax ventured from Harvard to the cattle range, many of the very musicians he sought were traveling in the opposite direction. They were in search not of American tradition but of access to the modern American theater, music publishing, and phonograph industries centered in New York. The generation of southern artists that arrived in New York between 1890 and 1920 participated in an important and contradictory reinterpretation of southern music and culture. They encountered a musical world that traded on stereotypes of rural and southern music, from hillbilly comedy records to the minstrel stage. As southern artists attempted to gain access to New York stages and recording studios, to make the shift from local to national markets, they discovered that their best chance often involved conforming to the prevailing stereotypes of southern culture.

Back home, southern musicians often had been the only show in town. They performed the best renditions of Tin Pan Alley, British ballads, or blackface routines available to audiences denied the originators of these genres. In New York, however, many of these same southern artists confronted steep competition in the performance of nationally recognized styles. What southern singer could hope to make opera recordings that could challenge the prestige and sales of Caruso's Red Seals? Or brave Broadway stars' recordings of stage hits? Instead, they turned to what distinguished them from the innumerable performers already on record: their southern heritage. Yet embracing this niche meant embodying the authentic "local color," "primitive" abandon, or "genuine" racial temperament associated with the rural South. Access to modern media—and the prospective pay that accompanied it—often was predicated on donning the mantle of the premodern, catching up by playing the role of the one left behind. Southern artists sold themselves as more authentic representations of the stereotypical minstrel or hillbilly of the urban stage. The result was a highly unstable new musical world in which weathered caricatures of southern culture were invested with the authority of folklore, claimed authentic by the very people they were created to ridicule.

James Weldon Johnson and J. Rosamond Johnson moved to New York in 1899. The African American brothers were well-educated scions of a Jacksonville, Florida, family, Rosamond a trained pianist and James Weldon a poet and lyricist. Like Dalhart, they moved to New York to break into the national entertainment industry. Neither knew what they were up against. "Two young Negroes away down in Florida, unknown and inexperienced, starting for New York thirty-three years ago to try for a place in the world of light opera. I can now recognize all the absurdities and count up all the improbabilities of it," James Weldon later marveled. Indeed, they faced serious obstacles upon their arrival. Musician unions, theaters, and phonograph studios often systematically excluded black artists.[4]

The brothers soon met a number of African American musicians who had come to New York before them and already were struggling to overcome industry segregation in the city. Bert Williams, born in Nassau, was a versatile actor and songwriter. His stage partner, George Walker, was a medicine show veteran and vaudevillian from Lawrence, Kansas. Ernest Hogan, born in Bowling Green, Kentucky, was an actor and comedian whose song "All Coons Look Alike to Me" (1896) had signaled the arrival of the coon song craze. The composer Will Marion Cook, a native of Washington, D.C., studied music at the Oberlin Conservatory and in Berlin before attending the New York National Conservatory in the mid-1890s. Cook had just produced *Clorindy: or, The Origin of the Cakewalk* (1898), a landmark show notable for its black cast, its Broadway debut, and a score that twisted minstrel stereotypes into a celebration of black culture. Hogan had starred in the debut. Paul Laurence Dunbar, a poet and lyricist born to former slaves in Dayton, Ohio, had supplied the libretto. These artists, whose pursuit of music careers had taken them along serpentine routes before landing them in New York, congregated around the Marshall Hotel, a boarding house and restaurant on 53rd Street in Manhattan. The Johnson brothers soon rented a room. Bob Cole, one of the stage veterans of the Marshall scene, lived two doors down from the boarding house. They became fast friends. The three would soon start writing songs together in an attempt to transform the meaning and measure of black music in the city. They had their work cut out for them.[5]

Coon Songs in White New York

New York at the time was awash in blackface and coon songs, what James Weldon Johnson later condemned as "crude" ditties "concerned with jamborees of various sorts and the play of razors, with the gastronomical delights of chicken, pork chops and watermelon, and with the experiences of red-hot 'mammas' and their never too faithful 'papas.' "[6] Blackface routines and coon songs had helped get the fledgling phonograph industry off the ground in the 1890s. Arguably the best-selling record of the decade was "The Laughing Song" performed by the African American singer George W. Johnson. Born around 1846, Johnson was a former Virginia slave who moved to New York in the 1870s and survived by singing hit songs in the Manhattan streets. His recording debut in 1890 was a performance of "The Whistling Coon" by the minstrel veteran Sam Devere. The song featured Johnson's melodious whistling and lyrics that described "a funny, queer old coon" with a "nose like an injun rubber shoe" and "a cranium like a big baboon." It was an instant hit. "The Laughing Song" followed the same mold, describing a "dandy darkey" and featuring a chorus full of Johnson's infectious laughter. It outperformed even its successful predecessor. The song remained available for years, was recorded by numerous different singers, and helped spread the novelty of the talking machine far and wide. Fred Gaisberg claimed that a version in 1900 by the white singer Burt Shepard sold 500,000 copies in India, where the record scout witnessed "dozens of natives seated on the haunches round a gramophone, rocking with laughter" to the disc. The song made Johnson a star, yet he remained one of the very few African American performers to cut records prior to the 1920s.[7]

Recordings of minstrel and coon songs were almost always by white musicians. Len Spencer was one of the most prolific. The Washington, D.C. native recorded in a huge variety of different styles, but he became known as a specialist in "Negro" material. Spencer began waxing miniature minstrel shows for Columbia around 1894. The popular sellers squeezed the familiar form—from the "Gentlemen, Be Seated" intro through the olio and finale—onto a three-minute cylinder. Some early releases featured a quartet that included George W. Johnson, making them perhaps the first interracial recordings. Spencer also recorded a large collection of coon songs, such as "A Hot Time in the Old Town Tonight" by Theodore Metz, "All Coons Look Alike to Me" by Ernest Hogan, and "My Gal Is a High Born Lady" by the white minstrel and dancer Barney Fagan.[8] Arthur Collins was another white recording artist known for his performance of minstrel and coon songs. The Philadelphia native, who liked to be called "The King of Ragtime Songs," recorded Hogan's "All Coons Look Alike to Me" in 1899. He continued to record similar songs, including "Just Because She Made Dem Goo Goo Eyes" and numerous versions of "I Got Mine," the song discovered so often by folklorists on southern collecting trips.[9] Spencer and Collins were but two of the myriad white artists who cut such material. Byron G. Harlan, J. W. Myers, Vess Ossman, Billy Murray, Billy Golden, S. H. Dudley: many of the popular recording artists of the day waxed coon songs and minstrel tunes. Their work helped the fledgling phonograph industry remain afloat by demonstrating that the new talking machine could deliver the latest and most popular hits from the theatrical stage.

While phonograph companies capitalized on coon songs, the epicenter of the craze was indeed the New York stage, the home of the white female "coon shouter."[10] Anna Held embodied one model of the coon shouter when she became a sensation in New York during the mid-1890s. Held used coon songs as part of a repertoire of tactics to project a simultaneously safe and transgressive sexuality to New York audiences. Despite Held's Polish birth and Jewish heritage, the impresario Florenz Ziegfeld promoted her as a Parisian chanteuse whose teasing eyes, luxurious milk baths, and beauty tips had a lot to teach American men and women about female desire. Her coon songs contributed to this image. One of her most popular was "I Want Dem Presents Back," a tale expressing a man's frustration over a woman's sexual independence:

> She skipped out wif a low down nigger,
> Ain't got half mah stack
> She kin go whar she's a mind to
> Fer I don't care whar she gwine ter
> But I want my presents back.

Held staged her performance to allow multiple interpretations of the song. The singer never wore blackface, but when she sang "I Want Dem Presents Back," she attached a mannequin to her waist to create the illusion that she was being carried on the back of a hunched black man. In one reading, the costume highlighted her white femininity by contrasting it to the mannequin's masculine and servile blackness. Yet Held also could be seen as the female character in the song, relating the words of her jilted lover to the "low down" man with whom she was running away. Suggesting such a relationship between a white woman and a black man (even a mannequin) was a highly charged contention in an age when white southerners often justified lynching as a means of protecting white women from African American sexual advances or rape. "I Want Dem Presents Back" revealed the desire that existed beneath the social scandal of interracial sex. Held was able to sing frankly about white female sexuality and autonomy while allowing nervous audiences to imagine that her words were simply those of the song's black characters. A stage backdrop through which black male actors poked their heads to represent notes on a giant musical staff reinforced this dualism. While Held's memoir described the scene as "thirty-three black noggins . . . rolling the whites of their eyes, to the rhythm of the song," the effect marked Held as an object of the black male gaze. The cover to one version of the sheet music emphasized this reading. Roughly mimicking the backdrop, it featured a photomontage of Held surrounded by six black men staring at her with expressions of surprise or desire. She turned slightly away from the camera, her trademark demure glance implying that Held remained in firm control.[11]

While coon songs helped Held challenge stereotypes of white female sexuality and decorum, coon shouting also offered rare access to the footlights for women who did not conform to the images of female beauty that dominated the commercial theater world. Few roles were available for women beyond those as pristine romantic leads or statuesque but interchangeable chorus girls. Clarice Vance failed in her bid to land such coveted roles. "I was too big to play a leading part," explained the six-foot actress. "Imagine a man making love to me on stage. It would have been hilariously funny." Vance, a white woman from Louisville, Kentucky, instead donned blackface and performed songs such as "I Can't Give Up My Rough and Rowd'ish Ways," a tune one reviewer described as a "tough negro oddity."[12] Playing the "tough negro" transformed Vance's large frame into a theatrical asset and made her a vaudeville star. Coon shouting helped her and other white women to expand the range of female physiques represented on stage—and the ranks of women who could sustain a musical career—by performing stylized caricatures of black masculinity rather than fulfilling stereotypes of white femininity.

Indeed, coon shouting helped some women create ostensibly positive representations of white femininity based on power rather than passivity. May Irwin may have been the most successful in this regard. Born in Canada in 1862, the singer had become a vaudeville celebrity by the early 1890s, helping to launch Tin Pan Alley hits such as "After the Ball." She later became known for her comedy farces, loosely knit plays that were primarily excuses for Irwin to command the stage with her dancing, off-the-cuff jokes, and coon songs. Newspaper critics went to lengths to call attention to Irwin's supposedly large body. "She weighs, perhaps, 197 pounds and a fraction, and she looks her weight," inveighed the *New York Times*.[13] "Would she be funny if she were thin?" asked the *Brooklyn Daily Eagle* before suggesting that her humor was directly related to her girth. "There are people who object to Miss Irwin as coarse, but that is a quality which she shares with many big, strong and natural things."[14] By inhabiting the "coarse" images of coon songs, Irwin transformed what many critics understood as her excessive, unrestrained body into a symbol of female strength and authenticity. She was natural, while thin chorus girls were not. This naturalism towered over other aspects of Irwin's productions. "It is not what May Irwin does which fills theaters, but what she is," insisted the *Daily Eagle*.[15]

Irwin's apparent realism as a female performer depended on the acknowledged deceit of her coon shouting. Like so many minstrels before her, the singer claimed that she learned her craft by directly observing black musicians.[16] Yet just as often, Irwin emphasized the theatricality of her coon songs and the work she put into their creation.[17] Reviews marveled at her apparent ability to act the black man. It was a feat reportedly more remarkable because she did not appear in blackface. "The spectacle of a plump, good-natured, blonde (or light-haired) woman in evening dress transforming herself, without aid of make-up or accessories, into a wicked colored person of the streets, is as startling and, seemingly, as gratifying to the public taste as ever," gushed one review.[18] Far from depicting an encounter with genuine black song, critics emphasized the skill required to pull off the coon song humbug. They expressed their wonder by reference to Irwin's white femininity. It was her apparent naturalness as a female personality that enabled them to recognize the ruse of the coon song performance even as they imagined that the songs themselves channeled black reality. Irwin's white womanhood was revealed through—and as proof of—her theatrical skills in portraying the black male characters of her coon songs.[19]

White female artists such as Vance, Held, and Irwin used coon songs to upset prevailing gender norms, exert their own personalities and sexuality, and expand the representation of women on New York stages. They depended upon the controversial violence and extreme racial stereotypes of 1890s coon songs to pull this off. These images remained dangerous, because many white listeners imagined them to be accurate depictions of black people. The *New York Times*, for example, claimed that Irwin's coon songs "illustrate the unconscious drollery, the lack of moral responsibility, the laziness, vanity, and other striking though reprehensible qualities of a recognizable type of darky."[20] White coon shouters converted the scandals of the coon song to serve their own ends, gaining an autonomous, even natural, voice, by perpetuating grotesque stereotypes of black people. They packed theaters in the process.

Coon songs were popular with a wide variety of New Yorkers. They quickly made their way out of the theaters and into residents' everyday lives, where they were used to negotiate racial, gender, class, and generational tensions in the city. Not long after May Irwin's "The Bully Song" became a hit, the *New York Times* reported that buskers in the city regularly were singing the song of black violence and bravado. An ordinance banning street singing had recently pushed them into performing in the courtyards of buildings, where they found that such songs could generate a rain of loose change from residents in the windows above. Yet they were just as likely to be met by a shower of garbage from tenement dwellers resenting the intrusion or pining for the nostalgic minstrelsy of "My Old Kentucky Home," a song some local black performers simply refused to acknowledge that they knew, the *Times* reported.[21] At least some African American residents apparently preferred to shout "My madness keeps a risin' " to the New York roof tops than to pretend "the darkies are gay" in their "old Kentucky home." In 1897, Irwin performed a charity concert at the Colored Home and Hospital in Manhattan for an audience of black patients and white philanthropists and staff. Both groups reportedly loved the show. While the white audience was "highly delighted but more subdued in its mirth," the African American attendees reportedly mouthed the words along with Irwin as she sang her most popular coon songs. Every time the stage star hit a phrase culled from African American slang, the black crowd "broke out hilariously." The penultimate line of "The Bully Song"—" I'm getting' so bad dat I'm askeer'd of myself"—was met with black cheers that lasted for three minutes.[22] The coon song could give voice to African American anger by portraying black characters who successfully protected themselves and their communities in the age of Jim Crow.

White New Yorkers embraced coon songs for a variety of contradictory reasons. In 1901, a German youth told the *Times* that in all of his social visits to New York's "nice and quite jolly" young women, he had never spent an evening without hearing coon songs sung beside the piano.[23] Like their southern counterparts discussed in chapter 1, white New York women turned to coon songs both to sustain and to upturn social expectations of female decorum while reveling in the humor of the songs' depictions of black foibles. Racially and sexually transgressive, coon songs enabled young women to act out the dangers and excitement of commercial popular culture while remaining firmly seated at the parlor piano. Yet if they used the songs to court visiting suitors, they also turned coon songs into weapons. A Coney Island woman took her three teenaged stepdaughters to court in 1901, claiming that the girls were purposefully irritating her by waking in the middle of the night and shouting coon songs at the parlor piano, refusing the exhausted woman's pleas for them to quit. The judge in the case dismissed the summons after making the girls promise that they would stop singing the offensive songs.[24] The same year, an African American pastor from Brooklyn testified against a white woman who allegedly sang coon songs from her open window on Sunday mornings as he passed on his way to church. The minister insisted that her songs were part of a campaign of local residents to get him to move out of the predominantly white neighborhood.[25]

Coon songs were equally suited for making friends or picking a fight. Listeners took to the songs because they expressed black power or black inferiority. Others rejected the genre because they believed coon songs distorted black culture or because they thought singing the songs signaled a dangerous embrace of it. One thing was certain: at the turn of the century, New York was busy singing about African Americans' supposed love for watermelons, straight razors, and stolen chickens.

Turning South to Soften the Coon Song

Bob Cole was determined to undermine the minstrel and coon monolith long before he joined forces with the Johnson brothers at the Marshall Hotel. Born in 1868 to former slaves active in the Reconstruction politics of Athens, Georgia, Cole became an accomplished multi-instrumentalist as a child. He headed to New York to forge a music career when he was in his mid-twenties. A few of his songs were featured in *Black America* during its run in 1895. Cole also became involved in a number of other productions important for their attempts to crack open the confines of minstrelsy. The Sam T. Jack Creole Show (1893), Sissteretta Jones' Black Patti Troubadours (1896), and Cole's own *A Trip to Coontown* (1897) appealed to white audiences raised on minstrelsy while enabling their black casts to perform an unprecedented variety of musical styles and character types. While African American actors had previously been limited to portraying only black characters, *A Trip to Coontown* featured them in Italian and Asian roles. Bob Cole appeared as Willie Wayside, a white tramp character that he had developed in the early nineties. Cole wore whiteface makeup for the part, critiquing the blackface tradition by turning it inside out. Musical selections ranged from John Philip Sousa's "The Stars and Stripes Forever" to popular songs, an operatic excerpt from Verdi's *Attila* to tunes with new ragtime rhythms and coon imagery. The show had its New York debut at a Klaw and Erlanger theater in 1898.[26]

In order to maintain access to theater bookings and publishing houses, African American musicians in the 1890s walked a tenuous line between portraying a complex black world and not starkly contradicting white assumptions about black life. Cole acknowledged this conundrum when he advertised his sheet music as "Genuine Negro songs by a genuine Negro Minstrel" in 1896.[27] It was a two-pronged sales pitch. Cole found the claim of black authenticity to be an important selling point. He was offering black music straight from the source. Yet he also placed his art squarely within the marketable genre of minstrelsy. His was an attempt to transform blackface from within: black performers made the most realistic minstrels.[28]

Many of Cole's 1890s compositions outwardly conformed to the conventions of the coon song genre. In his association with his stage and songwriting partner Billy Johnson, Cole penned "The Luckiest Coon in Town," "No Coons Allowed," "The Wedding of the Chinee and the Coon," and "Chicken," among others. Despite appearances, many of these songs were scathing satires that critiqued racism, Jim Crow segregation, or other social realities. "Mr. Coon You're All Right in Your Place," for example, took on class and color prejudice among African Americans by rendering a black-on-black lynching. It offered the story of a wealthy, light-skinned African American woman who rejected the courtship of a working-class black man, insisting,

Mister coon you're alright in your place
To associate with you would be disgrace
Don't come around my house again,
'Cause I belong to the upper ten.

When the suitor became a bit more insistent, her family formed a lynch mob and "strung that coon up in a pine tree very tall / The coroner said, 'There's another coon dead, that is all.' "[29] In a few short lines, the composers skewered segregationists, the black elite, W. E. B. Du Bois's "talented tenth" strategy of racial uplift, color prejudice among African Americans, and white officials' refusal to confront lynch law. Perhaps most notably, the duo was able to portray the racial terror of lynching from the New York stage—avoiding censure by having African American characters stand in for the white lynch mobs increasingly common throughout the South. They did all of this by twisting the widely recognized Jim Crow slogan into its own critique.

Unfortunately, the duo may have been too sly for its own purposes. Some listeners certainly understood and embraced the song's intended criticisms, but many others left the theater with only the title's ubiquitous segregationist mantra dancing in their heads. In 1903, the black attorney and former Illinois state legislator Edward H. Morris made reference to the song when he blamed Booker T. Washington for the current spate of lynching across the country. "The learned doctor teaches the colored people that they are only fit to fill menial positions," he argued. "The spirit of his teaching is illustrated by a rag-time song. 'Mr. Coon, You're All Right in Your Place.'" Insisted Morris, "The result is that the whites think the negroes are not entitled to the same considerations as themselves, but should be looked upon in about the same manner as a master looks upon a dog . . . If he is lynched they think, 'Oh, he's only a negro. It doesn't count much.' "[30] Morris largely reduced the meaning of the song to its title. He showed little solace in—or knowledge of—the song's satire. Bob Cole and Billy Johnson transformed the coon song into an antiracist weapon. In doing so they simultaneously perpetuated its pernicious effects.

Cole developed a gentler alternative to the coon song in collaboration with J. Rosamond Johnson and his brother James Weldon Johnson. Their first composition was "Louisiana Lize," published in 1899. It was a significant departure from Cole's satires:

E'ry thing around de ole plantation
Seems to tell me dat my darling lubs me true
All de birds a singing, an' de bumblebees a hummin',
Don't you worry, she lubs you.
Nighttime I starts my boat to floatin',
Nighttime, dats when I goes a co'tin',
Goes to cote my Louisiana Lize.

Written in "Negro dialect," "Louisiana Lize" traded the confrontational social commentary of Cole's earlier work for a hazy plantation nostalgia, the urban North for the rural South. The song could be heard as a reinvention of the sentimentalist vein of classic minstrelsy. It returned to Stephen Foster's "ole plantation," but the pastoral utopianism now articulated the universal theme of romantic love rather than a slave's longing for the landscape of his bondage. It was a formula the songwriters would employ again and again during their seven-year collaboration.

Perhaps their most explicit attempt to transform minstrelsy into love songs came with "Sambo and Dinah," written in 1904. The song exploited audiences' familiarity with stock minstrel characters.

No doubt you've heard of Sambo,
The lad who plays the banjo,
And sings sweet songs to his dusky lady love.
You've heard also of Dinah,
The gal from Carolina,
With pearly teeth and eyes just like the stars above.

It then asked the listener to imagine eavesdropping on these characters in a private moment. "Suppose you could be list'ning," the song suggested, when Sambo and Dinah were speaking to each other instead of to minstrel audiences. "Their love you'd hear them stammer / Without respect to grammar / For this is how these dusky lovers bill and coo." The chorus found the pair professing their love in conventional dialect and ended with Sambo's plea for marriage, "When you g'wine to let me change yo' name?"[31] "Sambo and Dinah" evoked the minstrel mask only to rip it off and reveal black southerners tenderly courting each other in a manner familiar to lovers everywhere. It emphasized human concerns common across the color line and insisted that black characters could do more than pine for the plantation or play with razors.

By writing these private moments in "Negro dialect," Cole and Johnson also tried to reconstruct minstrel conventions into a marker of the authentic black southern voice. James Weldon Johnson understood his dialect love songs as attempts to inject black folklore into popular music. This was only possible if he maintained a cultural distinction between southern African American folk culture and the sophisticated urban black world of which he was a part. "Negro dialect" was the way in which Johnson signaled this distinction. The "Sambo and Dinah" narrator sings in standard English, the southern characters in dialect. Johnson could equate dialect with black southern speech in part because his interest in black folklore was forged out of his New York experiences. The city, he explained, "showed me a new world—an alluring world, a tempting world, a world of greatly lessened restraints, a world of fascinating perils; but, above all, a world of tremendous artistic potentialities." It was these new freedoms, more than his own southern experiences, which inspired the recent migrant to cast his gaze southward in search of black history and heritage. "I now began to grope toward a realization of the importance of the American Negro's cultural background and his creative folk-art, and to speculate on the superstructure of conscious art that might be reared upon them," he later wrote.[32]

Johnson's approach to black southern culture was akin to that of the protagonist in his novel *Autobiography of an Ex-Colored Man* (1912), who travels from the South to become a celebrated ragtime pianist in New York. He gains popularity in both black and white circles by transforming classical compositions into ragtime. A turning point in his life occurs at a party when an unknown artist pushes him off the piano stool and commences playing. "I sat amazed," he explains. "I had been turning classic music into ragtime, a comparatively easy task; and this man had taken ragtime and made it classic." The experience—a lesson in forging an authentic, yet hybrid and highbrow, African American style—sends the protagonist on a quest into the deep South to study the roots of black music and black identity. "I made up my mind to go back into the very heart of the South, to live among the people, and drink in my inspiration firsthand," he explains. "I gloated over the immense amount of material I had to work with, not only modern ragtime, but also the old slave songs—material which no one had yet touched." Johnson's protagonist intends to use the musical examples he transcribes during his southern travels—"the spirit of the Negro in his relatively primitive state"—as the basis for his sophisticated compositions. The South, in Johnson's writing, was an imaginary land of isolation and primitivism, a cultural preserve that could be tapped to save New York popular music from itself.[33] Songs such as "Louisiana Lize" or "Sambo and Dinah" were the result. They offered the sound of the black folk conceived through its difference from the composer's "conscious art," the South heard by way of New York.

Johnson later rejected the formula he developed with "Louisiana Lize" as he struggled with his own complicity in the perpetuation of minstrel stereotypes. "I got the sudden realization of the artificiality of conventionalized Negro dialect poetry; of its exaggerated geniality, childish optimism, forced comicality, and mawkish sentiment," he recalled. One could excise the most heinous stereotypes, but dialect poetry could not escape its long associations with minstrelsy and its domination by white expectations. Johnson surmised that the dialect poet "was expressing what often bore little relation, sometimes no relation at all, to actual Negro life; that he was really expressing only certain conceptions about Negro life that his audience was willing to accept and ready to enjoy." It was, in some ways, one of the most southern things he could have said. Many local southern musicians had never embraced the use of Negro dialect in the first place, preferring to sing in their own voices and build broad repertoires that could not be contained by blackface. Migrant artists such as Johnson attempted to break into the New York industry by writing songs in dialect and playing toward Northern stereotypes of southern African American culture. Black artists who remained in the South often transformed these songs by extracting the very dialect and accommodations to minstrelsy that New York migrants used to signify black southern culture. Yet Johnson's rejection of dialect poetry did not open him to the complex musical lives of African American southerners. It rather thrust him into a deeper commitment to an isolated black folk, because they "though working in dialect, sought only to express themselves for themselves, and to their *own group*."[34] He had landed on yet another marker of black authenticity. While "Louisiana Lize" had appeared authentic in relation to the coon song, its artifice was revealed when compared to the work of black folk artists who supposedly lived more isolated and racially homogenous lives than did the New York poet.

By the time of his conversion, dialect love songs had made Johnson, Cole, and Johnson successful New York songwriters. The trio had developed their formula at the precise moment that several processes were bringing and end to the era of the raucous coon shouter. Vaudeville houses attempting to broaden the customer base began shunning acts that were too racially or sexually provocative. Their move ushered in an era of "polite vaudeville" far more comfortable with sentimental minstrel odes to the Old South than with controversial coon songs.[35] Clarice Vance gave up her rough and rowdy ways and stopped wearing blackface makeup on stage.[36] One newspaper critic noticing the shift stated, "At Miss Vance's hands the Southern 'coon' song loses all of its roughness and becomes a sort of negro classic to rank with the old-time plantation melodies."[37] In 1899, May Irwin also expressed the desire to change her act. "Yes, I want to get out of the coon songs if I can, or if the audience wants me to, which is more to the purpose. People hear them now everywhere they go, and I think they must be tired of them," she said.[38] The *Times* concurred. "The revived and modified negro minstrelsy, minus the burnt cork, has probably had its day. The 'coon song' is getting very tiresome," it declared. "Miss Irwin, if she does not stand in urgent need of something new, will surely need to change the form and quality of her entertainments before another season."[39]

These shifts made New York ready for Johnson, Cole, and Johnson's alternative to the coon song. Irwin found her new sound when she bought "Louisiana Lize" for fifty dollars in 1899. It was the composers' first New York paycheck. After the song became a hit, the trio wrote several more dialect love songs for Irwin, including "Ma Mississippi Belle" and "Magdalene, My Southern Queen."[40] Anna Held had an enormous hit with the trio's "The Girl with the Dreamy Eyes." The song's success led to the composers finding further work with Florenz Ziegfeld. Soon the trio had a three-year contract with the publisher Joseph W. Stern and Company as well as an agreement with Klaw and Erlanger that their songs would appear only in the booking giant's shows.[41] Marie Cahill was another early champion of Johnson, Cole, and Johnson. The white actress met the team at a party in 1902, where they offered her "Under the Bamboo Tree," a new composition that Stern had refused to release. Cahill loved the song, which traded plantation imagery for an equally imaginary Africa. She successfully threatened to quit her current production in order to convince her manager to allow it in the show. Stern scrambled to release the sheet music, which eventually sold 400,000 copies.[42] Cahill went on to sing the team's "Congo Love Song," a performance the New York *Evening Star* described as "another instance of Cole and Johnson to the rescue."[43] The new style of dialect song was helping to transform the New York music world and make a living for the three southern migrants.

The songwriters helped inaugurate an intricate web of associations and collaborations between African American composers and white performers. In the next six years, their songs were featured by a variety of white stage singers, including Irene Bentley, Peter F. Dailey, John McVeigh, Lillian Coleman, Christie McDonald, and Faye Templeton. Other African American composers also found their songs picked up by white stars. Will Marion Cook supplied songs to Marie Cahill and James Alrich Libby, the tenor who first agreed to sing Charles K. Harris's "After the Ball."[44] Cahill also sang tunes by the African American composer Chris Smith, including, "I Want a Little Lovin', Sometimes" and "He's a Cousin of Mine," an answer to "After the Ball" in which the protagonist utters the title every time she kisses a different man. Smith had traveled to New York from his hometown of Charleston, South Carolina, in 1900 to make it as a popular composer. One of his regular songwriting partners was Cecil Mack. Over the next decade, the two helped write a number of songs for the black comedy team of Bert Williams and George Walker, including "You're in the Right Church, but the Wrong Pew," "Good Morning, Carrie!," and "Just an Old Friend of the Family." They also placed a number of their tunes with white singers. "He's a Cousin of Mine," for which Smith and Mack collaborated with Cahill's regular songwriter Silvo Hein, became a big hit. It enjoyed performances by Clarice Vance, Bert Williams, and the white singer Bob Roberts. Mack and Smith songs were also performed by white artists Donald Brian, Wylma Wynn, and the dance team of Jean and Jeanette Warner.[45]

White recording artists who had been waxing minstrel shows and coon songs also seized on the new sound of black composers. The virtual exclusion of black artists from the recording studio meant that white performers maintained near-exclusive access to African American composers' material. Arthur Collins may have been the most prolific. After recording Ernest Hogan's "All Coon's Look Alike to Me" in 1899, Collins went on to record several songs by Johnson, Cole, and Johnson, including "Under the Bamboo Tree," "Tell Me Dusky Maiden," "Give Me de Leavin's," "Who Do You Love," "There's Always Something Wrong," and "Didn't He Ramble." He also cut songs by Cook, Mack, and Smith. He recorded Bert Williams's signature song "Nobody" in 1905, a year before the African American star cut his own version. "The song fits Mr. Collins like a glove," Edison promotional material insisted.[46] Collins was far from alone. White artists Edward Meeker, Billy Murray, Bob Roberts, and Harry MacDonough, to name a few, also recorded Johnson, Cole, and Johnson material. Many of these artists also cut tunes by Cook or Chris Smith.[47]

White singers so regularly featured songs by black composers that Mack and Smith gently spoofed the trend in their song "Scaddle-De-Mooch" (1915). It tells the story of "Joe Madoza, the black composer" penning a novelty number. "Sallie Skiplong sang the hit song" after "Mister Mooser, the big producer, thought the song would fit in his show." The white vaudeville star Nora Bayes featured "Scaddle-De-Mooch" in her Ziegfeld act, and the white singer George O'Connor recorded it for Columbia in 1915.[48] In the early years of the century, black composers forged tense but mutually beneficial bonds with white performers around the reconstructed coon song.

The industry hunger for songs by black composers did not always extend to the embrace of black artists themselves. Around 1910, William Marion Cook established an exclusive contract with the giant Harry Von Tilzer Publishing Company. The firm provided the successful composer with an office in their New York headquarters in which he could work and hold meetings. In 1911, Cook wrote a blistering letter to the *New York Age*, announcing that Max Winslow, the company manager, had complained to him "that entirely too many spades come into the office." "Inasmuch as music of the day is to a great degree popularized by the colored performer and café singer, and inasmuch as the majority of music firms cater to the colored actor and singer when they have new songs, I feel that the color prejudice of Mr. Winslow should be widely known," Cook wrote. He named several other publishing companies who "consider colored singers their most valuable asset." Black composers were providing companies with some of the most successful songs of the era, but as white singers increasingly turned a profit on black songs, companies saw less financial need to court the black performers than they had previously. "The color line is being drawn," noted the *Age*. Cook concluded his letter asking, "Should the colored composer and performer go where they are not wanted?" The *Age* forcefully answered, "No!" It then called for an artist boycott of the Von Tilzer Publishing Company.[49]

African American critics claimed that the collaborations between black composers and white singers robbed black performers of jobs. "The white men and women are browning up, blacking up and turning up and our colored men are training them to do the colored people's work. Therefore there is nothing for our acts to do," the African American promoter Sherman H. Dudley told the *Freeman* in 1914. Dudley, a southern native born in 1872, had followed a path similar to Bob Cole's. He traveled with carnivals and medicine shows before cracking into vaudeville in the 1890s. There he performed and composed for a number of black-cast musical comedies that helped expand the representations of black characters on stage. In 1904, he landed the lead in the Smart Set, a successful African American touring troupe organized by the *Black America* impresario Billy McClain. Dudley became a successful comic, earning comparisons to Bert Williams and Ernest Hogan. In 1912, he began developing the first African American vaudeville circuit. The *Freeman* celebrated the move, noting that many "white houses [had] closed their doors to the colored performer." By the end of 1914, Dudley's circuit consisted of twenty-three theaters concentrated along the East Coast. He saw the persistence of white acts performing black music as a constant threat to the livelihood of African American talent, and he refused to take part. "I . . . have had many big-time white women ask me to teach them how to do a coon song as I do," he wrote. "They have offered me much money but I have refused, for I never teach a white woman something to make about six hundred dollars per week, when for the same thing, the manager would not give me fifty dollars. Let us look at all these things which are killing us every day."[50]

Yet several black composers found that landing a song in a white celebrity's show promised the attention of publishers, the ear of theater managers, the potential of significant royalties, and a much larger audience for their efforts to transform stage representations of black culture. It also helped black composers finance projects that could speak more directly to the tastes and needs of African American audiences. Cecil Mack, born Richard C. McPherson in Norfolk, Virginia, helped to found the Gotham-Attucks Music Publishing Company, perhaps the first black-owned publishing house, in 1905.[51] Over the next four years, the small company was an outlet for the work of Will Marion Cook, Bert Williams, and George Walker, publishing individual selections as well as the music to their successful black-cast musicals *Abyssinia* (1906) and *Bandana Land* (1907–9). These successes were helped by the strong sales of the Cahill vehicle "He's a Cousin of Mine," an early Gotham-Attucks publication that remained one of the small company's biggest sellers.[52] Johnson, Cole, and Johnson turned their cachet with white singers into two shows of their own, *The Shoo-Fly Regiment* in 1906 and *The Red Moon* in 1908. Each attempted to push the innovations of the dialect love song into new territory. "One of the well-known taboos was that there should never be any romantic love-making in a Negro play. If anything approaching a love duet was introduced in a musical comedy, it had to be broadly burlesqued," James Weldon Johnson later explained. Otherwise, "managers feared they would displease white folks." Their two plays pushed this envelope by portraying black love as dramatic rather than comedic. It was something even their songs such as "Sambo and Dinah" had not attempted. Yet the composers remained acutely aware of the dangers of challenging white taboos. *The Red Moon*, for example, told a story of interracial love set in the Johnsons' hometown of Jacksonville, Florida. It focused on the relationships between black, Native American, Asian, and Mexican characters. "Do you catch the ingenuity of that device?" asked the *Washington Post*. "The offspring of Indians and Africans mate in love and wedlock without the color scheme of yellow, brown and red offending the taste of the white audience." It echoed the strategy Cole had pursued in "Mr. Coon You're Alright in Your Place," here the taboo of African American romance substituting for the portrayal of lynching. Black composers faced serious constraints on the content of their work when they performed for white audiences or collaborated with white artists. Yet some believed that the benefits they received—in terms of bookings, reviews, money, and a platform from which to subtly challenge white expectations—were worth it at least for a time. Johnson later rejected his formula for songwriting success. He finally found the freedom he sought from white expectations in the theaters of Harlem during the 1920s. It was a liberty Sherman H. Dudley had been trying to realize for several years.[53]

White singers gained their own advantages from their associations with black composers. On the one hand, black dialect songs allowed white singers to market themselves as willing and able to transgress sexual and racial norms. Cole and the Johnson brothers tried to reform the coon song from within by dispensing with the most explicit racism of the genre. Yet it was their very transformation of the genre that made the songs more attractive to May Irwin, Anna Held, and other singers attempting to keep their racy reputations while adhering to the new restrictions of polite vaudeville. White singers remained interested in the very exoticism and eroticism the composers attempted to downplay. On the other hand, dialect numbers enabled many singers to assert their own whiteness in contrast to the apparent blackness of their performances just as coon shouters had done in the 1890s. Recent Eastern European immigrants—from Sophie Tucker to Al Jolson—discovered that acting black was one of the most American things they could do. Figuratively or literally donning burnt cork and then taking it off helped ease their acceptance into the ranks of white America. Indeed, when African American composers slowed their production of dialect numbers and odes to the South in the years after 1910, Jewish songwriters, many of them first- or second-generation immigrants, took the reins. "Alexander's Ragtime Band" (1911) by Irving Berlin, "Oh, Tennessee, I Hear You Calling Me" (1914) by Harry Ruby, "Everything Is Peaches Down in Georgia" (1918) by Milton Ager, and "Swanee" (1919) by George Gershwin: Jewish songwriters penned a legion of ragtime paeans to a region many of them had never visited. Southern tributes enabled them not only to embrace supposed African American music. The writers also found in the South a means to express their desires for a romantic, pastoral America, one that often stood in stark contrast to their actual immigrant experiences.[54]

White singers who had migrated from the South took special advantage of the turn from coon songs to dialect love songs, identifying the latter as a new marker of southern *white* identity. Clarice Vance dropped her blackface makeup and began advertising herself as "The Southern Singer." Her new moniker effectively erased any apparent difference between the white and the black southern voice. "Miss Vance, judging by her speech is a Southron to manner born, for the darky twang is strongly evident in her singing," opined the *Los Angeles Times*.[55] If Vance put over the "darky twang," the critic implied, it was because of who she was rather than whom she was imitating.

Perhaps nobody identified black dialect as the sound of white southern culture more clearly than did Vernon Dalhart. After arriving in New York, the Texas transplant had little luck convincing phonograph companies to take him on. Dalhart unsuccessfully auditioned for Thomas Edison three times between 1911 and 1915. He believed that he had failed because Thomas Edison was not interested in hearing him sing opera. "Because of his deafness Edison holds a horn to his ear when he is listening to a new singer.

Time and again I sang opera into that horn while the old man listened, only to be turned away," Dalhart later explained. "Then one day I forgot all my high-falutin ideas of singing, and going back to my Southern accent, sang 'Can't Yo' Hear Me Callin', Caroline?' into his trumpet. I've been making Edison records ever since."[56]

The company released Dalhart's version of "Can't Yo' Heah Me Callin', Caroline?" in 1917. The composition was a black dialect love song in the mold pioneered by Johnson, Cole, and Johnson. Dalhart gave his all to the recording when he sang the lyrics:

Can't yo' heah me callin', Caroline,
It's mah heart a-callin' dine.
Lordy, how I miss yo', gal o' mine,
Wish dat I could kiss yo' Caroline!

Employing his clarion tenor and classically trained diction, he smoothly bent notes in legato phrases, increased his volume over sustained notes, and retarded rhythms of key phrases in a manner that had come to signify "Negro dialect." The record, which remained a popular seller for years, inaugurated a very fruitful collaboration with Edison that helped put the singer on a sound financial footing. Dalhart soon recorded light opera selections. He waxed foxtrots and sentimental ballads. Yet he became best known for his rendition of "Negro dialect" songs such as the one that had finally attracted Edison to the singer.[57]

The supposed value of Dalhart's performance was based on a tightening of the association between minstrelsy and the "real" culture of southern black people. Edison promotional literature insisted, "You must realize, even when you have only heard 'Can't Yo' Heah Me Callin', Caroline?' once that this is quite different from the usual 'coon song.' It is a really artistic, old-fashioned darky love song. Vernon Dalhart sings it with tremendous effect. He gets the real darky whine. This is probably the best rendition of its kind ever recorded." Edison asserted that Dalhart's "darky whine" was superior because it was authentic. It was "real" and "old-fashioned." Yet the language of authenticity Edison used remained that of minstrelsy. It was a circular argument: Minstrelsy was best when it gave a genuine depiction of black culture; genuine performances were those that adhered to the conventions of minstrelsy. Increasingly, white artists advertised that these conventions were the equivalent of southern culture. An Edison publication from

1918 found Dalhart responding to questions about how he learned to perform such convincing "Negro dialect":

> "Learn it?" he said. "I never had to learn it. When you are born and brought up in the South your only trouble is to talk any other way. All through my childhood that was almost the only talk I ever heard because you know the sure 'nough Southerner talks almost like a Negro, even when he's white. I've broken myself of the habit, more or less, in ordinary conversation, but it still comes pretty easy."[58]

Dalhart's assertion signaled a momentous shift. African American artists had seized the representation of black music from white minstrels in the late nineteenth century by claiming, in the words of Bob Cole, that genuine Negro minstrels should perform genuine Negro songs. White artists such as Vance and Dalhart reclaimed the authority to perform black song by insisting it constituted their own southern heritage. Dalhart did not follow James Weldon Johnson's formula, using black folklore as a basis for high art. His black dialect, he insisted, was a result of dispensing with "high-falutin'" pretensions and getting back to his southern roots. Gone were the conceits of white delineators, the "students of the Negro" whose practiced imitation of black performers defined nineteenth-century white minstrelsy. Gone too was the classic coon shouter whose white femininity emerged in contrast to the raucous black masculinity of the characters she portrayed. Here was the uncut authenticity of the white southern voice. Yet it was a voice dependent on continued African American support. When Dalhart was searching for a follow up to "Can't Yo' Heah Me Callin', Caroline?," he wrote a letter to Edison's head of A&R pleading to record "Lil' Gal" by Paul Laurence Dunbar and J. Rosamond Johnson. "Will you please look it over carefully as a favor to me, as I think it the most beautiful song of its kind I have ever heard," he wrote. "I believe I whip Caroline with it. I sing it, a slow 'two beats' to the measure, *as Johnson himself coached me in the number.*"[59] Johnson's bid for access, to succeed in the New York music world, enabled Dalhart's bid for authenticity, to propose a new sound of blackness through which he could define himself as a white southerner.

The Common Roots of Hillbillies and Minstrels

Dalhart's professed affinity between black and white sound was quite real. A long history of exchange and intermingling across the southern color line created commonalities between black and white southern speech and music. Yet even more important to his cultural claim to "Negro dialect" were the intertwined histories of minstrelsy and popular commercial stereotypes of rural white culture. Far less common than the blackface minstrel, the rural white hayseed or rube nevertheless was a standard stage character by the 1890s and it soon appeared regularly on phonograph records. Dressed in rough, shapeless garb, northern vaudeville and variety performers such as Josh Denman, Rose Melville, and Cal Stewart caricatured the dialects, clothing, and lack of sophistication audiences associated with rural white culture. Local color literature of the 1870s and 1880s had celebrated "our contemporary ancestors" in Appalachia for both their rural isolation and their distance from African American culture. By the dawn of the new century, these romantic images of rural racial purity had begun to give way to popular depictions of Appalachian or Ozark hillbillies, characters less interesting for their preservation of English culture than for their feuding, their willful disregard for modern ways, and their humorous inability to lift themselves out of poverty.[60]

One of the templates for the genre was "The Arkansas Traveler," a ubiquitous fiddle tune and comedy sketch that dated back to the 1840s. In its most common incarnations, the skit portrayed a traveler (usually from the city or the East) coming across a squatter in rural Arkansas. As the squatter repeatedly saws the first strain of the tune on his fiddle, the two engage in pun-riddled banter. "Where does this road go?" the traveler asks. "It don't go nowhere. Stays right where it is," comes the reply. Tension grows as the traveler's questions become more antagonistic and the squatter continues to dissemble. It is finally eased when the traveler takes the fiddle and plays the second strain of the tune. Upon hearing it, the squatter warms to the visitor and invites him to stay the night. The humor of "The Arkansas Traveler" cut two ways. The rural fiddler's apparent inability to comprehend the traveler's questions pegged him as comically unsophisticated thus reinforcing urban fantasies about the rural South. Yet it is easy to see the squatter's naiveté as an act. He feigned ignorance in order to deflect the city's slicker's condescension, deflate his pretensions, and get him to leave. The traveler looked down on the backwoods primitive without realizing that the joke was on him.[61]

"The Arkansas Traveler" spread far and wide during the second half of the nineteenth century, the music becoming a common stock fiddle tune throughout the South and the sketch providing a template for rube and hillbilly humor on the nation's stages. It was reborn in the talking machine age when Len Spencer recorded it for Victor in 1901 and released multiple versions of the skit for a variety of companies over the next several years. Instrumental versions of the song appeared when Eugene A. Jaudas, violinist and house orchestra leader for Edison, included it in 1913 in his recording of a "Medley of Country Dances," featuring it among ten fiddle standards such as "Little Brown Jug" and "Turkey in the Straw." The violinist Don Richardson recorded it for Columbia in 1916 as part of a recording repertoire of traditional fiddle tunes and minstrel favorites.[62]

This storied history suggests that rube recordings, including "The Arkansas Traveler," functioned in multiple ways during the first two decades of the century. They helped attract southern consumers to the phonograph by providing some of the only distinctively southern music available on record. Southerners apparently embraced them. In 1910, a Dallas retailer reported that two of the four most popular records in Texas were "Turkey in the Straw" and "Dixie."[63] They also helped urban consumers salve nostalgia for their rural roots and question their current conditions while ridiculing country folks. The Peerless Trio's "Three Rubes Seeing New York" (1907), for example, turned country folks touring the modern metropolis into a comedy of the absurd. "Say, this New York's a big town, Sy, but the streets is pretty well tore up, ain't they?" "Yeah, tore up just now, but it'll be a great town when they get it finished." The audacious outsiders on the recording thought they understood the city, but they had no idea. The real comedy of the bit, however, was that the bumpkins got it right despite their ignorance. As their tour passes Union Square, one exclaims, "I thought Tammany Hall was on the Square." "No," another replies, "Tammany Hall ain't on the square!" Arriving at John D. Rockefeller's home, one asks, "Ain't he the Standard Oil maggot?" Laughter ensues. "Three Rubes" was one of a collection of recordings that skewered urban pretensions and accumulated wealth by imagining rural misfits marveling at city ways. Cuts such as "Two Rubes at the Vaudeville," "Old Country Fiddler in New York," and "Uncle Josh on a Fifth Avenue Bus" helped New Yorkers see their city for what it was and embrace the homespun wisdom of their rural heritage even as they suggested that actual rural migrants were comically unprepared to live in the modern city. At the same time, the recordings helped listeners who had remained on the farm imagine that they had made the right choice.[64]

In all of these ways, the hillbilly shared a great deal with the classic blackface minstrel. Both stereotypes depicted southern characters as happy in their exclusion from urban civilization. The minstrel's plantation slave danced in a land of natural abundance and familial love, while the hillbilly simply laughed in the face of scarcity and family strife. Both traded on their difference from the urban North and granted urbanites the opportunity to fantasize about a pastoral ideal while maintaining a sense of superiority to those they imagined living in it. Minstrel and hillbilly caricatures also relied on a common set of conventional jokes and songs. In 1903, a white railroad worker, Thomas Jackson, published *On a Slow Train through Arkansaw*. The joke book, which eventually sold seven million copies, helped establish the hillbilly as the reigning stereotype of the poor white southerner. Yet much of the material in the book consisted of well-known bits from the minstrel stage. Indeed, Jackson subtitled his book, "Funny Railroad Songs, The Sayings of Southern Darkies; All the Latest and Best Minstrel Jokes of the Day." The book, which was one long list of jokes organized loosely around a narrative, made little distinction about which jokes were supposed to be about white Arkansans, black southerners, or minstrel delineators, reinforcing the notion that there was little difference among them.[65]

Commercial recordings of these stereotypes also shared a great deal in common, preparing northern listeners to expect little difference between the sound and content of black and white southern culture. Most of the recording artists who depicted rubes or hillbillies also regularly sang black dialect material, and they often did so in a similar manner. Arthur Collins maintained a distinction between his black and white southern dialects, performing black voices in a slow, low drawl while giving white characters a high-pitched speedy delivery. Yet this distinction did not characterize Collins's peers. When Byron Harlan sang "When Silas Did the Turkey Trot (to Turkey in the Straw)," for example, the accent and laugh he employed to represent a white hillbilly differed little from that he used on his coon song recordings. The content of rube and minstrel recordings also significantly overlapped. Singers traded on the same styles of jokes, puns, and malapropisms, just as Thomas Jackson had done in his book, to portray dim-witted black southerners and backward white hillbillies. Many rube and hillbilly recordings featured common stock tunes from the minstrel stage. Byron Harlan's "Scene in a Country Store" from 1903 found white southerners bonding while singing "Shew! Fly, Don't Bother Me," a minstrel tune first published in 1869. His recording of "Merry Farmer Boy" in 1907 presented a white southern youth whistling Stephen Foster's "Old Folks at Home." "Two Rubes at the Vaudeville" by Harlan and Frank Stanley portrays the characters taking the urban stage and singing "Don't Get Weary," a song related to the African American spiritual "Don't Be Weary, Traveler," first published in *Slave Songs of the United States* in 1867. It is unclear whether these depictions of hillbillies singing minstrel tunes or pseudo-spirituals were a result of the slippage between northern representations of black and white southern exoticism or of the fact that white southerners regularly sang minstrel tunes. Minstrelsy had long been a major component of southern white culture. In either case, the close association between commercial depictions of minstrels and hillbillies helped prepare northern ears to accept Vernon Dalhart's notion that black dialect songs were a natural and authentic representation of the singer's white southern identity.[66]

Yet the hillbilly ultimately told a story of commonality while the minstrel remained an exercise in difference. In "The Arkansas Traveler," the tensions between the urban and rural characters dissolved as the two discovered that they knew the same music. The white hayseed and city slicker were not so different after all. White rural listeners thus could imagine holding their own in cities populated by the likes of the gullible yet ultimately endearing traveler, and their urban counterparts could identify with the fiddler, who may have expressed shared contempt for urban pretensions and represented the simplicity and straight-talk of their own real or imagined rural heritage. White artists Cal Stewart and Charles Ross Taggart embodied such connections between white rural and urban residents. Taggart advertised himself as "The Man from Vermont." His stage persona adhered to the hayseed stereotype as he performed musical comedies bits such as "Old Country Fiddler in a New York Restaurant." Yet his promotional photographs featured him in a spiffy suit and tie. He was thus able to portray himself as both a genuine "old country fiddler" and an urban sophisticate who was merely acting a role. Stewart's career was based on a similar premise. The Virginia native had most of his success performing the role of "Uncle Josh," a comical resident of an imaginary New England village. Yet his act was supposedly informed by Stewart's own small-town experiences. When he died in 1919, a *Talking Machine World* obituary emphasized his studied performance while celebrating the rural life he depicted as the foundation of American civilization. "The 'Uncle Josh' of Cal Stewart was, in its fullest sense, not the portrayal of a humorous character only, but the reflection of a distinct type of simple, earnest hardworking Americans, crude and unsophisticated perhaps, but nevertheless responsible for much of the solid progress of the country," the author wrote. Stewart did a great service by enabling future generations to learn about the country's rural past "not through the medium of dry volumes of history, but through the actual living voice of one who lived among and studied these solid citizens."[67] Neither genuine rube nor mere actor, Stewart was reframed as an ethnographer whose fieldwork revealed the culture shared by white Americans across the rural and urban divide.

There was no corollary to this celebration of universal values in the minstrel world. White minstrelsy fans may have used blackface conventions to revel momentarily in the freedoms or hedonisms they associated with African Americans, but they rarely concluded that black and white people were the same under the skin. White delineators did not develop a tradition akin to the hillbilly's strategic use of feigned naiveté. Black characters said ignorant things, they implied, because black people were ignorant. The potential truth of their insights did not translate into the white celebration of the African American perspective. African American performers, as I have shown, did develop such a tradition. But bluffing ignorance to fool white characters on stage necessarily meant hoodwinking white audiences as well. Minstrelsy reinforced the color line. It was just this conundrum that the likes of Johnson, Cole, and Johnson attempted to address with the black dialect love song. They tried to bridge the racial divide by using the supposed voice of black America to express the universal theme of romantic love. Yet rather than admitting racial similarities, white southern artists such as Vernon Dalhart claimed the genre as their own. The moment that African American composers omitted specific references to black experience from their songs, white singers stopped acknowledging that black dialect had much to do with black people.

Enter the Blues

It is within the context of the white adoption of the black dialect love song that the blues became the new sound of black authenticity in the American music industry. In the decade 1910–20, African American commercial composers embraced the blues as a fresh new sound of the black South. They found that the blues was capable of articulating a wider range of thoughts and feelings and spoke more directly of the experiences and needs of African Americans than the dialect love song ever could. The blues ostensibly were by black southerners in a way that dialect songs were merely about them. They also promised a windfall to anyone who could figure out how to sell them in mass.

The shifting connections between race, music, and authenticity had everything to do with money. W. C. Handy, the African American composer who was one of the first to arrange and publish blues material, noted that his initial attraction to the genre was financial. Handy had formal musical training as a youngster, learning the piano, voice, and trumpet in his middle-class Florence, Alabama, home. As a young adult, he toured with Mahara's Minstrel Men and worked on the music faculty at A & M College in Huntsville, Alabama. In his own concerts he mixed classical compositions with ragtime and theatrical pieces. He did not have a high opinion of "low folk forms" such as the blues. "As a director of many respectable, conventional bands, it was not easy for me to concede that a simple slow-drag and repeat could be rhythm itself," he later explained. His opinions changed around 1903. When his dance orchestra performed in Cleveland, Mississippi, Handy was asked to allow a local black trio to perform a few songs. The rough group, with their "battered" and "worn-out" instruments, "struck up one of those over-and-over strains that seem to have no very clear beginning and certainly no ending at all." The audience showered coins on the stage. Handy was astounded. "There before the boys lay more money than my nine musicians were being paid for the entire engagement. Then I saw the beauty of primitive music," he recalled. "My idea of what constitutes music was changed by the sight of that silver money cascading around the splay feet of a Mississippi string band." Handy began writing arrangements of blues melodies similar to the one's he heard in Cleveland, and "the popularity of our orchestra increased by leaps and bounds."[68] Handy became one of the most successful of the early publishers of blues-inspired tunes, penning such standards as "Memphis Blues" (1912), "St. Louis Blues" (1914), and "Beale Street Blues" (1917). These songs were instant hits in his Memphis home, New York, and throughout the country.[69]

The "beauty of primitive music," Handy insisted, was its profit potential. Handy's revelation was not unique in its equation between black authenticity and marketability. Handy joined a strong tradition of white and black artists from the minstrel world marketing their music as genuine depictions of southern black culture. What set Handy apart was the way he described himself as a cultural middleman between "primitive" African American music and the nation at large. He insisted that his black identity was important, yet he did not claim to embody musical authenticity as much as discover it and package it for outsider consumption. "I am a Southern negro by birth and environments and it is from the levee camps, the mines, the plantations and other places where the negro laborer works that these snatches of melody originate," Handy told the *Chicago Defender* in 1919. Handy regularly incorporated these melodic "snatches" from southern African American singers into his own sophisticated compositions and arrangements. "I have heard on the Mississippi plantation the negro plowman, after a day's work which began at sunrise, sing just these little snatches, 'Hurry, sundown, let tomorrow come,' which means that he hopes tomorrow will be for him better than today," he continued. "It is from such sources that I built my 'SAINT LOUIS BLUES,' which begins, 'I hate to see the evening sun go down.'"[70]

While claiming a familiar intimacy with blues culture through his race and southern birth, Handy rhetorically placed himself (and the readers of the *Defender*) outside the world of the southern "negro laborer." Handy did not present warmed-over minstrel dialect as black folk song as did James Weldon Johnson. Nor did he declare his music was his own as did Bob Cole. The composer presented his blues compositions as elaborations of the music he witnessed southern black workers perform. In other words, he implicitly claimed his published songs were "genuine Negro music" but that he was not a "genuine Negro minstrel." Handy in some important ways fulfilled James Weldon Johnson's dream of combining conscious art with black folklore. He published his first hit "The Memphis Blues" in 1912, the same year *Autobiography of an Ex-Colored Man* found its narrator yearning to go into the heart of the South to find inspiration for his compositions. His songs had their roots in the same style of casual fieldwork Johnson's character envisioned but Johnson the lyricist could only imagine. His "snatches" thus hewed more closely to the music actually sung by black southerners. The blues initially lacked the sediment of white expectations and control that James Weldon Johnson had found an inescapable component of dialect poetry. They could therefore signal a distinctive African American voice in the precise way that Johnson had come to believe that dialect poetry could not.[71]

It is likely for this reason that African American audiences began encouraging black touring troupes to perform the blues on the vaudeville stage.

Handy was surprised that he initially had trouble convincing performers in black companies to sing his songs. "Having spent much time in Jim Crow towns, I was under the illusion that these Negro musicians would jump at the chance to patronize one of their own publishers," he surmised. "They didn't. The Negro musicians simply played the hits of the day, whether composed by me or someone else. They followed the parade."[72] Yet the parade had begun to change course even before Handy started publishing his music. In 1911, the African American vaudevillian Paul Carter lamented a new trend. "When a performer meets another that has played the theater he intends playing the next week, he will ask how things are over there. This will be the answer: 'Oh, they like a little smut, and things with a double meaning. If you don't put it on you can't make it there,' " Carter wrote in the *Freeman*. "He then lays aside his music for his regular opening, and when he gets to the theater for re-hearsal he will say to the piano player, 'When I come on just play the 'Blues.' "[73] Black audiences forced touring African American performers to replace stylized dialect pop songs with the blues, northern fantasies about the South with indigenous southern sounds. Between about 1910 and 1914, the blues became the new musical marker of black authenticity.[74]

Not to be left behind, white vaudeville singers incorporated the new sound of blackness into their own routines. "Many white bands and orchestra leaders . . . were on the alert for novelties," Handy noted. "They were therefore the ones most ready to introduce our numbers."[75] The blues were undeniably associated with African American culture. White singers did not claim the blues as their own as they were beginning to do with black dialect songs. They instead revitalized the tradition of racial masquerade that had long characterized white minstrel and coon song performances. When white vaudeville artists sang the blues in the early years, they were usually acting black.

White singers invested the blues with black stereotypes and epithets in order to portray a fundamental difference between themselves and the African American culture they were portraying. One of the most blatant examples was "Nigger Blues" ostensibly penned by the white blackface performer Leroy White. It contained many blues couplets that were well known by African American singers throughout the South. White may have picked these up in the same manner that W. C. Handy secured his "snatches": hanging out with black musicians around his hometown of Dallas. He submitted his composite song for copyright under the title "Negro Blues," yet a publishing house released it in 1912 under the new moniker, perhaps seeing the derogatory title as a way to attract white consumers. "Nigger Blues" had its recording debut in 1916, when a white blackface performer named George O'Connor recorded it for Columbia.[76] As "Nigger Blues" moved from Dallas to the national stage, and from "Negro" to "nigger," racist white epithets obscured the white awareness of southern African American blues lyrics in which it had its origins.

A similar process was already at work when W. C. Handy published his first composition. Two white men swindled Handy out of the copyright to "Memphis Blues" in 1912. One of them had another white writer add lyrics that celebrated Handy yet recast the song in a minstrel mold by depicting the white consumption of a darky act.

> I went out a-dancin' with a Tennessee dear,
> They had a fellow there named Handy with a band you should hear
> And while the whi' folk gently swayed
> All dem darkies played . . .
> I never will forget the tune that Handy called the Memphis Blues.

George Evans's Honey Boy Minstrels, a white company, began playing this version of the song in 1913. The lyric became the first vocal blues on record two years later when Midwesterner Morton Harvey waxed it for Victor.[77] Other white artists followed quickly. Arthur Collins and Byron Harlan soon cut the song for Columbia. New Orleans native Al Bernard, dubbed "the Boy from Dixie," became the first to wax Handy's "Beale Street Blues" and "St. Louis Blues."[78]

In the years after 1910, the blues was less a challenge to white minstrelsy than an important tool for its continuation, because it helped white artists reassert their authority as interpreters of black culture. Artists such as Marie Cahill, Vernon Dalhart, and Marion Harris gained accolades when they added blues to their repertoire of coon songs and black dialect numbers. The blues also enabled white artists to make a significant amount of cash by once again exploiting the gap between African American access to song publishing and virtual exclusion from the recording studio.

The blues again enabled white female performers to express their autonomy and sexuality through their supposed association with black culture. Gilda Gray became an icon when she introduced Handy's "Beale Street Blues" to Broadway in *The Gaieties of 1919*. The Polish migrant grew up in

Wisconsin before coming to New York sometime after 1915. Gray's "Beale Street Blues," declared a review, succeeded because of "the artistry and authenticity of her recreation of the fugitive songs of the underworld."[79] Gray claimed to know one hundred blues songs, and she used them to create a sense of racial danger and exoticism associated with a distant, mysterious world of black nightlife. The sense of scandal was enhanced when she danced the shimmy while singing the blues. The quick, seductive shaking of her shoulders took audiences by storm and came to define the libertine flapper on the dance floor. "There is something delightfully primitive about it," a critic opined. "It is real—and so is Gilda. And in this primitiveness and realness men and women hear the echo of their own yearnings—to be startling, unconventional, untamed as were the ancestors of centuries ago."[80] Gray insisted that the move was inspired by southern African American dance. "Go to any typical town of the old South, seek the outskirts some evening when the darkies are strumming the moonlight," she implored. "You will see dozens of pickaninnies shuffling the shimmy in doorways. It was from these kinky heads that I crystallized my first concrete idea of my present syncopated dance."[81]

Here we see the familiar interplay between the languages of minstrelsy and folklore: contemporary African American culture, in the guise of real-life "pickaninnies" associated with a white primitive past. The blues, like the coon song of the 1890s, became an open signifier of white desires and abandon, a safe way for those civilized too much to play with racial and sexual transgression in order to find their true selves. At the same time, W. C. Handy apparently appreciated Gray's performance of "Beale Street Blues." She introduced the song to Broadway and the world, increasing its sales and the stature of its composer. It was an achievement he later acknowledged when he wrote to the African American composer William Grant Still about his upcoming appearance on the aging Gray's episode of the television show *This Is Your Life*.[82]

This tension between the white exoticization and promotion of black compositions can be seen even more clearly in the work of Marion Harris. Born in Henderson, Kentucky, the white singer moved to Chicago and then New York in the hopes of breaking into theater. She became a vaudeville headliner and began making phonograph records for Victor in 1916.[83] On her early recordings, Harris featured sentimental songs about the South such as "There's a Lump of Sugar Down in Dixie" and "I Always Think I'm

Up in Heaven (When I'm Down in Dixieland)." She also recorded a significant amount of blues-related material. Several of her early songs represented black music as an emotional and physical release from the confines of white respectability. "Paradise Blues" (1916) tells the story of "Ragtime Lew" from Mobile who can "show you how to blue on that piano." It finds the singer rejecting the North for the South, white high culture for black barrelhouse.

Honey, don't play me no opera.
Play me some blue melody.
I don't care nothing about *Carmen*,
When I hear those harmonies.[84]

The singer "feels that feeling down in my knees" when Lew "plays right on those piano keys." On "When I Hear that Jazz Band Play" from 1917, Harris marvels at the effects of the imaginary band from Dixieland, whose "lazy," "out of tune" playing—exaggerated by the studio orchestra—"makes me feel so good I could just throw myself away."[85] Black music was a path to white ecstasy.

On the other hand, Harris was one of the most active white champions of African American blues composers between 1916 and 1922. She cut a number of their songs, including Spencer Williams's "I Ain't Got Nobody" and Henry Creamer and Turner Layton's "After You've Gone" and "Everybody's Crazy 'Bout the Doggone Blues but I'm Happy." She fought to record Handy's "St. Louis Blues" and defected to the Columbia label when Victor refused. She recorded the song in April 1920, several months before Mamie Smith's "Crazy Blues" inaugurated the race record era. Her recording reveals a relatively nuanced and controlled interpretation that displayed some familiarity with African American blues performances. She tended to push her relatively weak but clear voice to capacity, achieving a slight growl when attacking notes and sliding smoothly between pitches. Harris, like southerners Clarice Vance and Vernon Dalhart, claimed her facility with performing black song "just came naturally" as a result of her southern background.[86] In concert, she avoided many of the exaggerations of voice and movement that typically identified white performance as caricature. "Where the usual artist of this type must gallop around the stage and shout to get over, Miss Harris stands almost motionless, offering a few gestures with her hands, and her soft, mellow voice puts a hush over the house," wrote the *Los Angeles Times*.[87] Performances such as this that may have led W. C. Handy to comment, "She sang blues so well that people sometimes thought that the singer was colored."[88]

White artists such as Marion Harris and Gilda Gray turned the blues into a complicated symbol of black culture transforming the national music scene. On the one hand, they got the music of a new group of black composers onto phonograph records. This fact was not lost on black consumers. Evidence suggests that African Americans purchased blues records by white artists when they were the only ones available. "Marion Harris has the manner so at her command that thousands of Negroes make a point of buying her records, under the impression that she is one of them," noted the author Abbe Niles in the introduction to W. C. Handy's 1926 *Blues: An Anthology*.[89] They likely also understood the discs as the products of black composers, just as an earlier generation had celebrated the work of African American songwriters such as Gussie Davis or Johnson, Cole, and Johnson. White blues recordings were popular enough with African American consumers that an Atlanta dealer decried the trend in October 1920. He lamented that black record buyers displayed a "present craze for blues" (ostensibly by white performers at this date), but they could be trained to appreciate more serious, uplifting music.[90] On the other hand, Harris and Gray opened white critics—and perhaps white audiences—to the possibility that the blues was serious, uplifting music, an important art form worthy of study and preservation. Gray's "Beale Street Blues" debut in 1919 encouraged one critic to declare, "The archeology of these communal chants is worthy of as serious study as Cecil Sharp and others have given to the ballads of the Appalachians."[91] In a very limited sense, African American music had arrived. The pride of place enjoyed by the blues, of course, was seriously undercut by the fact that it represented a celebration of black culture at the expense of black artists. White critics exalted the songs yet excluded the singers. It was an issue of access as much as aesthetics.

In early 1920, few knew that the landscape of American recorded music was about to change. Blues records by white artists were flying off the shelves. The recordings of rural rube Cal Stewart were enjoying a renaissance following the press's career retrospectives and obituaries. Southern transplants to New York and other northeastern cities were performing Dixie-tinged pop songs from vaudeville, minstrel, and cabaret stages. They had transformed northern visions of southern primitive music from within. Their claims of authenticity—a minstrel more genuine, a hillbilly born from participant observation—helped shift images of southern music from strict caricature to a stylized presentation of southern music traditions. And many were paid for their efforts, even as their acts played primarily to mainstream buyers of novelty or nostalgia. At the same time, phonograph dealers were developing radical new strategies for selling their wares. Spurred by examples from around the globe and a fear of market saturation at home, they created new markets for the magic talking machine by offering selections that spoke to particular geographical or ethnic identities. In 1920, as the industry swooned over positive economic reports from the postwar South, these two fresh marketing models would collide. Pressures from southern migrant musicians, the almost frantic quest for market share, and an increasing association between genuine folk music and minstrel or hillbilly guises opened the door to the race record and old-time trade. Southern musicians who had honed their subtle skills with the mask were poised to walk on through. Vernon Dalhart, the aspiring opera singer who had found his white southern identity through black dialect songs, was paying attention.

TALKING MACHINE WORLD 5

Discovering Local Music in the
Global Phonograph Industry

In the summer of 1920, the *New York Evening Post* interviewed Edmond F. Sause about the state of the international recording industry. Sause was in a good position to answer the query. The middle-aged export manager had begun working in the phonograph trade in 1903 as a basement stock clerk at the Columbia Graphophone Company store in Manhattan. Eventually, Sause became a salesman and store manager. Literally rising through the ranks, he ascended to an office on the twentieth floor of the Woolworth building, where he oversaw one of the largest international departments in the business. "Like the sewing machine, typewriter and cash register, the talking machine can be said to be an American product," Sause told the *Post*. "Its possibilities in foreign trade were appreciated practically from the beginning. While the industry was still struggling in home markets, progress was being made in developing foreign trade. Few American industries can show as large a percentage of foreign trade to its total turnover as the talking machine industry during the last twenty years." Sause's comments were brief, yet his message was clear: the phonograph, invented by Thomas Edison in 1877, may have been an American product, but its early history was one of international success and domestic difficulty.[1] What did Sause mean by this?

First, Sause suggested that globalization and recorded music had been together almost from the start. This runs counter to most of what has been written about both the phonograph and musical globalization. Standard industry histories focus primarily on the United States with nods to Great Britain, Germany, and France. They rarely mention the foreign trade that Sause found so significant to the industry as a whole.[2] The large body of literature about musical globalization, on the other hand, is dominated by discussion of the years since the 1970s, an era noted for the rapid movement of media, people, and money, and the integration of global markets. For all its diversity, recent literature largely agrees that musical globalization is a story of the late twentieth century.[3] Yet Edmond Sause's comments in 1920 came after more than two decades of rapid global expansion by the fledgling phonograph industry. In these years, major patent-controlling firms such as Columbia, Edison's National Phonograph Company, the Victor Talking Machine Company, and its British affiliate Gramophone scrambled to establish markets throughout the world. Companies spread across Western Europe in the 1890s. They systematically expanded into Latin America, Asia, and Eastern Europe in the first years of the new century. Business grew quickly.[4] By 1910, companies had established sophisticated global networks of production and distribution for their machines and phonograph records. They had recorded thousands of musicians in dozens of countries, and the quantity of "foreign" or "ethnic" records in their catalogues outnumbered domestic releases by a significant margin. The industry's largest trade journal, founded in 1905, was called the *Talking Machine World*. The title was no mistake. Phonograph dealers and company executives understood themselves as part of a global industry.

Second, Sause implied that there was something wrong with phonograph marketing in the United States. Again, the current literature is little help here, for it focuses primarily on the internal development of the U.S. industry. It is only by contrasting the domestic situation to the global scene—something Sause no doubt did regularly—that the United States' problems come into focus. Sometime between 1901 and 1905, a major split occurred within companies in response to perceived market saturation. Domestic dealers began promoting the *universal* values of Western art music. They attempted to convince American consumers with little interest in the concert hall that they—lo, their very nation—would be better off if they acquired an appreciation for "serious" music. International dealers, on the other hand, developed concepts of *local* music, promoting American technology as a means of listening to native songs and styles. The concept of local music proved a more successful model upon which to build the phonograph business. As Sause implied, touting the universal value of Western music caused the domestic industry to falter. Promoting "serious" music did not create a nation of art-house patrons nor did it alleviate domestic dealers' fears about the future of their industry. In fact, by the time Sause talked to the *Post*, companies had begun importing the strategies developed internationally and applying them to domestic markets. It was a decision that would revolutionize American music.

Promoting Serious Music: Cultural Uplift in the United States

When the phonograph business was in its infancy, few people involved talked about the meaning of local music. Hardly any talked about music at all. Early advocates thought Thomas Edison's talking machine was remarkable enough to sell itself. *Scientific American* captured some of this excitement when it announced the invention in 1877. "It has been said that Science is never sensational; that it is intellectual, not emotional," the author began. "But certainly nothing that can be conceived would be more likely to create the profoundest of sensations, to arouse the liveliest of human emotions, than once more to hear the familiar voices of the dead."[5] The writer listed possible applications for the new machine: the recording of political speeches, great works of literature, business correspondence, and famous singers of the day. Possibilities were everywhere—in the business office, in the library, and in children's toys. One thing was certain: there was money to be made.

In the years that followed, dealers scurried to get their products in front of consumers, hoping to cash in on the wonder predicted by *Scientific American*. Nineteenth-century sales efforts focused on placing coin-operated phonographs in arcades, saloons, and other places of public amusement. People were willing to pay a nickel for the spectacle of sound emanating from a box. "When a man can hear the 7th Regiment Band of New York play the boulanger March, a Cornet solo by Levy, or the famous song, The Old Oaken Bucket, for five cents he has little desire to pay five cents to ascertain his weight or test the strength of his grip," wrote the Cincinnati *Gazette* in 1890. "That is the reason the musical machine has killed the business of other automatic machines."[6] Technological novelty—"arousing the liveliest of human emotions"—got the talking machine industry off the ground.

The music promoted by the early industry reflected this. Pushing their product as a novelty, companies recorded the variety of styles popular with the urban, working-class audiences who attended arcades. Tin Pan Alley songs, Broadway hits, light classical selections, and vaudeville-style racial and ethnic caricatures dominated catalogues, echoing the music popular in New York where Edison and Columbia were located. Victor had its home in nearby Camden, New Jersey. The tendency of record catalogues to look like cross sections of the New York theater world was reinforced by the limitations of recording technology. Early recording equipment was not portable. Almost every recording made in the United States was cut in New York or New Jersey.[7]

Early promoters did their job almost too well. By the first years of the twentieth century, pundits began fearing an industry based on novelty was destined to falter as consumers got used to the talking machine. Dealers decried "the popular impression that the talking machine is still only a scientific toy, and that anything to which the generic name of 'phonograph' can be applied is something capable of emitting only weird screeches and scratchings without the slightest pretensions to musical quality of tone."[8] The burning question confronting phonograph producers was how to build a consistent market for the invention as initial wonder wore thin.

Domestic salesmen responded to the waning novelty of the talking machine by launching what can be called a campaign of cultural uplift, repositioning their product as an educational tool rather than a parlor trick. In 1905, a vice-president of a major firm declared, "1904 can really, I think, go into history as the year when the talking machine first became generally recognized as more than a toy and as a medium not only of entertainment suitable for the home of the refined and artistic and when it first assumed its place as an educational force."[9] It signaled a reinvention of the industry.

At the heart of the cultural uplift campaign was a dedication to encouraging the use of "serious" art music in the private home. Victor led the pack by promoting its new Red Seal line of classical recordings. The company signed exclusive contracts with Enrico Caruso and other opera singers featured in New York's Metropolitan Opera House. Fine furniture makers designed beautiful cabinets, and interior designers began including the talking machine among the list of the modern home's essential accoutrements. Records by the great opera and concert artists of Europe sold heartily, and dealers often compared the talking machine to a home library of great literature. The industry also promoted the use of art music and opera recordings in public schools as a means of introducing young children to the cultural heritage of the Western tradition.[10]

The cultural uplift campaign had some economic motivations. Record companies often found classical selections cheaper to produce. Artists' fees, while often higher than in the popular field, could be spread over a longer time, because recordings did not go out of style. Local dealers also believed the classical music trade could be more profitable than the popular field. Until the mid-twenties, dealers were not allowed to return unsold records to the manufacturer. Classical records had a longer shelf life. While the latest ragtime or dance record could sell legions of copies, its time in the sun was usually limited to a few months. After the initial novelty of the tune subsided so did sales, and dealers' shelves were often stuffed with extra copies of yesterday's hit record. A Beethoven string quartet, on the other hand, did not fade from public favor. While it could not approach the sales figures of the current hits, over the course of several years it would continue to sell at a steady pace, and overstock would remain marketable until a superior recording of the selection was made.

The cultural uplift campaign was more rhetorical than reality. Pop music continued to drive the phonograph industry. In 1905, Victor Talking Machine Company issued a four-page advertisement in *Talking Machine World*. The ad copy stated, "Three [pages] show pictures of operatic artists, one shows pictures of popular artists. Three to one—our business is just the other way, and more too; *but there is good advertising in Grand Opera.*"[11] Victor acknowledged the overwhelming dominance of popular music within the industry even as it preferred to imagine itself primarily as a promoter of operatic music. Early opera recordings helped to legitimize the talking machine as a serious musical instrument.[12] They also achieved a similar end for the talking machine business. Characterizing their job as one of moral and cultural uplift helped phonograph producers and dealers to legitimize their own standing within a class of professional cultural workers, rhetorically distancing themselves from their customers, whose taste for popular music was filling company coffers.

Perhaps no one epitomized the cultural uplift campaign more than Frances E. Clark, the supervisor of music for Milwaukee public schools who in 1911 became the director of Victor's Public School Educational Department. In a speech in 1909 before the Wisconsin State Teachers' Association,

Clark directly tied American cultural uplift to technological innovation and serious music. "If music is to become the great force of the uplifting of this American people that I firmly believe that it will become, it must be brought about by the next generation knowing more about music and knowing more music itself," Clark declared. She found the phonograph an essential tool for this musical education. "It is necessary to reconstruct our old ideas of the wheezy, blaring, blatant, brassy thing we have known in the days agone," she insisted. "The new talking machine with its wood horn, its bamboo needle and the wonderful records obtainable is a joy and delight— an artistic success." With these technological improvements should come more uplifting listening habits. "The old was almost wholly given over to the lower class of music—the coon song, the ragtime, the cheap popular song heard in saloon and dance hall," maintained Clark. "The new talking machine is eminently respectable and worthy of a place as an educational factor in every school in the land. By the use of the machine we may enjoy opera, oratorio, orchestra, band, violin, 'cello, folk songs and ballets over and over again as many times as we like."[13]

Between 1905 and 1917, Clark's opinions about class, race, technology, and education became increasingly common within the domestic talking machine trade. A Columbia sales manager simply echoed standard industry hyperbole in 1917 when he declared: "Music in the home is the greatest addition to the education of man since the printing press was invented."[14]

The cultural uplift campaign seized the imagination of many within the United States industry for it soothed interrelated anxieties concerning American culture, consumerism, and their own identity as cultural brokers. At first glance, proponents of cultural uplift appeared to be picking sides in one of the era's fundamental battles over the meaning of culture. Whether identified in terms of art versus novelty, the highbrow versus the low, or even Matthew Arnold's "sweetness and light" versus the mundane, distinctions between that which uplifts and that which debases ran through American debates about the meaning and measure of culture in the early twentieth century. Industry advocate of cultural uplift, with their proclamations about "serious" music and education, fell largely within the Arnoldian camp. They hoped to deliver Culture to those who did not possess it by incubating an appreciation for musical sweetness and light among the American masses.[15]

Yet cultural uplift was not about transforming American consumer tastes but about changing the very meaning of consumption itself. As the historian Michael Denning has suggested, the turn-of-the-century vogue for Arnold and highbrow refinements was precipitated by uneasiness about the growing commodification of culture in industrial capitalist societies. Appeals to high art were, in part, attempts to locate cultural meaning outside the marketplace. Though difficult to glean from cultural uplift campaign materials, many citizens outside the industry saw the phonograph's commodification of music as symptomatic of the larger problem of mass-marketed culture. John Philip Sousa expressed a common feeling when he decried "mechanical music" in 1906. "Sweeping across the country with the speed of a transient fashion in slang or Panama hats, political war cries or popular novels, comes now the mechanical device to sing for us a song or play for us a piano, in substitute for human skill, intelligence, and soul," the composer wailed.[16] The commercial phonograph, mechanical reproduction itself, was antithetical to high art. Cultural uplift attempted to counter such attacks by imbuing the industry's products with the very "intelligence" and "soul" others reserved for human culture and interaction beyond the cash nexus. It was a bold bait and switch—a Trojan horse in the fragile fortress of uncommodified culture.[17]

The campaign worked as well as it did because it also buttressed the class and racial hierarchies that were marking out United States society and culture. On the one hand, it reinforced the class distinctions that had come to define "highbrow" and "lowbrow" culture during the latter half of the nineteenth century. As the historian Lawrence Levine has chronicled, opera itself went through a similar process of uplift in the late nineteenth century as American elites rescued it from popular audiences and recast it as symbol of their own superior social standing, complete with an emphasis on private consumption, a rhetoric of transcendent universal value, and a desire to evangelize the uninitiated about how to approach true art. Levine is quick to point out that the emergent cultural hierarchy was propelled by racial— as well as class—ideology. The terms "highbrow" and "lowbrow" themselves were borrowed from the racist pseudoscience of phrenology which posited that racial types and intelligence could be determined through cranial measurements. Opera and orchestral music may have epitomized upper-class refinement, but they also came to signify white cultural supremacy in an era characterized by the racial violence of lynching and Jim Crow segregation, as well as by the growing fear that white children were, in the words of an influential editorial in 1913, "falling prey to the collective soul of the negro through the influence of what is popularly known as 'rag time' music."[18]

Phonograph company spokespeople such as Frances Clark performed this script to perfection, regularly attacking African American and popular music, predicting national transcendence through the cultivation of high-brow culture, and convincing elite audiences that they could maintain class and racial dominance only by overcoming their misguided objections to cultural commodification and mechanical music. In the process, they pro-jected themselves into the ranks of the nation's cultural elite. This was a dramatic transformation for a group that until very recently had been defined as toy and novelty peddlers, a designation more likely to evoke patent medicine con games than upright professionals rubbing shoulders with renowned conductors and celebrity tenors.[19]

Yet in its explicit incarnations, the cultural uplift campaign was about transforming consumers. "The Prima-Donna and the Cowboy," a short story by Howard Taylor published in *Talking Machine World* in 1905, offers but one example. The story opens with Ike, a cowhand prone to cursing and hurling racial slurs, settling down with his friend the Kid to listen to a new talking machine sent from his boss, who has traveled to a roping contest in New York City. The first record they hear depicts a Wild West show. It culminates in a cavalry bugle cry and the wails of Indian warriors in retreat. "I've heard a lot about them talkin' machines, but reckoned they was a fake put up to sell like that blamed patent medicine that slick critter from the East pawned off on us down to Denver last winter," the Kid comments after a moment of silence. "When they kin git a whole tribe of Injuns, a full brass band, a regiment of cowboys an' the Lord knows what else in one of them black dinner plates, an' shoot it out at you through a funnel, an' make your hair stand up an' bring the sweat out on you in a minute more'n a whole blamed round up of mad steers would in a month, it's a tolerably hot article, ain't it, Ike?" he asks. " 'Them my sentiments, Kid,' " Ike responds. Here again is the initial contact with the phonograph spawning technological awe and arousing emotions. Previous products coming from "slick critter[s] from the East" had been disappointing ruses, the Kid contends, but the talking machine appeared to live up to its name.[20]

The mood of the story changes quickly when the pair listens to the next record. Technological awe is replaced with a cultural metamorphosis.

"Home Sweet Home" echoes from the horn, and Ike is transformed into an eastern middle-class college man. "His cowboy life fell away, and once more he was home from college on his first vacation home in the little New Hampshire village, and strolling up to the rustic cottage where dwelt Grace Brandon, the little New England maid who had promised to become Mrs. James in the far-distant, rosy future when his college days were o'er and he had made a fortune." The phonograph, Taylor suggested, held the power to civilize the frontier cowboy.

Advocates of cultural uplift believed one of their major obstacles was ordinary citizens' love of inferior novelty music. They reveled in reports of consumers—particularly those in remote rural locales—learning to appreciate serious music. A dealer in West Virginia, H. C. Farber, published a rebuttal to Sousa's critique of "mechanical music," noting that the talking machine had created legions of new Sousa devotees among the nation's rural residents. "The ruralite or hayseed," Farber wrote, "buys himself a 'talker' of some kind, and plays it to beat the band. He hears some of Sousa's pieces and then when the March King comes within one or two hundred miles of his lonely mountain home this very hayseed will put on his store suit and dig down into his jeans for the fare and go to hear the famous bandmaster, whom he would never have heard of if not for the 'talker.'"[21] Once exposed to the great artists of the Western tradition, others agreed, consumers would no longer remain satisfied with the sounds of the amateur or semiprofessional musicians from their own communities. "Only a few years ago, when the price of a talking machine was not within the reach of people of ordinary means, I noticed that most especially in the smaller towns and hamlets, a traveling musician, an organ grinder or a 'barnstormer' show proved a great attraction and was received with the warmest of welcome," explained the writer William F. Hunt in 1905. "The people, most in particular those of the rural class, were anxious to hear music, regardless of quality—anything, just so it had some of the characteristics of music about it." Audiences no longer settled for mediocrity now that the phonograph had arrived in homes across the country. Hunt continued, "The traveling musician is now rarely if ever seen, and poor class shows are getting scarce. People have been cultivated to the best class of music and entertainments through the marvelous little entertainer—the phonograph—and the above-named class of vendors could now not get a hearing, to say nothing of a recompense for their labor if they put in an appearance."[22]

Hunt was getting ahead of himself. Rural audiences still supported traveling musicians, street performers, and local bands. Live music offered a thrill and excitement that could not be banished by the scratchy sounds of the talking machine. It also offered local songs and styles not available on record at the time.

Yet United States dealers were blinded to the value of local music by the dichotomous categorizations behind the cultural uplift campaign. As a pamphlet titled "Helping Record Buyers" argued in 1917,

> There are two kinds of record customers, one who makes an initial purchase of the latest topical records, and then quickly tires of his Gramophone, and the other type of buyer who when purchasing his instrument selects a variety of good records, as the base of an ultimate collection. This is the class of customer that is a real asset. . . . The dealer has a Gramophone enthusiast in embryo, and according to the method of the training so the customer. When it comes to selecting records, the dealer should give his advice, and state his reasons for so advising. Fully 60 per cent of the customers do not know the type of record they require and are probably drawn to the topical and humorous because they have never had the opportunity of hearing good music.

There were two kinds of customers, and there were two kinds of records: topical novelty selections and uplifting classical recordings. This was the dichotomous vision of American music that drove the domestic phonograph industry. The dealer had a duty to instruct consumers how to make the right decision. It was a matter of economics as well as cultural education. The brochure concluded, "Neglecting an opportunity to familiarize a customer with higher class music than he is accustomed to buying, never did build a business and never will."[23]

Cultural uplift and education were the primary visions many domestic dealers had of the future of their industry and of themselves as professionals. Facing the waning novelty of their product, domestic dealers argued that they had to convince consumers to appreciate the music that they themselves found meaningful. The mission of cultural uplift precluded the possibility that dealers would look toward consumers themselves to determine what music would sell well. Local musical tastes in other parts of the country, when considered at all, were seen as part of the problem facing the phonograph industry rather than as a potential basis for phonograph sales. The industry was progressing very differently outside of the United States.

Imagining Local Music: The Creation of Global Markets

In 1902, Henry M. Blackwell, an engineer, accompanied a surveying company building a railroad track through eastern China. Soon after setting camp in a small village along the route, the crew was alarmed to hear "several hundred chattering Chinamen" gathered outside its quarters. The villagers had caught wind that the surveyors possessed a miraculous talking machine, their military escort explained. The crowd was demanding a demonstration. Once produced, the machine "received more reverence than an ancestor's tomb," recalled Blackwell. Events then took a turn for the worse. As Blackwell dropped the needle, there was a pop followed by stone silence. The machine refused to talk. "Muttering arose from the crowd and a spokesman addressed the interpreter, declaring that there had been unfair discrimination and that if their sovereign rights were withheld, they would 'get hung.' When the little file of soldiers attempted to disperse them the uproar became deafening and the engineers rushed out to find an incipient Boxer outbreak." Several people from the crowd tried to storm the house and take the machine by force, but the soldiers held their ground. Eventually, the crowd tired of the scene and dispersed but not before three "ringleaders" had been arrested. Blackwell and his associates worked half the night to repair the machine. They presented a concert of " 'coon' songs and comic opera trifles" the following morning to a "grateful, awestruck" audience. Not in attendance were the ringleaders, who had been sentenced to hang by their wrists for forty-eight hours for their offenses. "Every innovation is bound to have its martyrs," Blackwell concluded.[24]

Henry Blackwell's story of technology, wonder, and violence was not unique in the early years of the century. Stock narratives of distant people's first contact with the phonograph regularly graced the pages of *Talking Machine World*. From rural China to Chilean forests, Alaska to Central Africa, published stories and photographs depicted exotic foreign populations genuflecting before the talking machine. Phonograph dealers fetishized these images of "uncivilized" people marveling at the phonograph. Victor maintained a collection of such photographs that it would lend to various periodicals for publication.[25] These complex texts and images com-

municated several contradictory messages. The awe-inspiring magic of mechanical reproduction collided with violence and exploitation. Accounts of
racial difference and distance—often finding natives worshiping Western
technology or men—mingled with portrayals of the phonograph ultimately
smoothing uneasy encounters between civilization and primitivism, colonial powers and colonial subjects. Behind all these images crept the expanding market for music and machines, a force willing to overcome or reinforce
cultural difference as the situations dictated but always able to reframe
global cultural clashes as opportunities for consumption. The contradictions contained in these images enabled phonograph dealers to interpret
them in multiple ways.

First, stories such as Blackwell's fit into larger tropes about the uses of
Western technology in the colonial project. The phonograph joined the
rifle, dynamite, fireworks, and the pocket mirror as a tool to subdue primitive populations. It held a special place in such narratives for it was a
technology of culture rather than force, encouraging colonial metaphors of
exchange to eclipse those of conquest. The machine provided what the
anthropologist Michael Taussig calls "spectaculars of civilized primitivism,
exchanges of magic and of metamagic satisfying to both primitive and
civilized."[26] The talking machine, like the mirror, invested inanimate objects
with human form or function. Ghostly voices arose from a box possessed. It
thus could bridge the apparent divide between Western science and primitive superstition, and everyone could delight in its charms. Beyond the
scratchy sounds, however, the machine's true magic in these narratives was
its ability to evoke commonality while inscribing difference. All were in awe
of the talking machine, but there was no doubt that Blackwell and his
compatriots were in control. Backed by a military escort, they possessed the
machine and proved themselves midnight masters of the technology behind
its magic.

White explorers and colonists also controlled the voices emanating from
the phonograph, resulting in a firm association between its technological
brilliance and white racial superiority. "Huh! Him canned white man," an
"Alaskan Indian" reportedly declared upon hearing his first record.[27] The
racial ideology encoded in such stories suggested that white people created
and owned the machine, which in turn was haunted by white voices that
insinuated themselves into the consciousness of the listener. It was a short
leap to the suggestion that primitive people became more civilized through

exposure to American technology and culture. One photograph in 1905 displayed exotically clothed Aleutian Islanders cocking their heads toward a talking machine in the center of the frame, mirroring the stance of the famous dog in the Victor logo responding to "His Master's Voice." The accompanying article enthused, "It is possible they are hearing for the first time modern music of the leading orchestras, as well as the songs and witty sayings which are current in the large cities. What is true of the Aleutian Islanders is true practically of everywhere the talking machine becomes known. It is a great civilizer and its popularity is founded upon the substantial grounds of giving a tremendous value to every user throughout the world."[28] The author Howard Taylor's poem "A Phonographic Legend" (1905) further delineated the perceived congruity between the spread of the phonograph and the civilizing effects of American culture. The poem begins with a phonograph washing ashore on a remote island ruled by "King Jamboree." When the mysterious machine begins to speak, the gathered crowd "did not understand the words, / But felt that it must be / A command from their Fetish / To pray on bended knee." Thus, just as in Blackwell's story, Taylor's listeners first associate the talking machine with the supernatural. The mood quickly shifts, however, when the king eats one of the records, thinking it to be a pancake. Others follow, and the technological encounter acquires a specific cultural referent:

No sooner had they eaten it
And started for a walk,
Than with stirring eloquence,
They all began to talk.
Not in the savage guttural,
But in old U. S. A.
The kind you hear in Boston,
And that is swell, they say.[29]

The talking machine spoke with an American accent. To all others, the stories implied, it was a foreign technology representing an American modernity just now arriving on their uncivilized shores. They literally could consume it, but it would remain possessed by its American creators.[30]

Even as such stories celebrated the unifying magic of the talking machine and its power to transmit American culture, they reveled in their own absurdity. Blackwell's saga, like Taylor's poetic legend, was less reportage than a comedic set piece. It evoked what the historian Philip J. Deloria calls an "ideological chuckle" born from the recognition of a cultural anomaly. Stark juxtapositions of primitivism and civilization—chattering Chinamen listening to light opera or island monarchs sporting a Boston brogue— reinforced expectations of racial distance and domination by briefly over- coming them. The juxtaposition was funny exactly to the extent that one believed it could never happen. The laughter placed oneself and one's cul- ture above that of the primitive protagonists. These stories of first contact thus ambiguously professed a hope that cultural imperialism could make the world a more civilized place, yet they constantly expressed doubts that primitives would be able to appreciate American music when they heard it. The value of civilized culture was simply beyond many foreigners' comprehension.[31]

First-contact stories became popular among United States dealers at the precise moment that the novelty of the talking machine was waning among U.S. consumers. They helped express the longings many dealers felt for the not so distant past, an era when American consumers still marveled at mechanical reproduction and the machines sold themselves. In 1877, *Scientific American* had identified the emotional power the machine possessed in its introduction of Edison's invention. Domestic dealers recalled that even as expressions of awe and wonder depicted the complacent colonial subject, they also characterized the ideal consumer. As dealers swapped tales of distant phonograph encounters, they found in "primitives" the wonder and excitement about talking machines that they and their domestic customers no longer possessed. Yet they also read these fantasies of unspoiled con- sumers through their experiences with the U.S. market. Foreign wonder could not last. A new strategy would be required once international au- diences got used to sound coming from a box. It was with this realization that the international phonograph campaigns departed fundamentally from the path pursued in the United States. Initial impetus came from those working in local markets around the world.

In 1905, an anonymous phonograph dealer was asked by *Talking Machine World* to assess business prospects in the Philippines. "I should say, from my superficial investigation," the dealer noted, "that the possibilities for a large business here with talking machines is most encouraging. To begin with, the Filipinos take to novelties. They are like children in many respects, and to see them gather around some machine which is sending forth a reproduction of a famous American song, and note the childlike look on their faces, is interesting." The dealer struck the familiar chord of primitive wonder and American culture, but then departed from the score. "Of course, all of the records must be in Spanish," the author maintained. "I believe that if the talking machine manufacturers could get some noted Filipino to sing for recording purposes, or some native orator, the records and the machines would have an enormous sale. All people who can, would buy one simply to hear the local singer or speaker."[32]

Other dealers and investigators were coming to similar conclusions about the importance of recording local music in foreign markets. John Watson Hawd traveled to Calcutta on a fact-finding mission for Gramophone in 1901. He was alarmed at the number of talking machine dealers who were already present in the city. Furniture and bicycle salesmen were adding talking machines to their line of goods. He urgently wrote the home office in London suggesting that Gramophone establish an Indian branch office before other transnational and local firms flooded the market with rival machines. Some were using the recording capabilities of Edison's consumer phonographs to capture the singing of their friends and families. Such amateur recordings were selling crisply to Calcutta music lovers. Hawd thus insisted that Gramophone send recording experts to capture the sounds of "native" musicians. Gramophone responded immediately, offering to dispatch Fred Gaisberg, their most successful scout, fresh from recording tours of Europe. Hawd did not wait for Gramophone to act. After sending his request, he quickly befriended Amerendra Dutt, manager of the Classic Theatre in Calcutta. By the time Gaisberg and his recording equipment arrived, Dutt had selected and rehearsed a number of local artists for the scout to record.[33] Similar networks for finding local talent were established in other markets. Quite often these involved tapping into existing arts organizations or infrastructures: music schools in the Philippines, court musicians in India, noted scholars in China.[34]

The scramble for foreign sales was a highly competitive game. Heinrich Bumb, a scout for the German Beka-Record firm, arrived in Hong Kong in 1906 only to discover several other companies already ensconced there. "The Columbia Graphophone Company had just finished its latest recordings— said to be of 1,000 titles, for which fees of 50,000 dollars had been paid. 'Victor,' 'Grammophon' [sic] as well as 'Zonophon-Records' and 'Odeon' were represented in the colony," he recalled.[35] Successful phonograph companies designed detailed strategic plans for global expansion. In 1907, for example, Victor and its sister company British Gramophone agreed upon a global division of markets so they could spread the use of Berliner disc technology without directly competing with each other. Victor's sphere included North and South America, China, and Japan. Gramophone would sell the Berliner phonograph system in Europe, India, and other Asian countries.[36] Gramophone soon recorded a significant number of musicians in India, Turkey, and Egypt as well as several other smaller national markets. The company cut 14,000 discs in Asia and North Africa during the first decade of the century. Phonograph companies moved throughout Latin America with almost equal speed. Columbia established a presence in Mexico by 1903. Victor and Edison followed within a few years. The Latin American trade grew quickly. In 1913, Argentina imported an estimated 2.7 million phonograph records. Companies that could not afford to set up their own international offices expanded their catalogues by signing licensing agreements with other labels. General Phonograph, the maker of the popular Okeh records, increased its catalogue and cache in this way when it became the U.S. distributor for the European Odeon label. By 1915, when almost all United States recordings were made in a handful of urban centers, the major phonograph companies had made thousands of records in countries around the world.[37]

As the industry expanded, companies developed international networks of production, distribution, and information sharing. Gramophone's production chain provides but one example. Gramophone constructed its machines and cabinets out of wood harvested from around the world: mahogany from Africa and South America; oak from Great Britain, North America, and Russia; and walnut from southern Russia and the United States. Recorded discs themselves were manufactured out of raw materials gleaned from East Asia, India, Spain, France, and the United States. The company maintained even more sophisticated global networks for the production of its recorded music. International recordings were made through the collaboration of company scouts and recording experts with local agents, dealers, and talent. Once initial recordings were made, commercial discs were pressed in Hanover, Germany, although by 1912 Gramophone had expanded disc production to plants in France, Spain, Germany, Austria, Russia, and India. Discs then were distributed along with machines to exclusive dealerships for sale in the country of origin and migrant communities throughout the world. Gramophone also licensed large portions of its ethnic and classical catalogues to Victor for production and distribution in the United States. This transnational production network was essential to the growth of both Gramophone and Victor. Victor's access to international opera stars through the Gramophone catalogue enabled them to dominate the United States opera trade, and the combined geographic reach of the two powerhouses allowed them to claim one of the most comprehensive catalogues of "ethnic" music.[38]

In the beginning, United States recording engineers had a very difficult time comprehending the music they encountered on their international expeditions. "Generally they are strangers in the countries to which they may be despatched [sic], knowing little, if anything, of the language or customs of the people and ignorant of the material from which to choose suitable record-making talent," confessed Edward Burns, manager of Columbia's Export Department.[39] Fred Gaisberg concurred, "On the first day [in Shanghai in 1903], after making ten records we had to stop. The din had so paralyzed my wits that I could not think . . . Up to the 27th of March we made 325 records for which we paid $4 each. To me, the differences between the tunes of any two records were too slight for me to detect."[40] Kathleen Howard, a popular contralto, wrote of an experience her favorite engineer had while recording in China:

> They had been working for some time, the Chinese musicians sitting in utter stolidity round him, twanging and scraping when told to, laying aside their instruments in the pauses, all with no show of interest or spark of enthusiasm. The singers would record impassively amid the same dull atmosphere, and the recording manager began to grow discouraged. Some of the songs were supposed to be comic, and he thought, "Well, they can't be very successful or at least one musician would crack a smile."
>
> At last up stepped a little Oriental and began to sing. One musician smiled, another grinned—at last they were all chuckling, then roaring.
>
> "Aha," thought the manager, "This man is really good. At last I have a true comedian. We must do lots of his songs and make them especially carefully."
>
> After the session he said to the interpreter: "That last fellow was a good one, wasn't he? He must be very funny to make them laugh so—a really good comedian."

"Oh, no," said the interpreter quietly, "they were laughing because he was so bad!"[41]

American scouts were out of their element. Their skills in assessing and recording musicians from Western art traditions had helped them rise within the ranks of the growing recording industry. Their initial recording successes in the United States and Europe had convinced industry executives that they were the right people to carry out similar ventures throughout the world. Yet they had no framework or aesthetic criteria with which to judge the strange sounds they encountered. "We entered a new world of musical and artistic values," recalled Gaisberg. "One had to erase all memories of the music of European opera houses and concert halls: the very foundations of my musical training were undermined."[42] Many questioned whether the sounds they captured on disc—often based on complex, unfamiliar rhythms and quarter-tone scales "sounding to the Western ear constantly out of tune"—could be considered music at all.[43]

Confronted with such musical and cognitive dissonance, scouts and dealers escaped into the logic of the free market. John Watson Hawd wrote back from India to his Gramophone superiors in 1902, "The native music is to me worse than Turkish but as long as it suits them and sells well what do we care?"[44] S. Porter, a recording engineer working in India, echoed this sentiment in 1905: "To be sure the selections are weird, if not altogether grand, gloomy and peculiar, but they sell like hot cakes." Since "American records are absolutely unknown" and "orchestral records are also little in demand," Porter saw no alternative to supplying the "weird" music to Indian consumers willing to pay the price. In fact, once he focused on "native music," the demand was great enough for him to declare: "India is the best place on earth for talking machines . . . I have made records in Russia, Sweden, Norway, in fact all the principal countries of Europe, but India tops them all, and appears to me a great field for American enterprise in this line."[45] Such declarations suggest what American scouts may have been thinking during their international adventures. Hawd and Porter first pronounced disgust for local musical tastes. Yet failing to arouse interest in American or orchestral music, they threw up their hands, surrendered their own musical tastes, and succumbed to local consumer desires. This new premium placed on local music was born not from an ideology of cultural relativism or equality but from a reassertion of cultural and racial hierarchy,

The primitivist rhetoric perfected in the stories of first contact enabled talking machine men to focus on local music. A subtle but unmistakable alchemy was occurring as international scouts explained their experiences to domestic readers. From one sentence to the next, stock descriptions of ignorant natives transformed into detailed analyses of local musical styles and tastes. Primitive stereotypes—particularly the denial that foreign peoples could comprehend Western art traditions—became the justification for taking local music seriously. Reporting on scout Henry Marker's trip through China, one author asserted, "Talking machine exporters know only too well that the most insignificant nations will buy talking machines if they can hear records made by their own people. A cannibal would flee from a record of Cavalieri but would go almost insane with delight at hearing his own tongue emerge from the horn of a machine." The author then parsed the Chinese population into a variety of distinct markets, revealing his knowledge of Chinese society and geography. "One of the first things that strikes the foreigner when he travels about the Chinese Empire is the lack of homogeneity. This is particularly noticeable in the languages. There is the Pekin dialect and the Canton dialect, and so many others that only a skilled linguist can distinguish them . . . so in making talking machine records it is necessary to have actors in all the dialects of the provinces where the goods are to be sold," the author explained.[46]

Edward Burns, Columbia's export manager, likewise began his summary of the company's Asian expeditions by evoking standard images of foreign superstitions. "In fact, in some countries in the far East," he announced, "the people looked on the talking machine not only with wonder, but positive awe, and approached it with fear and trembling, regarding the mysterious voice from the horn as that of a god." Burns then insisted that Columbia's success throughout East Asia was dependent on a broad and detailed knowledge of local cultures. He offered a running list of his company's work toward this end. In the four years of its campaign, Columbia had studied a variety of local dialects and musical styles; charted the internal and international migration patterns of different ethnic groups; categorized the musical tastes of different economic and social classes; compared the use of music in different religious traditions; chronicled local trade and distribution networks; invented a new recording diaphragm to accommodate the broad dynamics of some local singing styles; learned to promote loud records in areas favoring open air architecture; and even surveyed different locales regarding the colors consumers preferred to see on their record labels.[47] International campaigns were producing serious students of foreign cultures even as they maintained a deep investment in racial and cultural hierarchies.

Some scouts even began to acknowledge the artistic qualities of the music they encountered abroad. T. J. Theobald Noble recorded extensively throughout Europe and Asia in the years after 1910. The prominent engineer chronicled his dawning comprehension of the Hindustani music he captured in Calcutta. "At first I found it unmusical and weird, but eventually began to follow the songs with keen enjoyment and appreciation," he explained. Noble was particularly impressed by an amateur singer accompanied by a harmonium and a set of tabla drums, or "tum-tum."

> These instruments are very curious for, although the playing of them appears to be simple, they are in reality extremely difficult . . . It was many days before I could follow even to a small extent—how the tum-tum was supposed to accompany the singer, and I do confess that to this day I cannot fathom how it is possible to accurately accompany an Indian song on such an instrument. The artist sings up and down the keyboard, and to my mind there are no bars, rhythm or tempo, yet the tum-tumist crescendos, stops, commences and synchronises perfectly with the singing. It was and still is an enigma to me.[48]

Here was the culmination of the industry's slow recognition of local music and cultural difference. Noble's comments represented a profound, if subtle, change in the conception of foreign sounds. It was a shift from *noise* to *music*—from Fred Gaisberg decrying a paralyzing "din" to the acknowledgment of a conscious, skilled performance. Noble began to hear Hindustani music on its own terms, discovering its difficulty and appreciating its internal logic. In the process, he relinquished some of his power to define cultural value. Even as he acknowledged the music's merits, he admitted that full comprehension and mastery was beyond him. While not admitting its transcendence or even its parity with Western music traditions, Noble allowed that Indians had their own culture and that native musicians understood its artistic characteristics better than American scouts.

At the same time, the local music paradigm placed serious constraints on the music that foreign musicians were allowed to record. It defined local music through its isolation from scouts' own culture and civilization. On the prowl for music that could charm local consumers into purchasing a talking machine, scouts regularly ignored or suppressed evidence that the musicians they encountered in distant lands had already forged their own extralocal connections and cultures. Fred Gaisberg, for example, had no patience for Indian musicians enamored with Western music. Soon after arriving in Calcutta in 1901, he was treated to a female chorus singing "And Her Golden Hair Was Hanging Down Her Back" accompanied by a brass ensemble. Gaisberg cringed. "I had yet to learn that the oriental ear was unappreciative of chords and harmonic treatment and only demanded the rhythmic beat of accompaniment of the drums," he recalled. "At this point we left."[49] Often, such reactions arose out of corporate strategies of market development. Phonograph companies saw little money to be made from recordings of Indians singing British music hall ditties.

Just as often, scouts' reactions in the field were driven by their assumptions about music, race, and primitivism. Henry L. Marker, for example, traveled over 12,500 miles making records for Columbia between 1910 and 1912. In Singapore, Marker arrived for a recording session wearing his standard pith helmet, white suit, and matching shoes. He was surprised to discover the scheduled Malay ensemble similarly decked in identical trousers and boots. The scout believed the Western clothes would inhibit the passions of the performers. "Tell that bunch of misguided heathens to take off their boots or there will be no more records made," he declared. The musicians quickly complied.[50] Casting themselves as savvy globetrotters confident in the artistic supremacy of their own Western music traditions, phonograph company scouts imagined they were introducing modern technology to isolated, primitive people around the world. Well-shod Malay musicians or Indian brass bands challenged such conceits. They not only demonstrated the worldliness of supposedly isolated, racially inferior people but also suggested that white talking machine scouts were not as superior or as unique as advertised. Artists or music that challenged scouts' understanding of the dichotomy between primitivism and civilization rarely got recorded.

The global expansion of the phonograph industry thus launched a new conception of local culture. In this new configuration, the local was something separate. It was a distinct, circumscribed space that contained its own musical culture, one demonstrating little apparent relationship to either that of its neighbors or to the music emanating from the United States and

Europe. Second, the local was something deeply private. Local culture was known and understood only by insiders and represented something of the essential identity of its practitioners. Finally, local culture was inferior. Scouts did not promote local music because they believed it was equal to the universal values of the Western music tradition. They embraced it because they understood it to be the best that racially inferior foreign populations could achieve. Lacking the capacity to comprehend civilized art, they could be sold music from their own lands.

This local music paradigm closely paralleled the folkloric paradigm developing within the academy. Some within the industry were well aware of the similarities. They began to talk about local music—developed out of market-driven desire—as folk music. Talking machine dealers invested the music they recorded internationally with cultural importance by claiming it represented various national folk traditions. Talking machine dealers may have acquired their understanding of national folk music from two major sources. First was the concert hall. Ideologies of "national races" and national folk cultures that drew close associations among race, geography, and culture had been gaining influence within art music circles since the late nineteenth century. Within the classical music that many phonograph dealers held so dear, folk song traditions were venerated and integrated into larger concert works. Antonín Dvořák's celebrated tenure in New York had made such combinations big news. Phonograph dealers thus could portray their international recordings as folk music and claim to be continuing their mission of cultural uplift by providing source material for serious composition.

Second, and perhaps more important, was the connection many within the phonograph industry tried to forge between their machine and the fields of anthropology and folklore. In 1890 the Harvard anthropologist J. Walter Fewkes sang the praises of the new invention to his peers in the pages of the *Journal of American Folklore* and *Science*. He urged them to use the phonograph while collecting in the field, contending that "the phonograph imparts to the study of folk-lore . . . a scientific base which it has not previously had, and makes it approximately accurate."[51] Fewkes originally turned his eye toward Native American culture through the encouragement of the Boston philanthropist Mary Hemenway. In addition to her support of ethnological research, Hemenway was a major shareholder in Edison Phonograph Company. She convinced several scholars to take the new machine into the field. Of the 158 extant field recordings made during the first five years of the phonograph, Hemenway funded 141 of them.[52]

By 1905, industry odes to their vaulted role in the academy were commonplace. A typical editorial enthused:

> Folk songs and racial music would be lost entirely were it not for the perpetuating power of the talking machines. Through the agency of these marvelous reproducers of music and sound it is possible to transfer from one country to another an accurate idea of the music of remote countries of earth . . . The anthropologist and the philologist also are finding it a great aid to their investigations. The Academy of Sciences in New York City has made a collection of the various dialects of Austria, Germany, France, India, and Northwest American Indian. This, of course, the future historian will find of great value in his studies.[53]

Associating themselves with the academy helped phonograph companies promote their product as a scientific and educational tool. For many dealers, this association continued through their own international recording expeditions. Even when scholars were not present, commercial scouts claimed they were doing important work preserving national folk music as they developed new markets for the phonograph by recording "native bands" throughout the world.

An appeal to the concepts of cultural distance and difference promoted by anthropologists and folklorists assuaged much of the discomfort American dealers felt upon hearing strange music from different lands. Folklore's veneration of isolated, uncivilized cultures provided dealers a language to talk about musical difference and a conceptual basis for marketing music that they did not like or understand. It also helped dealers distance themselves from the obligation to provide a cultural education to their new nonwhite consumers, while holding themselves up as preservers of folk culture.

Talking machine scouts and dealers did not adhere to the definitions of folk music then being propagated in the social sciences, however. Their use of the term had little to do with claims of isolation from the market. Rather, the terms "folk" and "national" were used more sweepingly to denote aural difference from the fare offered in the companies' popular and classical catalogues. Many of the "traditional" tunes that Fred Gaisberg recorded during his initial visits to India, for example, were recent selections from the popular theater.[54] Concepts of folk and national music, forged by scholars to establish the limits of acceptable, isolated national cultures, thus became in the hands of the international phonograph industry catch-all marketing terms to denote difference from the norms of Western art music. It was a concept of folklore born from the local music imperative to give distant, supposedly primitive people what they wanted to hear.

Importing the Local: Selling Foreign Music at Home

The conceptions of local music that were developed internationally slowly began to influence phonograph marketing in the United States. As global expansion progressed, industry employees crossed borders with ease through travels, transfers, and promotions. A stratum of middle-level administrators and technicians thus became well versed in sharing knowledge about selling phonographs and records within a variety of ethnic and national markets. They increasingly brought their international experiences to bear on the domestic market in the United States. U.S. native Raphael Cabanas, for example, was the president of the Compania Fonografica Mexicana, the exclusive distributor for Columbia in Mexico. In the years between 1910 and 1915, Cabanas made frequent trips to the home offices in New York and Washington, D.C., where he created collaborative marketing campaigns with the Columbia advertising department. In 1913, Cabanas extended the reach of his company by purchasing Columbia dealerships in Texas and Arizona. His Dallas store significantly increased its business following a spate of innovative billboard advertisements, a strategy Cabanas had perfected earlier in Mexico City.[55] Edward N. Burns, Cabanas's chief contact at Columbia, boasted one of the most significant international résumés in the business. Burns was the founding manager of the Columbia Phonograph export department around 1902. He held the position until 1915, when Edmond Sause replaced him so that Burns could be promoted to the vice presidency of the company. In addition to supervising exports, Burns served as an advisor to domestic dealers hoping to increase sales among immigrant populations.[56]

It was through fostering sales among U.S. immigrants that international experts had their most direct influence on U.S. sales strategies. Talking machine companies began to realize the potential markets that existed in the nation's immigrant neighborhoods during the first decade of the cen tury. Early rhetoric about immigrant sales reflected the emphasis on local singers or speakers developing in the international campaigns. "Remember that in all large cities and in most towns there are sections where people of one nationality or another congregate in 'colonies,'" explained a writer in the *Columbia Record* in 1909. "Most of these people keep up the habits and prefer to speak the language of the old country . . . To these people REC-ORDS IN THEIR OWN LANGUAGE have an irresistible attraction, and they will buy them readily."[57]

The arrival of ethnic recordings in the United States was disorienting to some in the industry. Many dealers invoked caricatures of ethnic difference similar to those of the foreign first-contact stories when they imagined domestic consumers of foreign records. One dealer related the apocryphal tale of a traveling salesman who sold a machine and twelve records to an Irish immigrant, a Mr. O'Toole. The customer was very excited that the traditional Irish songs he ordered arrived in time for his daughter's birthday party. At the appropriate moment, Mr. O'Toole hushed the gathered crowd and placed the first record on the machine, stating ""Oi will now give yez Chauncey Olcott's latest song av th' ould country." To the party's surprise a "mysterious tinkle of bells" came forth from the horn, followed by "a series of barbaric shouts." After a second record brought similar results, the crowd demanded the worthless machine be thrown out the window. Just in time, the salesman appeared at the door and breathlessly apologized for mixing up Mr. O'Toole's order with that intended for a local Chinese restaurant. The party proceeded as planned.[58] The tone of such stories closely echoed both the violent confusion of Henry Blackwell's Chinese villagers and Fred Gaisberg's disorientation while recording the paralyzing "din" of different music traditions.

Yet the role of talking machine dealers in such tales is notable for two reasons. First, in stark contrast to international scouts, the phonograph company employees in these stories were no longer the ones experiencing anxiety. The shock of encountering the strange music of another ethnic tradition was reserved for other immigrants. The talking machine man negotiated between multiple ethnic groups, containing and channeling ethnic anxiety by teaching immigrants to be more informed consumers. Second, such stories reveal an important loophole in the industry's cultural uplift campaign. Here are domestic dealers gladly giving customers what they want. It was a double-edged sword. The same racism displayed in the international campaigns excluded many immigrant groups from the possibility of cultural uplift in the eyes of the industry. Yet this very exclusion enabled American immigrants to demand that phonograph companies grant them recordings of their unique musical traditions.

Companies dramatically accelerated efforts to sell "ethnic" music in the United States following the outbreak of war in 1914 in an effort to protect themselves from the possible interruption of global trade networks. As editorialists pleaded for calm and predicted a growing U.S. economy, phonograph companies moved to make up for endangered international profits through increased domestic business. Companies immediately placed their sights on fostering immigrant consumption. "The immense stirring of patriotic fervor due to the European war has given an impetus to the sale of Columbia records of foreign music which is truly phenomenal," a Columbia publication announced in 1914. Victor and Columbia expanded their recording of international material in the United States, setting up recording studios in Chicago to complement their primary New York and New Jersey facilities. Anton Heindl of Columbia's International Record Department was named director of the company's new Chicago studio and promised to place special emphasis on recording the "folk songs, the dances, and the religious hymns" desired by U.S. immigrant populations.[59]

In 1917, Columbia launched a major campaign to pressure their dealers to take advantage of underexploited immigrant markets. "This is a harvest time for foreign record business," its advertising copy announced. "Our International Record Department issues records in 37 different languages, and thousands of Columbia dealers in this country are making good, regular money on these records."[60] In the fall, Anton Heindl organized an unprecedented, week-long conference that brought together Columbia executives from both the domestic and international departments to share experiences and develop joint marketing strategies. It was attended by regional sales managers and featured a series of lectures by Edward Burns, the architect of Columbia's global expansion. The conference had the explicit purpose of fostering foreign record sales in the United States. Following the conference, sales managers were to take its message to dealers throughout their territories. Samuel Lenberg, a sales manager out of Chicago, left the conference with orders to "study the conditions in the dealers' territory, collect data and show them how to cultivate successfully trade to which they have not hitherto catered" and "seek to establish new Columbia dealers in localities where there is a large foreign trade and in which the company is not now represented."[61]

It was through this concerted push to increase foreign record sales during the First World War that conceptions of local music and difference—born in companies' international expeditions—came to dominate the U.S. talking machine business. First, the campaign changed the way many dealers conceived the history of the industry. Previous dealers had characterized it in terms of its oscillating commitment to cultural uplift, themselves as soldiers in the fight to protect serious, transcendent culture from class or racial degradation. Others now identified the motivating force behind the industry as the search for new markets. "The secret of increasing business lies not alone in redoubling efforts in accepted and familiar fields, but in discovering and operating in new fields where it is possible to create a fresh demand for a product," one author argued. Distinct ethnic markets offered just such possibilities, the author concluded.[62] Second, the foreign record campaign introduced domestic dealers to the marketing magic of local music, the idea that consumers would line up to purchase music that represented their own identity. As one advertisement explained in 1917, "The big foreign-born population of the United States is hungering—yes, *actually hungering*—for its own native music . . . These are not just records sung in foreign languages. They are records that have been actually *made in their native land*. That is why they have the indefinable atmosphere which the purchaser immediately recognizes and cherishes."[63]

These were lessons that international scouts had learned many years before, yet they represented a revolution of values to domestic dealers reared on the rhetoric of cultural uplift. Odes to "native music" not only shattered the dichotomous definitions of music behind cultural uplift; they also insisted that consumers—not talking machine dealers—were in the best position to recognize musical quality. Harry A. Goldsmith, a Milwaukee Victor wholesaler, made this point forcefully:

> Tony Andrianopolis shyly enters your store, hat in hand, and asks if you have some Greek records. Of course you have none, and in the past simply told him so and turned away from him. He slinked out of your store. You soon forgot the incident. Now, had you invited Tony into your office, inquired from him about how many Greeks, for instance, lived in your city, and put it up to him squarely if he thought it would be profitable for you to carry Greek

records, you might sit up surprised that you had wasted some wonderful opportunities . . . Just hand him a Greek catalog and ask him to mark in this what records he thinks you ought to carry for a starter . . . Have faith in Tony. Order every single record he tells you to . . . When you get these Greek records in stock let Tony know. Tony will do the rest.[64]

The dealer's role in this transaction was far different from that proposed during the educational and cultural uplift campaigns. The dealer looked to the immigrant customer for musical guidance. By focusing on consumers' current desires rather than trying to foster new ones, American phonograph dealers could profit in the foreign record business.

Conclusion: Globalization and Local Music

Edmond Sause was interviewed at an important moment in the history of music in the United States. Even as he spoke of foreign success and domestic difficulties in 1920, the local music model invented in the global marketplace was coming to dominate the phonograph business within the United States. This process, begun by targeting immigrant populations, reached a turning point little more than a month after Sause's words appeared in print. On August 8, 1920, Mamie Smith and Her Jazz Hounds recorded the song "Crazy Blues" for Okeh Records. It was the first significant blues record by an African American singer and backing band. "Crazy Blues" helped to inaugurate the "race" record industry that sold music made by and for African Americans. It was a market conception that owed a lot to the local music paradigm developed internationally. Race records were soon followed by "hillbilly" or "old-time" tunes marketed to rural white audiences. For many Americans, these products traded on their racial, class, and regional authenticity in new ways. Here was music made by artists who lived and performed in the same milieu as their audiences. If previous commercial recordings represented national culture imposed on consumers in every city, race and old-time music often were marketed as local sounds writ large—the triumph of local authenticity over homogenizing bids for universal value.[65] Edmond Sause and others involved in the international industry may have understood these products differently. Race and old-time records in part signified global marketing strategies coming home to roost.

This story suggests some general conclusions about globalization and the local music paradigm. First, American music is a product of globalization. Global markets were a major concern of the industry practically from the start, and global experiences were intimately intertwined with the conception and development of music markets in the United States. Some scholars have attempted to locate the emergence of the local music paradigm within the history of American popular music. A number of scholars have emphasized the 1950s rise of rock and roll, along with its attendant valorization of local "roots," its global appeal, and its apparent anticommercialism.[66] Others have insisted that the 1920s witnessed the birth of the local music paradigm as race and old-time records began selling briskly. Unfortunately, such explanations suggest that the local music paradigm developed in isolation within the United States and was then exported. As surely as we must question images of discrete, isolated cultures prior to contact with the phonograph, we should be skeptical of these portrayals of local U.S. music developing in isolation from or prior to globalization.

Second, within the phonograph industry, concepts of universal and local music did not arise in opposition to each other. Both were driven by a fundamental faith in racial and cultural hierarchy. Both shared contempt for earlier marketing strategies that pitched the talking machine as a piece of awe-inspiring technology. Both insisted that the future of the machine was as a carrier of culture. The fact of mechanical reproduction mattered less than the ways in which consumers were moved by the music emanating from the horn. Likewise, both spoke to uneasiness about the growing commodification of culture in industrial, capitalist societies. Each identified culture as that human activity existing outside the marketplace: the uplift program found it in the fine arts; the international campaigns located it among isolated, supposedly primitive peoples. What is significant about the campaigns for cultural uplift and local music is not that one faltered as the other came to dominate the United States record charts. It is that the industry so quickly was able to commodify two realms of music celebrated for their existence beyond the commercial nexus.[67]

Finally, local music was produced by corporate globalization. Local culture has played a defining role in the recent literature about musical globalization. At its most basic, the local has stood for everything the global is not: rooted in place and tradition, uncommodified, and uninterested in empire building. Many scholars have challenged the simplicity of this formulation, suggesting that the local emerges through its opposition to globalization or as the specific ground upon which globalization occurs. Yet for all the theorizing, scholars have had a difficult time escaping the basic idea of the local as a thing apart. It remains a way a particular place is defined against the global. The story of the early-twentieth-century phonograph industry suggests otherwise.[68]

The local music paradigm within the phonograph industry arose out of a particular two-pronged historical process. First, the identification of local music was a story of discovery. It involved the slow determination that different locales (defined according to geography, nationality, race, or class) had developed their own unique musical styles. This discovery of local sounds was partially a byproduct of the capitalist tendency toward differentiation common to the historical quest for new labor and consumer markets. It was also spurred by the Western intellectual revolution in the concept of culture that challenged Arnoldian visions of transcendent "sweetness and light" with anthropological notions of distinct customs and folkways. The identification of local music also was accomplished through a process of erasure. Once phonograph companies identified unique musical styles, they limited their depictions of local cultures to these aspects of the scene by ignoring or eliminating musical evidence of outside influences—particularly that of the Western "serious" music they were promoting back home. This aspect of the "local" is rarely discussed in the literature about globalization, yet it is vitally important. Within the commercial recording industry, the local did not develop in opposition to the universal claims of the Western music tradition. On the contrary, it was born out of the belief that some racial or ethnic groups lacked the capacity to comprehend Western civilization. Local music offered a way to increase consumption among inferior populations. The local music paradigm thus reinforced the superiority of the West, the divide between primitivism and civilization, and the Western tendency to hear foreign sounds through the prism of exoticism. Local music was deeply inscribed with the racialism and racial hierarchies of its day. Recent scholars have had a difficult time defining a local culture that does not perpetuate exoticizing tendencies in part because that was what the concept—like the folkloric paradigm developing simultaneously within the academy—was designed to do.

RACE RECORDS AND OLD-TIME MUSIC **6**

*The Creation of Two Marketing
Categories in the 1920s*

By early 1920, the national music industry had developed a number of models for selling music to the American public. It had perfected the mass production of sentimental ballads to pull on the heart-strings of consumers across the nation. It had sold stylized black music in the form of coon songs, Negro dialect ditties, and blues numbers to audiences both black and white. It had featured wise-cracking hillbillies in the big city and fiddle breakdowns to enter-tain urban audiences pining for a taste of the backwoods. And it had learned to expand into new geographical areas by employing native singers to cater to local racial or ethnic markets.

Two more strategies emerged in the 1920s. "Race" records, as discs by African American performers came to be called, grew into a significant segment of the market. Beginning in 1920 with Okeh's release of Mamie Smith singing "Crazy Blues," the marketing cate-gory became quite broad, including everything from show tunes, urban religious services, and Smith's vaudeville-inspired blues to an assortment of sounds associated with the South: jubilee choirs, country blues, the occasional black string band, and many others. White southern artists also enjoyed a vogue during the decade, beginning with the recording debut of Fiddlin' John Carson in 1923. Recordings of "old familiar tunes," "old-time," or "hillbilly" music captured white fiddlers, guitarists, and banjo pickers who had been plying their trade in the streets, nightspots, and medicine shows of the South. Previously viewed by industry insiders as untalented

hacks in need of cultural uplift, these artists became the down-home dar-
lings, some even claimed saviors, of the talking machine world in the 1920s.
By the end of the decade, legions of black and white southern artists had
recorded commercial discs. Later scholars would identify this body of work
as a watershed, the fundamental transformation of the American recording
industry marking the triumph of authentic southern music over the nefari-
ous pseudo-hillbilly and minstrel-styled stereotypes that previously had
passed for the real thing.

Race and old-time records launched a new way of organizing American
popular music and, by extension, the American public. Most companies
separated race and old-time records from their general popular music recordings. They gave records in each category a unique series of serial numbers, and they printed separate catalogues and flyers to promote the discs.
This was new. Earlier record catalogues had listed domestic releases according to musical genres, distinguishing "Dance Hits" or "Marches" from "Minstrel," "Novelty," or "Classical" selections. Yet they had offered all of a company's products in one place. Such inclusive catalogues reflected the way in
which phonograph dealers had imagined their customers. They had courted
the total, undifferentiated American buying public. It was a sales model
based on the notion that individuals had broad musical tastes. Any particular
person might buy selections from any or all of the genres that shared space in
the catalogue. Indeed, the primary distinction that had concerned dealers
was the one between customers who invested in classical recordings and
those who preferred everything else. The decision to separate race and old-
time music from the general catalogues marked a pivotal change in approach, the implications of which spiraled through the music industry in the
1920s. Separate catalogues suggested a correspondence between consumer
identity and musical taste, one that was both holistic and exclusive. They
implied that unique segments of the population were satisfied by particular
kinds of records yet uninterested in others. Musical tastes were assumed to be
narrow rather than broad. The race and old-time categories were the industry's biggest experiment in market segmentation to date.

In practice, separate race and old-time classifications functioned as both
advertisements and censors. They simultaneously defined the scope of a
musical category (those records included in the catalogue) and a unique
segment of the population (the buyers targeted by it and the artists it
promoted). One defined the limitations of the other. The significant variety

of musical sounds and styles that stuffed race record catalogues were held together and advertised as a cohesive whole by the fact that they were all created by African American musicians. Companies, however, often refused to allow black artists to record selections the musicians held dear—from pop songs and arias to hillbilly breakdowns—but did not fit within corporate conceptions of black music. African American musicians made race records, the argument went, and race records contained race music. The old-time category functioned in a parallel way. Consumers looking for the sounds unique to the white rural South could find them in old-time catalogues, but the musicians who made these discs were discouraged from recording material that smacked too much of Broadway, Tin Pan Alley, or any of the other musical imports that had peppered their performances back home.

The race and old-time categories sold millions of records and profoundly shaped Americans' understanding of the nation's vernacular music, yet they corresponded to the musical lives of no particular sets of artists or audiences. They resided at the edge of the difference between the music African Americans or white southerners loved and what predominantly northern corporate record men imagined that they did. Race and old-time records held the promise of greatly expanding phonograph sales. By targeting specific groups with their own unique music, companies could draw the attention of untapped consumers to the wonders of the talking machine just as they had done in their international campaigns. Yet black America and the South were not China. They had each been common subjects of popular musical stereotypes for the better part of a century. Writers and academics had developed theories of cultural isolation and collections of southern folklore to explain them. Minstrels on the ole plantation, black dialect love songs, and southern primitives: As industry insiders began imagining how to appeal to African American and white southern consumers they were influenced by the myriad fantasies they for years had been pushing on record buyers. When the industry began courting their prospective race and old-time consumers, it imagined buyers who looked a lot like the stereotypes that filled northern stages, record catalogues, and folklore collections.

From Dialect Songs to Race Records

The race record trade arose directly out of the networks developed between the African American composers and the publishing companies that had sold coon songs and black dialect numbers in the first two decades of the twentieth century. Perry Bradford had become an integral part of the black musical community in New York before he convinced Okeh Records to record Mamie Smith in 1920. Born in Montgomery, Alabama, in 1895 and raised in a working-class home in Atlanta, Bradford followed a now-familiar path in pursuit of a music career. He joined a local minstrel troupe, toured throughout the South and Midwest with a number of companies, and eventually settled in New York City. He became involved in the city's African American theater and vaudeville scene, performing in several shows, composing songs, and hanging out at the Colored Vaudeville and Benevolent Association (CVBA). There he befriended a bevy of successful African American performers and composers, including Bert Williams, J. Rosamond Johnson, and Chris Smith.[1]

Bradford had campaigned for years to get record labels to take a chance on an African American blues singer. Nothing had worked. Columbia repeatedly turned him down. He could not get past the secretary at the Okeh office. Victor recorded a test pressing of Smith but refused to approve it for release. "I'd kept on 'gum-beating' in the C.V.B.A. Club every night that something ought to be done to crack that solidly entrenched recording monopoly wide open, until it seemed to be getting on the members' nerves," Bradford recalled. On one particular night, he happened to mention the name of Fred W. Hager, the Okeh manager with whom he was getting nowhere. The composer Chris Smith's ears perked. "I've known him for a long time," he declared. Bill Tracey was also at the CVBA Club that night. The white composer had written tunes for Bert Williams, including the hit "Play that Barbershop Chord" published in 1910 by the Helf and Hager Company. "Next time you talk with Fred Hager," Tracey insisted, "tell him that I asked that he give you an audition for your colored girl singer."[2] The generation that had used ragtime and the coon song to propel African American composers and performers onto Broadway provided Bradford an introduction to the music publisher turned record man. It was all the help he needed.

At their meeting, Bradford pushed Hager to record Mamie Smith, an Ohio native and veteran of the black vaudeville circuit. The Okeh executive was intrigued, but he fell short of booking Smith a studio date. Instead, he offered to have the popular white coon shouter Sophie Tucker record two of Bradford's compositions. Bradford agreed. As he walked out of the office, the potentially historic meeting looked like just another case of a white singer commissioning songs from an African American composer. However when Tucker could not make it to the recording session, Bradford was quick to suggest Smith as a replacement. "She will do more with these songs than a monkey can do with a peanut," he recalled telling Hager. "She sings jazz songs with more soulful feeling than the other girls, for it's only natural with us."[3] It was an echo of Bob Cole: African American artists could perform genuine black music better than white imitators. The pitch worked.[4] Mamie Smith recorded Bradford's "That Thing Called Love" and "You Can't Keep a Good Man Down" with a white studio band in February 1920. When the record sold well, Okeh allowed Smith to cut her next session with an African American band. Bradford was ecstatic. He had successfully drawn on the arguments and the business networks developed by a previous generation of black composers to break the color line in the phonograph industry. "Crazy Blues" was the result.

The record remains open to wildly divergent interpretations. Scholars have labeled it alternately a "period novelty" and an "insurrectionary social text." On the surface, "Crazy Blues" fit tidily into the existing collection of vocal blues records. Smith delivered the lyrical lament for a missing lover in a plain, unwavering tone, her vocal projection and clear diction pegging her as a veteran of the New York stage from which both she and the song had come. If "Crazy Blues" is remembered as the first blues record featuring a black singer, the actual contents of the disc might sound less than revolutionary. The historian Adam Gussow, however, finds that the song contributed to a larger conversation about the use of "black violence as a way of resisting white violence and unsettling a repressive social order." After the grief-stricken narrator imagines her lover dead and contemplates suicide, she threatens to "get myself a gun and shoot myself a cop." The bold endorsement of violence retribution by a gun-toting black woman, Gussow argues, spoke to the particular needs and desires of black New Yorkers who had recently braved race riots, police violence, and a resurgence of the Klan. "Crazy Blues" was nothing if not a break from the norm.[5] Each of these interpretations has merit. Indeed, part of the power of "Crazy Blues"—like race records as a whole—was its openness to multiple interpretations, its appeal to different consumers for different reasons. It was an ambiguity record labels would learn to foster.

By any account, the disc was a breakaway seller throughout the country.

A reported 75,000 copies sold in Harlem in the first few weeks. Sales soared in Chicago and Philadelphia. "We'd . . . get in 500 of those records," recalled a retailer in Atlanta. "The clerk wouldn't even put them in a bag. Just take a dollar and hand them out—just like you were selling tickets."[6] The immediate sales took Okeh by complete surprise. Ralph Peer, Hagar's assistant, admitted, "We didn't know it. We don't know where these records were going." He only later discovered that African Americans quickly developed their own word-of-mouth campaigns and distribution networks. "The porters on the Pullman trains would make a fortune just by carrying the records out." Peer recalled. "They'd pay a dollar a piece for them. Sell them for two dollars, because the Negroes in the South had the money."[7]

Published accounts suggest that African American consumers bought the record because they were enthusiastic about a black singer gaining entry to a field previously closed to African American performers. The *Chicago Defender* dubbed Smith "Our Race Artist." The nationally distributed African American newspaper celebrated Smith joining the ranks of white coon and blues singers. "Well, you've heard the famous stars of the white race chirping their stuff on the different makes of phonograph records . . . but we have never—up to now—been able to hear one of our own ladies deliver the canned goods," it began, before announcing Smith's debut. "At last they have recognized the fact that we are here for their service." The paper emphasized labor rather than art. Black singers could do the job. Smith's "capable" vocal recording was notable because it cracked the industry color line, not because it necessarily signaled a significant shift in the sound or meaning of blues recordings. When the paper reviewed her Chicago appearance in 1921, the critic positively dubbed Smith "a splendid reproduction of May Irwin, who made this class of amusement what it is today and what it will remain." The *Defender* insisted that black singers could make the grade and integrate seamlessly into the existing music industry based on the white performance of songs by African American composers.[8]

As black buyers were scooping up copies of "Crazy Blues," Okeh offered little indication that Mamie Smith's records were anything out of the ordinary. Industry press and advertisements carefully opened the possibility of an African American market for her records while promoting "Crazy Blues" to white consumers through the models they had developed for selling blues, coon songs, and minstrel records by white artists. " 'Mamie' Smith, Whose 'Blues' Songs Are So Popular, Joins General Phonograph Corp.

Roster of Artists—Many Jobbers Make Calls" ran the announcement of the collaboration in the October 1920, issue of *Talking Machine World*. The article did not mention Smith's race.[9] The following issue included a full-page Okeh advertisement for "Mamie Smith Blues." The ad featured a drawing of a blackface minstrel in top hat and white gloves labeled "Mr. Public Opinion." He exclaimed, "I's heard Blues, but I's telling you Mamie's beats 'em all." The ad cut two ways. The blackface character and his dialect implied that Smith's records continued the trend of selling minstrel material. Such imagery had been ubiquitous in music advertisements for decades. Yet, contrary to previous imagery, the minstrel in the ad was not a performer but a consumer. "Mr. Public Opinion" spoke for African American buyers. The troubling advertisement suggests Okeh's initial ambivalence about their new recording star. Excited about the possibility of tapping an African American market, the company could only imagine black consumers as the embodiments of blackface stereotypes. It inaugurated a trend that would continue in blues advertising through the decade.[10]

Other labels quickly tried to replicate the success Okeh had with Mamie Smith. Almost every recording company produced its own version of "Crazy Blues" within months of the Okeh release.[11] Labels scurried to add at least one African American singer to their rosters. Columbia grabbed Mary Stafford. Gennett recorded Daisy Martin. The small Arto label from New Jersey snagged Lucille Hegamin. And Black Swan, the historic African American–owned and operated company founded in 1921, featured Ethel Waters among others. Smith hadn't opened a door. She had knocked it down. Over night, being black did not mean being barred from the record business.

Black recording artists rushed to support the African American composers who had pioneered black participation in the national music industry and eased the way for race records. They cut songs by the likes of Chris Smith and Spencer Williams, African American writers who had successfully supplied songs to black stage acts and white recording artists for years. Others featured songs by successful white composers who had supplied Negro-tinged material to African American performing artists. Mary Stafford's brief discography from 1921 offers just one example. In addition to "Crazy Blues," the New York cabaret singer recorded "Strut Miss Lizzie" by black songwriting veterans Henry Creamer and J. Turner Layton, "If You Don't Want Me, Send Me to My Ma" by Chris Smith, Cecil Mack, and Silvo Hein, and "I'm Gonna Jazz My Way Right Straight Thru Paradise" by Will

E. Skidmore, the white composer whose songs had been performed by Bert Williams, Marion Harris, and Nora Bayes. Stafford was far from alone. A critic dubbed Ethel Waters "the ebony Nora Bayes," just as the *Defender* had compared Mamie Smith to May Irwin, because her material was similar to that of the white vaudeville star.[12] Many African American recording artists of the early 1920s sang songs by established black and white composers whose work was recorded almost exclusively by white artists just a few years before.

Taken together, they suggest both the power and the limits of Perry Bradford's and Mamie Smith's assault on Jim Crow in the music business. On the one hand, black artists finally were able to record in significant numbers. Smith and Bradford cracked the color line in the phonograph industry just as a previous generation of black artists and composers had breached the walls of segregation in musical theater and publishing. Ecstatic African American consumers—not to mention black composers themselves —could finally hear recordings of their songs sung by "one of our own," and black musicians could begin to leverage the incredible marketing muscle of the phonograph. "Crazy Blues" made Perry Bradford and Mamie Smith known throughout the country. The composer suddenly spent his time managing lucrative song licensing contracts, and Smith's appearance fee skyrocketed to one thousand dollars a show.[13] The record also marked the beginning of the end for the crop of white blues singers who had dominated phonograph catalogues before 1920. Marion Harris, Gilda Gray, and Al Bernard could not compete with African American blues recordings. They retreated to singing other genres, from sentimental love songs to Broadway novelties. The opera singer turned Negro dialect performer Vernon Dalhart eventually reinvented himself again—as a hillbilly star. Race records dealt a serious blow to white artists who traded on the authenticity of their portrayals of black music.

On the other hand, African American recording artists confronted—and in some ways perpetuated—the compromises and stereotypes that had plagued the earlier generation of black composers. Supporting the black songwriters who had paved the way for African American participation in the pop music industry meant giving voice to the residues of minstrelsy the composers had found necessary to include in their songs. Two of the biggest blues hits of 1921 were "Arkansas Blues" and "Down Home Blues." Their syncopated melodies, clever rhymes, and lyrics shared a lot with the nostalgic odes to the South that had become Tin Pan Alley staples. "There's no use in grievin', because I'm leavin'. I'm broken-hearted and Dixie-bound," declared "Down Home Blues." Mamie Smith, Mary Stafford, and Ethel Waters each recorded the song in 1921.[14] The same year, Anton Lada and Spencer Williams penned "Arkansas Blues (A Down Home Chant)." Smith, Stafford, and Lucille Hegamin recorded it soon after.

> Homesickness has got me down in mind
> 'Way down in old Arkansas
> In old Dixie, My log cabin home,
> Where the Southern folks are good and kind, I find . . .
> I'm tired of roamin'
> I'm tired of roamin'
> I long to see my mammy and my home in
> Old Log Cabinland 'Way down there in the Dell
> I've Got the Arkansas Blues.[15]

Log cabins, mammies, and Dixie: "Arkansas Blues" traded on the age-worn clichés that New York composers had used to talk about the South for decades. Its depiction of a migrant's longing for her southern home expressed a genuine feeling shared by many sojourners to the urban North. But its simplistic assumption of regret about leaving the land of Jim Crow also echoed the legion of nineteenth-century minstrel tunes in which a freed slave pined for the old plantation.

The industry remained deeply committed to interpreting black music as an extension of minstrelsy. *Talking Machine World* declared that listening to a Mary Stafford record "one would suppose that this artist had been reared down South with some Alabama mammy to understudy, instead of being a native of Missouri."[16] An Okeh advertisement in August 1921 for a record by an African American group called the Norfolk Jazz Quartette declared, "It is an appeal to the white people to revive negro minstrelsy. It is the old-fashioned folk music of this country. And they are responding. They are buying eight to one of an average popular hit."[17] The group was a male a cappella quartet, featuring the tight harmonies and propulsive rhythms that had remained a signature sound of black southern singing at least since legions of similar quartets had been featured in *Black America*. Yet its recent release was "Strut Miss Lizzie," the Tin Pan Alley tune by the African American composers Henry Creamer and J. Turner Layton recently recorded by

Mary Stafford and the white singer Al Bernard. The other side of the record featured the song "My Mammy."[18] The company insisted that the Norfolk Jazz Quartette's music was not a departure from standard blackface depictions of black culture. It, in fact, was a nostalgic return to minstrelsy. The authenticity of the quartet's music did not challenge the cultural authority of blackface acts. It could not, the sales pitch implied, for minstrelsy and black folk music were the same thing.

The sudden insurgence of African American singers into the recording realm invested such minstrel rhetoric with new life. Ethel Waters understood this better than most. The Pennsylvania native had moved through the black vaudeville circuit before making it in the white theatrical world and recording for Black Swan. In 1925, the white songwriters Harry Askt and Joe Young asked her to try their tune "Dinah." The song, whose title character of course resided in Carolina, was the latest in a long list of Young's southern-themed ditties that included "Rock-a-Bye Your Baby with a Dixie Melody," "My Mammy," and "Tuck Me to Sleep in my Old 'Tucky Home." Waters thought the composers sang the song "fast and corny," but they encouraged her to sing it her own way. Her slow, lilting interpretation helped make the song an international hit. Waters's "Dinah" marked a new relationship between singers and songwriters. White singers used to flock to the songs of black composers to give a sense of legitimacy to their black imitations. Now white songwriters searched for African American talent to invest their compositions with a sense of black authenticity.[19] Pioneer black recording artists found themselves deeply entangled in popular music's continuing commitment to minstrel imagery. They had fought for their inclusion in a business that had sold rich but distorted fantasies about African American music and culture to white consumers. Once in the door, they discovered just how entrenched those fantasies were.

It is within this context that the composition "Down South Blues" acquires special significance. The song, written in 1923 by Waters, Alberta Hunter, and Fletcher Henderson, replicated many of the familiar themes about unsuccessful migration: alienation from the urban North, a desire to see one's parents, and catching a south-bound train. Two features distinguish it from the previous crop of tunes. First, the lyrics were completely devoid of minstrel imagery or pop music cliché. Second, the bulk of the song consisted of the twelve-bar, three-line verses that characterized the blues throughout the rural South.

I'm goin' to the station and get the fastest train that goes,
I'm goin' to the station and get the fastest train that goes,
I'm goin' back South where the weather suits my clothes.
Because my mamma told me and my daddy told me too,
I say my mamma told me and my daddy told me too,
Don't go North and let them make a fool of you.[20]

"Down South Blues" featured a number of lyrics that had traveled widely through southern oral culture. It spoke in the language not of minstrelsy but of black migrants and the families they left behind. "Down South Blues" was a big hit and quickly recorded by a variety of singers.[21] It offers one small sign that 1923 was a major year in the phonograph industry's slow realization that it was more profitable to approach African Americans as buyers in their own right and the South as a region of consumers rather than as a subject of nostalgia or fantasy.

The year would also see the phonograph industry's first recording sessions in the South. Companies would soon traverse the region and record legions of local artists performing a wide variety of African American songs and styles indigenous to the region, including gospel quartets, string bands, and solitary blues singers accompanying themselves on a guitar. The music of the latter group, performed by artists such as Charley Patton, Blind Lemon Jefferson, and Robert Johnson, would eventually become known as country or down-home blues. Its raw power and simple instrumentation would cause later listeners and scholars to associate blues singers such as Mamie Smith and Ethel Waters with the city, the North, and the professional theater and publishing industries that drew them there rather than with the South that they sang about in their songs.

Finding Native Southern Singers:
The International Campaign Heads South

For decades, southern musicians interested in participating in the national music business had packed up and moved to New York. From Billy McClain and Bob Cole through the Johnson brothers, Clarice Vance, and Vernon Dalhart, artists came to New York looking for an entrée into the national theater, publishing, and phonograph industries. They succeeded by negotiating the differences between their previous southern experiences and the industry's expectations about the South. The trend partially reversed itself in 1923, as phonograph companies began heading south in search of talent. Over the next nine years, record companies conducted dozens of field recording trips throughout the region. The number and variety of race and old-time records blossomed during these years as the phonograph industry attempted to increase penetration into southern markets by selling the unique music of the region back to itself. It was something the industry had tried before.

"I saw that this was really a business like our foreign record business," Ralph Peer noted about Okeh's race record list. "We put out German records, Swedish records and what have you. So I decided that, like the German records were all in let's say the 6000 series, I said well we need another number series so I started using this 8000. That was the theory behind it." Peer continued, "And when the hillbilly came along and I quickly saw the analogy and I gave that a separate number series almost immediately. The first record was Fiddlin' John Carson and they were so terrible I just didn't dare put any of them in the regular list."[22]

Race and old-time music, in part, was a result of the industry revelation that the American South—particularly the rural South—might be a distinct market, one in which New York pop music was as foreign as it was in India or China. Inklings of this began to pepper industry press as early as 1907. The writer Howard Taylor Middleton, the visionary of the industry's international campaign, suggested that a rural market existed for chestnuts such as "Old Folks at Home" and "Silver Threads among the Gold." Previous articles about rural marketing had envisioned the talking machine bringing the modern sounds of the city to isolated consumers. Here Middleton insisted that white rural residents could be wooed by bringing them songs of a bygone era rather than the latest hits.[23] A few years later, he suggested that African American consumers constituted another neglected niche market. He interviewed an Edison retailer who had increased sales among black consumers by hiring an African American salesman in 1913. The rare records featuring African Americans such as the poet Paul Laurence Dunbar and the composer James Timothy Brymn were particularly popular among black consumers, they discovered. "The black man is greatly misunderstood. He is not nearly so ignorant and unappreciative as the world in general would have us believe," the retailer insisted. "The negro knows his music." Middleton concluded, "A talker man who is fortunate enough to obtain the services of an intelligent colored salesman, can win a large amount of trade from the negroes of his city."[24]

Middleton's discoveries went largely unacknowledged until the trade disruptions of the First World War forced the industry to strategize about increasing domestic consumption. Rural residents, just like immigrant populations, became a major focus for future development. "Helpful Suggestions on Getting Farmer Business," "How Exhibits at State and County Fairs Help to Boost Your Business," "Reaching the Country Consumer through the Agency of the Automobile": numerous articles replaced Middleton's anecdotal fiction with detailed and proven strategies for getting the talking machine into rural homes. *Talking Machine World* reported that a *Farm Life* survey in 1920 found that about one-third of surveyed households contained a phonograph. A survey in 1921 asked, "Do you think that musical instruments could be advertised and sold successfully to farm people through farm papers?" Eighty-two percent of respondents answered yes. Rural America, the conclusion ran, was primed for market development.[25]

Industry pundits became particularly interested in the South. Reports on the region's economic conditions suddenly appeared in the pages of *Talking Machine World*. Previous attention to the South in the trade journal had been intermittent and usually consisted of anecdotal depictions of forbidding terrain and romantic, alien people.[26] Now references were to hard statistics: oil and crop prices, laborers' wages, and the industrial boom. "On the whole, I found the South very optimistic," wrote Edwin Boykin, who traveled to Alabama and Georgia for Edison in 1917. "It has practically adjusted itself to war conditions, and is looking forward to a real era of prosperity. Crops are good, and with the establishment of several large training camps in the South, many millions of dollars will be put into circulation there."[27] An Atlanta jobber argued this new prosperity should not go unnoticed. "The South is virgin territory to most Northern manufacturers," he wrote. "Do you realize that the South produces 44 per cent of the agricultural wealth of the country?"[28] Reports swarmed in about record-breaking sales in Texas, Florida, Alabama, North and South Carolina, and Georgia. Virginia dealers were unable to keep a stock of records and machines. The Victor distributor in Richmond boasted that his company was beating Edison at attracting African American consumers. A Nashville dealer reported that new retailers were cropping up in the villages outside the city as fast as overextended factories could supply them with products. "This kind of business can be traced directly to the high price of cotton, and the large amount of money in circulation," came a report from Atlanta in October 1920, the same month Okeh announced the release of "Crazy Blues." "The South, as a section, has more money than in fifty years, and the eyes of the nation are turned this way."[29]

Race records offered an important opportunity to tap this southern market. Perry Bradford had forecast the possibilities of southern sales when he first pitched Mamie Smith to Okeh. "There's fourteen million Negroes in our great country," and most lived in the South, he remembered telling Fred Hager. "The southern whites will buy them like nobody's business. They understand blues and jazz songs, for they've heard blind-men on street-corners in the South playing guitars and singing 'em for nickels and dimes ever since their childhood days." Here was the familiar "native singer" argument that had fueled the phonograph industry's global expansion, now applied to the American South. "What really got the butter and sold Mr. Hager was the big surprise of learning about that big Southern market that no one up North had ever thought of," Bradford recalled.[30] After "Crazy Blues" was released Mamie Smith almost immediately launched a southern tour, garnering rave reviews from Virginia to Dallas. By the time the tour ended in May 1921, she reportedly had sold over half a million records, many of them in the South.[31]

Over the next couple of years, companies pushed the same songs and musicians on southern consumers that they were selling throughout the nation. Just as the international campaigns had first promoted U.S. products around the globe, the industry did not distinguish clearly between southern music and renditions of southern music coming out of the northern theater world. This changed in 1923, when the retailer Polk C. Brockman convinced Ralph Peer to come to Atlanta and record the local street musician and fiddle contest champion Fiddlin' John Carson.

Brockman was a scrappy businessman with a holistic vision of the phonograph industry shared by so many of the local scouts who had propelled the international expansion of the industry. When a young man, he canvassed the South as a sales representative for Simmons beds and determined that there was a strong potential market for wholesale phonographs in the region. In 1921, he got a job in the in Decatur Street furniture store his grandfather had founded in 1888 and quickly established a phonograph department selling records and needles wholesale by mail. Within six months he had signed a deal with Okeh to be its exclusive distributor in the area. A significant portion of Polk, Inc.'s business growth can be attributed to the rising popularity of Okeh's race records. The exclusive distribution rights for the Atlanta area put Brockman and company in a strong position to profit from this trade.[32] Yet race record sales were but one part of Brockman's designs to expand business. He traveled extensively, courting distribution contracts with Okeh but also with Sonora and Caswell phonograph companies, Mastercraft accessories, and Wall-Kane needles. Profits soared. From 1923 through 1925, the firm charted sales growth between 58 percent and 120 percent annually. Polk sold the furniture division of the business in 1924 so the firm could concentrate on the talking-machine trade. Sales increased as Brockman expanded the scope of the firm. He began dealing in all aspects of the trade including portable machines, custom cabinets, and accessories. He also expanded geographically, opening branches in Dallas, Richmond, and Memphis. By 1928, Polk, Inc. was one of the biggest and most celebrated distributors in the country.[33]

On a business trip to meet with Peer in New York in 1923, Brockman caught a newsreel of a Virginia fiddling contest and thought of the stir caused in Atlanta by Carson's contest championships. He reportedly scribbled a note to himself, "Fiddlin' John Carson—local talent—let's record."[34] He convinced Peer to bring recording equipment to Atlanta and commit the popular fiddler to record in the summer of 1923. "When I heard this stuff back in New York, it was so horrible that I couldn't possibly put a number on this thing," Peer recalled. "So we just put a label without a number on it and made up a thousand records and sent them off to the distributor."[35] Soon Brockman was ordering more copies.[36] Yet he had little stomach for the sound of the tunes that he was hawking. "My interest in hillbilly music and black music is strictly financial," he later explained.[37] "He liked the sound of the cash register," his wife concurred.[38] Like Fred Gaisberg and other international scouts in the early years of the century, Peer and Brockman found they could overcome their distaste for native music if the products sold well. Peer released the record in Okeh's regular catalogue and called Carson up to New York to record more selections. It was the beginning of the old-time music craze.

While the industry did not respond to the surprising success of Fiddlin' John Carson's debut as quickly as it had to Mamie Smith's "Crazy Blues," over the following months several firms released discs by rural southern white musicians to capitalize on the newly discovered market. Victor had been sitting on unreleased selections from the Texas fiddler Eck Robertson, born in 1887 in Delaney, Arkansas. Robertson had traveled with medicine shows, provided music for silent movies, and built a regional reputation through fiddle contests before he arrived unannounced at the New York Victor headquarters in 1922. He recorded several fiddle pieces for the company who did not find them worthy of release until after Carson's debut.[39] Okeh had a similar experience with Henry Whitter, a mill hand from Fries, Virginia, who had traveled to New York and convinced Fred Hager to record some test sides. Nothing was done with the recordings until after Carson's debut. Then Peer, on Brockman's advice, released Whitter's "Lonesome Road Blues/The Wreck on the Southern Old 97" in early 1924. Brockman was soon funneling a number of Atlanta artists into the Okeh recording studio. Columbia, which would become the industry leader in the old-time trade, snagged up the Atlanta fiddle contest veteran Gid Tanner and the blind singers and guitarists Riley Puckett and Ernest Thompson, among others. Vocalion jumped into the trade in 1924 as well, releasing a version of Whitter's first record by the singer George Reneau and corralling fellow Tennessean Uncle Dave Macon, who would become one of the most prolific old-time recording artists. Companies released their initial old-time selections on their general pop music lists. By late 1924 and 1925, they developed separate marketing strategies for the music, first advertising them in their own booklets and eventually separating old-time tunes from their pop selections by placing them in their own unique series.[40]

Fiddlin' John Carson was the perfect artist to inaugurate the new trade. He had built two professional musical careers, one catering to textile workers around Atlanta and another feeding the southern embrace of hillbilly stereotypes. Born about 1868 in the Blue Ridge Mountains of northern Georgia, Carson had learned the fiddle at an early age. He held railroad jobs and stumped for populist politicians before taking a job at a textile mill outside Atlanta in 1900.[41] After hours, he worked the "kerosene circuit," traveling from one mill village to the next and playing in small halls or houses far too crowded to admit all the mill hands who wanted to join the party.[42] In 1913, Carson went on strike to support unionization at his mill. He turned to busking on nearby Decatur Street, the commercial drag in Atlanta dubbed "the melting pot of Dixie" for the interracial and interclass crowds it attracted.[43] Carson maintained a remarkably broad repertoire. In addition to writing his own songs, he knew hundreds of ancient fiddle breakdowns, minstrel standbys, and Tin Pan Alley hits. Brockman first may have heard John Carson playing outside his grandfather's furniture store on Decatur Street.[44]

Carson also built a regional reputation by participating in fiddling conventions. In 1913 he entered the first annual Atlanta fiddling contest, winning the fourth prize of twelve dollars. He continued to enter the annual contests, several times winning first prize, and he eventually became the contests' master of ceremonies. The Atlanta fiddling contests were an important site for the construction of a regional identity based on rural life, traditional folk music, and the image of the white hillbilly. Many participants lived and worked in the city, but they created stage personas as hayseeds humorously unacquainted with modern urban ways. In 1914, *Musical America* covered the Atlanta contest and ran photos of several "picturesque figures of [the] old fiddlers' convention." Deacon Ludwig, convention chairman, sported a long brambling beard and a smile. Gid Tanner, who would later gain fame with his recording band the Skillet Lickers, mugged for the camera, his exaggerated expressions looking by turns ecstatic and unhinged. Debates raged in the local press about whether contestants should be allowed to enjoin their coon dogs to sing along during the competition. Such hayseed stereotypes were encouraged by audience members, many of whom came from Atlanta's social elite. The contests were touted in the society pages and reviews repeatedly emphasized the upper-crust enthusiasm for the event. *Musical America* reported: "From front row to back row sat richly gowned society leaders, side by side with working folk in rough attire. The big auditorium was packed with 5,000 persons, and on the stage sat the most picturesque looking bunch of 'fiddlers' imaginable."[45] Atlanta's fiddle conventions gave promising exposure to some of the area's best instrumentalists, yet they also gave white Atlanta residents a strong sense of local identity and character. The images and music of "plain folk" served as rollicking entertainment for all who attended. Carson was the most decorated participant in contests that could fill the local auditorium with Atlanta residents from every economic class. When Polk Brockman jotted "Fiddlin' John Carson—local talent—let's record," he determined to tap a local Atlanta celebrity to help sell talking machines.

Okeh's Atlanta trip in 1923 was the first major field recording expedition conducted by a phonograph company. It set the pattern for many that followed. Companies used local or regional scouts—often their own dealers in the area—to find promising musicians in anticipation of the recording trip. Companies sometimes placed advertisements in a local paper announcing the recording session and encouraging hopefuls to audition. Sessions lasted from a couple of days to a few weeks, before the equipment was packed up and master recordings sent back to the home plant for assessment, production, and release. It was a process similar to the one that companies had used in their foreign expeditions since 1901 but had not attempted previously in the American South. Competition for talent was fierce. Companies canvassed the same areas, poached each other's artists, or recorded contracted musicians under pseudonyms. Nevertheless, companies soon established patterns of regular visits to particular cities. Columbia scoured Atlanta and Dallas. Okeh moved through New Orleans, Atlanta, and San Antonio. Victor was known for mining talent in Memphis and Atlanta, Birmingham, Charlotte, Savannah, and a handful of other cities hosted recording trips but received less regular attention. Paramount, the race record leader by the late 1920s, was the only major company not to conduct field recording trips. However, its network of dealers and scouts— as well as appeals to the public for suggestions—alerted the company about southern musicians to bring into their permanent recording studios.[46]

The strategies of the international campaigns had come home to roost. Recording southern black and white musicians offered the possibility of tapping niche markets separated by geography and race from the popular and classical music that previously had dominated company interest. Promoting native singers to different locales could expand sales in the previously unexplored South. Companies acknowledged the connections they saw among the newfound niche markets when they made joint efforts to enter the foreign, race, and old-time trade. The same month Okeh began advertising Smith's "Crazy Blues," the company got into the international record market by acquiring the distribution rights to seven foreign-language labels. "Okeh enters the foreign language field," announced full-page advertisement in *Talking Machine World*. "Thousands of songs and instrumental selections in more than twenty languages, recorded by artists in their native countries, are now offered to the American trade. There is a market of over thirty million foreigners that can be reached by these repertoires."[47] Emerson made a similar move in 1924 when it simultaneously started a race record line and expanded its number of foreign record releases.[48]

These joint entries into the race record and foreign trade were no coincidence. Companies saw both markets as important means of protecting themselves against fickle tastes of popular music audiences and the growing threat of radio. By 1922, radio had severely affected the sales of phonograph records. Many companies voiced concern, feeling that their businesses were under attack by the new medium.[49] "Many talking machine dealers are at sea over the question as to whether the radio broadcasting of music helps or injures record sales, the majority being inclined to the latter viewpoint," reported *Talking Machine World* in the spring of 1924. "But there is one field wherein the radio has made little impression and that is the foreign record field."[50] The following year, Otto Heineman, president of Okeh's parent corporation General Phonograph, addressed a stockholders' meeting. "Our company has not been affected perhaps as much by the so-called radio competition as other phonograph record manufacturers, as this company has a list of records catering to certain classes of our population which have not been and will never, in our opinion, be taken in by radio," he explained. "Our company is issuing a list of records in over twenty-three languages, in addition to a repertoire of race records and so-called 'Hill Country' records."[51]

Perhaps the best evidence of the phonograph industry's association between the three niche markets is Victor's decision to send Ralph Peer to Mexico in 1928. "I never did understand how they got this idea," recalled Peer. "I'd never been in Mexico, and I don't speak any foreign languages, and I'd never talked to anybody about the subject—had no ideas about Latin American music." Peer had helped produce Mamie Smith's "Crazy Blues" and been an early advocate of race records while at Okeh. In 1927 he had discovered the old-time artists Jimmie Rodgers and the Carter Family for Victor. In 1928, he sat on the Victor advisory board for record sales. When the company sought to expand its market share in Mexico, it turned to the scout who had twice proven himself as a creator of niche markets. "Because I'd solved the hillbilly position, and their distributors were so well satisfied with what was being done, they thought, 'Well, maybe Peer can help us about Mexico.'" Peer took two weeks in Mexico to discover that Victor was losing out to Aeolian, a company that had established a relationship with a Mexican distributor. He went back to Victor with a solid, well-rehearsed plan: open a branch of their own publishing company in Mexico and find some local musicians to record. "We did just that," Peer recalled. His venture into Mexico helped secure the composer Augustin Lara for the label and Peer's Southern Music Publishing Company, a firm that would later branch out into Puerto Rico, Cuba, and Argentina.[52]

Advertising Race and Old-Time Records

At the dawn of the race record trade, many southern dealers were loath to sell records by African American artists for fear that black consumers would drive away white business. Phonograph companies had dealt with a very similar problem in previous years as they promoted the sale of foreign or ethnic records to doubtful dealers. In their promotional material they suggested that sales among black patrons could increase, while claims of the "wide appeal" or "supreme popularity" of black artists—euphemisms for white consumption—assured that the records would not alienate dealers' white customers.[53] Yet phonograph dealers—like their retail peers at general, furniture, or clothing stores—depended upon African American business. Few storeowners were willing to lose sales by banning black customers completely. Some southern stores capitulated to Jim Crow by allowing black customers but installing separate entrances and listening booths for black and white patrons.

As a possible concession to dealers' concerns, Okeh unveiled a new advertising strategy in early 1922. Previously, the company had supplied dealers with a single window display advertisement announcing all the new Okeh records that were available. Now the company offered separate placards for each selection, allowing the individual dealer to decide which record would be featured in the store's display. It was an acknowledgment that local retailers had different needs and clientele and that a general list of records would not appeal to all consumers. The change also enabled retailers to avoid advertising records by black artists if they so chose.[54]

Okeh simultaneously announced that their placards would begin featuring humorous cartoon illustrations for each new release rather than "pretty pictures that don't make sales." The decision to use humor to sell black music was of course nothing new. Companies had been using blackface humor to sell music for some time. Okeh's cartoon illustrations simply perpetuated this trend. Pictures of thick-lipped minstrel men, smiling blackfaced dandies, and bandana-wearing mammies filled Okeh's race record advertisements in window displays and in newspapers such as the *Chicago Defender*. Other companies soon followed Okeh's lead. The use of minstrel imagery in race record advertisements was but one more way in which the industry signaled that its new trade in black music would not upset previous marketing strategies or the conventions of segregation.[55] Joseph Sullivan helped design most of Okeh's race record advertisements. Reporting his departure from the company in 1924, *Talking Machine World* noted that Sullivan had "lived in the Southern States for many years" and was "thoroughly familiar with the peculiarities of Southern negro dialect." More likely, but unreported, was that Sullivan understood that minstrel imagery would stroke white southerners' sense of racial superiority and make it less likely that they would protest African Americans' successful assault on segregation in the recording industry. Black artists had made it onto records, the ads implied, but they were still playing minstrel buffoons.[56] Some African American observers were not amused. "This ad is an offense and an insult to the race," a black writer for *Half-Century Magazine* stated flatly after confronting a blues record advertisement featuring antebellum mammies waving at a "flashily-dressed gambler" prone on a giant set of dice. "Records of this kind and their highly descriptive ads do much to increase hatred and widen the breach between the races."[57]

Race record advertisements nevertheless attempted to appeal to black consumers in a number of ways. Many advertisements were benign. They did not feature minstrel imagery but simply announced new selections, either without illustrations or with a realistic portrait of the artist.[58] Other advertisements directly addressed black consumers. Black Swan promoted itself in the *Chicago Defender* as the "Only bonafide Racial Company making talking machine records. All stockholders are Colored, all artists are Colored, all employees are Colored."[59] In 1925, Paramount ran a large ad in the *Defender* celebrating the sixtieth anniversary of emancipation and extolling "Paramount's Part in the Advancement of Music of the Race."[60] Other ads tried to appeal to black buyers by attempting to replicate contemporary African American slang. An Ajax Record Company advertisement in 1924 insisted, "Talk about syncopatin' the 'L' out of Louisville—man, they'll pull your feet right out of your shoes if you don't 'step to it' when you hear that medicine music. Stand pat til you've got this one going."[61]

Even advertisements sporting minstrel imagery could court black allegiance by allowing consumers in on the jokes at the center of the advertisements themselves. Illustrators often were willfully—sometimes ridiculously —literal in their interpretation of blues lyrics. The ad for "Death Letter Blues" showed the Grim Reaper writing a note. "Rumblin' and Ramblin' Boa Constrictor Blues" sported a picture of a woman confronting a snake in the jungle. "Spoonful Blues," a song about cocaine, featured a picture of a waitress serving a man a bowl of soup.[62] Consumers possessing a bare familiarity with the blues and its use of metaphor and double entendre could see through these simplistic illustrations. The ads invited them to read against the grain, to imagine the unstated—possibly subversive or scandalous—meaning that lurked behind the apparently innocuous implicit message. Promotional copy, on rare occasions, acknowledged the game. An ad for the Hokum Boys' "I Had to Give Up Gym" depicted a woman walking away from an exercise session. "No, it isn't spelled 'J-I-M,'" the copy ran, "but if you're smart you know what she means."[63] Such strategies enabled companies to court white buyers without alienating black initiates to the blues. While minstrel imagery promised nervous white readers that black artists remained in their place, the visual double entendres tried to assure African American consumers that the blackface was a front, a mask that camouflaged the true meaning and value of the music on offer.

Industry strategies for selling old-time music paralleled the methods employed to market race records. The press recognized that the records found their most immediate sales in the South, among the existing local fans of the new recording artists. "To the folks down North Carolina way these ladies need no introduction," *Talking Machine World* wrote about Samantha Bumgarner and Eve Davis from Silva, North Carolina. "They have played and sung their way into such local fame that the demand for their records was big, even before their first recordings were released."[64] In September 1924, the journal reported that Atlanta record sales were increasing because local artists such as Gid Tanner and Riley Puckett had "recorded for some of the large record manufacturing companies and, as was but natural, their recordings were in great demand by their townsfolks."[65]

Old-time records soon came to dominate sales among white consumers in the rural and small-town South. "Take for example the 'Mountain Whites', who buy a considerable number of Columbia records," suggested Columbia advertising manager James Duffy in 1925. "Among them symphony concerts, jazz, popular songs and the old songs well rendered make little appeal. Apparently they do not care for music they do not know or the sort of playing they are not accustomed to. They want special records of 'Familiar Tunes,'" the company's name for their old-time records. "These records are made from playing by blind artists in many cases on homely instruments, such as guitars and harmonicas."[66] "Virginia mountaineers are cagey buyers," concluded Ulysses J. Walsh, who worked at a record shop in Marion, Virginia, population 3,500. "The manufacturer's advertising appearing regularly in the county papers was prepared in New York and boosting, as it did, only the late song hits and fox-trots, was ill-adapted to a community where, even among the townspeople, three 'old-time' tunes were sold to one modern number."[67]

Even as consumers scurried to purchase old-time records, such comments signaled a shift in industry conceptions of the southern market. The realization that locals would support local artists subtly morphed into the position that southerners wanted little but local music. It was a reversal of the cultural uplift strategy that dominated the industry just a few years before. Victor Talking Machine Company had celebrated the potential of opera records to transform the listening public into art music patrons when opera discs were outsold by popular selections by only three to one. The industry reveled in evidence that rural residents bought classical music records and were coming to appreciate serious music. Walsh, on the other hand, considered the modern numbers that constituted 25 percent of his trade negligible. Virginia mountaineers liked old-time music, he concluded.

Some southern musicians had different stories to tell. They spoke glowingly about their interest in the wide variety of music available on phonograph. Maybelle Carter, who rose to fame as a member of the Carter Family, enjoyed a phonograph in her Maces Springs, Virginia, home before she began recording for Victor in 1927. "In fact, my husband had this victrola and a gang of records when we got married," she recalled. Carter remembered owning records by Vernon Dalhart as well as "popular" tunes such as "Dinah," the hit by Harry Askt and Joe Young first recorded by Ethel Waters.[68] The aspiring white musician Jimmie Rodgers, born in Meridian, Mississippi, in 1896, had a fanatical love of phonograph records. He bought them "by the ton," according to his wife Carrie, and his collection included old sentimental songs, current New York stage hits, and novelty numbers.[69] Some future musicians leaned toward classical music in their phonograph listening. The Mexican American singer Lydia Mendoza recalled, "My father liked the theater and music very much, and during those times when he owned a phonograph, our home was always full of music from records as well as what we would play ourselves. For instance, when I was young I listened a lot to Caruso, Enrico Caruso. My father was a fanatical *aficionado* of his. At one time, he had the entire collection of Caruso's recordings."[70]

Even while southern musicians loved, performed, and bought old-time records, they also embraced a wide variety of other kinds of music, from classical selections to northern commercial fare. Folklorists were only too aware of the southern love for mass-produced music. The same year that James Duffy insisted that rural southerners were uninterested in "popular songs," the folklorist Dorothy Scarborough lamented being "tricked into enthusiasm over the promise of folk-songs only to hear age-worn phonograph records" and "Broadway echoes" as she attempted to collect songs in the South.[71] Indeed, almost all of the Tin Pan Alley compositions that made it onto the old-time music lists had also been featured on phonograph records by the likes of Billy Murray, Arthur Collins, Marie Cahill, and, of course, Vernon Dalhart.

While fostering a market for old-time music throughout the South, record companies regularly insisted that the records had a broad appeal to buyers outside the region—just as they had emphasized the white consumption of race records. "Hear these Tanner and Puckett records," urged Columbia ad copy. "No Southerner can hear them and go away without them. And it will take a pretty hard-shelled Yankee to leave them. The fact is that these records have got that 'something' that everybody wants."[72] Columbia later advertised their "records of old-fashioned southern songs and dances," announcing, "The fiddle and guitar craze is sweeping northward!"[73] On June 15, 1924, a year after Carson's initial Atlanta recordings, Okeh declared the national popularity of the records by Carson and fellow old-time singer Henry Whitter. "The craze for this 'Hill Country Music," their ad insisted, "has spread to thousands of communities north, east and west as well as in the south and the fame of these artists is ever increasing."[74]

Courting national consumers, companies pitched the music as an ambiguous combination of folklore and hillbilly stereotypes that ultimately denied much difference between the two. Promotional materials initially contained little of the humor found in race record ads or in previous depictions of comical rube stereotypes. This marked an important distinction between race and old-time marketing. While the industry promoted early race records as a continuation of minstrelsy, companies suggested that early recordings of southern white audiences constituted a break from earlier stage stereotypes. They introduced old-time records as upstanding and serious folklore. Advertisements featured photos of recording artists dressed in suits. Catalogue covers offered noncaricatured portrayals of white couples dancing to a country fiddler in rustic barns or houses, pictures that implied wholesome fun set in a previous era. Okeh announced that its field trip to Atlanta to record Carson and other singers had led to the discovery of "these mountaineers" and "uncovered a brand new field for record sales."[75] No mention was made of Carson's experiences in textile factories and the streets of Atlanta. Advertising copy rather emphasized the obscurity and age of Carson's material, as well as Okeh's efforts to bring this ancient music to the attention of the public. "Minstrel from the mountains of Georgia strikes public's fancy in Okeh recordings of quaint and little-known numbers," an article declared in 1925. It continued, "The majority of these songs belong to the early period of pioneer life in the mountains; many of the numbers have been collected in the hills, and many of them have been written by Carson himself."[76] The copy suggested that Carson was a holdover from a previous era, a vessel not unlike many folklorists' informants whose music was collected in the backwoods and was defined by its difference from modern popular music. The article explained Carson's music through its isolation from urban life, industrial work, and popular music, when it was in fact a product of Carson's extensive experience in these realms.

In 1925, Okeh began using hillbilly stereotypes in reference to the music. Ralph Peer recorded a white string band from Galax, Virginia, composed of Tony Alderman, John Rector, and Al and Joe Hopkins. Peer asked the name of their group and the musicians met him with stone silence. "There hadn't been anyone that ever mentioned we ought to call ourselves something or other growing up, cause we didn't think we needed that," recalled Alderman. "Finally Al Hopkins says, 'Well, we're only a bunch of hillbillies from North Carolina.'" A few months later Okeh released their first record with the name "The Hill Billies" blazoned across the label. Southern musicians had been playing upon hillbilly stereotypes for years at fiddle conventions, but the bold moniker worried Alderman. "We didn't know whether to leave home or what, because that was sort of fighting words if you said it just right."[77] He stayed away from Galax for a few years. Upon his return, he was surprised to discover that local residents had embraced the term. "Things happened so fast that by the time I did get home the name was real dignified," he marveled. "Country people would go into a music store, ask for Hill Billy records, and the salesman would show them all the new country records just out. They just didn't bother with the ritzy kind. The name "Hill Billy" sort-of classified them."[78]

White southern musicians themselves soon noticed the marketing value of hillbilly imagery. They partially embraced the stereotype just as African American artists had latched onto minstrel imagery in the coon song era. Groups adopted tongue-in-cheek names that played upon hillbilly clichés: the Georgia Crackers, the Fruit Jar Guzzlers, Chenowerth's Cornfield Symphony Orchestra, the Carolina Tar Heels, Chitwood's Georgia Mountaineers, the Blue Ridge Cornshuckers, the Mississippi Possum Hunters.

Many of these monikers cut two ways, advertising both a general hillbilly image and a specific state or local identity. The combination corresponded to the industry strategy to sell old-time tunes simultaneously as local music for hometown fans and as comical yet nostalgic hill country music for the masses. The pitch worked. Ulysses J. Walsh of Marion, Virginia, began rewriting the standard ad copy provided by New York firms to appeal to his local consumers. "Special emphasis was laid on the hill-billy records and it immediately began to evince more pulling power," he maintained. Walsh's store mailed circulars to local residents describing hillbilly records in "a light and rather humorous fashion": " 'The Big Rock Candy Mountains' describes Hobo Heaven. There hooch gushes through rocks, you don't have to change your socks, and indignant citizens have hanged the Turk who invented the work."[79] Like the use of minstrel clichés to sell race records, hillbilly humor confirmed caricatures of white rural culture while assuring white southern audiences that they were in on the joke.

Nowhere were old-time music's connections to this dual legacy of hillbilly stereotypes more evident than in the collection of what came to be known as rural drama recordings. Inserting snatches of music into comedy skits, these discs were reinventions of the rube records popular in the early years of the century. The new records traded the rube, often a character from the Yankee North, for the southern mountaineer or hillbilly. Indications are that the skits were often encouraged and sometimes written by record producers and scouts, helping southern string bands project a hillbilly image palatable to record buyers across the nation. Some rural drama recordings attempted to portray artists in their natural southern habitat, employing an almost folkloric or ethnographic tone as they explained what occurred at southern general stores, bee hunts, or corn shuckings. "Now folks, you know it's a custom in these here mountains to shuck old people's corn when they're old and can't work," began a recording by the Blue Ridge Corn Shuckers in 1927. "We will begin now with what we call a regular old corn shucking ceremony. We want everyone to take part in this for everyone in these mountains can play some kind of music." Other records depicted southern musicians' local performances, be they dramatizations of medicine shows, county fairs, or fiddling conventions. Some of the most successful rural drama recordings, however, traded in hillbilly comedy. Earlier rube recordings had sold the supposed humor of isolated rural residents in their own milieu or encountering the big city and modern civilization. The new recordings did the same. Yet they added moonshine to the mix, transforming their protagonists from naïfs to rebels, defiant lawbreakers who chose and defended their own isolation from government authorities in the age of Prohibition.[80]

An early adopter—and perhaps the master—of the form was a Georgia string band called the Skillet Lickers. In 1926, Gil Tanner, a veteran of fiddling conventions, formed the Skillet Lickers with the guitarist Riley Puckett and the fiddler Clayton McMichen. The group became one of the most successful old-time string bands of the 1920s. Among their best-selling records were the nineteen rural drama discs they released between 1927 and 1930, including "A Fiddler's Convention in Georgia," "Kickapoo Medicine Show," and "A Corn Licker Still in Georgia," a series eventually running to seven discs, the first of which reportedly sold 250,000 copies. The Skillet Lickers' rural drama recordings often adhered to the conventions of the rube genre while subtly transforming them. Several featured pun-infested repartee between the band of hillbillies and a clueless urban straight man. When a government agent arrives to take the census, one of the band members replies, "Come up and get what senses we got, I don't know what we will do." Such bits echoed not only "The Arkansas Traveler," the ubiquitous nineteenth-century template for hillbilly humor, but also the standard minstrel show banter between the dignified interlocutor and the blackface end men. Yet the Skillet Lickers often would follow such passive aggressive punning with explicit assertions of their own power. "Well, we don't usually talk to strangers up here. We know our racket, and know what we going to do," another band member quickly tells the census taker. "Be careful about the questions that you ask, and don't ask too many of them. And sit down over there and keep quiet 'til we get this fiddling over, and we'll try to fix you up." Such bold demands were unheard of in rube recordings or blackface routines. They enabled the Skillet Lickers to inhabit the hillbilly stereotype in a new way, to lay claim to a popular genre of commercialized humor while demonstrating that their embrace of the hillbilly guise was one of many tactical maneuvers they employed to challenge the authority of the state or the pretensions of city slickers. Indeed, on their recordings the band usually greeted revenuers and other authorities with shotguns in addition to puns.[81]

Throughout their recordings, the Skillet Lickers never disappeared into their hillbilly caricatures. Listeners were constantly reminded that they were hearing professional musicians at the top of their game. After the group is hauled into prison for moonshining in the popular "Corn Licker Still" series, for example, they gain an early release when fan mail swamps the warden's desk. By maintaining these dual personas, the band could trade on the popularity of hillbilly stereotypes without being reduced to them. Perhaps the clearest example of this came not from the Skillet Lickers but from Charlie Poole and the Allegheny Highlanders. In 1929, the popular string band released a four-side series titled "A Trip to New York." Its premise of rural yokels encountering the city echoed a legion of earlier cuts such as "Two Rubes at the Vaudeville" (1904), "Three Rubes Seeing New York City" (1907), or "Old Country Fiddler in New York" (1914). Yet the Highlanders did not come to the city to marvel at the metropolis. They came to get paid. The series dramatizes a successful audition and recording session with the Brunswick Record Company. While waiting for their audition, the band decides to make a little cash busking in the city streets. They drop right into "The Sidewalks of New York," the Tin Pan Alley tune written in 1894 by James Blake and Charles Lawlor that had just been resurrected as part of New Yorker Al Smith's 1928 presidential campaign. Here were hillbillies who knew what they were doing. They not only had a firm grasp of American popular music; they also knew how to appeal to New Yorkers with the same ease and expertise they had used to court consumers back home in the hills.[82]

BLACK FOLK AND HILLBILLY POP 7

Industry Enforcement of the Musical Color Line

The first selection on Columbia's old-time music list, inaugurated in 1925, was "Alexander's Ragtime Band." Jewish immigrant Irving Berlin composed the song in 1911. While lacking the polyrhythms or syncopation that characterized its titular genre, "Alexander's Ragtime Band" did fit within Tin Pan Alley's long tradition of representing African American music through minstrel imagery. Alexander was a common name for blackface characters. Berlin's lyrics featured familiar minstrel dialect, and the melody quoted Stephen Foster's "Old Folks at Home" in case listeners cared "to hear Swanee played in ragtime." The composition was a breakaway hit and helped establish Berlin as one of the most popular and prolific songwriters in the country.[1]

The Columbia recording of "Alexander's Ragtime Band" was by the white artist Ernest Thompson, born in 1892 near Winston-Salem, North Carolina, performing on guitar, harmonica, and kazoo along with whistling. After learning to play the guitar as a youth, the blind musician spent years as a street singer coaxing money from passing crowds by performing popular hits on a wide variety of instruments. "A lot of times when he'd be out there playing, people would gather around him," his sister later recalled. "He'd sing 'It's a Long Way to Tipperary' and all these songs, like 'Smile Awhile.' All those people who listened would pay him for singing. That's the way he made a living." Thompson came to the attention of William Parks, Columbia's regional representative, who took the singer to the company's New York studio in April 1924.[2]

Accompanying himself on guitar and harmonica, Thompson cut twenty sides during the visit. A large number of the selections were relatively recently minted Tin Pan Alley compositions: the anti-Prohibition song "How Are You Goin' to Wet Your Whistle" (1919); the snappy ode to the South "Are You from Dixie?" (1915); the Native American exotica number "Snow Deer" (1913); and others, including "Don't Put a Tax on the Beautiful Girls" (1919) and "Coon Crap Game," a version of the ubiquitous "I Got Mine" (1901). Thompson delivered these tunes with a smooth, high tenor that betrayed his southern accent yet remained faithful to the original compositions. His steady eighth-note guitar rhythms and harmonica distinguished the discs from earlier recordings of the songs by industry stalwarts such as Billy Murray even as Columbia released them on the popular music lists.[3] Upon his return home, the Winston-Salem newspaper ran a story celebrating the local recording artist who sang "old southern melodies and folk songs." A promotional story in *Talking Machine World* dubbed Thompson's music "old southern songs, dances and ballads."[4]

These were inaccurate descriptions of Thompson's repertoire, yet they illustrated what was becoming a common interpretation of white southern musicians who attempted to enter the popular music business. Regardless of their apparent love for mass-produced pop, southern musicians were portrayed as folk musicians. Their isolation from the currents of popular music was a major selling point—at the same time that their recorded music may now appear to contradict the sales pitch. This was no mistake and it was no ruse. It was a result of the evolving relationship between the minstrel and the folkloric paradigms, between the notion that genuine music was an act and the insistence that it was not. When Columbia decided to consolidate its list of records by white southern musicians into a separate category in its catalogue in 1925, the company suggested no incongruity in touting Irving Berlin's minstrel-inspired ode to black dance music as the sound of the white rural South.

The commercial recordings of the 1920s offer dramatically different portraits of black and white southerners' musical worlds. Industry enforcement of racial and marketing categories on race records left relatively little evidence of black southerners' long investment in commercial pop or their participation in the region's interracial music culture. Old-time catalogues of white southern music, on the other hand, were stuffed with evidence of both. Phonograph companies gave white southerners more freedom to record a wide variety of music. A number of factors influenced the industry's decision: the treacherous politics of segregation, the breakaway popularity of the blues, a regional market segmentation strategy, a belief in the importance of native singers, concerns about the redundancy of songs across a company's catalogues, and the desire to control copyrights. Above all, the different characters of the race and old-time lists were the results of the uneven replacement of the minstrel paradigm of performative authenticity by the folkloric paradigm that connected racialized music to racialized bodies. The transition was messy and incomplete resulting in a series of folkloric/minstrel mongrels. Nevertheless, the folkloric paradigm came to dominate industry approaches to southern black music in the mid-1920s, well before it gained ascendancy in the old-time trade. Scouts demanded that African American musicians perform what they considered to be black music. They understood hillbilly music, with a few important caveats, to be whatever hillbillies played.

Enforcing the Color Line on Race Records

The Columbia record scout Frank Walker claimed that the separate race and old-time categories did not represent the music he heard while traveling through the South. The southern color line was permeable, he insisted, and black and white musicians often influenced each other. "In those days in the outskirts of a city like Atlanta, you had your colored section full of colored people and you had your white, I am sorry to use the word, they used to call them 'white trash', but they were right close to each other," he explained. "They would pass each other every day. And a little of the spiritualistic singing of the colored people worked over into the white hillbilly and a little of the white hillbilly worked over into what the colored people did, so you got a little combination of the two things there."[5] Such close proximity made recording trips much easier. Local record dealers serving an interracial local clientele knew most of the strong musicians in their area and could bring them together when the recording engineers arrived. "If you were recording in Texas, well, you might have a week in which you recorded your country music, cowboy music thrown in, and a little Spanish music from across the border," Walker noted. "And your next week might be devoted to your so-called 'race music.' Because they both came from the same area, and with the same general ideas."[6]

African American musicians recorded some evidence of this interracial music culture during the 1920s, but it was relatively rare. Both black and white artists recorded examples of the string band styles that had developed throughout the South. String bands utilizing combinations of fiddles and guitars were among the major features of old-time catalogues. They performed a variety of tunes, from traditional fiddle pieces and hoedowns through minstrelsy, rags, blues, and popular songs. Black artists made a number of records that revealed their debt to the same musical traditions as their white counterparts on hillbilly records. The guitarists Henry Thomas from Texas and Blind Blake from the Southeast each recorded songs with square dance calls. Peg Leg Howell, from Georgia, released a version of the standard "Turkey in the Straw" titled "Turkey Buzzard Blues" featuring the fiddler Eddie Anthony. Mississippi John Hurt cut a version of the ubiquitous "Frankie and Johnny." Julius Daniels, from South Carolina, recorded a handful of riveting fingerstyle piedmont blues, but he also cut "Can't Put the Bridle on the Mule This Morning," a song with common stock ancestry that could have fit nicely on an old-time list.[7] A few recordings feature white and black musicians performing this music together. The black fiddler Jim Booker joined white musicians to form Taylor's Kentucky Boys in 1927. The same year found the African American harmonica player El Watson recording with white musicians for Victor in Bristol, Tennessee. In 1928, the Georgia Yellowhammers featured the black fiddler Andrew Baxter on "G Rag." Such direct collaborations were extremely rare.[8]

More common were black and white renditions of similar songs or styles forged during the late nineteenth or early twentieth centuries. Ragtime provided one base of commonality. Ragtime developed among black composers and instrumentalists in the late nineteenth century. By the 1920s, both black and white southerners had converted ragtime to the string band format. African American musicians such as Blind Blake or Coley Jones, the leader of the Dallas String Band, recorded a number of rags, as did white string bands such as the Skillet Lickers.[9] Older mass-produced pop songs provided the largest source of common stock tunes on 1920s recordings. "I Got Mine" (1901) was recorded by the black artist Frank Stokes and by the white performers John Carson and the Skillet Lickers.[10] White singers Ernest Thompson, Henry Whitter, and Cliff Carlisle, and the Leake County Revelers recorded the coon song ditty "Chicken (You Can Roost behind the Moon)," as did black artists such as the Beale Street Sheiks (with Frank Stokes).[11] "Hesitation Blues," versions of which were published almost simultaneously by W. C. Handy and by the composers Billy Smythe, Scott Middleton, and Art Gillham in 1915, was cut by a variety of black performers including James Reese Europe, Esther Bigeou, and Sam Collins as well as white performers ranging from Charlie Poole and the Reaves White Country Ramblers to the Grand Ole Opry regular Uncle Dave Macon, whose version was released under the title "Hill Billie Blues," perhaps the first use of the hillbilly moniker to describe the old-time trade.[12] One of the most popular interracial compositions was the medicine show stalwart "In the Jailhouse Now." A number of white and black southerners cut versions of the tune. The music and lyrics differed from one recording to the next. The black artists Blind Blake and the Memphis Jug Band featured lyrics about African American electoral politics in the age of segregation and disfranchisement. Blake depicted a black porter in the Northeast who lands in jail after convincing others to vote twice for a black candidate. The Memphis Jug Band depicted a similar scene before singing, "Instead of him staying at home / Letting those white folks' business alone / He's in the jailhouse now." The explicit political context was absent from white renditions of the tune. White singers such as Jimmie Rodgers or the duo of Darby and Tarlton sang of less politicized crimes such as gambling. The musical commonalities across the various versions of the song, however, leave little doubt as to the presence of overlapping racial music cultures in the South.[13]

Some of the most successful African American recording artists to feature common stock tunes were the busking denizens of Beale Street in Memphis. The Memphis Jug Band led by Will Shade; Gus Cannon's Jug Stompers, including the guitarist Ashley Thompson; the Beale Street Sheiks featuring the singer and guitarist Frank Stokes: the recorded repertoire of these artists contained a wide variety of blues, minstrelsy-inspired tunes, popular coon songs such as "The Bully Song," "I Got Mine," and "Chicken You Can Roost behind the Moon," and even the Tin Pan Alley–inspired tune by the Memphis Jug Band, "I'll See You in the Spring, When the Birds Begin to Sing." The diversity of the selections suggests some of the sounds they used to court passing listeners or to entertain crowds at local picnics and frolics. Here was the sound of southern working musicians intent on making money with their music.[14]

Race records that revealed their commonalities with hillbilly music were the exceptions that proved the rule of the musical color line. Phonograph companies largely did what they could to enforce categorical and marketing distinctions between race and old-time records. Companies listed them in separate categories, advertised them in different niche-marketed periodicals, and promoted them as representative of distinct musical traditions. Part of the impetus for creating distinct race and old-time catalogues stemmed from the fear of alienating consumers in the Jim Crow South. Frank Walker recalled that he often came across what he considered black hillbilly bands, yet he could not market them as such. "You had to be very careful about it, you see," he explained, "because there were many laws in the Southern states, which for instance, if I recorded a colored group and yet it was of a hillbilly nature, I couldn't put that on my little folders that I got out on hillbilly music or visa versa."[15]

Walker learned the importance of separating race and old-time records in 1928, when he released "Laughing and Crying Blues" by Lee and Austin Allen in Columbia's race record series. The Allen brothers, a white duo from Sewanee, Tennessee, were accomplished musicians who had worked dances, medicine shows, and radio gigs in Chattanooga and other cities. Their quick, well-executed "Laughing and Crying Blues" sounded a lot like many of the blues already on record by black artists such as Papa Charlie Jackson, Blind Blake, or Gus Cannon. Lee laid down a solid guitar rhythm as Austin embellished the harmony with eighth-note arpeggios on his banjo. Austin's vocal followed the familiar three-line blues format until he erupted in melodic crying and laughter, a familiar convention ever since George W. Johnson recorded "The Laughing Song" in the 1890s. Lee responded with improvised lines on his kazoo.[16] Columbia promoted the recording with a *Chicago Defender* advertisement featuring a caricatured drawing of two identical black men, one laughing and the other, of course, crying. "What a laugh you will get out of this sobbing, weeping, laughing, howlingly funny record by Austin and Lee Allen," the copy promised. No mention was made of the brothers' race.[17] The Allens threatened to sue Columbia for $250,000. Musical commonalities did not mitigate the corporeal color line. "We were trying to get into vaudeville back then. It would have hurt us in getting dates if people who didn't know us thought we were black," Lee later explained. They never filed the suit, but they left Columbia for Victor where they worked with Ralph Peer, who had recently begun freelancing as a scout for the company. Peer kept the duo off of the race record list, but he insisted that they "stay on the blues."[18] The lesson was clear. The label "race record" did not identify a musical sound or style. It defined the race of a musician.

Yet while the race record moniker identified the race of performers, it also shaped the sounds they were able to make. Most companies attempted to limit African American musicians to recording material that would fit easily within corporate conceptions of black music. They thus denied black artists the opportunity to wax the variety of classical, Tin Pan Alley, or hillbilly music many of them had been performing for years on the nation's stages. Industry censorship of black artists was so ubiquitous that Black Swan Records made it a point of their advertising campaign in 1923. "This company made the only Grand Opera Records ever made by Negro," an ad maintained. "All others confine this end of their work to blues, rags, comedy numbers, etc."[19] J. Mayo Williams, the African American scout at Paramount, was only too familiar with the censorship of black repertoires. As a black executive he was allowed to work only with black artists. "They didn't want me to be identified with the white records, or the white side of the situation at all," he explained. While companies segregated black and white musicians, the industry also worked to confine African American artists to recording selections it had come to associate with black music. Williams knew that artists such as Alberta Hunter "could sing as many popular numbers as blues." Yet when a black performer came to him with a ballad or pop song, "I would very quickly say: 'Well, we can't use it . . . write me a blues.' In doing it that way I'd save a lot of embarrassment for myself, the company, and the person," he explained.[20] Williams ultimately frowned on the race record designation, finding it both artistically limiting and demeaning to black people by insinuating a gulf between black music and the popular music field that African American artists had done so much to help build.

It was, of course, not the goal of phonograph companies' southern strategy to chronicle the region's links to Tin Pan Alley or to capture black musicians' diverse repertoires. Scouts sought songs that would sell, and the industry had determined that African Americans singing the blues sold. When they headed into the southern climes, record scouts sought regional versions of the blues, both one of the most popular musical styles in the land and the new marker of black authenticity.

Southern African American artists, similarly, had no intention of committing their entire repertoire to wax. They often approached record scouts as they did other paying audiences: musicians gave listeners what they wanted and took the money. Mississippian Samuel Chatman, for example, recalled an early recording session for Okeh as something of a con game. Chatman was part of a loose coalition of musicians surrounding the popular string band the Mississippi Sheiks that included guitarist Walter Vinson and two of Sam's brothers, the fiddler Lonnie Chatman and the guitarist Bo Carter. The men were musical omnivores. Plying their trade in streets, storefronts, and cafes, they performed blues and ballads, fiddle tunes, coon songs, and the latest Broadway hits. It is useful to recall Samuel Chatman's summation of his early years of hustling for tips: "You take a fellow that can play anything, he can get a job more or less anywhere." The musicians became some of the most prolific artists on the race records of the late 1920s and early 1930s. They cut a number of fiddle features and pop tunes, but the blues dominated their recorded output. Chatman did not seem to notice. When he arrived at his first Okeh recording session, music was less on his mind than money. He was discouraged to learn that Polk Brockman was not paying much per selection. Chatman and his fellow musicians changed their arrangements on the spot—creating a number of different combinations of musicians so they could record more selections and make more cash. "They wouldn't give you but $20, so I'd get with two here and other two or three'd get together over there and that's the way we made us money. Sort of stretch it, you know, so all of us would have some." Chatman gave Brockman what the record scout wanted to hear, but he used his musical skill and flexibility to get the most out of the encounter. He had been doing the same thing with live audiences for years.[21]

The industry expectation that black artists should record the blues was also propelled by a shift from minstrel to folkloric marketing strategies in the mid-1920s. The shift was subtle and always incomplete. It culminated at the same time that companies were enacting a number of other changes in their marketing of southern music: the inauguration of Southern recording expeditions; the separation of race and old-time selections from their pop catalogues; the expansion of minstrel imagery to advertise blues records; and the identification of what came to be known as rural or country blues. Even as companies expanded their minstrel marketing tactics, they increasingly identified rural southern blues as folk music.

Record companies advertised their expertise in black music by using the language folklorists had developed regarding purity, isolation, and timelessness. This was first evident in industry promotion of spiritual recordings. Spirituals, for many within the industry, were unique both for their unquestionable morality and their long acceptance as folk songs within the world of high culture. In 1920, Columbia promoted songs of the Fisk University Jubilee Singers as retentions from ancient Africa. "Where for ages the Congo has cut its golden thread through the dark green of the African jungles negro music was born," a Columbia catalogue claimed. "In the singing of the Fisk University Jubilee Singers there is a rhythm as of vanished beating feet and the monotony of the simple three chord harmony of primitive music. The singing of this negro quartette is very appealing."[22] The industry touted the African origins of the black spirituals as evidence of the songs' uncontrived emotionalism and timeless value. In an article in 1926 discussing Paul Robeson's sophisticated presentation of the spirituals, *Talking Machine World* quoted an editorial by E. H. Droop. "Many of these melodies are unquestionably of ancient tribal origin and were brought to this country more than 300 years ago by those poor beings who, torn from their homes, were sold into slavery," wrote Droop. "Added to and taken from as time went on, they gradually became a fountain of hope and consolation—always expressing the negroes' faith in God and belief in immortality."

This lineage, combined with the spirituals' expression of Christian faith, resulted in music that was far more important, lasting, and pure than other race records, the article claimed. "Those music lovers with a proper appreciation of music values have always ranked 'spirituals' in their proper position as classics, with a distinctive and everlasting appeal. Others, however, were apt to confuse this type of record with the more widely know 'race' record which has a wide appeal but is as different from the 'spiritual' as a jazz or 'nut' song of the present day is from an operatic selection rendered by Caruso."[23]

Some associated the folk purity of the spirituals with their roots in the American South, a land separate from the urban black cultural centers of the Northeast. In 1921, *Talking Machine World* announced the availability of Okeh recordings by the Virginia Female Jubilee Singers. The copy touted Okeh's lengthy field trips through the South in search of authentic black music, a goal more often associated with folklorists than phonograph companies. "For months the company's representatives had been touring the South in search of artists who were capable of interpreting realistically the old-fashioned negro spirituals and they recently discovered this quartet of singers in the country regions of Virginia and engaged them for the Okeh library," the article reported. Okeh argued that the group was important for its religious devotion and its command of an orally transmitted repertoire. "These four young girls are so filled with the true religious spirit that they have an extensive knowledge of all the spirituals which have attained any degree of popularity, and which have been handed down in folk-song fashion from one generation to another," the article declared.[24] Borrowing arguments from the academy, Okeh insisted that its discovery and preservation of ancient, orally transmitted material set the company apart from its peers in the industry.[25]

In the mid-twenties, the industry tentatively began to apply these arguments about black musical authenticity to the blues. This shift was encouraged by an increasing acceptance of the blues as legitimate folk song by prominent scholars and writers. Mirroring the reevaluation of the blues within the academy, people in the phonograph industry began describing the blues in folkloric terms as a creation and cultural tradition of African Americans rather than as a reflection of minstrel-styled stereotypes. Perry Bradford, the southern migrant, promoter, and songwriter who used arguments about black primitivism to convince Okeh to record Mamie Smith, was one of the first to argue that the blues were folk music in the industry press. "Blues originated from old darky folklore in slavery times. It, therefore, becomes natural for colored people to sing and play 'blues' numbers," he declared in 1921.[26] Beginning two years later, industry press used the language of folklore to celebrate the blues singer Bessie Smith. *Talking Machine World* announced, "Miss Smith is the possessor of a voice of that peculiarly desirable quality for which the old-fashioned colored folks of the South were noted, and her records reflect her individual personality." Smith, the author claimed, particularly impressed many white musicians, who "seem to recognize and appreciate her unique artistry."[27] No longer representing minstrel stereotypes, her blues provided "an opportunity for white people to see the progress made by the colored performers," explained a synopsis of Smith's sold-out concert for a segregated white audience in Atlanta.[28]

If it gave white listeners a new way to interpret the blues, the industry's shift toward folklore also was propelled by the desire to attract black consumers. A few years after "Crazy Blues" shook the nation, companies could no longer deny the African American market for race records. In an article in 1923 announcing Aeolian's entry into the race record business, *Talking Machine World* declared that the records were designed for black consumption. "It has been recognized for some time that the negroes had their own favorites among artists of their own race and that records by such artists, particularly of 'blues,' had a much stronger appeal than similar records made by white singers," the writer explained. A month later, the journal reported, " 'Blues' are distinctly the creation of colored people. They live them, they breathe them and they write them and from this viewpoint some of the best 'blue' numbers, naturally, will come from colored writers."[29]

In 1925, Okeh advertised its "Great Blue Book of Blues" by claiming "the delicate passions of humanity—all have been made real and articulate by our exclusive Okeh Artists." The evocation of a universal humanism echoed the folkloric quest for fundamental human truths and stood in stark contrast to minstrelsy's performance of racial difference. The campaign's slogan touted, "Genuine Race Artists Make Genuine Blues for Okeh."[30] It was a telling departure from Bob Cole's self-identification as a "genuine minstrel" and Okeh's previous blackface advertisements for "Crazy Blues." Cole's "genuine Negro songs by a genuine Negro minstrel" had made the argument that African American artists were better interpreters of minstrel material than were their white counterparts. It nevertheless maintained a relationship between genuine black song and minstrelsy. The new slogan from Okeh severed this very connection. It equated black artists with black music and left white performers—and the entire blackface tradition—out of the picture entirely.

At the same time that the industry stopped rooting the blues in minstrelsy, it began promoting a categorical distinction between the sophisticated and modern urban blues developed by the likes of Mamie Smith and Ethel Waters and the raw rural blues of musicians who lived in the South. Companies began suggesting that the region's blues represented the music's more authentic past, just as they had suggested about the spirituals a few years before. In 1926 Paramount offered another twist on Bob Cole's bid for genuine minstrels when it advertised Blind Lemon Jefferson's debut as "a real old-fashioned blues by a real old-fashioned blues singer."[31] The previous crop of urban blues was the product of the commercial theater and professional songwriters, the pitch implied. Jefferson, isolated from modern civilization and the modern blues, sang the older music of the southern folk.

The difference between urban and country blues often was more about marketing than music. Indeed, it is difficult to draw a definitive distinction between southern musicians who might represent the region's milieu and their northern counterparts who were deeply invested in the national music industry. Southern musicians had been listening to mass-produced music for decades. Folklorists regularly wrote of hearing commercial pop songs from their southern black informants. In the 1920s, black southerners bought urban blues records and integrated the modern music into their lives. At the same time, the urban blues was crafted with the help of a legion of southern migrants to northern cities. Papa Charlie Jackson, whose recording debut for Paramount in 1924 helped alert the industry to the sales potential of what came to be known as country blues, spent most of his professional career in Chicago. Jackson, believed to be a New Orleans native born around 1895, spent years touring with medicine shows and music troupes through the nation, and his music reveals the imprint of the commercialized minstrelsy so popular in the early twentieth century. A recorded duet with the southern guitar virtuoso Blind Blake, another southern migrant to Chicago, finds the pair exchanging comic patter in the stylized dialect of minstrel show veterans. At the same time, Jackson squeezed complex rhythms and harmonies out of his banjo—his instrument of choice—on recordings that often sounded like solo performances of the blues arrangements being recorded by urban blues singers such as Bessie Smith—from Chattanooga, Tennessee. Indeed, Paramount touted Jackson as both a break from and a continuation of the blues recorded by urban female singers. "Only man living who sings, self-accompanied, for Blues records," an ad for his debut disc exclaimed. "Be convinced that this man Charlie can sing and play the Blues even better than a woman can."[32] Jackson, in fact, recorded with several musicians involved in the urban blues scene, including Ida Cox, Ma Rainey, and Freddie Keppard. His recording with Keppard, a cornet player, bandleader, and giant of the New Orleans jazz scene, was a slow-drag reimagination of Jackson's popular number "Salty Dog Blues," a tune later reimagined again by the Allen Brothers. It was a transformative performance. Jackson's controlled and laconic delivery positioned him as the sophisticated voice against Keppard's unhinged interjection, "Sing it, Papa Charlie!," performed with enough gusto to disintegrate any distinction between rural primitivism and urban cool.[33] Moving to Chicago, Jackson was only one step removed from numerous other race record artists who had spent formative years performing in streets, storefronts, and medicine shows yet did not make the sojourn north.

The uneasy fusion of the minstrel and folkloric paradigms in the phonograph industry's promotion of race records tied southern African American artists to stereotypes of black isolation. It set them apart from both mass-produced music and the white patrons who had dropped coins in their cups and now bought their records. Ironically, race record manufacturers asked black southerners to embody minstrel stereotypes constrained by folkloric values. The results of these policies were profound. Johnnie Temple, Johnny Shines, Charley Patton, Blind Lemon Jefferson, Blind Willie McTell, Jim Jackson, Robert Johnson, and a host of other black southern musicians—artists who had performed a wide variety of music during their live performances— recorded blues material almost exclusively. "If I could record whatever I want to play, I would have recorded some great numbers. Ballads and things like that," lamented the pianist Little Brother Montgomery, born in 1906 in Louisiana, who began his recording career in 1930. "But they have had us in a bracket: If you wasn't no great blues player, or played some hell out of a boogies or somethin', they wasn't gonna let us record no way." African American musicians left a remarkable and rich musical legacy on race records, but their recorded blues did not begin to chronicle the diverse and complex body of music with which they had forged their earlier careers as live musicians.[34] White southern artists faced a different challenge. They had to paint the pop tunes they loved with a patina of down-home credibility. Southern black recording artists were encouraged to pretend they did not know about modern pop music. White southerners had to make Tin Pan Alley sound like a farm road.

Old Time Pop Songs

Hillbilly catalogues were overrun with mass-produced pop songs. Sentimental ballads, coon shouts, snappy odes to the South, love songs, Broadway ditties, and contemporary dance hits: southern white artists recorded them in droves. When the country music historian Charles Wolfe tabulated the sources of the 732 releases in Columbia's "Familiar Tunes—Old and New" series, the most successful old-time list in the industry between 1925 and 1932, he found that approximately 27 percent of the songs had begun their lives as conventional pop songs. About 34 percent were traditional songs and instrumentals, while the remainder consisted of original hillbilly compositions, event songs, comedy numbers, and, the largest remaining category, gospel tunes, a species he did not parse according to commercial or traditional origins.[35] Wolfe's figures testify to the long history of pop music in the South. Many of the songs recorded by early old-time artists were mass-produced compositions that had already circulated throughout the nation through the mediums of sheet music, touring shows, and phonograph records. Southern musicians and audiences had been imbibing and reproducing Tin Pan Alley songs for decades before the invention of the old-time and race record trade, and musicians who had been entertaining audiences on southern street corners brought this music with them into the recording studio. Its presence, in the face of some industry attempts to discourage it, suggests that southern musicians understood themselves as part and parcel of the national music business, and by extension the national cultural conversation—even as they recorded a healthy amount of the traditional music of the region.

Charles Wolfe's tabulations also suggest a significant difference between the recorded outputs of black and white southerners. Phonograph company expeditions captured only scant evidence of black southerners' engagement with Tin Pan Alley, while they apparently embraced that of white southerners. Pop tunes constituted over 25 percent of the Columbia old-time catalogue. The difference emerged for a number of reasons. Perhaps most revealing, the difference suggests the uneven development of the minstrel and folkloric paradigms in industry approaches to black and white southern repertoires. While the combination of minstrelsy and folklore discouraged southern black artists from revealing their pop music credentials, the combination encouraged white southern artists to do so. As Vernon Dalhart and Clarice Vance already had demonstrated, commercialized minstrel masquerades were a constitutive component of the white southern tradition.

Evidence of pop music on old-time records is abundant. Fiddlin' John Carson, for example, had a long personal history of performing commercial songs as well as traditional numbers before he entered the Okeh studio. His early recorded repertoire featured a wide variety of mass-produced music, including classic minstrel tunes such as "Old Dan Tucker" and Stephen Foster's "Old Folks at Home" (dubbed "Swanee River"), rural nostalgia pieces such as Will Hays's "Little Old Log Cabin in the Lane" (1871), sentimental ballads such as Gussie Davis's "In the Baggage Coach Ahead," coon songs such as "I Got Mine," a version of "I'm Glad My Wife's in Europe" (1914), a wartime vehicle for Al Jolson, as well as relatively new compositions such as "It Ain't Gonna Rain No Mo'," a refashioning of a common stock song published by the singer Wendell Hall in 1923 and recorded by a number of black and white southerners during the 1920s.[36] Carson delivered all of this material with his signature raspy voice and raw violin sound. There was no mistaking his recordings for those echoing from the Broadway stage, yet his engagement with the broad expanse of American popular music was not in doubt. If his sound separated him from his peers on the Okeh popular music list, his choice of material revealed his commonality. Carson's signature caterwaul was the product not of isolation from the popular music of the day but of his long-sought integration into it. He was a practiced musician. Even today his recordings sound brash, dissonant, and under-rehearsed. These are the exact qualities he cultivated to win numerous fiddle contests in Atlanta, coon dogs notwithstanding.

Other early old-time artists shared Carson's love of Tin Pan Alley tunes yet presented them with far clearer voices and smoother deliveries. Ernest Thompson's "Alexander's Ragtime Band," the inaugural release on Columbia's old-time list, was no mistake. A majority of the songs the North Carolinian recorded in his first session for Columbia in 1924 originated with commercial publishers. The guitarist and singer Riley Puckett also recorded a legion of popular songs for Columbia during the 1920s. In addition his work with the popular string band the Skillet Lickers, Puckett regularly recorded by himself or in duets with the fiddler Bob Nichols. Puckett, like Thompson, had a much smoother delivery than did John Carson. His popular material stuck relatively close to the published compositions. He recorded classic sentimental ballads such as Charles K. Harris's "Hello Central, Give Me Heaven" (1901) and "In the Shade of the Old Apple Tree" (1905), but he also recorded relatively recent compositions, including "I'm Drifting Back to Dreamland" (1922), "I'm Forever Blowing Bubbles" (1919), "Let the Rest of the World Go By" (1919), and "Don't You Remember the Time" (1919), to name only a few examples out of his extensive list of pop song recordings.[37]

The white old-time artist Charlie Poole, born in 1892 in Randolph County, North Carolina, also waxed a significant number of mass-produced pop songs for Columbia during the 1920s. He tended to favor coon songs from the previous generation of white and black Tin Pan Alley composers. Poole cut "You Ain't Talkin' to Me" (1909) by Shelton Brooks, the African American performer and writer who also penned the popular "Darktown Strutter's Ball" (1917) and the Sophie Tucker vehicle "One of These Days" (1911). He recorded "Good Bye Booze! A Coon Temperance Ditty" (ca.

1901), "The Girl I Loved in Sunny Tennessee" (ca. 1899), and "Sweet Refrain," Gussie Davis's ode to Stephen Foster (1894). Poole's "Coon from Tennessee" was a version of "I'm Goin' to Live Anyhow, 'til I Die," a song written around 1901 by Shepard N. Edmonds and performed by the African American singer Ernest Hogan and the white singer Clarice Vance. Poole's recording "He Rambled" was a version of "Oh! Didn't He Ramble" by Johnson, Cole, and Johnson.[38]

Carson, Puckett, and Poole were some of the most prolific and successful old-time artists of the 1920s, and it may be tempting to hear their broad repertoires as a byproduct and a cause of their success. It is instructive to look at some artists who were not particularly successful in their recording careers, musicians who cut a few songs and never recorded again. These lesser-known musicians might give us a better picture of the variety of music performed by southern artists whose careers were not dramatically affected by their recording experiences. The singer Connie Sides, for example, cut only six selections for Columbia in 1925. Included were "You're as Welcome as the Flowers in May" (ca. 1903); "Underneath the Southern Moon" (1905); the song of Irish longing "Where the River Shannon Flows," composed by James I. Russell (ca. 1906) and recorded by the celebrity John McCormack; "They Made It Twice as Nice as Paradise (And They Called it Dixieland)," a 1916 minstrel-inspired ode to the Old South; the Al Jolson vehicle "Mammy's Little Coal Black Rose" (1916); and "In the Shadow of the Pine," which would become an old-time standard recorded by, among others, Kelly Harrell, Fiddlin' Doc Roberts, the Carter Family, and Gene Autry.[39] Sides was accompanied by the guitar and harmonica of Ernest Thompson, with whom she recorded a few duets, including the ubiquitous minstrel-inspired song "At a Georgia Camp Meeting" (1897) by the Tin Pan Alley composer Kerry Mills, a song that enjoyed vocal recordings as well as instrumental renditions by John Philip Sousa and the Edison Military Band.[40] Little is known about Sides. Her delivery on "They Made It Twice as Nice as Paradise" features a rather weedy voice comfortable with the rhythmic complexities of the Tin Pan Alley song, yet her unsure intonation and weak breath control suggest that the young singer probably was not a veteran stage performer. But when she stepped in front of the whirling recording disc, Tin Pan Alley was on her mind.

Emery and John McClung, born in 1910 and 1906 respectively, were far more confident performers but left only a slightly larger recorded legacy than Connie Sides. The brothers began their musical careers playing their guitar and fiddle on the streets in the small town of Beckley, West Virginia. As the McClung Brothers, the white duo cut fourteen songs for the Brunswick and Paramount labels in the late 1920s. In addition to the traditional standard "Liza Jane," the duo recorded a few gospel tunes, some of their own compositions, and a number of well-known popular tunes. Selections included "It's a Long Way to Tipperary" (1912), the First World War anthem that fast became a fiddle favorite, "Chicken (You Can Roost Behind the Moon)" (1899), one of many versions of the coon song recorded by southerners in the 1920s, and the vaudeville hit "When You Wore a Tulip and I Wore a Big Red Rose" (1914), a Tin Pan Alley love song set in Kentucky whose lyrics declared, "You made life cheerie, when you called me dearie, 'twas down where the blue grass grows."[41]

The recorded repertoires of Riley Puckett and Charlie Poole, Connie Sides and the McClung Brothers show that southern artists chose to represent their musical worlds by singing pop songs. Even as their selections reached broadly across the spectrum of popular song from sentimental ballads to Irish-themed material, they gravitated toward Tin Pan Alley's depictions of southern music and culture. Southern artists used professionally penned odes to the region to celebrate and assert their own southern identities. In 1924, Ernest Thompson sang:

My home's a way down in Alabam'
On a plantation near Birmingham.
And one thing's certain.
I'm surely flirtin'.
With those southbound trains.

He was walking a well-trod path. From black artists such as Bob Cole, the Johnson Brothers, and Ethel Waters through white artists such as Clarice Vance and Marion Harris, southern musicians made names for themselves in the national music business by embracing commercial popular music while emphasizing their southern roots. Mamie Smith's recording of "Arkansas Blues" in 1921 shared a great deal with Thompson's cut. Each imagined the South from a northern clime and used the words of Tin Pan Alley to assert southern longing. "Are you from Dixie?" Thompson asked through the words of the Tin Pan Alley composer Jack Yellen. "Well, I'm from Dixie, too."[42]

Thompson's performance suggests the importance of a structural difference between the race and old-time marketing categories and reveals some of the nuances of the emerging musical color line. Both categories were defined by race, yet only the old-time list had a built-in presumption about the artists' regional affiliation. Race record artists were black. Old-time artists were white southerners. This distinction may have had a significant effect on southern musicians' ability to record pop music. Companies headed south to discover native singers who could sell phonographs to local consumers. Regional distinctions thus were very important for marketing purposes. Companies had to maintain these regional distinctions within the race record category, distinguishing black southern artists from their northern counterparts. They accomplished this distinction largely through the evocation of folklore. Race records, of course, featured a bounty of compositions by professional songwriters. Yet these songs almost exclusively were recorded by urban or northern artists. Black northerners performed modern music, marketing suggested, while black southerners performed old-fashioned blues. Selling regional distinctions through genre had two effects. On one hand, it discouraged "southern" black artists from recording Tin Pan Alley music. On the other, it suggested that black artists who played "northern" styles were not southern. White southern artists, on the other hand, enjoyed a structural separation from the pop catalogues. Regional distinctions were suggested by the separation of the popular and the old-time lists. Ironically, this distinction enabled white southern artists to record Tin Pan Alley tunes while maintaining their regional distinctiveness. Ernest Thompson's take on "Alexander's Ragtime Band" was marketed as southern in a way that Chattanooga native Bessie Smith's version of the tune was not. The first suggested Tin Pan Alley was part of the sound of southern white folk music; the second suggested Smith's migration away from the southern folk roots of the blues.

Nowhere is the integration of popular music into the old-time catalogue more evident than in the recorded work of Vernon Dalhart. The Texas opera singer turned "Negro dialect" performer made his final transformation into an old-time singer in 1924. Dalhart waxed the song "The Wreck of the Southern Old 97" for Edison after being pushed from the performance of Negro dialect and blues numbers by the emergence of race records. Already cut by Henry Whitter and Ernest Thompson, the song was fast becoming the "Crazy Blues" of the old-time trade, the song that every up-and-coming artist must record. In 1925, Dalhart recorded the song again, this time for Victor. Coupled with "The Prisoner Song," it became one of the best-selling discs in the history of the industry. Dalhart embraced his new home in the hillbilly business.[43]

Dalhart was the most prolific artist on the most successful old-time series, Columbia's "Familiar Tunes," between 1925 and 1932. Charles Wolfe estimates that his recordings constituted one third of the Columbia old-time list prior to 1928 at the same time that Dalhart was recording material under his own name and pseudonyms for a number of other labels. In some important ways, Vernon Dalhart was old-time music. His trained tenor accompanied by a simple guitar and harmonica was one of the most common and most commercially successful sounds of the old-time craze. After his transformation into a hillbilly singer, Dalhart largely recorded topical songs and old-time standards. Yet the singer continued to record Tin Pan Alley classics such as "After the Ball" and "In the Baggage Coach Ahead" as well as new compositions like "Ain't Gonna Rain No 'Mo" and the Eddie Cantor vaudeville vehicle "Doodle Doo Doo," selections from the Tin Pan Alley catalogue that he, and many of his southern fans, had known and loved for decades.[44]

If record companies enabled old-time artists to sing pop songs, they also encouraged white southerners to perform music that emerged out of the interracial music culture of the South. As the story of the Allen Brothers illustrates, white southern artists had far more freedom to record blues than black artists had to record ostensibly white styles. Legions of blues performances peppered old-time lists. Between 1925 and 1931, there were seventy-three blues titles on the Okeh old-time list alone. Old-time blues selections ranged wildly. Some had nothing to identify them as blues other than their title, just as many pop songs were dubbed "blues" in order to help sales. However, the sound of some sides—such as Henry Whitter's early classic "Lonesome Road Blues" or cuts by the guitarists Frank Hutchison and Riley Puckett and fiddlers such as Gid Tanner—suggest that they arose out of the contested interracial music culture of the early twentieth century. Others arose out of white artists gaining inspiration from race records. The Virginia banjoist Doc Boggs, for example, recorded a stirring version of the Ethel Waters and Alberta Hunter composition "Down South Blues" in 1927. Blind Lemon Jefferson records provided inspiration to a number of white southern artists. His influence can be heard in records such as Larry Hensley's version of "Match Box Blues" or Debs Mays's nuanced interpretation of the Jefferson style on "Soap Box Blues" under the pseudonym "Slim Jim."

White players listened and learned from black musicians and then used the blues to express their own feelings of longing or loss, joy or desire. Other old-time blues recordings chart the profound popularity and influence of the blue yodel style of the white singer Jimmie Rodgers, a native of Meridian, Mississippi, who developed his unique style through musical contact with fellow black railroad workers, his obsession with phonograph records, and his work in blackface. Indeed, many white southern blues recordings reveal their roots in minstrelsy. Herschel Brown's "Talking Nigger Blues," for example, offers conventional blackface patter delivered in the stuttering speech familiar to listeners through the long history of minstrel performance from Arthur Collins to Emmett Miller. White southern artists used the blues to perpetuate blackface stereotypes just as white recording artists used blues to reclaim their authority as imitators of black music prior to 1920. These interpretations were not mutually exclusive categories. In 1927, Riley Puckett recorded a solo guitar arrangement of the common stock song "John Henry." His intricate fingerstyle arrangement featuring a bottleneck slide technique revealed him to be a serious student of African American blues styles, yet he prefaced the performance with a speech noting how he learned the piece from "an old southern darkey I heard play coming down Decatur Street." Columbia released it under the title "A Darkey's Wail."[45]

The preponderance of blues and pop tunes on commercial old-time records does not mean that companies gave white southern artists free rein to record what they wished. Record scouts attempted to censor old-time artists' repertoire and shape the sound of their music in order to conform to industry marketing strategies. Clayton McMichen, a fiddler for the Skillet Lickers, recalled that Columbia's Frank Walker pushed the group away from recording some jazz-influenced numbers favored by McMichen in order to maintain the group's traditional image. McMichen wanted to perform "modern" music by replacing the horns in jazz arrangements with fiddles. The folk music historian Norm Cohen explained, "Walker assured them that there were far better bands in New York playing pop music; Columbia, he said, brought their recording equipment to Atlanta to record country music, not popular music.[46] McMichen's story reveals the limits of industry willingness to record hillbilly pop. Artists could wax popular songs, but they needed to maintain the sounds and instrumentation associated with southern tradition. At the same time, McMichen's tale demonstrates how race affected the conceptual categories of both popular and hillbilly music. While J. Mayo Williams lamented the ways in which the race record designation obscured the long African American influence on the sounds of popular music, the politics of the old-time trade may have involved the same process. Black music, defined by blues and jazz, in large part became the sound of popular music during the 1920s. Dubbing this music "modern" rather than jazz not only distanced it from the old-time music designed as a market alternative. It also severed the link between black music and popular music.

Yet by the late 1920s the censorship of old-time artists had less to do with maintaining racial distinctions than with maximizing profits. The music business was driven by copyrights on songs. Composers' royalty payments were often far more lucrative than profits from record sales. Companies therefore sought to control the copyrights on as many of the songs they recorded as possible. In the early days of race and old-time records, companies rarely mentioned copyrights or royalties to musicians who did not already know how the system worked. They simply paid artists a flat fee for each selection that they released. Payments ranged widely from five to one hundred dollars but usually sat somewhere around twenty-five dollars a selection. The fee essentially purchased both the recorded performance and the song (if composed by the performer), assuring that all future profits would accrue to the company rather than the artist. Musicians eventually got wise to the scam and demanded composer credit and copyright control. When he became a freelance scout for Victor in 1927, Ralph Peer pioneered the method of leasing copyrights from artists. For an additional upfront payment, Peer personally acquired the rights to the copyright for a limited time, usually about five years, after which the copyright reverted to the composer. Excluding the occasional monster hit, a song typically enjoyed the vast majority of its sales in the first five years after its release. Leasing copyrights made Peer a rich man. The industry was quick to adopt his strategy.[47]

Copyright concerns were a far weaker restriction than the demand for the blues that met black southern artists. They did, however, shape old-time catalogues in two important ways. Copyrights made record scouts more willing to record traditional folk songs than to allow hillbilly artists to sing popular tunes. Folk songs were cheap. "They were getting that stuff without royalties," Polk Brockman explained. "If they put on the pop tunes they'd naturally have to pay royalties on them."[48] This was unacceptable to Ralph Peer. He encountered a lot of white southern singers who wanted to record popular songs. "They never got a chance," he insisted.[49] Peer's distaste for southern renditions of pop songs stemmed partially from concern about catalogue redundancy. "We wouldn't let them record 'Home Sweet Home.' We found out the hard way that we wouldn't sell any of them. There's always been better records of 'Home Sweet Home,'" he claimed. "So by insisting on new material and leaning towards artists who could produce it for us, their own compositions, that created the so-called hillbilly business, and also the nigger business," he concluded.[50]

Yet Peer was perfectly willing to claim a copyright on someone else's song if he could get away with it. "When I worked with Fiddlin' John Carson, I wouldn't let him record a thing like 'Silver Threads among the Gold' or anything that already had wide distribution. He had a repertoire of about three hundred songs that you've never heard of before, things he'd acquired in his circus days, from other performers. Of course, they were all duly copyrighted and put over as new songs."[51] Peer also filed copyright claims on traditional folk songs. He later stated that half the selections he recorded with the white artists G. B. Grayson and Henry Whitter were "probably traditional songs, but these men, being what they were, didn't get the words from a book or from anybody else. They heard them and then they would forget part of them, and they'd make up their own version. These are all versions. I'll put it that way."[52]

The scramble to discover and define new music in the South put commercial record scouts in the folklore business. Identifying the provenance of songs put money in their pockets. The folklorist Robert W. Gordon asked the Victor Talking Machine Company to underwrite his collecting trip in 1925, arguing that his findings and expertise would be useful to the phonograph giant. "I knew that in a number of cases the firm was paying royalty to unscrupulous pretenders who had no [vestige] of right in the texts they sold; and I knew that in other cases there were ample grounds for suit for infringement if only the facts happened to fall into the hands of the right parties," Gordon later wrote to the company.[53] Ralph Peer took a different tack. He sought new versions of traditional songs because they could be claimed as original compositions even while folklorists such as Gordon and John Lomax argued that separate versions were evidence of a living folk tradition. "It amuses me—people like Lomax," Peer exclaimed, "They hear one of these songs, and it's always 'legendary.' I've always taken the position, 'Well, I don't know whether it's legendary or not. Now you prove it. I've got a contract on it.' And you'd be amazed the number of times that nobody's been able to bring up anything to show that it was legendary. They just assume that it is."[54] Peer's is a rare admission. It is an important corollary to the frustrations many folklorists expressed about the ubiquitous spread of commercial music throughout the South. While John Lomax lamented that southerners had forsaken authentic folk music for the phonograph, Peer decried folk song collectors who claimed too much as traditional. Peer underestimated the ballad hunter. Lomax eventually would claim copyrights on the songs he discovered during collecting trips through the South.

Peer also may have underestimated the ability of the old-time musicians he found to reimagine pop tunes as traditional fare. One of Peer's most successful collaborations was with Jimmie Rodgers. Peer met the former railroad brakeman in 1927 when Rodgers auditioned at a now-famous Victor recording session in Bristol, Tennessee, in which the Carter Family also made their recording debut. At the time, Rodgers was leading a group of musicians who enjoyed a regular job as a dance band at a resort outside Asheville. The Jimmie Rodgers Entertainers performed a wide variety of tunes at the resort. Group member Claude Grant recalled, "We would play just about everything, square dancing music and other dance numbers. When we played for dinner it would be popular music, some country music also." Rodgers was not satisfied with the ninety dollars a week his band was receiving. He repeatedly attempted to break into the talking machine business. He wrote letters to a number of phonograph companies requesting an audition yet received nothing but rejections. When he discovered that Peer would be recording in Bristol, Rodgers convinced his partners to make the trip.[55]

They auditioned for the Victor scout on August 3, 1927, singing the popular songs that had gone over well at their resort gigs. Peer was uninterested. "We ran into a snag almost immediately," he recalled, "because in order to earn a living in Asheville, he was singing mostly songs originated by the New York publishers—the current hits."[56] Rodgers convinced Peer that they could come up with some old-time material by the following day. By the time the second audition came around, Rodgers had split from his musical companions and decided to audition as a solo act. Peer worked with the singer to develop the type of material he wanted: music that sounded old yet was original enough to be copyrighted. Rodgers accommodated—almost. He recorded two selections based on older compositions: "The Soldier's Sweetheart," a reworked lyric based on a First World War–era theme and sung to the tune of "Where the River Shannon Flows," and "Sleep, Baby, Sleep," a refiguring of a composition dating back to 1869. Peer copyrighted the first. The second, Peer determined, was in the public domain. Rodgers walked away from the sessions with a royalty deal and $100 cash—more than his band's weekly salary—as well as the satisfaction that his recording career had begun.[57]

Rodgers's music, despite or perhaps because of his willingness to bend to Peer's desires, continued to foster the interracial southern music culture out of which it had sprung. After his successful audition, Rodgers went on to record a series of yodeling blues discs. They featured his simple guitar plucking out a steady twelve-bar blues while the singer recited standard three-line blues verses, many of which had floated through the South for years. He interspersed gentle, clarion yodeling into each performance to craft the sound that would become his trademark. Jimmie Rodgers's blue yodels became wildly popular and influential. Cliff Carlisle, Tom Darby and Jimmie Tarlton, Roy Harvey, the Leake County Revelers, and many other old-time artists copped Jimmie Rodgers's sound to make the yodel an essential component of the white country blues. Later white artists continued to be fascinated by Rodgers's sound. The future singing cowboy, Gene Autry, began his career as a yodeling Rodgers clone, as did the honky-tonk legend Ernest Tubb. Rodgers's influence reached well beyond country music. The Tejano duo Valentin and Pete Martinez recorded exclusively in Spanish for a variety of labels' Mexican lists, yet in 1928 they cut "Yodeling Blues" for Okeh. It was a spot-on impression of Rodgers. As far away as South Africa, the singer William Mseleku recorded songs based on Rodgers's blue yodel in 1932. Black southern artists also embraced the sound of the blue yodeler. The Mississippi Sheiks recorded "Yodeling Fiddling Blues," a clear homage, in 1930. Huddie Ledbetter, Tommy Johnson, Skip James, Mississippi John Hurt, Muddy Waters, Johnny Shines, and Robert Johnson each recalled singing Jimmie Rodgers songs. The fact that these African American artists were unable to release their own versions of Rodgers's blue yodel reveals the uneven enforcement of the musical color line in the race and old-time trade.[58]

At the same time, the roots of Jimmie Rodgers's yodel bespoke a long history of black and white southerners' interaction with each other and with mass-produced commercial music. Rodgers was not the first to inject yodeling into popular music in the United States. Yodeling in American popular music reaches back to Tyrolean groups influenced by the famous Rainier Family, who visited the United States in the 1840s. Minstrel troupes soon took to parodying the fad and yodeling became a regular feature in their shows. Lynn Abbott and Doug Seroff have shown that African American vaudeville performers had featured yodeling along with coon songs, ragtime, and other popular genres in the early years of the twentieth century. Several had begun combining yodeling with the blues before 1920. One of the most successful was the African American singer Charles Anderson from Birmingham, Alabama. Anderson received regular notices in the black press as he played vaudeville circuits across the nation. His featured songs included "In the Jail House Now" and "Sleep, Baby, Sleep." Anderson recorded the popular lullaby for Okeh, along with seven other selections in 1923 and 1924. Another African American yodeler named John Churchill recorded "Sleep, Baby, Sleep" for Paramount in 1923. While Anderson's full-throated tenor and peppy rhythmic attack reveal his roots in pre-blues vaudeville, Churchill's laconic, understated delivery is remarkably similar to the one Rodgers would use when he sang the song for Ralph Peer. It is impossible to know if Rodgers, with his gang of phonograph records, had heard Anderson, Churchill, or any of the other African American yodelers. Nevertheless, black performers had sung something very similar to Rodgers's blue yodel—the sound that would help make the singer one of the biggest stars of old-time music—on commercial stages for years. Ralph Peer went looking for new music that sounded old. He had no idea what he was getting himself into.[59]

Rodgers's experience at the Bristol sessions reveals the extent to which some southern musicians were willing—and able—to shape their art to the needs of commercial companies in order to build their careers. He became one of the most successful southern performers of the era. Yet his initial desires and decision to travel to Bristol were similar those of the seventeen other acts Peer recorded during his stay in Bristol as well as the legion of artists who attended other field recordings throughout the South. They had built local reputations for their music. They had been exposed to a variety of tunes through their travels and their phonographs. And they seized the opportunity to record when it was presented. Some also exhibited business savvy when dealing with phonograph companies. They learned how to turn the demands of the phonograph industry to their own advantage. Rodgers, versed in current styles, was willing to transform his image and material in order to accommodate Peer's desire for old-time material. Like many of his peers, he understood the economics of the new old-time music craze: sounding out of synch with modern culture could put money in his pocket.

The race and old-time categories, as they developed in the phonograph industry, each created an image of southern artists isolated from popular music, yet they accomplished this through divergent combinations of the minstrel and folkloric paradigms. Black southern artists entered an industry that portrayed them as minstrels while discouraging them from performing anything that could not be interpreted as folk blues. White southerners, on the other hand, found an industry willing to allow them to play Tin Pan Alley tunes as long as they did not acknowledge the music's commercial pedigree. Each project offered distorted, incomplete portraits of the musical lives developed by both artists and audiences. They obscured the long southern embrace of American popular music, creating false impressions of black singers and consumers willfully isolated from the sounds of Tin Pan Alley. They omitted evidence that African Americans excelled in all fields of music, that black culture and consciousness had never been limited to the spirituals, the blues, and the remaining handful of genres that had come to define the scope of African American expression in race record catalogues and folklore collections. And they masked the long history of southern musical interaction across the color line, suggesting that the music of black and white southerners was defined by their differences from each other rather than through their common histories, sounds, and relationships to American popular music.

Home, home on the range,
Where the dear and the antelope play
Where seldom is heard a discouraging word
And the skies are not cloudy all day.

LOMAX, *COWBOY SONGS* (1918), 39

REIMAGINING POP TUNES AS FOLK SONGS 8

The Ascension of the Folkloric Paradigm

In the midst of a song-collecting trip through the South in the summer of 1933, the folklorist John Lomax penned one of his regular letters to his sweetheart Ruby Terrill. "I was told in New York recently that a frontier song, *Home on the Range*, was now the most popular song in this country," he wrote. "The words and the music of that song I took down in 1909 from a negro saloon-keeper in San Antonio. Only recently have the public discovered it." Lomax had included "Home on the Range" in his collection *Cowboy Songs and other Frontier Ballads* (1910), where it had sat relatively unnoticed until its sudden popularity in 1933. Trudging through the South, far from the woman he would soon ask to be his wife, Lomax was disheartened by the news of the song's ascendance. "What we find this summer that seems worth while I shall see is better protected for our own benefit," he assured Terrill.[1]

Lomax found his chance less than a month later, when he met Huddie Ledbetter in Angola State Prison. The African American musician, who went by the name of Leadbelly, was a Louisiana native and Texas resident who had spent years singing in streets, saloons, and anywhere else he could find a paying audience. He commanded a massive repertoire that ranged from British ballads and blues to spirituals and popular hits of the day. In 1933, Ledbetter was serving time on an assault conviction. Lomax wrote Terrill, "He knew so many songs which he sang with restraint and sympathy that, accepting his story in full, I quite resolved to get him out of prison and take him along as a third member of our party." He then promised, "He sang us one song which I shall copyright as soon as I get to Washington and try to market in sheet form."[2]

The folklorist left no doubt that money was on his mind. "Home on the Range" and Huddie Ledbetter represented the nation's musical heritage to Lomax. Yet his different reactions to the two were all about the timing of their discovery. In 1909, Lomax saw little need or justification for copyrighting the traditional songs he collected. He left "Home on the Range" in the public domain even as he published it in *Cowboy Songs*. By 1933, his uncovered folk songs offered potential revenue streams for the scholar, whose commitment to chronicling the nation's traditional music left him constantly struggling to make ends meet. He soon would copyright a number of Ledbetter's songs, which would prove a source of royalty payments for years to come. As we will see, Ledbetter had his own designs on the aging ballad hunter. He understood the potential windfall their relationship represented and doggedly pursued work with the scholar. Each used the other to gather audiences and get paid, even as Lomax attempted to remain firmly in control of the partnership.

By the time Lomax met Ledbetter, the folkloric paradigm had largely supplanted the minstrel tradition of depicting musical authenticity. This chapter charts how this change occurred. It explores a series of debates and negotiations over the connections among race, folklore, and commercial music that resulted in the tentative victory of folkloric authenticity and the solidification of the musical color line in the 1920s. By the end of the decade, blackface was no longer the primary means by which the music industry, audiences, performers, or intellectuals debated the meaning of genuine music. Folklore had taken its place. The shift was neither triumphant nor complete. The border between folklore and minstrelsy had been quite fluid since the early days of the American Folklore Society, when scholars used their academic authority to validate common blackface stereotypes and theater companies touted the folkloric or ethnographic value of their plantation shows. A great deal of folklore in the 1920s continued to promote nostalgic blackface fantasies. Indeed, Leadbelly's public reception in New York—"Here to Do a Few Tunes between Homicides" announced the *Herald Tribune*—was deeply shaped by minstrel stereotypes of black male violence and primitivism.[3] Many folklorists of the 1920s, particularly African American collectors and authors, contested these visions. They used folklore to forge positive, holistic portraits of black music and its relationship to the nation's culture. These were precisely the arguments that used to be framed in terms of minstrelsy. By the 1920s, arguments about genuine black music were conducted through appeals to folklore. Most observers identified minstrelsy as an act.

The shift from minstrelsy to folklore marked the culmination of two long processes I have traced throughout this book: the growing association between racial music and racial bodies and the distinction between mass-produced music and southern culture. For all its similarities with minstrelsy, folkloric authenticity alone promoted these two ideas. The connection between racial bodies and racial music was long in coming. The tenacious minstrel conceit that black music could come from white singers underwent a series of attacks. African American performers such as Bob Cole asserted that black people made the most genuine minstrels. White singers such as Vernon Dalhart insisted that blackface dialect should be considered a marker of white identity. Race record artists showed up white delineators on phonograph records. The disabling blow came from folklore, which rooted traditional music in racial cultures and often explicitly in racial bodies. Folklorists, black and white, vigorously debated the value and meaning of black music, but on this they largely agreed: African American music was performed by black people.

The process of distinguishing southern music from mass-produced music underwent a series of transformations during the 1920s. The distinction was one of the foundational premises of the American Folklore Society, and scholars continued to hold it dear. Yet folklore emerged as the dominant framework for interpreting musical authenticity only when folklorists began to reinterpret the relationship between folk and commercial music. The change happened in a couple of phases. First, a commercial market developed for folk music. Published song collections, newspaper feature articles, phonograph records, and live performances: American consumers bought products when they were touted as authentic folklore. Initial evidence of the change can be found in the explosion of interest in African American and southern folk song during the 1920s. "The 'discovery' of the American Negro . . . has taken place in scientific as well as popular circles," noted the anthropologist Melville Herskovits in 1926.[4] Between 1914 and the year of his writing, a reported fifty-nine books had been published on African American music, many by authors steeped in the discipline of folklore. About a third of the books were by African American authors. "Manifestly the Negro is no longer merely the singer of his folk-songs," declared the white scholar Newman White in 1928.[5] These books marked a popular watershed for folklorists. No longer confined to the esoteric *Journal of American Folklore*, collectors published their work with prominent presses and garnered reviews in popular magazines and newspapers. The distinction between folklore and the media crumbled when folk music became a hot commodity. John Lomax was, perhaps, the most notable beneficiary of this development. In 1935, he became what the founders of the American Folklore Society could hardly imagine: a celebrity folklorist.

Second, and more importantly, folklorists in the 1920s began to incorporate popular commercial styles into their portraits of American folk music. This became possible when communalists largely won their battle against degenerationists over the origins of folk songs. While the new generation rarely invoked Gummere's dancing throng or other of the more controversial elements of communalist theory, most prominent writers came to embrace some version of the communalist paradigm that located the creation of folk songs among the folk rather than the elite. Communalism was based on the premise that isolated musicians were still creating folk songs. It thus opened the possibility that commercially successful genres were the products of the folk rather than slick professional songwriters. Communalists were aided in their fight by the sudden popularity of race and hillbilly records, discs sold as the uncut music of local artists operating outside the conventional music industry. Some commentators used folkloric paradigms to root popular music in deep and abiding folk traditions—to suggest that mass-produced tunes could be used as folkloric evidence of distinct, essential racial culture and consciousness. Other writers became more willing to explore the ways in which mass-produced pop penetrated the world of the folk, to amend their theories of folk isolation from modern media. Several black commentators used folkloric arguments to assert African American ownership of popular commercial styles. Together, folklorists of different bents helped to galvanize and propagate folklore as the primary frame through which to interpret southern song.

The contested partnership between Lomax and Ledbetter that began in 1933 was both a product of the shift to folkloric authenticity and one of its clearest manifestations. Over the next few years the two cut a convoluted path through American folk and commercial music. Their relationship is easily the most chronicled and analyzed pairing between a folklorist and an informant in U.S. history. Ledbetter took a job as Lomax's personal driver upon his release from prison. Joined by John's son Alan, the men collected songs throughout the South and began performing for academic conferences, society parties, and anyone who would pay them. Upon their arrival in New York City in 1935, they were touted in the local papers and chronicled by *The March of Time*. They became famous. Throughout, Lomax and Ledbetter maintained a division of labor within their "joint performances." Lomax introduced a song, stating its title and providing historical and musical contextualization. Then Ledbetter performed it, occasionally inserting his own spoken explanation of the lyrics. Ledbetter succinctly dubbed the act: "He named 'em and I whipped 'em."[6] If the singer wowed the New York literary world with his music, the scholar was always at the ready to tell the audience what that music meant—and exactly how much it was worth.[7]

The Problem of Pop Songs in Folklore Collections

Toward the end of their association, Huddie Ledbetter and John Lomax collaborated on what would become the book *Negro Folk Songs as Sung by Lead Belly* (1936). The folklorist's unpublished notes for the project reveal a large body of Ledbetter's repertoire that the scholar did not deem appropriate for the collection. "Many of the songs he sings do not appear in this volume because they are copyrighted. Prime examples are the yodeling blues and ballads of Jimmy Rogers [*sic*] of recent fame, whose ardent admirer Lead Belly still remains," Lomax wrote. "His favorite song, we hate to say, is 'Silver Haired Daddy,' a favorite with yodelers and only too familiar to everyone who has a radio. He also likes certain jazz tunes, i.e., 'I'm in Love with You, Honey,' but he sings them so vilely and with such little understanding that he himself cannot enjoy the performances."[8]

Lomax rejected both commercial tunes and songs associated with white artists or composers.[9] While Lomax may have excluded copyrighted material simply because he was unable or unwilling to pay for its inclusion in the book, his denigrating remarks implied that it did not belong in a collection of "folk" songs. Throughout his life, Lomax decried how the profusion of commercial music had made his job of ballad hunting more difficult. He often opposed the two, suggesting that the rise of commercial music meant the fall of the folk ballad.[10] Music understood as white, be it the yodeling of Jimmie Rodgers or "Silver Haired Daddy of Mine," a song written and popularized by the Hollywood cowboy crooner Gene Autry, did not fit with the image of the African American folk songster that Lomax tried to portray through Ledbetter. The singer tried several times to get the folklorist to allow him to sing "Silver Haired Daddy" at their joint concerts.[11] When Lomax refused to allow him to sing such songs, "he could never understand why we did not care for them," Lomax recalled.[12] Finally, jazz numbers and popular hits of the day were desired by the patrons at dances at which Ledbetter had often performed before meeting the folklorist. Ledbetter had these and other songs at his disposal when performing for audiences in the South and later throughout the nation. Under the watchful eye of Lomax, however, the singer's vast repertoire was kept in check. The singer who provided more songs than any other Lomax informant apparently was unable to judge which of his songs were of interest to the scholar. As Lomax stated in the published collection, "We held him to the singing of music that first attracted us to him in Louisiana, some of which he had 'composed,' at least partly."[13] Lomax's censorship propagated an image of a racial and market isolation that contradicted Ledbetter's musical experiences and the long history of commercial music in the South.

Folklorists had long policed the line between folk and commercial music by systematically excluding mass-produced fare from their collections. The products of Tin Pan Alley and commercial theater were ubiquitous and valued throughout the South, and scholars regularly, and often to their considerable annoyance, encountered such material as they traversed the region in search of song. Yet the collector Newman White stated a common goal when he declared, "I want no material from printed sources" to be included in his published folk song collection.[14] Just as John Lomax chose to print only the portion of Ledbetter's repertoire he deemed to be folk songs, many scholars in the 1920s were far more interested in defining songs according to their supposed origins than by their living usage. They thus left many of the songs they heard out in the field.

Reviewers took glee in discovering pop songs or other widely circulated tunes that had made their way into published collections despite song catchers' demonstrative disavowals of such material. A review of John Harrington Cox's *Folk Songs from the South* (1925) asserted, "There are some half-dozen or more songs which seem to have no business in the book, such as 'The Dying Californian' and 'Just before the Battle, Mother.' Surely there can be no ground for calling these folk songs?"[15] A review of a Dorothy

Scarborough collection of black folk material in 1925 noted rather drolly, "One can hardly blame Miss Scarborough for making a few mistakes as to the origins of her songs. For example, 'I Ain't Goin' To Work No Mo' '" is not a folk song, but was composed and published about fifteen years ago by James Weldon Johnson and his Brother Rosamond Johnson."[16] While this reviewer criticized the inclusion of the May Irwin vehicle because of its known authorship, others maintained that the inclusion of songs enjoyed across the color line polluted a presentation of distinct African American music. "That many of Miss Scarborough's songs are too obviously not strictly Negro pieces but rather songs partly taken over and sung by Negroes, tells somewhat against her anthology" complained one reviewer.[17] "It is extremely questionable . . . whether such songs as 'The Lost Youth' . . . should be considered the work of the negro singer," stated another before noting that the song "has been a favorite of the mountain whites in the isolated valleys of east Tennessee for many years."[18] The speed and assurance of such critiques suggest that folklorists censored many more examples of commercial or interracial repertoires from their collections long before their books went to print. Such examples are testament to the fact that black and white southerners inhabited far more complex and interrelated musical worlds than those portrayed in folk song collections.

Indeed, folklorists were able to depict pure racial repertoires only by omitting or eliding evidence of music shared between black and white southerners—some of which was essential to their own collection processes. Newman White, for example, noted with mild amusement that he learned many African American songs from white singers. "The first time I heard 'Alabama Bound' and 'Dr. Cook's in town,' they were sung by white men on the vaudeville stage," he admitted. "The song, 'Well de Good Book say dat Cain killed Abel,' enters this collection *via* a Jewish student of the College of the City of New York, who taught it to me as a current campus song."[19] White was far from alone. Many collectors used white informants—including friends, students, and unsolicited contributors—to find African American songs. These instances of music shared across the color line never convinced scholars that they were dealing with interracial repertoires, however. Even when white informants had learned a song in childhood and had sung it throughout their lives, folklorists could determine that it was in essence an African American song, eclipsing the prevalence of common stock repertoires to maintain a distinction between black originators and white carriers. A similar process could separate black informants from the songs that they sang. While John Lomax acknowledged that he learned "Home on the Range" from a "negro saloon-keeper," he never considered it a "Negro folk song." Dorothy Scarborough likewise penned an innovative chapter on the preponderance of old English ballads performed by black southern singers. Rather than analyzing these tunes as integral elements of black southern culture, she defined the phenomenon in terms of the black transmission of ostensibly English songs: the ballads were "obviously not a natural part of the Negro repertoire."[20] The communalist emphasis on folk song origins obscured repertoires known across the color line. Folklorists collected songs from both white and black informants but rarely talked about their informants' diverse repertoires as evidence that contradicted their own racial musical categories.

These maneuvers echoed the tactics of the previous generation of folklorists, yet 1920s collectors became more willing to address the complex relationship between folk and commercial song. In some regards, folklorists had little choice but to deal with mass-produced music. When race and old-time music emerged as significant commercial forces in the mid-1920s, it became impossible to ignore their popularity among the folk previously thought isolated from the mass media. Dorothy Scarborough, for example, suggested several ways to reimagine the relationship between folk music and commercial tunes. "Of course, many pieces thought to be authentic folk-songs are undoubtedly of minstrel origin, no matter how sincere the collector may be in his belief that they are genuine folk-material," she wrote. "On the other hand, may not folk-singing and change make a folk-song out of what was originally a minstrel-song? And certainly there are cases where the folk-song came first—where the folk-song was taken over in the whole or in part and adapted to the minstrel stage."[21] Speculations such as this helped open the door for popular music's entry into discussions about folk music and culture. Folklore, in part, became the primary paradigm through which cultural authorities interpreted southern music not by denying the presence of mass-produced music but by expanding the definition of folklore in order to embrace the very music that scholars had previously condemned as inauthentic commercial fare. It constituted a momentous shift.

African American writers were at the forefront of the movement to bring popular commercial music into the folkloric fold. Thomas W. Talley, a chemistry professor at Fisk University, became one of the first to do so when he published *Negro Folk Rhymes (Wise and Otherwise)* in 1922. Talley, born in 1870, assembled his collection of 349 songs from numerous sources, including former students, friends, field trips in and around Tennessee, and his own memory. The country music historian Charles Wolfe notes that Talley may have gained his interest in collecting folk music in 1915 and 1916, while studying science at Harvard, the longtime center of American folk song studies. Yet Talley's catholic approach to southern black song did not reveal a serious debt to the strict definitions of folk song then being proffered by the profession. Talley apparently printed it all. Several selections were related to Tin Pan Alley or minstrel songs that had circulated commercially in the previous decades. Others were songs popular with white singers in the area and were recorded by white hillbilly artists during the 1920s. He gave little indication that he knew or cared that his collection contained songs originating with music publishers.[22] Talley did not provide notes about individual selections, and his concluding essay did not address explicitly the distinction between folk and commercial songs beyond his passing comment that "a few of the Rhymes bear the mark of a somewhat recent date in composition."[23] The book nevertheless maintained an attitude of inclusiveness that separated it from many of the folklore collections of the era. "All nature is one," Talley insisted in a passage critiquing the limits of standard folkloric categories. "Though we arbitrarily divide Nature's objects for study, they are indissolubly bound together and every part carries in some part of its constitution some well defined marks which characterize the other parts with which it has no immediate connection."[24] While not directly attacking the divide between mass-produced music and folklore, Talley offered a holistic portrait of African American folk music defined by commonalities in form and function rather than through differences in origin.

James Weldon Johnson was far more explicit in his expansive portrait of African American musical traditions. Perhaps no one better exemplifies the shift from minstrelsy to folklore than Johnson, the dialect love song composer who became one of the major champions of black folk song in the 1920s. Appearing the same year as Talley's collection, Johnson's *The Book of American Negro Poetry* began with his essay "The Negro's Creative Genius," in which he attempted to demonstrate African Americans' capacity to create great art—works at once racially specific and universal in their import. "No people that has produced great literature and art has ever been looked upon by the world as distinctly inferior," he noted. Johnson strategically defined ragtime, "the one artistic production by which America is known the world over," as African American folk music. It was a bold assertion, for many Americans conceived of ragtime as a commercial fad, on the one hand, or a product of white composers, on the other. "For a dozen years or so there has been a steady tendency to divorce Ragtime from the Negro; in fact, to take from him the credit of having originated it," Johnson wrote. He briefly detailed ragtime's genesis among black pianists in the "questionable resorts" of Memphis, St. Louis, and other cities. Lacking musical education, ragtime composers drew on generalized racial gifts, African Americans' "natural musical instinct" and "extraordinary sense of rhythm." From these humble beginnings, Johnson argued, ragtime expanded into an international sensation dominated by white composers and performers—including his former customer May Irwin, whose hit "The Bully" (1895) had been sung by black roustabouts long before it made her rich.[25]

The folkloric paradigm enabled Johnson to describe and condemn the white co-optation of ragtime. Older models of minstrel authenticity were not as well suited to the task. Black responses to white minstrelsy often were ambivalent, veering between accusations of cultural poaching and angry denials that minstrel stereotypes had anything at all to do with authentic black music. Johnson's early experiences as a songwriter were marred by this very dualism. Defining ragtime as black folklore, Johnson could avoid the conundrum and clearly identify white ragtime compositions as a form of racial theft. Yet in order to pull this off, he had to diminish the role of professional African American songwriters such as himself. While *The Auto-biography of an Ex-Colored Man* (1912) emphasized the sophisticated artistic work necessary to lift folk materials into the realm of serious art, Johnson now suggested that published ragtime compositions were simply versions of uncut black folk songs. He offered his own "Oh, Didn't He Ramble!" as an example. "It was a song which had been sung for years all through the South," he explained. "We took it, re-wrote the verses, telling an entirely different story from the original, left the chorus as it was, and published the song."[26] Professional composers added little value to the music in this equation. More important were "those artistic expressions which sprang from folk origin rather than from individual origin."[27]

Hit Broadway numbers reimagined as folk songs: Johnson's essay symbolized the expanding scope and influence of folkloric notions of authenticity. Not everyone was happy about the change. It not only called out white appropriators of black song. It also challenged the foundational premise of academic folklore that defined authenticity through cultural and racial isolation. Henry Edward Krehbiel, a white author and long-time music critic for the *New York Tribune*, wrote a scathing review of *The Book of American Negro Poetry* devoted almost entirely to Johnson's interpretation of ragtime. In 1914, Krehbiel had written one of the first substantial treatises on black folk music. It was a devoutly communalist work, emphasizing the anonymous, collective nature of folk songs: "the music of the folksong reflects the inner life of the people that gave it birth."[28] He could not stomach what he saw as Johnson's insistence that the "vulgar music which has taken possession of the vaudeville stage and the dance halls" should be claimed as an African American creation or equated with the "unperverted" musical elements of the spirituals. Krehbiel labeled Johnson a poor historian and a sloppy author. Hit songs such as "The Bully" and "There'll Be a Hot Time in the Old Town Tonight" were not folk songs but commercial ditties penned by individuals—some of them white. Krehbiel knew, he claimed. He had met the authors.[29]

Krehbiel's review was something of a rear-guard defense of the boundary separating folk from commercial music. Johnson and Krehbiel shared more in common than their exchange would suggest. Both celebrated the power and beauty of black folk music. Both were deeply influenced by the founding debates in academic folklore and anthropology. And both emerged embracing some version of the communalist theory of folk song origins. They differed, however, over the work they hoped that folklore could accomplish. Krehbiel remained wed to the conviction that folklore could give insight into the racial mind. If black folk song had any hope of representing "the inner life of the people that gave it birth" it could not include ragtime—a music bought and sold on the open market that, in Johnson's own words, had become "national rather than racial."[30] Krehbiel's position was forged through the early debates and designs of the discipline of folklore. It remained popular among folklorists and social scientists interested in using music as evidence in their larger arguments about racial capacities and the developmental history of modern civilization. The sociologist Robert E. Park, for example, hit a similar chord when he celebrated Thomas Talley's collection for its emphasis on black secular, rather than religious, song. "It reveals, therefore, a quite different aspect of the Negro 'mind,' and is, for that reason, a valuable contribution to the materials which students have been accumulating in recent years for the understanding of the cultural evolution of the Negro race and of all races," wrote Park.[31] Johnson, on the other hand, hoped folklore could help overcome white racism and establish black ownership of American popular music. Ragtime, he argued, was important precisely because it was known and loved by white Americans. Its very universality helped to establish "the Negro's Creative Genius" and black people's contribution to American culture.

A related distinction between black folk and commercial music animated debates within the New Negro Renaissance in the 1920s. The historian Paul Allen Anderson has demonstrated that a number of writers in the movement shared Alain Locke's marked disdain for commercial genres. Locke saw popular jazz and blues recordings promoting an exotic primitivism through which white listeners could confirm their romantic, reductive stereotypes of black culture and consciousness. For Locke, the music's popularity with white listeners did not signal the black ownership of commercial styles but the rejection of folk authenticity for stereotypes. He thus spent very little time addressing mass-produced music during the decade. Locke instead promoted the evolution of pure African American folk idioms into a high African American art music in the mode advocated by Antonín Dvořák in the 1890s. His language in some ways echoed that of turn-of-the-century advocates of nationalist music and high art based upon folk sources. He desired not a "cultivation of the last decadences of the over-civilized, but rather a deep realization of the fundamental purpose of art and of its function as a tap root of vigorous, flourishing living." Turning to vigorous folk music as an antidote to overcivilization, Locke largely bypassed the decadent and compromised music of the marketplace in his writings from the 1920s.[32] The Negro Renaissance writer Sterling Brown, on the other hand, offered an alternative to Locke's distinction between black folk and commercial music during the twenties. Brown measured ragtime favorably compared to European "classics," and, Anderson demonstrates, valued black music without resorting to simple visions of folk authenticity. But he remained wary of white listeners' and critics' tendency to hear a romantic primitivism when listening to black music in the commercial sphere.[33]

The slow rise of the folkloric paradigm during the 1920s occurred through such quests for an African American music tradition that could not be reduced to minstrel stereotypes of black inferiority. James Weldon Johnson's reevaluation of ragtime as folklore promised to seize the sound of the coon song away from minstrel delineators by asserting its origins among the black folk. It was a dramatically different strategy from the one he had employed when writing "Louisiana Lize" in 1899, but it attempted to produce a similar rebuttal to white racism through a depiction of black musical authenticity. The process of reimagining pop tunes as folklore worked to defend the distinction between folk and commercial music in an era of popular music's ascendance. It maintained that there was a major difference between the two, but it shifted the border to bring some genres into the folkloric camp. Ultimately, many folklorists in the 1920s sided with Krehbiel regarding ragtime. The music had been entangled with minstrelsy, coon songs, and Tin Pan Alley far too long for them to suddenly interpret it as folk song. They were far more willing to accept into the folkloric fold the other recent commercial phenomenon addressed by James Weldon Johnson in *The Book of American Negro Poetry*: the blues.

How the Blues Became Folk Song

Prior to the mid-twenties, practically every commentator, with some minor exceptions, understood the blues as a commercial style.[34] The blues were a successful, almost viral, product of the music industry and professional songwriters. Academic collectors were particularly slow to associate the blues with folklore. Between 1888 and 1930 the "blues" were only mentioned in eleven articles in the *Journal of American Folklore*. E. C. Perrow's landmark collection of southern folk songs (1912) never used the word except in the middle of one song lyric: "I've got the blues; I'm too damn mean to talk."[35] Howard Odum's important collection of black secular songs (1911) printed the word twice, again in lyrics: "I got the blues, but too damn mean to cry" and "I got de blues an' can't be satisfied."[36] Perrow and Odum published their collections before the blues craze had taken hold, and they probably remained unaware that such lines might belong to a new genus of southern folk song. Neither provided any commentary on the subject. The white folklorist Walter Prescott Webb, on the other hand, published a monumental example of blues-like lyrics in 1915, well after the beginning of the commercial craze. He transcribed the "ballad" from a black Texan named Floyd Canada, who, Webb tells us, "says it is sung to the tune of 'The Dallas Blues.'"[37] Webb called Canada's song "The Railroad Blues." These solitary uses of the term "blues" are telling. "The Dallas Blues," supposedly known to Webb and his readers, was one of the earliest commercial blues hits. The tune interestingly enough begins with a line echoing Perrow and Odum: "I've got the blues but I'm too mean to, I said mean to, I mean to cry." The white composer Hart A. Wand published the song in 1912, and African American touring groups, including the popular Rabbit Foot Minstrels, were performing it on the road by 1914. The song was closely related to "The Nigger Blues," published by Leroy White in 1912.[38] It was familiar enough to operate as a shorthand for identifying a song's melody, but it did not fit within the folk framework. Webb thus employed the blues as a popular commercial genre. "Ballad," the term he used to describe Canada's song throughout the article, suited his needs much better. This would change within a few short years.

W. C. Handy was more responsible than anyone for establishing the blues as folk music. The successful composer helped inaugurate the commercial blues craze with songs such as "Memphis Blues" and "St. Louis Blues." Eventually, he became a major advocate for applying the folkloric paradigm to the blues. Handy did not use the term "folk" to describe the blues in his earliest writings on the subject. In newspaper articles written between 1916 and 1919, Handy began to establish his reputation as an authority on the history and meaning of the genre. What would become some of his most famous anecdotes—indeed some of the most important and ubiquitous early blues narratives—first appeared in print in these articles. He related first hearing the blues around southern plantations and train depots and told the now-infamous story of being upstaged by a local blues band in Clarksdale, Mississippi, during a performance in 1903. Handy clearly identified the blues as a collective invention of the African American South. He deflected apparent suggestions that he alone had created the form by insisting that the blues were a product of the "peculiar harmonies and perfect rhythmic characteristic of our race." He nevertheless framed the music as a commercial genre, both in its local southern habitat and in the nation at large. As a writer for the *Freeman* explained in 1917, Handy "is known the world over for his success in writing a number that was destined to set everybody dancing or trying to refrain from making an effort to dance. This dance success is The Memphis Blues. But he did more than write a dance. He ushered into musical composition a new FORM." Neither Handy nor writers profiling the composer identified the blues as folk music.[39]

When he published the first major collection of blues songs in 1926, however, Handy explicitly framed the blues as folk music. *Blues: An Anthology* featured fifty piano arrangements that outlined a history of the genre. The anthology began with several spirituals and work songs. It then provided a large number of blues songs, featuring several of Handy's own compositions, before concluding with complex, blues-inspired compositions, including some by white composers. This evolutionary narrative leading from simple folk songs to sophisticated compositions was reenforced by a substantial introductory essay by the writer Abbe Niles based on his conversations with Handy. Niles launched his essay by unequivocally stating, "To summarize the story of the blues: They began as a form of Afro-American folksong." Niles then detailed the lyrical and musical development of what he called "folk-blues."[40] The song collector Guy B. Johnson began a review of the anthology by declaring, "The blues present the unique spectacles of a form of Negro folk song becoming the most important single type of popular song in America."[41] It was a dramatic reinterpretation of the music that had first attracted Handy for its "commercial potential."

A number of things had changed between Handy's first articles and the publication of his anthology. The explosion of race records in 1920 had established urban blues as one of the most popular genres in the country. This made Handy's argument that the blues was a distinctive dance music rather passé. Everybody had the doggone blues. At the same time, the commercial success of the blues, Handy feared, obscured its roots in southern black culture and among African Americans in general. Just as Johnson was doing with ragtime, Handy searched for a way to reestablish the black ownership and character of the blues during the early 1920s. One minor attempt involved his effort to create a new genre he called "gouge," a synthesis of black musical styles that, according to the African American *Pittsburgh Courier*, "is a bit above the level to which his beloved blues have descended." Handy published "The Chicago Gouge" in 1924. Its chorus outlined a recipe for combining blues, jazz, ragtime, and the Charleston in one musical stew. The gouge never caught on with the public.[42] Yet if his attempt to define a pan-generic black music in the commercial realm failed, he had more success when he began having conversations with folklorists about his beloved blues.

Between 1923 and 1926, a handful of significant writings characterized the blues as folklore. W. C. Handy made his mark on every one of them. Works by the white authors Dorothy Scarborough, Carl Van Vechten, and the team of Howard Odum and Guy Johnson began from the presumption that the blues a was commercial entity that did not belong in a collection of folk music. They each used interviews with Handy or descriptions of his music to reframe the blues as folklore. Dorothy Scarborough helped set the formula with an article aptly titled "The 'Blues' as Folk-Songs" in 1923.[43] The article gained larger circulation when she included it in her book *On the Trail of Negro Folk Songs* (1925). "Blues, being widely published as sheet music in the North as well as the South, and sung in vaudeville everywhere, would seem to have little relation to authentic folk-music of the Negroes," Scarborough began. "One might imagine this tinge of blue to the black music to be an artificial coloring—printer's ink, in fact." She then told of tracking down Handy, "the man who had put the bluing in the blues," and interviewing him on the subject.

> To my question, "Have blues any relation to Negro folk-song?" Handy replied instantly:
> "Yes—they are folk music."
> "Do you mean in the sense that a song is taken up by many singers, who change and adapt it and add to it in accordance with their own mood?" I asked. "That constitutes communal singing, in part, at least."
> "I mean that and more . . . They are essentially racial, the ones that are genuine,—though since they became the fashion many blues have been written that are not Negro in character,—and they have a basis in older folksong."[44]

The rest of the article used the interview with Handy as its main evidence to describe the form and function of "this modern folk-music." Carl Van Vechten, the white music critic, novelist, and ubiquitous Harlem presence, followed the same formula in a pair of influential articles for *Vanity Fair* in 1925. After talking with Handy, Van Vechten declared, "Like the spirituals, the blues are folksongs . . . although those that achieved publication or performance under sophisticated auspices have generally passed through a process of transmutation."[45]

Perhaps the most dramatic reinterpretation of the blues as folk songs came from the sociologists Howard Odum and Guy Johnson. They collaborated in 1925 to publish *The Negro and His Songs*, a large collection of African American religious and secular selections, many of which were culled from Odum's previous academic journal articles. They equated "blues" with "popular hits" and emphatically insisted that they were "not folk songs."[46] By the following year, the authors had reversed their opinion. Citing Handy and Scarborough, their next book maintained that the blues were "straight from the folk as surely as the old spirituals." The shift provides a clear example of the emerging recognition of the blues as folk music. For illustration, the duo culled lyrics from various sections of their previously published collections and recategorized them as examples of the blues. They then provided a fascinating analysis of the ways in which informants had remembered and combined lyrics from blues recordings and sheet music. Commercial songs had become the raw material for orally transmitted folk songs. Odum and Johnson declared, "It is no longer possible to speak with certainty of the folk blues, so entangled are the relations between them and the formal compositions." They failed to acknowledge that neither they nor anybody else had ever talked about "folk blues" until well after the music had been established as a top-selling genre.[47]

Segregation and the Validation of the Musical Color Line

Labeling the blues and other genres as folk music implied far more than that it existed prior to its incorporation into the national music industry. It suggested that all of the folkloric assumptions about racial isolation and character could be applied to the music. Most fundamentally, the folkloric paradigm drew a distinction between genuine music and the market, and it identified authentic song as a product of racial isolation rather than contact. Segregation, a relatively new phenomenon in the first decades of the century, became an important tool for folklorists interested in finding music supposedly forged by racial and commercial isolation. With the rise of Jim Crow, scholars turned toward segregated spaces to find isolated racial cultures. It made the job of identifying separate racial repertoires—and by extension racial capacities and temperaments—much easier. Likewise, many white scholars began to suggest that their authority as cultural commentators was based upon their ability—some argued courage—to pass into segregated black spaces to record a culture invisible to most white people.[48]

In her collection *On the Trail of Negro Folk-Songs* (1925), the Texas native and Columbia University professor Dorothy Scarborough detailed her adventures hunting folk songs in the segregated South. "I myself haunted all sorts of places where Negroes gather for work or play," she recalled. The white song catcher, who began collecting around 1915, traipsed through rural Texas and Louisiana, visiting areas "where few white people live." She went "strolling leisurely through the colored section of town to hear what I could hear" while in Birmingham, Alabama. She followed an aged man in Louisville to hear the lyrics he was singing to himself. She attended a baptismal ceremony in Natchez, Louisiana, where she attempted to take photographs until "the crowd surged against me, and I had to put up my Kodak hastily and become as inconspicuous as possible," she recalled. "Even my pencil taking down songs upset them."[49]

Crossing over into segregated spaces enabled Scarborough to grapple with her own history as a white southerner and scion of slave owners. She reveled in nostalgic memories of white leisure and black labor upon hearing African American singing. "I see a procession of black and yellow and cream-colored faces that have passed through our kitchen and house and garden—some very impermanent and some remaining for years, but all singing," she wrote. "I can project myself into the past and hear the wailful songs at Negro funerals, the shouting songs at baptizings in the creek or river, old break-downs at parties, lullabies crooned as mammies rocked black or white babies to sleep, work-songs in cottonfield or on the railroad or street-grading jobs."[50] It was imagery borrowed whole cloth from minstrelsy's sentimental odes to the old plantation, yet it was imbued with a highbrow legitimacy that could only come with an academic pedigree. Scarborough, like her predecessors in the early twentieth century, helped to make black song a safe, moving talisman for white southern identity.

While she used the geography of segregation to target potential informants, Scarborough never mentioned Jim Crow. The closest she came to discussing the racial regime that white citizens had brought upon the South was in a passage about Sebron Mallard, a former slave of her grandfather's whom she encountered while collecting in Louisiana. Her family "was allus so good to their pore slaves," Mallard reportedly told her. "White folks and black folks look like they ain't live lovely together like they used to," he lamented after blaming current racial tensions on the younger generation of black southerners' lack of manners. Scarborough's understanding of the supposed interracial harmony of the slave era, her narrative implied, granted her a special ability to bridge the twentieth-century color line. She could uncover buried folk songs by reverting to the racial intimacy of the southern plantation and ignoring the racial violence and segregation surrounding her. Indeed, folklore provided a suitable platform for these rhetorical gymnastics. The field regularly presented folk culture as an outgrowth of essential racial temperaments and capacities rather than a result of contemporary social and political contexts. Scarborough followed this tradition when analyzing the songs that filled her collection. Her discussion of railroad songs, for example, gave no indication that black southerners might have considered the train an important means of leaving the segregated South. She rather turned to generalizations about the African American character. "The Negro, an imaginative being, delights to personify the things that enter his life," she began, "so he makes a dramatic figure out of such a thing as a railroad train." He is attracted to its "shining rails" and the "unknown objectives" they imply. "The Negro, while often outwardly lethargic, is restless of heart; is it because he feels that he has never found his true place in life?"[51] Folklore's focus on racial character and causation enabled Scarborough to celebrate black creativity while ignoring the effects of white oppression.

Walter Prescott Webb, on the other hand, acknowledged some of the realities of segregation in order to demonstrate the authenticity of his collection and his own authority as a scholar. In his article published in 1916 in the *Journal of American Folklore* featuring his encounter with Floyd Canada, the white scholar evoked segregated space for a number of rhetorical purposes. Within his narrative, segregation established a mood of immediacy and danger, an image of a genuine, uncontaminated black culture, and a white scholarly authority born from the transgression of Jim Crow boundaries. While visiting Beeville, Texas, Webb heard a young schoolboy singing a series of blues stanzas. He asked "Harry, where did you learn that [song]?" "From a negro here in town," the boy replied. The exchange began Webb's venture into a separate black space, one that revealed a black culture more authentic than the coon songs digested by white Americans' unwilling peek behind the veil, Webb maintained. Floyd Canada had just finished serving time in prison for shooting craps. "I located him, through Harry, over across the railroad track, in a negro pool hall," Webb recalled. "We found him with a band of his comrades, including the hotel waiter, making merry with guitar, banjo, harp, and song,—as merry as though a jail had never been." Segregation afforded Webb the opportunity to step into what he considered an uncontaminated black world. The African American pool hall was a space that erased white contact and control ("as though a jail had never been"), leaving a black culture more authentic for its absence. Webb emphasized the danger of crossing to the other side of the tracks by insisting on a hasty retreat: "In a small town one cannot spend much time in a pool-hall, and especially a negro pool-hall. The near-by depot offered the solution, for it is the common meeting-ground of all the races; and to the depot I invited Floyd." Canada recited his song for Webb in the train depot.[52]

"The song tells no connected story, any more than the ruins of Rome tell a story, or the grave of an American Indian, with its bones, arrow-heads, beads, and pottery, tells a story." Like these material artifacts, Webb implied, Canada's song provided a glimpse of a world not seen or experienced by his readers—a dim and murky world that could be clarified only with the proper insight. "But a story may be drawn from it,—the story of the modern negro," Webb insisted. "If the race should be blotted out and its history lost and forgotten, much of it could be reconstructed from this ballad," he continued. "We could learn what the negro held to be of highest importance, we could learn of his desires and aims, his love and hate, his ethical and chivalrous ideas, his philosophy of life, code of morals, and idea of the future."[53] While imagining a future without African American people, Webb rhetorically made it so. Canada, the individual singer, disappeared from Webb's narrative. He was replaced with a composite "negro," a generalized author whom the scholar assembled out of Canada's song. Webb thus constructed an artifact out of an encounter. He met a man across the tracks and brought back his bones for analysis.

Scarborough and Webb used their brief sojourns into a segregated black world to assert their authority as scholars and the isolation of authentic black folk culture. John Lomax perfected the systematic presentation of these interrelated claims in the 1930s. When Lomax sought African American folk songs he turned toward the sites in which he believed cultural isolation was the most complete: the nation's jails and prisons. "Folk songs and folk literature flourish, grow—are created, propagated, transformed—in the eddies of human society, particularly [prisons] where there is isolation and homogeneity of thought and experience," he wrote in 1934. "These communities of Negro men and women, shut out from the clamor of the world, thrown back almost entirely on their own resources for entertainment, lonely, few with any background of reading, naturally resort to song."[54] Prisons, Lomax argued, actually transformed black culture by separating African American prisoners from the white influences they had previously embraced. "[A] long-time Negro convict spends many years with practically no chance of hearing a white man speak or sing," he explained. "Such men slough off the white idiom they may once have employed in their speech and revert more and more to the idiom of the Negro common people."[55] Isolation from popular music and white influences, Lomax believed, made black prisoners ideal repositories and creators of authentic folk songs.

Outside the prison walls, Lomax had difficulty transgressing racial boundaries and recording black music. In June 1933, for example, he became frustrated when he could not extract folk songs from African American teachers at a meeting he attended in Prairie View, Texas. "They are naturally suspicious of the whites and just as naturally somewhat ashamed of the creations of their people—the uneducated group known as the 'folk,'" he wrote to Ruby Terrill.[56] A few weeks later, Lomax was again frustrated by his inability to extract folk songs from educated African American informants. "A bit of shallow instruction has had its inevitable result in a crop of false ideals," he insisted. "These negroes are ashamed of their heritage and make themselves ridiculous (in most cases) when they attempt to ape the whites in the field of music."[57] The black informants with whom he had easy contact were unwilling or unable to provide authentic folk songs. Conversely, Lomax had difficulty accessing black cultural spaces less contaminated by white influences. In the Brazos River valley he met a black guitarist and, with Alan's help, transcribed a number of songs. They then followed the artist to a crowded party. The folklorists waited outside:

> As I sat in the car and listened to the steady monotonous beat of the guitar accented by hand claps and the shuffle of feet, the excitement growing as time went on, the rhythm deeper and clearer, I again felt carried across to Africa, and I know I was listening to the tom-toms of savage blacks and when I peered through the door and windows and saw the grotesque postures and heard the jumbled and undistinguishable cries of jubilant pleasure, I realized that Alan and I were really enjoying a unique experience amid a people we really know little about.[58]

The passage clearly displays Lomax's romantic vision of African primitivism. Yet the story is also a telling parable about cultural access and academic authority. Excluded from the party, only catching the sound from afar and glimpses through a window, Lomax admitted that he knew very little about

African American people and their culture. In prisons, Lomax would finally find the intimacy with black informants that would enable him to record their music and speak authoritatively about it.[59]

Lomax was able to collect songs in southern prisons because black inmates, far from isolated from white influence, were under constant white supervision and control. While visiting the Nashville Penitentiary, Lomax met an inmate named "Black Sampson" who could sing a number of work songs. Sampson was not interested in performing for the folklorist. His religious beliefs kept him from committing "sinful songs" to Lomax's phonograph, though he taunted the collector by singing them out of the range of the microphone. Lomax turned to the warden for help.

> Soon the big black man, frightened but smiling ingratiatingly, came into the room. "Black Sampson," said the Warden, "stand up before the microphone and sing whatever this white man tells you." Black Sampson shambled up to the microphone . . . He prayed: "Oh Lawd, you see what a fix yo po black man is in. Heah he is down in do world where he has to do ev'ything this white man tells him to, But Oh Lawd, I hope you will understand and forgive me for de sin I is about to commit and not charge it up against a po negro who caint hep hissef. For jesus' sake, Amen," and then he sang some beautiful work song. Meanwhile our machine had recorded both the prayer and the songs.[60]

Lomax's authority as a scholar and collector of black folk songs was deeply intertwined with the authority white guards practiced over black inmates. His use of the warden's power enabled him an intimacy with black culture that he had difficulty attaining outside the prison walls. At the same time, Black Sampson was not only forced to sing for the collector. He was forced to perform songs that were not to his liking. Lomax extracted songs and styles that, far from representing the everyday culture of his informant, were morally repugnant and consciously avoided. Nevertheless, Lomax considered his encounter with Black Sampson an unqualified success. "I call this my prize record," he boasted.[61]

Black prisoners were far less musically isolated than Lomax imagined. In 1934, he wrote to prison wardens throughout the country, asking if their inmates knew the folk songs for which he was searching. Many were baffled by the request and told of black prisoners' love of popular music. The warden of the Maine state prison replied, "Having made a canvass among the prisoners of this institution I do not find that there are any real Folk-Songs or similar airs sung by the inmates. About the only thing heard among them is snatches from popular airs."[62] Word came from upstate New York that "this institution is surprisingly free from this type of song. Perhaps the fact that our inmates enjoy the music of our orchestra and band, then also listen to the radio nightly, might influence this condition."[63] A superintendent in Iowa claimed, "We just sing the good old songs and also popular, up to date ones."[64] E. McFate, the director of musical instruction at the Michigan state prison, apologized, "We have music in this prison—but not the type sought by you." He then listed a bevy of musical activities at the prison, including a military band, an orchestra, a "colored dance or rhythm orchestra," a "Hill-Billy group of 7 real hill-billies," a church choir, a violin virtuoso, and a "colored quartette" specializing in written arrangements of spirituals.[65] It is very likely that prison wardens and supervisors did not know all the music that inmates sang. Such responses do not mean that prisoners at these institutions did not know the type of folk songs that interested Lomax. They do suggest, however, that prisoners had very broad musical experiences—the "isolation and homogeneity" that attracted Lomax to prisons was not in evidence. M. F. Amrine, the superintendent of the federal jail in New Orleans, made this point forcefully. "If the idea of Dr. John A. Lomax regarding prisoners' songs is based on the idea that prisoners, as a class, are different from the general run of humanity in regard to musical taste, I think he will find his idea is not correct," Amrine wrote. "People in prison are a cross-section of society, more nearly than they are any one classification. They have such songs as have the people outside of prisons, and for the same general reasons."[66]

Despite this evidence to the contrary, Lomax, like many of his peers, used his transgressions into segregated spaces to portray separate black and white musical cultures. Part of Lomax's theoretical connection between black isolation and authenticity may have stemmed from his romantic nostalgia for a past era of race relations in the South. The historian Jerrold Hirsch argues that Lomax, driven by a conservative nostalgia, sought an antidote to modernity in the primitive, unselfconscious art of black Americans. He found in black folk songs an "artless simplicity" that, like the cowboy songs he published in 1910, spoke of a life lived outside of modern contrivances.[67] Yet in the process, Lomax created a dichotomy between black culture and black freedom and progress. "Implicitly, Lomax contended that anything that changed the African-American's traditional place in southern culture would destroy his folk traditions," Hirsch explains.[68] Education, well-paying jobs, and any form of participation in the larger society caused African Americans to lose their racial core, a core Lomax repeatedly associated with poverty, isolation, and pathos. While his encounters with educated black people often left him cold and unsatisfied, the prison environment encouraged nostalgia for his childhood similar to that expressed by Dorothy Scarborough. Writing from Parchman farm in 1933, he explained to Ruby Terrill, "When I was about one year old my parents immigrated from near here to Texas. Queerly enough I feel that I am visiting an old home. Sometimes such visits are not saddening. This visit is not so."[69] Part of the reason for this response was the heartfelt songs of tribulation and longing that he collected from black prisoners. " 'Lifetime' looked at me with his one good eye—a sinister immobile face rendered more unattractive by a white film-covered eye," his letter continued. "He was singing in a deep and tremulous voice an epic about 'The Midnight Special' (train) which suggested to him freedom with all its opportunities."[70]

Throughout his writing, Lomax struggled to come to terms with the relationship between freedom and authenticity in black folk songs. In 1917, he insisted that the pathos in black song arose from an unconscious sense of self-pity and racial inferiority born out of constant comparison to white people.[71] As his letter suggests, the longing for an unattained freedom was an important element for Lomax in the songs that he heard from African American informants. Yet he repeatedly insisted that the pathos he detected in almost all black music was not a result of white oppression. "And yet the sadness, the melancholy, did not, it is believed, grow out of brutal treatment," he explained while discussing his experiences with black prisoners. "The men were well fed and their sleeping quarters looked comfortable . . . no case of cruelty was noted. The Negro makes a model prisoner, as one guard said, easy to control, but in his singing he abandons himself to a brooding hopelessness, as though freedom were beyond reach."[72] Through such rhetorical gymnastics, Lomax identified the pain at the heart of much black folk music, but he found it a result of racial psychological tendencies rather than the experience of racism. Though black prisoners supposedly were treated well, their songs nevertheless slipped into a "brooding hopelessness." It was a characteristic that for Lomax, as for Dorothy Scarborough, could be found in segregated spaces but was not caused by the enforcement of them.

While the scholar did not acknowledge the relationship between segregation and black music, some African American musicians realized their own
connections. Black Sampson, after singing for Lomax at the insistence of the
prison warden, hoped that his relationship with the ballad hunter could
help reduce his sentence. Lomax reported him stating, " 'Boss, you please
tell some o' dem big mens up in Washington, when dey hears my songs on
the record, to please he'p me get out of dis place, I jes' nachully don' like
it.' "[73] Sampson's request gave lie to the image of the black inmate's isolation. The singer attempted to parlay his brief encounter with the collector
into a reprieve from his local conditions.[74] Sampson's request, of course,
echoed the legend of Huddie Ledbetter's release from prison after singing
for the governor of Louisiana, a tale Lomax regularly repeated even as
he maintained that black prisoners were isolated from the outside world.
Other musicians also understood how national connections held the possibility of alleviating local racism. The African American musician Willie
Blackwell, for example, told Alan Lomax that he could not be reduced to
white locals' impressions of him. "These Memphis cops call me vagrant, but
I'm a musician," he declared. "I'm a recording artist for the Vict'ry company. Known all over the world. But these Southern laws don't recognize a
man by his talents."[75] Segregation did not produce the isolated black culture
imagined by collectors. Racial contact and white oppression infused and
shaped the sound and meaning of black music in the age of Jim Crow.

Folk Singers and the Academic Market

If southern musicians contested folkloric assumptions about racial isolation, they also taught scholars that folkloric encounters were commercial
encounters. The relationships between folklorists and their informants were
often predicated on the hope or promise of money. Mrs. M. B. Wright, a
casual collector from Fort Thomas, Arizona, wrote a letter to John Lomax
in 1910 wishing him luck on his ballad-hunting trips through the area.
"Don't tell the public what you want," she warned. "I could have got more
but I told that you intended having them printed in book form[.] the
parties said you would make money out of them and they would not furnish
the songs without pay."[76] A. P. Welchman, from Grover Wyoming, wrote to
the scholar in 1907 after seeing a newspaper announcement that Lomax was
collecting songs. "It stated in the News article that your object is the 'preserving from extinction this expression of American literature.' That is well,

so far," Welchman wrote. "But it is also stated that—'eventually it is expected that' the ballads will be published in book form." He continued, "As a rule, publications are expected to render some return, when published, in some manner, and to some party or parties. Question: will such be the result in this case of publication? If so, what will be the nature of the return; and to whom will it be made; [s]hall I be a sharer in the benefits accruing? If so, how, and in what degree? And I may ask when?"[77]

Welchman's concerns apparently were quite common. Lomax scribbled across the letter, "Noteworthy among my replies came replies from young authors who prompt publication through me. Here is a sample." The black songwriter Wallis Sanders of Canton, Mississippi, reportedly was far less long-winded when approached by O. S. Miller, who was acting as an agent for Lomax. Miller wrote, "I read your letter to Wallis + [he] said Boss is there anything in it[.] I told him no money but lots of fame + he said what dat Boss."[78] Lomax dismissed informants' desires to get paid. He thought that such requests demonstrated informants' incomprehension of his project and the quality of the songs he was attempting to preserve. Yet informants often were quite aware of the folklorists' project. They demanded access to the rewards they believed collectors would certainly reap. John Harrington Cox was confronted with these demands when collecting in Clarksburg, West Virginia, in 1921. When he visited Nancy McAtee's home in Clarksburg, West Virginia, her son immediately turned the conversation toward money and "told me a regular hard-luck story about unemployment." Cox shirked off the hint. His retelling shows the folklorist impatient with the intrusion of informants' financial need in his quest for ancient songs. Yet McAtee kept at it. She was cold and unresponsive, Cox reported, until she requested a Christmas gift. Once he promised to give her one, she became animated and shared many of her songs with the collector.[79] Southern singers understood folk song collections as financial ventures for the collectors, and they tried to get in on the action.

Many of the black southern singers who spoke to the sociologist Howard Odum during his collecting of secular songs insisted that they should be paid for sharing them with the scholar. "The singers are often conscious that they are singing folk-songs, and they attempt to pose as the authors," Odum asserted. One informant declared, "Song composed by Will Smith of Chattanooga, Tennessee," before every song he sung into Odum's graphophone. "He maintained," Odum explained, "these songs would be sung all over the world, and he deserved the credit for them." When challenged, Smith backed off his claim of authorship. Yet some informants insisted that they be paid even when they had not written the song. Odum recalled one singer explaining that he got a song from a nearby town "and that he had been forced to pay dearly for it (therefore he should be rewarded accordingly)." Odum concluded from these encounters that black informants tended to deceive. They claimed credit for songs that were not theirs, "misleading the investigator by misquoting the songs" or "giving verses which they have got from books or papers, or heard from 'coon songs.' "[80]

These accounts suggest that many southern musicians understood their encounters with folklorists to be professional or commercial events. Artists who had attempted to make their music pay at their worksites, on the streets, and in makeshift theaters saw performing for scholars as another professional opportunity. Many artists understood that folklorists had an access to the mass media that they themselves lacked. Publishing held the possibility of money and exposure as surely as commercial recording did. The artists who contributed their music to both mediums often considered them the same. The African American blues musician Son House was apparently quite dismayed in 1942 when John's son Alan Lomax recorded his music all day for the Library of Congress yet gave the guitarist nothing more than a cold Coke.[81] Likewise, the black singer Willie Blackwell waxed a song for Alan Lomax yet insisted that the collector not circulate the performance, for he intended to record it for a commercial label. He understood that recording for a folklorist could conflict with his contract with the commercial label, so he insisted that Lomax not use his real name.[82] Both Lomax and the commercial scouts were making a living off of recording his songs. Blackwell did not see the difference.

Even when they did not request payment, informants reminded folklorists that they understood the assumptions of the collector's project and that their participation should not be taken for granted. "You're jes' lucky I happened to want to sing this mornin'. Maybe to-morrow I wouldn't 'a' sung you nothin'," an African American woman in a Texas levee camp warned John Lomax. "Anyhow, maybe to-morrow I won't be here. I'm likely to git tired, or mad, an' go. Say, if I got mad, I'd about dump that tub o' wet clo's there in that bed, an' I wouldn't be here by night."[83] Dorothy Scarborough recalled gathering songs from black Texans to be presented at a meeting of the Texas Folklore Association. When she requested songs from an African American woman sitting on her front porch, Scarborough wrote,

> She desired to know why I wanted them. I explained elaborately that I *liked* old songs.
>
> "What you gwine to *do* with 'em?" she persisted.
>
> "Oh—er,—remember them and write them down so I can keep them," I parried.
>
> She gave me a glance of scorn for my subterfuge, as she grunted, "You's Miss Dottie Scarber, and that mettin' of yores is on the twenty-fust!"
>
> I had over looked the fact of my press announcements!
>
> But she consented to give me some songs.[84]

In 1936, Elizabeth Gordon, a white collector for the Works Progress Administration, transcribed several songs from Carrie Richardson, an elderly African American woman who lived in Jackson County, Mississippi. She reported an incident that occurred during her transcription of Richardson's "Don' Call de Roll." "Of course, I wanted it, so she sang it over for me and then I tried to get it down," Gordon explained. "I was very much amused when she was giving me the words. She said, 'Goin' to make a lit'l inquirashun' stopped and asked, 'I guess you want 'gwine' instead of 'goin', don't you?' Rather nonplussed I dubiously answered, 'I guess so', so she nodded her head and much to my amusement, 'Gwine' it was until I had it all written down—words and music— to her complete satisfaction."[85] Richardson and the others, it appears, understood that their words and their art were escaping them into a form—be it phonograph record or hastily scrawled notes—over which they would have little control. Richardson also understood that the collector was not interested in notating songs as she sang them as much as in creating a stylized vision of black folk culture out of her raw material. Asserting their presence and cognizance of the collecting process, these informants challenged the authority of folklorists to control the representation of their culture. However, it is important to note that they also accommodated the desires of the collectors. Richardson's fluid conversion to standard dialect not only showed Gordon that she was aware of the assumptions and distortions involved in the folkloric process. It also demonstrated the singer's ability to shape her performance to the needs and expectations of a particular audience—a hallmark of professionalism in local southern music markets.

Huddie Ledbetter used many of the same techniques in his dealings with John Lomax as he turned the role of folk informant into that of paid working musician. The folklorist noted the profit potential of Ledbetter's songs as soon as he met the singer. Ledbetter was equally excited about the financial prospects of his relationship with the aging ballad hunter. He began writing to Lomax while he was still in Angola. "Com Back after me if not now find out when they are going to turn me out and send me a tick[et]," he wrote in 1934. On August 10, 1934, he wrote to announce he was out of prison, stating, "i am looking for you[.] i am going to work for you."[86] The following month he wrote with more urgency: "let me here from you com after me soon as you can[.] im not got no job waiting on you so i haven got any money."[87] Lomax later lamented, "He confessedly cares for me only because I am 'the money man.' "[88]

Ledbetter was adept at playing up the role of the loyal servant to the white Lomax once he was hired as the scholar's driver and assistant. He often praised Lomax's kindness, repeatedly referring to him as "kind Boss." Early in their association, Lomax quoted him as saying, "You got me out of the pen. Ise yo man. You won't ever have to tie yo shoes again if you don't want to. I'll step in front of you if ever anybody tries to shoot you. I'm ready to die for you, Boss."[89] Yet the singer would also skip out on Lomax as they were traveling in new cities, forcing the collector to stop working and search for him. Ledbetter would then suddenly return, a night or a few days later, and be sternly unapologetic for his absence.[90] Lomax interpreted these absences in terms of Ledbetter's racial character, fiscal irresponsibility, and ego. "I regret to say that I probably will not be able to keep [him], partly because the praise of his music spoiling him and partly because of his Shreveport woman. If I understood the nature of a negro," he lamented, "I could perhaps do something with him to the end that I could sell his product. But he is too much of a child to wait."[91] Yet Lomax continued to employ the singer. In the early months of their association, at least, Ledbetter was able to balance his two stances: appeasing Lomax with gratuitous praise and subservience while carving out at least some time and space to do what he wished.

Lomax and Ledbetter needed each other's help reaching audiences to which they would not otherwise have access. As they toured southern prisons in search of songs in the fall of 1934, Ledbetter proved invaluable to Lomax. The singer often began their prison visits by performing a brief concert. The show would put other black performers at ease, as well as demonstrate the kind of material Lomax was after.[92] Lomax could not have recorded all the music he did without Ledbetter's assistance. At the same time, Lomax provided Ledbetter with larger and better-paying audiences than the singer had ever known. In December, they presented at the annual Modern Language Association meeting in Philadelphia. John and Alan Lomax read "Negro Folksongs and Ballads," as Ledbetter demonstrated the material with song. The event was a novel mix of scholarship and theater. Following the presentation, Ledbetter passed his hat and received $47.50 in donations from the academic crowd—not a paltry sum. When passing the hat at society gatherings, Ledbetter turned toward the tricks of the minstrel trade he had learned in his Texas busking days. Lomax explained, "He never failed to delight his audience when he 'passed his hat' at the end of his program. Then he always became the smiling cajoling Southern darky minstrel extracting nickels from his 'White folks.' He would bow and thank each visitor with amusing comments, 'Bless Gawd, dat's a dime! Where is all de quarters? Thank you, boss! Thank you, missy, thank you! Wait back dere, don' you see me comin'?' "[93] The money made from passing the hat at such meetings was kept by Ledbetter and may go a long way toward explaining his attraction to Lomax. "Even when I had agreed on a fixed fee he seemed always disappointed when he could not pass his hat," Lomax recalled.[94] As the singer's notoriety began to grow in early 1935, however, Lomax insisted that the proceeds from the hat should be split evenly between Ledbetter, John, and Alan.[95]

Ledbetter's well-documented trip to New York in 1935 was an economic boon to both the singer and the scholar. They took New York and the nation by storm, filling papers with stories of the convict in town to sing a few songs between homicides—and the ballad hunter by his side. In January, Lomax exclaimed to Terrill, "Leadbelly at this moment is the most famous nigger in the world and I the most notorious white man. Where does this leave you? I have just *sold* him for cash money to a party on Sunday January 20 at which the Mayor of New York is the guest of honor."[96] The pair was inundated with performance opportunities and book deals, and they were the subjects of a major newsreel feature. Their standard rate for concert appearances was between $50 and $100, plus the proceeds from the hat.[97]

The story of Lomax and Ledbetter, scholar and musician, suggests many of the tensions and expectations found in similar (if less sensational) relationships. The two came to each other with dramatically different agendas and expectations. Lomax had been struggling financially before he met Ledbetter. He wrote of the economic possibilities of their relationship the very day he met the singer. Here was the isolated primitive he had been touting for several decades. Lomax would become famous bringing his songs to the world. Ledbetter imagined Lomax to be a ticket out of the world of work, poverty, and prejudice that had twice landed him in prison. Lomax maintained the rights to many of Ledbetter's songs and benefited more from their publication. The two were in no way on equal economic footing. Yet each transformed the relationship into a continuation and escalation of the careers they had been building before they ever met. Folk music had become a way to get paid. One could sell books, records, and concert tickets by promising genuine music untainted by the marketplace.

As the bright lights of the photographers' flashbulbs began to dull, so did the relationship between John Lomax and Huddie Ledbetter. Beyond the spotlight (and maybe because of the pressures the spotlight entailed), the one who whipped became increasingly insolent and uncontrollable in the eyes of the one who named. In March 1935, the duo pressed through severe weather during a series of engagements in upstate New York. In Rochester, Ledbetter skipped out on Lomax, heading to the African American section of town. Lomax wrote,

> After breakfast yesterday he had proved so angelic that I allowed him to take the car for a short drive into the negro section. At noon, four hours later he was still out of pocket. I waited awhile and then my host and I set out on a search for him. He could not be found. Next a police station where my car number was flashed over the city. I waited until 6 p.m. in that dreary station. No Huddie; no car. Finally we drove sadly back to my room where we found him and a negro tramp both half drunk. We got through . . . when Huddie announced that he was taking his friend back to town where they had been invited to a party. I objected and almost begged him to spare himself.[98]

Eleven days later, things had gotten worse. "About Huddie," Lomax wrote, "he got entirely out of hand, sat up and sang all night to negroes in low barrel houses, stayed drunk four days, disobeyed me and finally, after various threats became ugly and dangerous." In an echo of their original encounter, the law stepped between the two. "For the last 24 hours in Buffalo he was under arrest, the Chief of Detentions brought him to his last concert with his voice all gone from laryngitis developed from shouting his songs in the open air. Until the last moment the chief had planned to drive to Buffalo with me. Without money and sober again Huddie became humble again," Lomax explained, before concluding, "You need not worry about the future either, for he is afraid of the law or rather what the law can do to him. I'll tell him that he must never be found in Austin."[99]

One can only imagine how Ledbetter might have told the story differently. He was a singer used to performing what he liked reduced to singing what he was told; a veteran of countless black house parties being booked at white society functions and academic conferences; a southerner on a road trip to Buffalo, about as far away from friends and family as he could imagine. Control of his money, his mobility, and his schedule were in another's hands, even as he saw New York clamoring to glimpse his face. The bottle, the fleeting visits to local African American neighborhoods, the all-night sessions in barrelhouses may have been his way of coping with the strange, uncontrollable world in which he found himself. His reaction was testament to the ways in which folklore had beaten minstrelsy at its own game. While it held the potential of identifying and celebrating the black musical tradition, folklore also provided a potent means to define black inferiority and control African American artists. Ledbetter's drunken binges recalled nothing more clearly than Gus Cannon's reaction to wearing burnt cork for his patent medicine gigs in the South. "I had to have a shot of liquor before the show," Cannon recalled. "If I didn't it seemed like I couldn't be funny in front of all them people. When I had one it seemed like them people was one and I would throw up the banjo in the air and really put on a show."[100]

Even as the relationship between Ledbetter and Lomax was swinging from triumph to tragedy, controversy surrounding another Lomax discovery was developing into an illustration of folklore's new relationship to commercial music. "Home on the Range" became the subject of a copyright lawsuit that found the folklorist defending a phonograph company and commercial publishers celebrating the public domain. The song had attracted little attention in the two decades after it appeared in *Cowboy Songs*. In 1925, David Guion of Texas, a friend and correspondent of Lomax's, quietly published an arrangement of the song in sheet music form. Vernon Dalhart made the first commercial recording of the tune in 1927. "Home on the Range" was one of a number of western-themed ditties that Dalhart, the former "Negro dialect" singer, released in the late twenties as part of a successful bid to reinvent himself as an interpreter of hillbilly and cowboy fare.[101] The record was not a big seller. The song's fortunes changed abruptly when Franklin Delano Roosevelt, responding to a softball question on the night of his election in 1932, dubbed "Home on the Range" his favorite song. Soon everyone wanted to hear it. Radio stations featured it nightly. At least twenty-five publishers released sheet music scores. Every major recording company issued a version of the song, including a particularly popular rendition by the crooner Bing Crosby in 1933. The song spread quickly precisely because it was considered a folk song in the public domain. It lacked copyright protection, thus companies could reap large profits without paying composer royalties.[102]

In May 1933, Ralph Peer wrote a letter to John Lomax requesting the ballad hunter's help in determining the origins of "Home on the Range." The successful record scout and founder of the Southern Music Publishing Company was preparing to file a suit on behalf of clients William and Mary Goodwin, who claimed to have written and copyrighted a version of the song in 1905. Lomax shot back a terse reply. "I am under obligations to the RCA-Victor Company and would, therefore, take unusual pleasure in serving them in the matter," he wrote. He told of learning the song in 1908 or 1909 from a saloonkeeper in San Antonio. The African American man claimed to have learned it on the cattle drives of the 1880s. Knowledge of its provenance in oral tradition, Lomax implied, should thwart any attempts to extract money from the commercial publishers, record companies, and radio stations that had featured the song.[103] Peer, not satisfied with Lomax's response, continued to prepare the suit. As word spread, potential defendants contacted Lomax for help in establishing legal proof that "Home on the Range" was indeed a folk song.[104] All he could offer was his story of discovery, a tale that did not directly contradict the Goodwins' claims. Peer filed the suit in the spring of 1934. It demanded $500,000 in damages from thirty-five defendants: major radio broadcasting companies, publishing houses, and individuals who had published or performed the song, including Vernon Dalhart's regular collaborator Carson G. Robison.[105] Overnight, the song disappeared from the airwaves as the industry scrambled to avoid potential infractions and craft an organized response. John Lomax, himself convinced that the song was a folk song but uncertain about the outcome of the suit, pulled "Home on the Range" from his book *American Ballads and Folk Songs* right before it went to press.[106]

This is when commercial publishers got into the business of folklore. The Music Publishers Protective Association (MPPA) took over the defense of the suit. The organization hired a New York lawyer named Samuel Moanfeldt to investigate the origins of the song in the hope of contradicting the Goodwins' claim. In February 1935, Moanfeldt launched a three-month-long journey through Missouri, Kansas, Colorado, and Pennsylvania that resembled nothing so much as John Lomax's own collecting trips in search of folk songs. Following a series of leads given to him by MPPA researchers and correspondence sent from all over the country, Moanfeldt wound up in Dodge City, Kansas, the center of "cowboy country" in his own estimation. "There I interviewed a great number of people such as ex-cowboys, people who were employed as cooks in cowboy camps, ex-stage coach drivers and Buffalo hunters," Moanfeldt reported to the MPPA. "A great number of written statements were procured by me from these people and they all agreed that this song was well known to and generally sung by cowboys and other people traveling through that section of the country in stage coaches prior to 1890 and that the lyrics and music were practically identical with those now generally used by radio singers and they all stated that they recognized the tune as soon as the same became popular over the radio." Moanfeldt believed such testimony was sufficient to challenge the Goodwins' copyright claims, but he continued on his journey in search of more information. He eventually determined the song was probably written by Brewster Higley and Daniel Kelly of Kansas in the 1870s, long enough ago for any copyright to have elapsed. His investigation convinced Peer and the Goodwins to drop the suit. Determined to be in the public domain, "Home on the Range" could once again reap profits.[107]

AFTERWORD

"All Songs is Folk Songs"

"I guess all songs is folk songs. I never heard no horse sing 'em." Bill Broonzy's remarks leapt from the pages of *Time* magazine on November 23, 1962. James Meredith, a twenty-nine-year-old African American man, recently had braved riots to register at the University of Mississippi. Federal troops had confronted segregationist mobs as word of Meredith's struggle spread across the South and the evening news. The previously temperate *Time* was warming to Meredith's cause. The magazine chided Mississippi judge Walter O'Barr, a vocal fan of the state governor's attempt to refuse Meredith admission. "Laughable, but Not Funny," the headline read. Broonzy's comments appeared elsewhere in the issue as part of a cover story on the burgeoning folk song revival. "Removed from its natural backgrounds, folk singing has become both an esoteric cult and a light industry," the magazine reported. "Purists" gathered around college campuses and urban coffeehouses were learning to cherish folk songs for their simplicity, spirituality, and antiquity. Folk singers represented and preserved a holistic culture that had survived generations. Their songs flowed from a deep source a world apart from the products of the modern commercial music industry, they insisted. Broonzy, "the unwashed darling of purist fans," disagreed. The African American singer claimed that his world was larger than that. He insisted that all songs were folk songs. His rebuke may have been funny, but it was no joke. Broonzy knew exactly what he was saying.[1]

The two stories in *Time* were intertwined more deeply than many readers may have recognized. Purist visions of American folk culture developed at the same time that Jim Crow segregation put its stranglehold on southern states. Their histories were deeply intertwined. I have attempted to trace the emergence of a new musical color line in the first decades of the twentieth century. The musical color line emerged out of a number of processes that combined to replace minstrel notions of authenticity based on racial and market contact with folkloric ones that valued isolation. We have seen a number of groups come to this conclusion through various means between the 1880s and the 1930s. Southern segregation in law and practice; the corporate quest for niche musical markets; and the theoretical delineation of separate racial cultures in the discipline of folklore: each constructed divisions among American citizens, attempting to organize culture and society according to categories that did not reflect many southern people's complex lives. Broonzy spent a good part of his life challenging them all.

Bill Broonzy's words have enjoyed a long life in academic studies of folklore, popular culture, and African American music. Scholars from the 1960s through the first decade of the new century have invoked and repeated his "all songs is folk songs" as they have grappled with the irreducible dichotomies of the musical color line: the split between black and white expression, on the one hand, and between folklore and commercial culture on the other. Following his phrase through time reveals both the central interpretive role that the folkloric paradigm has continued to play in American music scholarship and the persistent inadequacy of these central dichotomies to explain or contain U.S. music history.[2]

Every decade since Broonzy uttered his words, scholars have invoked his "all songs" bit to poke holes in someone else's purist vision of folk music or culture. In 1963, the *Time* author used the quote to skewer what the writer considered the pretension and hypocrisy of the folk song revival. Slumming college students "sipping Java at 60 [cents] a cup" deified the "shiftless geniuses who have shouted the songs of their forebears into tape recorders provided by the Library of Congress." They had an odd love for Woody Guthrie, "who never held a job more than a week or so, always needed a shave, and sang for anybody who cared to listen." Such romantic valorization of poverty and sloth, the article concluded, was "closely allied with social protest and liberal politics" among folk song revivalists. The author used Broonzy's joke to cast aspersions on the whole lot.[3]

Broonzy's words performed a similar function in the ethnomusicologist

Charles Keil's book *Urban Blues* in 1966. Keil leveled "all songs is folk songs" as a critique of the blues scholars of the 1950s. "No neater summary of the present chapter's argument could be found," he wrote. White writers such as Samuel Charters, Paul Oliver, and Harold Courlander, insisted Keil, were preoccupied with a romantic quest for the " 'real' blues," which they identified as an early-twentieth-century music that had become diluted through commercialization, electrification, and pandering to mass audiences. Charters later acknowledged the romanticism in his seminal book *The Country Blues* (1959) that came under Keil's attack. In his own defense, he claimed that the book was designed to make folk song collecting attractive to new recruits; to open white youth to the power of black music and black voices during the civil rights struggle; and to escape the academic tendency to reduce vernacular music to "sociological" meanings. Charters and his 1950s peers attempted to reclaim a certain universal value for African American folk music, to free it from the grip of Popular Front–influenced writers who, in their estimation, had heard the music as a mere function of southern racial and class politics.[4]

In 1966, Charles Keil was having none of this. He insisted that the group valorized ancient blues singers because they were old, poor, and obscure and ignored the vibrant contemporary blues scene. Locating black musical authenticity in the past, Keil charged, white scholars could assuage their liberal guilt while averting their eyes from the contemporary plight of African Americans. "All songs is folk songs" enabled him to critique the romance of folk purity, while extending the model of folklore into the commercial marketplace. *Urban Blues* attempted to reveal a generalized vision of black masculinity through an exploration of the professional African American bluesman. In order to do this, Keil argued that folk culture was not destroyed through commercial mass-mediation. It was perpetuated and even intensified. "The strands of a folk tradition have been brought together; the music of a people has been unified, energized, amplified, and disseminated with an efficiency that seems fantastic," he wrote. In a strategy first pursued by folklorists during the 1920s, Keil insisted that folk culture was alive and well on the commercial urban blues stage. Professional musicians performed the traditional roles of shamans and griots, educating and exorcising African American blues listeners from the concert stage. Their work thus enabled Keil to extrapolate the concerns of African American men from the words and actions of blues singers. It might come as no surprise that he found black men to be preoccupied with sex, heartache, and itinerant travel.[5]

The urge to access listeners' thoughts through musical lyrics flowered in the 1970s as one of the methodological innovations of the new cultural history. The historian Lawrence Levine, for example, used song lyrics to locate "black culture and black consciousness" in his landmark study of that name, published in 1977. Levine believed Broonzy's "all songs" barb came out of the singer's "exasperation with those folklorists who insisted that a true folk song had to be of unknown authorship and be transmitted through the oral tradition." He immediately backpedaled away from the import of the joke, however, by insisting that the singer meant to endorse Levine's own vision of a communal black folk culture. "While his interpretation of folk music may have been too all-inclusive," Levine wrote, Broonzy meant that African Americans understood music as a "*participant* activity." The non sequitur did little to illuminate Broonzy's remark, but it did enable Levine to identify black consciousness through the interpretation of folk song lyrics. "This folk quality of black music is precisely what makes it such an important medium for getting at the thought, spirit, and history of the very segment of the Negro community that historians have rendered inarticulate through their neglect," he contended.[6] Levine proceeded to use the folk song collections from the late nineteenth and early twentieth centuries to provide evidence of "black culture and black consciousness." Considering his sources, his equation between culture and consciousness was no surprise.

We get far closer to the radicalism of Broonzy's message in the work of Andrew Ross and Robin D. G. Kelley. Each invoked "all songs" as part of a critique of "folk" as a category that assumes purity and authenticity. Ross argued that standard narratives equate commercial music with white tastes and desires to such an extent that it becomes impossible to local black authenticity anywhere but outside the commercial marketplace in an idealized "folk" culture. He challenged these presumptions by demonstrating how shifting "black" and "white" meanings get circulated through the commercial music industry. Far from being devoid of authentic black voices, commercial popular culture remains the central channel through which these voices circulate and negotiations about what gets valued as authentic take place. Commercial music, Ross insisted, matters in people's lives in a way we used to think only folk music could. Kelley quoted Broonzy (and Ross) in order to demonstrate how what we have come to see as "folk" culture operates in the same way. Never pure of outside influences, "folk" cultures have always been assembled from various influences, shifting scope and meaning over time. They are also constantly engaged with commercial media and technology. The question for Kelley was how technology influences "orality," how "mass-mediated forms" alter "the conditions in which culture is made, revised and contested." So-called folk music, Kelley concluded, has always been as messy, convoluted, and full of power plays as scholars used to imagine only commercial music could be. Kelley found that Broonzy's line offered "perhaps the most powerful challenge to the social construction of 'the folk.' "[7] Yet even Ross and Kelley, two authors intent on "deconstructing the folk," maintained an ur-culture at their respective points of origin. Kelley quoted Ross on the complex historical interaction between black and white styles: "Elvis's rockabilly hair, greased up with Royal Crown Pomade to emulate the black 'process' of straightening and curling, itself a black attempt to look 'white.' " While finely attuned to the ways in which socially constructed "folk" and "pop" music discourses wield power, they suggested that the myriad "hybrid cultural forms" that constitute pop music's convoluted racial history are the result of endless border raids across an identifiable cultural color line: white style imitates black style imitating white style.

What these authors invoking Broonzy share is a commitment to the concept of a folk tradition not only as a historical reality but also as the primary way in which to examine people's relationship to each other, their past, and commercial culture. Racial traditions function as the frames for their studies, defining their object and scope of inquiry. And racial traditions historically have been defined through or against the folk discourse that is the object of Broonzy's ridicule. The folk discourse cannot contain or refute his critique on its own. Attempts to embrace the singer's demolition of the folk category without moving beyond the frame of a racial tradition inevitably circle back to a restatement of the premise of racial folk cultures. These cultures may be more broad and diversified than previous writers had acknowledged. They may be modern and commercialized, hybrid and omnivorous, but they remain knowing and knowable communal cultures bounded by race and sound. The musicologist Richard Middleton may have summarized this problem inadvertently when he began his book *Studying Popular Music* (1990) by paraphrasing Bill Broonzy. Middleton substituted the word "popular" for "folk" in the "all songs" joke only to dismiss the significance of Broonzy's remark. "Unfortunately," he wrote, "this would be to empty the term of most of the meanings which it carries in actual discourse." The incantation of Broonzy's joke again functioned as an inoculation. Acknowledging the fallacies of simplistic conceptual categories protected the writer as he maintained the importance of categorical boundaries. Yet Middleton's comments, as usual, were informative. He rejected Broonzy's definition, not because it misrepresented the music or musicians but because it did not correspond to the "discourse" about music that was his primary concern.[8]

This book began with an imaginative leap. Instead of assuming that Broonzy anticipated the critique of the 1960s blues revival, 1970s desires to write history from below, or the deconstructionism of the late twentieth century, I wondered if his words might better be understood as a reflection of attitudes that prevailed during the singer's southern youth around the dawn of the twentieth century. It was a formative musical era that gave birth to the blues, country music, and an array of associated sounds. Here, before the erection of the folklore paradigm later writers repeatedly invoked and dismantled, black and white southerners did not talk about music in the terms of folklore. They acknowledged no operative difference between folk and nonfolk songs, between music made and music acquired by other means. All songs were equally available to help them make sense of their worlds.

Southern musicians and audiences at the beginning of the twentieth century willingly, even eagerly, imbibed all the music they could find. In addition to the styles originating in the South, southerners seized on sounds of the commercial music industry. Southerners thirsted for novel sounds, soaking them up from whatever sources they could find and integrating them into the musical worlds. Yet they often found different meanings in the variety of music they performed. Some, like Bill Broonzy, broadened their culture to deny the politics of exclusion that drove Jim Crow. Others embraced new tunes to help perpetuate it. Southerners turned to new songs to declare their own sophistication or to bring new communities into being, to articulate a southern identity or to ally themselves with the North, the nation, or the wider world. Some even sang new songs simply because they were pleasurable.

Bill Broonzy was hip to Richard Middleton's distinction between discourse and lived experience. The singer prefaced his concerts in the 1950s with a critique of the "folk songs" he was about to sing. "They name them that. We'll have to call them that," he demurred before dropping his "horses don't sing songs" bit. Acknowledging that "they"—academics, record executives, concert promoters, perhaps—held the power to define music, Broonzy incorporated the new category into his own performance and twisted it to fit his musical, economic, and political purposes. "So I call them all folk songs," he explained. "If you hear a song you like, well, sing it. If you don't like it, don't sing it."[9] His broad definition of folk songs combated not only academic pigeonholes but also the musical color line that helped define the Jim Crow era.

Born around 1893 in Scott, Mississippi, Broonzy learned early what it meant to be a black resident in the segregated South. He encountered Jim Crow every day. He was denied entrance to his local church. He could not travel to nearby towns without fear of white violence. His parents, barred from purchasing nearby farmland, struggled to escape the cyclical debt that was the common curse of black sharecroppers. Broonzy began working at the age of seven, caring for community children, helping his family in the cotton fields, and looking for a way out. He soon discovered that he could use music to mitigate and circumvent Jim Crow. His musical life began when he constructed a homemade violin at the age of ten and began entertaining friends and family. Local white residents soon noticed his skills, and they asked him to play for their dances and "two-way" picnics attended by the area's white and black communities. Performing for white listeners had its advantages. "We would be playing and sitting under screened porches while the other Negroes had to work in the hot sun," Broonzy recalled. After stints sharecropping, coal mining, and in the army, Broonzy moved to Chicago in 1920 and became a key figure in that city's burgeoning blues scene. He came to the attention of a national white audience in 1939, when the promoter John Hammond included him in the famous "Spirituals to Swing" concert at Carnegie Hall. By the 1950s, Broonzy was a popular performer on the folk revival circuit, playing not only the country blues that he recorded while in Chicago but a wide variety of American popular and folk songs. Broonzy's career confounded musical categories. The musician repeatedly reinvented himself and his sound, using his music to circumvent the color line, travel where he wanted to go, and eventually get paid for the strength of his singing instead of his back.[10]

Broonzy spoke from decades of experience in using music to forge and express his own freedom when he declared "all songs is folk songs." His simple definition did not make any distinction regarding the origins or the performance context of folk songs. Folk songs were simply whatever the folk sang. Yet central to the humor of his remark was a resoundingly broad conception of "the folk." The folk included everyone from the sharecropper humming behind a tuneless mule to the singer whose opening night at New York's Hippodrome was heralded in the papers. "All songs is folk songs" was an argument against reductive cultural categories. It was akin to the writer Ralph Ellison's equally snappy response in 1964 to folklorists who mistook the "prefabricated Negroes" they created for actual black people: "Watch out, Jack, there's people living under here." Each identified cultural and conceptual categories as ways to wield power rather than reflections of people's actual lives.[11] Broonzy's was also an argument about musical ownership. People could claim a song simply by performing it. They could make it their own, both in terms of refiguring it within their own artistic style and in terms of claiming it as part of their cultural possessions and heritage. Sheet music, a phonograph record, or a family gathering: where they learned the song was irrelevant. Broonzy insisted that all culture—and by inference all society—belonged to the folk. "I guess all songs is folk songs. I never heard no horse sing 'em." With these words Bill Broonzy joined a legion of artists intent on maintaining unique aspects of their culture without being reduced to them.

Introduction

1. Interview with Ralph Peer, 1959, Hollywood, California, by Lillian Borgeson, Tape #FT2772c, Southern Folklife Collection.
2. Scarborough, *On the Trail of Negro Folk-Songs*, 3.
3. Quoted in Barlow, *Looking Up at Down*, 46.
4. Important studies of Jim Crow segregation include Woodward, *Origins of the New South*; Woodward, *The Strange Career of Jim Crow*; Tindall, *The Emergence of the New South*; Ayers, *The Promise of the New South*; Hall, *Revolt against Chivalry*; McMillen, *Dark Journey*; Litwack, *Trouble in Mind*.
5. A number of scholars have emphasized the importance of the cultural aspects of southern segregation. Key works include Kelley, *Hammer and Hoe*; Kelley, *Race Rebels*; Hale, *Making Whiteness*; Dailey, Gilmore, and Simon, eds., *Jumpin' Jim Crow*; Tyson, *Radio Free Dixie*; Blue, *The Dawn at My Back*; Green, *Battling the Plantation Mentality*.
6. Ferris, *Blues from the Delta*, 96–97.
7. My interpretation of antebellum minstrelsy in this and the following paragraph is influenced by Toll, *Blacking Up*, 66–71; Nathan, *Dan Emmett and the Rise of Early Negro Minstrelsy*; Hamm, *Yesterdays*, 118–22; Denison, *Scandalize My Name*; Roediger, *The Wages of Whiteness*; Lott, *Love and Theft*; Saxton, *The Rise and Fall of the White Republic*; Lhamon, *Raising Cain*; Mahar, *Behind the Burnt Cork Mask*; Bean, Hatch, and McNamara, eds., *Inside the Blackface Mask*.
8. Hamm, *Yesterdays*, 118–22; Nathan, *Dan Emmett*, 50–52; Lott, *Love and Theft*, 18–19; 51–62; Toll, *Blacking Up*, 43–46; Roediger, *Wages of Whiteness*, 116–17.
9. Lott, *Love and Theft*, 16, 20; Toll, *Blacking Up*, 38.
10. Radano, *Lying Up a Nation*; Toll, *Blacking Up*, 51; Cruz, *Culture on the Margins*.
11. Potter, *The South and the Sectional Conflict*, 181–82; Cobb, *Away Down South*, 2; Ayers, *What Caused the Civil War?*, 41.
12. Wilgus, *Anglo-American Folksong Scholarship since 1898*; Bronner, *American*

Folklore Studies; Bendix, *In Search of Authenticity*; Graff, *Professing Literature*; Fabian, *Time and the Other*; Clifford, *The Predicament of Culture*; Rosaldo, *Culture and Truth*; Kirshenblatt-Gimblett, "Folklore's Crisis"; Baker, *From Savage to Negro*; Cruz, *Culture on the Margins*.

13. Kirshenblatt-Gimblett, "Folklore's Crisis," 286; Baker, *From Savage to Negro*, 2.

14. Lears, *No Place of Grace*; di Leonardo, *Exotics at Home*; Torgovnick, *Gone Primitive*.

15. Nicholls, *Conjuring the Folk*; Favor, *Authentic Blackness*; Whisnant, *All That Is Native and Fine*.

16. Levine, "The Folklore of Industrial Society"; Levine, *Black Culture and Black Consciousness*; Lipsitz, *Time Passages*; Lipsitz, *Footsteps in the Dark*; Keil, *Urban Blues*; Keil and Feld, *Music Grooves*; Frith, *Performing Rites*.

17. Critiques of romantic depictions of folk music from writers include Abrahams, "Phantoms of Romantic Nationalism in Folkloristics"; Kirshenblatt-Gimblett, "Folklore's Crisis"; Kelley, "Notes on Deconstructing 'The Folk'"; Ross, *No Respect*, 65–89. Explorations of commercial depictions of folk authenticity include Peterson, *Creating Country Music*; Becker, *Selling Tradition*; Titon, *Early Downhome Blues*, 218–60; Rosenberg, ed., *Transforming Tradition*; Cantwell, *When We Were Good*; Pecknold, *The Selling Sound*.

18. This study thus joins a growing number of works that carry the story of minstrelsy into the twentieth century. See Toll, *Blacking Up*; Rogin, *Blackface, White Noise*; Abbott and Seroff, *Out of Sight*; Sotiropoulos, *Staging Race*; Chude-Sokei, *The Last "Darkey."*

19. Szwed, "Race and the Embodiment of Culture," 27; Lott, *Love and Theft*, 7. For a similar invocation of this passage, see McCracken, " 'God's Gift to Us Girls,' " 370.

20. Painter, *Southern History across the Color Line*, 2. See also Brundage, *The Southern Past*.

21. The list of musical genre studies is vast. A few books that I have not already cited but that have been particularly important to me include Evans, *Big Road Blues*; Malone, *Country Music, USA*; Peña, *The Texas-Mexican Conjunto*.

22. Otto and Burns, "Black and White Cultural Interaction in the Early Twentieth Century South," 407; Gilroy, *The Black Atlantic*; Fields, "Slavery, Race and Ideology in the United States of America," 95–118.

23. Russell, *Blacks, Whites, and Blues*, 26–31, quote on 31. Russell's study, for all of its slapdash prose and maddening refusal to cite sources, remains one of the major inspirations for this book. Other studies of the interracial character of southern music and cultural traditions include Malone, *Southern Music/American Music*; Malone, "Blacks and Whites and the Music of the Old South"; Trietler, "Toward a Desegregated Music Historiography"; Daniel, *Lost Revolutions*; Joyner, *Shared Traditions*; Sobel, *The World They Made Together*; Abrahams, *Singing the Master*; Cohen, "The Folk Music Interchange"; Abbott, " 'Play That Barber Shop

Chord.' " Important works that extend the scope of inquiry to include Mexican, Latino, and Eastern European cultural influences include Roberts, *The Latin Tinge*; Greene, *A Passion for Polka*; Navárez, "Afro-American and Mexican Street Singers"; Navárez, "The Influences of Hispanic Music Cultures on African-American Blues Musicians."

24. Genovese, *Roll, Jordan, Roll*, 316.

25. Born and Hesmondhalgh, eds., *Western Music and Its Others*; Radano and Bohlman, eds., *Music and the Racial Imagination*; Radano, *Lying Up a Nation*; Lott, *Love and Theft*; Cruz, *Culture on the Margins*; Hall, "What Is This 'Black' in Black Popular Culture?"; Harkins, *Hillbilly*; Grundy, " 'We Always Tried to Be Good People' "; Carby, *Race Men*. For a critique of extreme racial constructivism and anti-essentialism, see Ramsey, "The Pot Liquor Principle."

26. Radano, *Lying Up a Nation*; Cruz, *Culture on the Margins*; Epstein, *Sinful Tunes and Spirituals*.

27. A useful overview of the spiritual origins controversy can be found in Wilgus, *Anglo-American Folksong Scholarship*, 344–64. See also Epstein, "A White Origin for the Black Spiritual?"; Levine, *Black Culture and Black Consciousness*, 19–25.

28. Leonard, *Jazz and the White Americans*; Ogren, *The Jazz Revolution*; Gennari, *Blowin' Hot and Cool*.

29. Three studies that directly counter this point of view are Rose, *Black Noise*; George, *Hip Hop America*; Walser, "Rhythm, Rhyme, and Rhetoric in the Music of Public Enemy."

30. Nathan Glazer and Daniel Patrick Moynihan, *Beyond the Melting Pot* (Cambridge, Mass.: MIT Press, 1963), 53; quoted in Levine, *Black Culture and Black Consciousness*, 443. For an earlier critique of their position, see Herskovits, *The Myth of the Negro Past*. For a concise summary of the debates surrounding Herskovits and black culture, see Joyner, *Shared Traditions*, chap. 2.

31. Jones, *Blues People*; Levine, *Black Culture and Black Consciousness;* Floyd, *The Power of Black Music*; Ramsey, *Race Music*.

32. Christopher A. Waterman, "Race Music: Bo Chatmon, 'Corrine Corrina,' and the Excluded Middle," in Radano and Bohlman, eds., *Music and the Racial Imagination*, 167.

33. A nice overview of this literature can be found in Kapchan, "Performance." See also Rudy, "Toward an Assessment of Verbal Art as Performance."

34. This literature is vast. I have cited it throughout the book. For a useful introduction to the promise and perils of defining black music through a focus on performance characteristics, see Wilson, "Black Music as an Art Form."

35. Steven Feld, "Communication, Music, and Speech about Music," in Keil and Feld, *Music Grooves*, 77–91, quote on 91. See also Frith, *Performing Rites*, 18.

36. Interview with Samuel Chatman, November 14, 1973, by Margaret McKee and Fred Chisenhall, "Beale Street Black and Blue," oral history transcripts.

1. Peabody, "Notes on Negro Music," 149. Examples of blues scholars' use of Peabody's article include Evans, *Big Road Blues*, 33–34; Barlow, *Looking Up at Down*, 27–28; Lomax, *The Land Where the Blues Began*, 231.

2. Peabody, "Negro Music," 148–49,

3. John Queen and Hughie Cannon, "Just Because She Made Dem Goo-Goo Eyes" (New York: Howley, Haviland and Co., 1900). The song was popular enough to inspire a sequel. See Thomas D. Buick, "You Needn't Make Dem Goo Goo Eyes" (Detroit: Thomas D. Buick Publishing Co., 1900). Charles E. Trevathan, "May Irwin's 'Bully' Song'" (Boston: White-Smith Music Publishing Co., 1896). See also Handy, *Father of the Blues*, 118–19; Sanjek, *American Popular Music and Its Business*, 2: 291; Oliver, *Songsters and Saints*, 48–49.

4. Interview with Ralph Peer, 1959, Hollywood, California, by Lillian Borgeson, Southern Folklife Collection, tape #FT2772c; Scarborough, *On the Trail of Negro Folk-Songs*, 3. Later authors commenting on the existence of commercial popular music in the South during the early twentieth century include Cohen, "Tin Pan Alley's Contribution to Folk Music"; Cohen and Cohen, "Folk and Hillbilly Music"; Wolfe, "Columbia Records and Old-Time Music."

5. Peabody, "Negro Music," 152.

6. Ayers, *The Promise of the New South*, 9, 19–20, 81–100, 111–14; Campbell, *Music and the Making of a New South*, 3.

7. Hamm, *Yesterdays*, 284–325; Crawford, *America's Musical Life*, 471–91; Charosh, "Studying Nineteenth-Century Popular Song," 459–92.

8. Harris, *After the Ball*, 233, 212; "How Singers Get New Songs," *Billboard*, February 16, 1901, 10.

9. Hamm, *Yesterdays*, 284–90, 299; Harris, *After the Ball*, 212–14, 233, 65–73; Randle, "Payola," 106; Abbott and Seroff, *Out of Sight*, 327, 336.

10. Bernheim, *The Business of the Theatre*, 20–31; Poggi, *Theater in America*; Durham, "The Tightening Rein," 388–89.

11. Bernheim, *Business of the Theatre*, 35.

12. Ibid., 80.

13. Ibid., 34–40, 49; Lippman, "Battle for Bookings, 38–45.

14. Quoted in Bernheim, *Business of the Theatre*, 43–44.

15. Ibid., 46–61; Travis, "The Rise and Fall of the Theatrical Syndicate," 35–40.

16. B. Jacks to Klaw and Erlanger, August 9, 1910, Squires (Art and Barbara) Papers, Center for American History, University of Texas at Austin, box 3G20, Klaw and Erlanger Papers, folder: Business Correspondence, 1910 (March–December).

17. Edwin Flagg to Klaw and Erlanger, May 13, 1906, Klaw and Erlanger Papers, folder: Business Correspondence, 1906.

18. Albert Weiss to Klaw and Erlanger, May 11, 1912, Klaw and Erlanger Papers, folder: Business Correspondence, 1912 (January–August).

19. "Routes," *Billboard*, December 1, 1900, 9.

20. "Vaudeville," *Billboard*, December 1, 1900, 7.

21. For examples of the variety of attractions featured in southern theaters, see "Gainesville, Ga. Theatres," *Billboard*, December 1, 1900, 7; Waller, *Main Street Amusements*, 4–8, 42. Regarding interpolation of songs, see Hamm, *Yesterdays*, 256; Mott, "A Bibliography of Song Sheets," 410; Riis, "The Music and Musicians in Nineteenth-Century Productions of *Uncle Tom's Cabin*," 268–86.

22. Abbott and Seroff, *Out of Sight*, 65, 117–19; Handy, *Father of the Blues*, 34–37.

23. Otto and Burns, "Black and White Cultural Interaction in the Early Twentieth Century South," 410. Otto and Burns note that only Louisiana and South Carolina passed laws segregating tent shows. The laws in these two cases related only to ticket windows and theater entrances, not to the entire theater. See also Barlow, *Looking Up at Down*, 119–21; Lieb, *Mother of the Blues*, 23–25. For a similar discussion about the African American experience in segregated movie theaters, see Regester, "From the Buzzard's Roost." For a discussion of segregated seating in New York theaters, see Vincent, *Keep Cool*, 17–19; Nasaw, *Going Out*, 31–32. For the legal segregation of public amusements, see McKay, "Segregation and Public Recreation," 697–731; Murray, *States' Laws on Race and Color*. For a discussion of the relationship between the law and social practice regarding theater admissions, see Conrad, "The Privilege of Forcibly Ejecting an Amusement Patron," *Indianapolis Freeman*, March 23, 1889, and *Detroit Plaindealer*, October 3, 1890, both quoted in Abbott and Seroff, *Out of Sight*, 41, 101.

24. Abbott and Seroff, *Out of Sight*, 41, 338.

25. Fletcher, *One Hundred Years of the Negro in Show Business*, 57–59.

26. Handy, *Father of the Blues*, 43–44.

27. Krummel, "Counting Every Star," 186.

28. Bernheim, *Business of the Theatre*, 35, 65, 75–80. See also Poggi, "The Beginnings of Decline," 88–94; Menefee, "A New Hypothesis for Dating the Decline of the 'Road,'" 343–56. For more on the competition between the Syndicate and the Shuberts, see Grau, *The Business Man in the Amusement World*; Stagg, *The Brothers Shubert*; Hirsch, *The Boys from Syracuse*.

29. The synergy between stage singers and songwriters initially developed during the era of the minstrel show. By the 1840s, minstrelsy was easily the most popular and profitable form of entertainment in the United States. Large companies toured the United States and Europe, taking increasingly elaborate production companies with them and receiving generous coverage in the nation's press. Songwriters contracted famous minstrel companies to feature their songs on the road. Stephen Foster, for example, used the Great Southern Sable Har-

monists and E. P. Christy's Minstrels to launch several of his minstrel tunes, including "Old Folks at Home," "Old Uncle Ned," and "Susanna." See Hamm, *Yesterdays*, 109, 206–15; Toll, *Blacking Up*, 34.

30. Harris, *After the Ball*, 57–62.
31. Ibid., 57–58.
32. Gussie L. Davis, "Sing Again That Sweet Refrain, or Far From the Old Folks at Home" (New York: W. B. Gray, 1894).
33. Davis, Wright, and Lucas, "Gussie Lord Davis (1863–1899)," 213–16.
34. *Kansas City American*, August 30, 1895, quoted in Abbott and Seroff, *Out of Sight*, 428–29.
35. Loesser, *Men, Women and Pianos*, 64–67; Roell, *The Piano in America*, 13–17.
36. Hartley, *The Ladies' Book of Etiquette and Manual of Politeness*, 186.
37. Ibid., 188.
38. "Irene, Good Night," *Cleveland Gazette*, February 4, 1888; reprinted in Davis, Wright, and Lucas, "Gussie Lord Davis," 191.
39. Loesser, *Men, Women and Pianos*, 549; Roell, *Piano in America*, 32.
40. Wells, *Manners, Culture and Dress of the Best American Society*, 389–90; Hartley, *Ladies' Book of Etiquette*, 188.
41. Person, "The Chivalry of Man, as Exemplified in the Life of Mrs. Joe Person," 1, 4, 48–55; Goertzen, "Mrs. Joe Person's Popular Aires," 31–53.
42. Person, "The Chivalry of Man ," 52, 54–55.
43. Dormon, "Shaping the Popular Image of Post-Reconstruction American Blacks," 453.
44. William F Quown and Sam Lucas, "De Coon Dat Had De Razor" (Boston: White, Smith and Co., ca. 1885).
45. Trevathan, "May Irwin's 'Bully' Song."
46. Ayers, *Promise of the New South*, 156–59; 495; Litwack, *Trouble in Mind*, 280–325.
47. "He Squeals Hard," *San Antonio Light*, July 24, 1893, 6.
48. Chestnutt, *The Colonel's Dream*, 49.
49. "Nordica's 'Coon Song' (From the Baltimore Herald)," *Atlanta Constitution*, December 1, 1901, 16.
50. "International Festival of Music is to be Held in Berlin Next Year—Americans' Chance: This Country to be Represented by Southern Plantation Melodies," *Galveston Daily News*, November 23, 1902, 16.
51. "This Music Had Charms but It Made 'Em Savage," *Atlanta Constitution*, February 10, 1906, 7; Andrew Sterling and Harry Von Tilzer, "What You Goin' to Do When the Rent Comes 'Round? (Rufus Rastus Johnson Brown)" (New York: Harry von Tilzer, 1905).
52. Sotiropoulos, *Staging Race*, 104; Du Bois, *The Souls of Black Folk*, 182.

53. Roberts, *From Trickster to Badman*, 174–75; 210–12; Levine, *Black Culture and Black Consciousness*, 407–20; O'Meally, " 'Game to the Heart,' " 43–54.

54. Trevathan, "May Irwin's 'Bully' Song."

55. Handy, *Father of the Blues*, 118–19; Oliver, *Songsters and Saints*, 48–49.

56. White, *American Negro Folk-Songs*, 195–99. For another version of the song, see Odum, "Folk-Song and Folk-Poetry as Found in the Secular Songs of the Southern Negroes—Concluded," 369. See also Oliver, *Songster and Saints*, 87–89; Fiddlin' John Carson, "I Got Mine" (Okeh 40119, 1924); Frank Stokes, "I Got Mine" (Victor 38512, 1928); Gid Tanner's Skillet Lickers, "I Got Mine" (Columbia 15134D, 1926).

57. Odum, "Folk-Song and Folk-Poetry as Found in the Secular Songs of the Southern Negroes," 259.

58. Abbott and Seroff, *Out of Sight*, 41.

59. Ibid., 338.

Chapter 2: Making Money Making Music

1. Transcribed from the original recording reissued on Henry Thomas, *Texas Worried Blues: The Complete Recordings, 1927–1929* (Yazoo 1080/1) with the help of William Barlow's transcription in *Looking Up at Down*, 63–64.

2. Barlow, *Looking Up at Down*, 60–65; Calt liner notes to *Texas Worried Blues*; Oliver, *Songsters and Saints*. The literature on black migration is vast. Three examples offering different angles on the process are Painter, *Exodusters*; Griffin, *"Who Set You Flowin'?"*; Gregory, *The Southern Diaspora*.

3. For a discussion of the continuum between amateur and professional musicians in a contemporary context, see Finnegan, *The Hidden Musicians*, 12–18.

4. Roell, *The Piano in America*, 8–11, quote on 9.

5. For a discussion of erasure of functionality in Western music aesthetics around 1800, see Goehr, *The Imaginary Museum of Musical Works*, 152–63. For a critique of the tendency to interpret African music as functional, see Agawu, *Representing African Music*, 98–107. For a discussion of the long debates about functionality in ethnomusicology, see Nettl, *The Study of Ethnomusicology*, 147–61.

6. For an insightful recent book that nevertheless conforms to the traditional mold of organizing music according to occupation, see Gioia, *Work Songs*.

7. Palmer, *Deep Blues*, 101. See also Lipsitz, *The Possessive Investment in Whiteness*, 124–25.

8. Interview with Sam Chatman, November 14, 1973, "Beale Street Black and Blue," oral history transcripts.

9. Quoted in Calt, Kent, and Stewart, liner notes to *Stop and Listen*.

10. Broonzy, *Big Bill Blues*, 35.

11. Morton with Wolfe, *DeFord Bailey*, 33–34.

12. Coleman, "Carl Van Vechten Presents the New Negro," 92.

13. Porterfield, *Jimmie Rodgers*, 34–5, 54–55.

14. Charles Wolfe, "Uncle Dave Macon," in Malone and McCulloh, eds., *Stars of Country Music*, 40–43, quote on 40.

15. Interview with Roosevelt Sykes, November 2, 1973, New Orleans, Louisiana, "Beale Street Black and Blue," oral history transcripts.

16. Interview with Ashley Thompson, October 27, 1973, Ripley, Tennessee, "Beale Street Black and Blue," oral history transcripts.

17. Evans, *Big Road Blues*, 43

18. Armstrong, liner notes to *Hobart Smith*, 2–3.

19. Ross Russell, "Illuminating the Leadbelly Legend," *Downbeat*, August 6, 1970, 33; Wolfe and Lornell, *The Life and Legend of Leadbelly*, 195.

20. Interview with Ashley Thompson.

21. Calt et al., *Stop and Listen*.

22. Interview with Ashley Thompson.

23. H. Allen Smith, "A Crooner Comes Back," *Saturday Evening Post*, August 31, 1957, 66–67; Agan, "The Voice of the Southland," 123–37. Austin quite possibly referred to the song "Hard Times" by Stephen Foster, but there may have been other songs with similar titles.

24. Armstrong, liner notes to *Hobart Smith*, 2–3. See also Russell, *Blacks, Whites, and Blues*, 48–49. Russell suggests that echoes of Jefferson can be heard on Smith's "Six White Horses," "Railroad Bill," and "Graveyard Blues."

25. Govenar and Brakefield, *Deep Ellum and Central Track*, 66.

26. Otto and Burns, "John 'Knocky' Parker," 25. Parker expanded his explanation of playing like a stringed instrument: "All those people were trying to play the guitar like Blind Lemon . . . it was just easy for me to play in the keys of A and E—it was just mother's milk to play in those keys [that fall naturally on the guitar]." Quote on 24.

27. Govenar and Brakesfield, *Deep Ellum*, 66.

28. Arthur Warner, "Traveling with a Band," *Nation*, April 27, 1932. Reprinted in *JEMF Quarterly* 3, no. 7 (December 1967): 42.

29. Wolfe and Lornell, *Leadbelly*, 46. For a similar example of musicians exchanging performances for free train travel, see Handy, *Father of the Blues*, 25.

30. Charles Edward Smith, "Forword," in Broonzy, *Big Bill Blues*, 16; Broonzy, *Big Bill Blues*, 34.

31. Quoted in Marcus, *Invisible Republic*, 150–52.

32. Mendoza, *Lydia Mendoza*, 28. A childhood friend of Huddie Ledbetter recalls that he made similar arrangements: "As time rolled on, the white people with stores and drugstores asked Huddie to play Saturday evening and nights at their places to draw the crowd. In that way he made nice change." Quoted in Wolfe and Lornell, *Leadbelly*, 18

33. "Columbia Signs Artists from Hills of Georgia," *Talking Machine World,* May 15, 1924.

34. Cohen, "The Skillet Lickers," 229–44; Cohen, "Riley Puckett."

35. Govenar and Brakefield, *Deep Ellum*, 62, 66.

36. Ibid.; McKee and Chisenhall, *Beale Black and Blue*; Miller, "Mexican Past and Mexican Presence."

37. Mendoza, *Lydia Mendoza*, 58.

38. Wolfe, *Tennessee Strings*, 18.

39. Interview with Bukka White, November 24, 1972, "Beale Street Black and Blue," oral history transcripts.

40. Interview with Sam Chatman.

41. Interview with Ashley Thompson. For a similar impression regarding the difference between white and black cafes, see Ferris, *Blues from the Delta*, 95–96.

42. Interview with Nat Williams, "Beale Street Black and Blue," oral history transcripts.

43. Interview with Arthur Crudup, September 27, 1973, Exmore, Virginia, "Beale Street Black and Blue," oral history transcripts; interview by Sam Chatman.

44. Interview with Arthur Crudup.

45. Interview with Sam Chatman.

46. A significant number of southern artists who would later record for the fledgling phonograph industry played on the medicine show circuit earlier in their careers. White singers Jimmie Rodgers, Clarence Ashley, Vernon Dalhart, and Buell Kazee each spent time with medicine shows. Many African American artists shared the formative experience of medicine show work, among them Joe Williams, Papa Charlie Jackson, Furry Lewis, Gus Cannon, and William Harris. See Malone, *Country Music, USA*, 6–7; Charters, *The Country Blues*, 101. See also Johnston, "Medicine Show," 394.

47. Oliver, "Med Show," 12.

48. Ibid., 169, 174.

49. This fluid movement between different entertainment circuits did not mean there was not a hierarchy of prestige among entertainers. As a show operator in Sinclair Lewis's *Main Street* explained, "Stock company actors felt superior to tent repertoire; musical tab and repertoire actors looked down on each other and both felt superior to carnival people, who felt superior to medicine show people." Even at the bottom of this hierarchy, medicine show performers were at least part of it, leaving singing laborers and street performers out of the picture. Quoted in McNamara, *Step Right Up*, 123. See also Oliver, "Med Show"; Oliver, "Alagazam," 26ff.

50. Oliver, "Alagazam," 79; Oliver reprints several job ads from *Billboard*. See also McNamara, *Step Right Up*, 123–25.

51. McNamara, *Step Right Up*, 108, Evans, *Big Road Blues*, 184–85.

52. Patterson and Tullos, *Born for Hard Luck*, 3–7; Tullos, "Born for Hard Luck," 40–45. For another example of the broad repertoires of black medicine show performers, see Evans, *Big Road Blues*, 184–85.

53. Patterson and Tullos, *Born for Hard Luck*, 7.

54. Quoted in Oakley, *The Devil's Music*, 153.

55. McKee and Chisenhall, *Beale Black and Blue*, 195–96; McNamara, *Step Right Up*, 123. McNamara notes that the manual labor required of medicine show performers was one of the reasons those in the "legitimate" theater looked down upon them.

56. McKee and Chisenhall, *Beale Black and Blue*, 196.

57. Calt, liner notes to *Texas Worried Blues*; Place, "Supplemental Notes on the Selections," 50; Russell, *Blacks, Whites, and Blues*, 47; Barlow, *Looking Up at Down*, 61–65.

58. Interview with Sam Chatman.

59. Charles Wolfe, *Tennessee Strings*, 18.

60. Interview with Roosevelt Sykes.

61. Interview with Ashley Thompson.

62. Small, *Music of the Common Tongue*, 45.

63. Carby, "It Just Be's Dat Way Sometime," 13.

64. Barlow, *Looking Up at Down*, 4.

65. This problem is not limited to blues scholarship. In his critique of the history of Western scholarship on African music, Kofi Agawu makes a similar point: "The pious dignifying of all performances as if they were equally good, of all instruments as if they were tuned in an 'interesting' way rather than simply being out of tune, of all informants as if a number of them did not practice systematic deception, and of dirge singing as if the missed entries and resulting heterophony did not result from inattentiveness or drunkenness: these are acts of mystification designed to ensure that the discourse about African music continues to lack the one thing that would give it scientific and hence universal status, namely, a *critical* element." See Agawu, *Representing African Music*, 386.

66. Thus while Christopher Small's analysis of African diasporic music focuses on "the creative powers of each individual performer, in contrast to the white tendency to think in terms of fixed entities," his steadfast equation of racial identity with cultural practice risks reifying the very processes he attempts to keep fluid. See Small, *Common Tongue*, 92.

67. Ellison, *Shadow and Act*, 130.

68. In a sense, this involves turning some of the more interesting examinations of audience responses on their head. As the editors of the groundbreaking study *My Music* make clear, contemporary individual listeners take part in many constantly shifting worlds of music—listening to concertos in the morning, the Grateful Dead on the way to work, and playing in a string band in their leisure

hours. With this fluid image of people's everyday relationships to music in mind, this study seeks to take seriously the multiple listeners with whom individual artists interact. See Crafts, Cavicchi, Keil, and the Music in Daily Life Project, *My Music*.

69. Interview with Bukka White.

70. Interview with Cliff Carlisle, August 18, 1962, Lexington, Kentucky, by Eugene Earle and Archie Green, Southern Folklife Collection FT#4068.,

71. Interview with Roosevelt Sykes.

72. Jeff Todd Titon makes this point very well in his *Early Downhome Blues*, 39–40. Sara Carter, of the famous Carter Family, noted that musicians looked toward aesthetic criteria rather than biographical accuracy when choosing material: "A good song is one that sounds good to you, one you like best. If you like the tune, whether it is true or not isn't important." See transcription of Sara Carter interview with Ed Kahn, June 3, 1961, Carter Family Artist File, Southern Folklore Collection, 4.

73. Small, *Common Tongue*, 69.

74. Zwigoff, "Black Country String Bands." Some examples of African American square-dance calling recorded commercially in the 1920s give clues to how earlier black square dance tunes may have sounded. See Blind Blake, "West Coast Blues," Paramount 12387 (1926); Henry Thomas, "Old Country Stomp," Vocalion 1230 (1928); Andrew Baxter with the Georgia Yellow Hammers, "G Rag," Victor 21195 (1927).

75. Interview with Sam Chatman.

76. Ferris, *Blues from the Delta*, 96–97.

77. Quoted in Evans, *Big Road Blues*, 47–48.

78. Quoted in Levine, *Black Culture and Black Consciousness*, 224.

79. This story is one of the most often cited stories in all of blues history, but it is rarely noted that the audience was white. Abbe Niles, "Introduction," in Handy, *Blues: An Anthology* (1926), 12; Abbe Niles, "Introduction," in Handy, *Blues: An Anthology* (1990), 24–25; Handy, *Father of the Blues*, 76–78.

80. Wolfe, "The White Man's Blues." See also Johnson, "Double Meaning in the Popular Negro Blues," 13.

81. "Atlanta," *Talking Machine World*, July 15, 1923, 142.

82. Oliver, *Songsters and Saints*, 47–77; Ferris, "Racial Repertoires among Blues Performers."

83. Johnson, "Double Meaning," 442.

84. See chapter 4 for more information.

85. Transcribed from Blind Willie McTell, "Monologue on Accidents," *Library of Congress Recordings, 1940* (RST Records BDCD-6001, 2000); originally recorded by John Lomax, Atlanta, Georgia, November 5, 1940. "Ain't It Hard to Be a Nigger" was a reported as "well known" by Howard Odum in his 1911 collection

of African American secular songs. See Odum, "Folk-Song and Folk-Poetry as Found in the Secular Songs of the Southern Negroes," 267. Sam Chatman similarly dissembled when questioned by Margaret McKee and Fred Chisenhall in 1973:

> MCKEE: Can you give us an example of a song in the later days, past slavery times, when a colored man was saying something, telling a white man he didn't like what he was doing but he was singing it?
> CHATMAN: Well, how would you like me to give you one about the colored man singing it to his girlfriend, would that be alright?

Chatman then sang the pop love song "I'm Gonna Sit Right Down and Write Myself a Letter" (1935) by the songwriters Fred Alhert and Joe Young. Interview with Sam Chatman.

86. I transcribed this conversation from "Interview and Strayhorn Mob," on *Field Recordings Vol. 15: Mississippi 1941–1942* (Document Records DOCD-5672, 2002). Original recording made by Alan Lomax in Sledge, Mississippi, August 15, 1942. See also Lomax, *The Land Where the Blues Began*, 323–24.

87. Niles, "Shout, Coon, Shout," 523–24.

88. Russell, *Blacks, Whites, and Blues*, 48.

89. This and the following paragraphs are based on the following sources from the Archie Green Collection, Southern Folklife Collection, series 3, folder 530: Handwritten notes about Mike Seeger interview with Sherman Lawson (August 2, 1964); Tony Russell, "Frank Hutchison: The Pride of West Virginia," *Old Time Music* 1 (n.d.): 4–7; "Hutch: Sherman Lawson Interview," *Old Time Music* 11 (winter 1973/74): 7–8.

Chapter 3: Isolating Folk, Isolating Songs

1. Lomax, *Cowboy Songs* (1910).

2. Anonymous letter to John Lomax, May 2, 1910, Lomax Family Papers, box 3D174, folder 2.

3. See, for example, letters from J. M. Grisby, Lomax Family Papers, box 3D169, folder 8.

4. John A. Lomax to W. P. MacLaughlin, March 27, 1911, Lomax Family Papers, box 3D169, folder 8.

5. "Rules," *Journal of American Folklore* 1, no.1 (1888): 2; Newell, "On the Field and Work of a Journal of American Folk-Lore," 7 (the original essay had no byline, but later scholars have been unanimous in attributing it to Newell); Bronner, *American Folklore Studies*, 18. On the growth of professionalization in folklore studies, see Williams, "Radicalism and Professionalism in Folklore Studies"; Seeger, "Professionalism and Amateurism in the Study of Folk Music"; Darnell, "American Anthropology and the Development of Folklore Scholarship, 1890–1920."

6. Wilgus, *Anglo-American Folksong Scholarship since 1898*; Zumwalt, *American Folklore Scholarship*; Bronner, *American Folklore Studies*.

7. Newell, "On the Field and Work of a Journal of American Folk-Lore," 3–7.

8. Graff, *Professing Literature*, 22, 28–35, 41–44; Kirshenblatt-Gimblett, "Folklore's Crisis"; quote in Alter, *Darwinism and the Linguistic Image*, 14. Kittredge, "James Francis Child," in Child, *The English and Scottish Popular Ballads*, vol. 1, xxv. For a discussion of the meaning of "origins" to nineteenth-century scholars, see Rehding, "The Quest for the Origins of Music in Germany circa 1900," 346–49.

9. The innovative English professor Frances A. March said one of his typical classes involved "hearing a short Grammar lesson, the rest of the hour reading Milton as if it were Homer, calling for the meaning of words, their etymology when interesting, the relations of words, parsing when it would help, the connection of clauses, the mythology, the biography and other illustrative matters, suited to the class." Graff, *Professing Literature*, 38–41, 65–69, quote on 38; Kirshenblatt-Gimblett, "Folklore's Crisis," 288.

10. Bernal, *Black Athena*, 2–3, 217–27; Alter, *Darwinism*, 31–32.

11. Graff, *Professing Literature*, 69–72, quote on 71.

12. Emerson, "New England Reformers" (1844), in Emerson, *Essays and Lectures*, 599; Emerson, "The American Scholar," in Eliot, ed., *The Harvard Classics*, vol. 5, 21; Matthiessen, *American Renaissance*, 34–35; Bendix, *In Search of Authenticity*, 73; Graff, *Professing Literature*, 21, 44–46; Bledstein, *The Culture of Professionalism*, 259–68.

13. These characterizations of Child and his collection were evident as early as 1884. One reviewer of Child's first volume praised the deep commitment and knowledge Child had brought to the study of the ballad. "We find that what once seemed almost too slight and common to deserve serious consideration or study can lay claim to long descent and widely spread relations—that ballads have had a growth, and a history as interesting as that of ideas, polities, religions or languages." However, the writer found it odd that Child "does not even discuss the nature of ballad, as distinguished from other species of popular literature." The writer was quick to recognize Child's silence as an opportunity for future speculation. "There grows upon us the conviction that, if what the author is doing for the ballads of Scotland and England . . . were done for the ballads of other countries, it would not be difficult to construct a theory, and a profoundly interesting one, of ballads." See Thomas Davidson, "Prof. Child's Ballad Book," *American Journal of Philology* 5, no. 4 (1884): 466–67, 468–69; Child, *The English and Scottish Popular Ballads*, vols. 1–5.

14. Quoted in Zumwalt, *American Folklore Scholarship*, 48.

15. Zumwalt, *American Folklore Scholarship*, 46–48; Bendix, *In Search of Authenticity*, 85–86; Wilgus, *Anglo-American Folksong Scholarship*, 174; Kittredge, "Francis James Child," in Child, *Popular Ballads*, vol. 1, xxvii.

16. Kittredge, "Francis James Child," xxx.

17. Quoted in M. J. Bell, " 'No Borders to the Ballad Maker's Art,' " 295.

18. Newell, "Early American Ballads," 241–54; quote on 241.

19. Wilgus, *Anglo-American Folksong Scholarship*, 147.

20. See Pound, "The Southwestern Cowboy and the English and Scottish Popular Ballads," 195–97; Wilgus, *Anglo-American Folksong Scholarship*, 80–81.

21. Gummere, *The Popular Ballad*, 19.

22. Quoted in Krehbiel, *Afro-American Folksongs*, 2.

23. Ibid., 4.

24. Ibid., 3.

25. Gummere, *The Popular Ballad*, 21. See also Bendix, *In Search of Authenticity*, 89–90; Wilgus, *Anglo-American Folksong Scholarship*, 9–32.

26. In 1881, Tylor drew a "connexion between a more full and intricate system of brain-cells and fibres, and a higher intellectual power, in the races which have risen in the scale of civilization." See Stocking, *Race, Culture, and Evolution*, 26–27, 115–20, quote on 116; Bronner, *American Folklore Studies*, 60–61; Baker, *From Savage to Negro*, 27–31; Wilgus, *Anglo-American Folksong Scholarship*, 22.

27. With the suggestion that races were "sub-species" of humanity, Brinton loosely echoed the polygenist thought of pre-Darwinian anthropology. See Stocking, *Race, Culture, and Evolution*, chap. 3; Fredrickson, *The Black Image in the White Mind*, chap. 3; Haller, *Outcasts from Evolution*, chap. 3.

28. Brinton, "The Aims of Anthropology." For background on Brinton, see Darnell, "Daniel Garrison Brinton"; Darnell, *And Along Came Boas*; Baker, *From Savage to Negro*, 32–37; Bronner, *American Folklore Studies*, 14–15, 55; Stocking, *Race, Culture, and Evolution*, 23. For another significant example of the theory that precivilized ways persisted on the margins of civilized society, see Mason, "The Natural History of Folk-Lore." See also Buettner-Janusch, "Boas and Mason."

29. Boas, "The Limitations of the Comparative Method of Anthropology," 901–8, quote on 905. For general background on Boas, see Stocking, *Race, Culture and Evolution*; Handler, "Boasian Anthropology and the Critique of American Culture"; Willis, "Franz Boas and the Study of Black Folklore"; Baker, *From Savage to Negro*.

30. Boas, "Limitations of the Comparative Method," 907. On another occasion, Boas wrote, "Before we seek for what is common in all culture, we must analyze each culture by careful and exact methods." Quoted in Zumwalt, *American Folklore Scholarship*, 112.

31. "Wild Negro Chants and Dances," *New York Times*, May 25, 1895, 9.

32. Silber, *Romance of Reunion*, 135–38; Webb, "Authentic Possibilities"; Hall, " 'Black America' "; Toll, *Blacking Up*; Riis, *Just before Jazz*, 22–24.

33. "Wild Negro Chants and Dances."

34. "Black America," *Brooklyn Daily Eagle*, June 11, 1895, 6.

35. Advertisement in *Brooklyn Daily Eagle*, May 25, 1895, 3.

36. "Black America."

37. Lindfors, "Ethnological Show Business," 208–11. See also Lindfors, ed., *Africans on Stage*.

38. Rydell, " 'Darkest Africa': African Shows at America's World's Fairs, 1893–1940," in Lindfors, ed., *Africans on Stage*, 136–41, quote on 140; Rydell, *All the World's a Fair*, 55–60; quote on 55.

39. Advertisement in *New York Times*, June 30, 1895, 11. Salsbury quoted in Silber, *Romance of Reunion*, 135. On Buffalo Bill, see Rydell and Kroes, *Buffalo Bill in Bologna*.

40. *Brooklyn Daily Eagle*, June 2, 1895, 9.

41. "Slave Life in the South," *New York Times*, June 9, 1895, 13.

42. Quoted in Silber, *Romance of Reunion*, 135.

43. Black America.

44. Untitled review. *New York Times*, May 26, 1895, 16.

45. Merwin, "On Being Civilized Too Much," 838–46. See also Bronner, *American Folklore Studies*, 10–11.

46. Bendix, *In Search of Authenticity*, 73–74.

47. Shapiro, *Appalachia on Our Mind*, 3–16; Ayers, *The Promise of the New South*, 339–49; Kaplan, "Nation, Region, and Empire"; Ammon and Rohy, eds., *American Local Color Writing, 1880–1920*.

48. Shapiro, *Appalachia on Our Mind*, 77–79; Ayers, *Promise of the New South*, 362–65; Frost, "Our Contemporary Ancestors in the Southern Mountains."

49. Mooney, "Folk-Lore of the Carolina Mountains," 95–97.

50. Moffat, "The Mountaineers of Middle Tennessee," 314. On "The Arkansas Traveler," see Bluestein, " 'The Arkansas Traveler' and the Strategy of American Humor"; "From the Archives: 'The Arkansas Traveler' by H. C. Mercer," *JEMF Quarterly* 6, no. 2 (summer 1970): 51–57; Harkins, *Hillbilly*, 26–29. One of the standard jokes of the sketch finds the traveler asking, "Why, how long have you lived here?" The squatter replies, "You see that hill over there? . . . That was here when I come." See Len Spencer, "Arkansas Traveler," Edison Amberol: 181 (1909).

51. Parker, "Folk-Lore of the North Carolina Mountaineers," 242. For another example, see Porter, "Notes on the Folk-Lore of the Mountain Whites of the Alleghanies," 105–17.

52. Bascom, "Ballads and Songs of Western North Carolina," 239.

53. Perrow, "Songs and Rhymes from the South" (1912), 137–38. See also Wilgus, *Anglo-American Folksong Scholarship*, 81–82.

54. Perrow, "Songs and Rhymes from the South" (1912), 144.

55. Whisnant, *All That Is Native and Fine*, 7, 51–58.

56. Perrow, "Songs and Rhymes from the South" (1912), 138.

57. Allen, Ware, and Garrison, *Slave Songs of the United States*, i, vi–viii, ix.

58. Ayers, *Promise of the New South*, 342; Silber, *The Romance of Reunion*, 138–39; Harris, *Uncle Remus*, 4.

59. Harris, *Uncle Remus*, vii–viii, 16.

60. Ibid., ix; Silber, *Romance of Reunion*, 139. For a discussion of the significant history of Brer Rabbit tales within African American oral tradition, see Levine, *Black Culture and Black Consciousness*.

61. Newell, "Myths of Voodoo Worship and Child Sacrifice in Hayti."

62. Other early reports regarding black witchcraft and voodoo include "Conjuring in Arkansas," *Journal of American Folklore* 1, no. 1 (1888): 83; Newell, "Reports of Voodoo Worship in Hayti and Louisiana"; Stewart Culin, "Reports Concerning Voodooism," *Journal of American Folklore* 2, no. 6 (1889): 232–33; W. Nelson, "Superstition Concerning Drowning," *Journal of American Folklore* 2, no. 7 (1889): 308; "[Report of Voodoo Ritual]," *Journal of American Folklore* 3, no. 8 (1890): 67; Louis Pendleton, "Notes on Negro Folk-Lore and Witchcraft in the South," *Journal of American Folklore* 3, no. 10 (1890): 201–7.

63. Fortier, "Customs and Superstitions in Louisiana," 136–37.

64. Hawkins, "An Old Mauma's Folk-Lore," 129. Other employments of the mammy stereotype include Mary Mann-Page Newton, "Aunt Deborah Goes Visiting: A Sketch from Virginian Life," *Journal of American Folklore* 4, no. 15 (1891): 354–56; Mrs. William Preston Johnson, "Two Negro Tales," *Journal of American Folklore* 9, no. 34 (1896): 194–98; Frank Russell, review of *Devil Tales* by Virginia Frazer Boyle, *Journal of American Folklore* 14, no. 52 (1901): 65. For the history of the mammy stereotype, see Morgan, "Mammy the Huckster"; White, *Ar'N't I a Woman?* 27–61.

65. Lee Baker notes that in 1900 Franz Boas began to insist that only credentialed collectors could contribute to the journal. This ultimately resulted in a severe decline in the coverage of African American folklore. See Baker, *From Savage to Negro*, 147–48.

66. Brinton, *Races and Peoples*, 192. See also Baker, *From Savage to Negro*, 34–37.

67. O. T. Mason, review of *Ethnology in Folklore* by George Laurence Gomme, *American Anthropologist* 5, no. 4 (1892): 384–85.

68. Johann Tonsor, "Negro Music," *Music* (December 1892). Reprinted in Beckerman, *New Worlds of Dvořák*, 229. Beckerman identifies Tonsor as the pseudonym of the writer Mildred Hill.

69. "Real Value of Negro Melodies," *New York Herald*, May 21, 1893, 28.

70. Charles Hamm, "Dvořák, Nationalism, Myth, and Racism in the United States," in Beveridge, ed., *Rethinking Dvořák*, 275–80. See also Mark Germer's "Dvořák among the Yankees: George Chadwick and the Impact of the Boston School" in the same collection, 237–44; Abrahams, "Phantoms of Romantic Nationalism in Folkloristics"; Moore, *Yankee Blues*; Beckerman, *New Worlds of Dvořák*.

71. "Real Value of Negro Melodies."

72. Beckerman, *New Worlds of Dvořák*, 87, 229–32.

73. Antonin Dvořák, "Music in America," *Harper's New Monthly Magazine* (February 1895), 429–34. My argument here owes a great deal to my reading of Hamm, "Dvořák, Nationalism, Myth, and Racism in the United States." Hamm argues that Dvořák was not promoting the use of black folk music as much as hybrid American popular music. I, of course, am questioning the dichotomy by demonstrating folk music's debt to commercialized minstrelsy.

74. Cruz, *Culture on the Margins*.

75. *Popular Science Monthly* 48, no. 1 (1896): 59–72. All citations continue to refer to the page numbers in the *Proceeding of the American Association for the Advancement of Science*. See Baker, *From Savage to Negro*, 37.

76. Brinton, "Aims of Anthropology," 13.

77. Shufeldt, *The Negro, A Menace to American Civilization*, 76.

78. Sumner, *Folkways*, 109, 81. See also, Hofstadter, *Social Darwinism in American Thought*, 51–66.

79. Du Bois, *Black Reconstruction in America, 1860–1880*, 719, 723.

80. Baker, *From Savage to Negro*, 34–37; Woodward, *Strange Career of Jim Crow*, 94–96.

81. Trotter, *Music and Some Highly Musical People*. For discussion of Trotter, see Stevenson, "America's First Black Music Historian"; Ramsey, "Cosmopolitan or Provincial?" 15–19; Southern, *The Music of Black Americans*, 261.

82. Trotter, *Music and Some Highly Musical People*; excerpted in Southern, ed., *Readings in Black American Music*, 142–43.

83. Terry, "The Negro Music Journal"; Vincent, *Keep Cool*, 92–105.

84. Franz Boas, "The Negro and the Demands of Modern Life," *Charities* 25 (1905): 86–87.

85. Baker, *From Savage to Negro*, 121–22.

86. Willis, "Franz Boas," 315; Baker, *From Savage to Negro*, 146; Cruz, *Culture at the Margins*, 168–73.

87. Bacon, "Work and Methods of the Hampton Folk-Lore Society," 17.

88. Ibid., 19–20.

89. Du Bois, *The Souls of Black Folk*, 177–79; Bell, "Folk Art and the Harlem Renaissance," 155–58; Herring, "Du Bois and the Minstrels."

90. Du Bois, *Souls of Black Folk*, 177–79, 186.

91. Lomax, *Cowboy Songs* (1918), xxiv.

92. Wilgus, *Anglo-American Folksong Scholarship*, 79–80; Lomax, *Cowboy Songs*, xxiii, xxiv. For Lomax's relationship with Kittredge, see Porterfield, *The Last Cavalier*, 119–30. Pound, "Southwestern Cowboy Songs," 13.

93. Lomax, *Cowboy Songs* (1918), xxiii.

94. Huntly Murray, "Cowboy Songs," *The Bookman* 32 (February 1911): 636. For discussion of other reviews of *Cowboy Songs*, see Porterfield, *Last Cavalier*, 157.

95. John Lomax to Francis James, August 8, 1911, Lomax Family Papers, box 3D169, folder 8.

96. A report of a stabbing incident that occurred between two cast members noted the local intersection at which the alleged perpetrator resided. See "Harrod Stabbed a Woman," *Brooklyn Daily Eagle*, July 2, 1895, 14.

97. Fletcher, *One Hundred Years of the Negro in Show Business*, 91–94.

98. For reprints of the *New York Clipper* coverage, see Abbott and Seroff, *Out of Sight*, 391–95.

Chapter 4: The Lure of New York City

1. Palmer, *Vernon Dalhart*, 1–17, quote on 16–17; Walter Darrell Haden, "Vernon Dalhart," in Malone and McCulloh, eds., *Stars of Country Music*, 64–68. See also Walsh, "Favorite Pioneer Recording Artists: Vernon Dalhart."

2. Bob Dumm, "Two Men Who Sell New Songs for Old," *Farm and Fireside Magazine*, May 1927, 19.

3. Palmer, *Vernon Dalhart*, 19–30.

4. Johnson, *Along This Way*, 150; Abbott and Seroff, " 'They Cert'ly Sound Good to Me' "; Vincent, *Keep Cool*; Riis, *Just before Jazz*.

5. Johnson, *Along This Way*, 150–51, 170–74; Riis, *Just before Jazz*; Sotiropoulos, *Staging Race*, 53–56.

6. Johnson, *Along This Way*, 152–53.

7. Brooks, *Lost Sounds*, 15–71; Gaisberg, *The Music Goes Round*, 41, quoted in Brooks, 62. Brooks has done an incredible job uncovering black artists who made recordings prior to 1920, yet the number of such artists remains tiny compared to that of black stage performers or white recording artists during the time period. See also Leonard, "An Introduction to Black Participation in the Early Recording Era, 1890–1920." For a brief profile of Sam Devere, see Rice, *Monarchs of Minstrelsy*, 152.

8. Gracyk, *Popular American Recording Pioneers, 1895–1925*, 314–19; Brooks, *Lost Sounds*, 36–43. On Fagan, see Rice, *Monarchs of Minstrelsy*, 216–18.

9. Gracyk, *Recording Pioneers*, 65–85.

10. My focus here is on white female performers. For an excellent study of female African American performers of the era, see Brown, *Babylon Girls*. For an early analysis of the methods of "coon shouting," see Niles, "Shout, Coon, Shout."

11. Mizejewski, *Ziegfeld Girl*, 41–64; Glenn, *Female Spectacle*, 48–49, 55–56; Paul West, "I Want Dem Presents Back" (New York: M. Witmark and Sons, ca. 1896). See also sheet music graphic in the *New York Journal*, January 23, 1897; Graziano, "Music in William Randolph Hearst's New York Journal," 402. On lynching, see Royster, ed., *Southern Horrors and Other Writings*; Hall, *Revolt against Chivalry*.

12. Abbott and Seroff, *Ragged but Right*, 15; George Graham, "I Can't Give Up My

Rough and Rowd'ish Ways" (Spaulding, 1897); Graziano, "New York Journal," 401.

13. "Home-Made Comic Plays: May Irwin in McNally's New Farce at the Bijou Theatre," *New York Times*, September 17, 1895, 5.

14. "Three New Plays Here, May Irwin and 'A Dangerous Maid' Make Fun and Andrew Mack Sings," *Brooklyn Daily Eagle*, February 21, 1899, 5.

15. "May Irwin and Other Fun: Good Humor and Negro Ditties at the Montauk," *Brooklyn Daily Eagle*, February 22, 1898, 7. See also Kibler, *Rank Ladies*, 128–31; Glenn, *Female Spectacle*, 51–52.

16. "Gathered about Town," *New York Times*, November 4, 1896, 8.

17. "Some of May Irwin's Ideas," *New York Times*, November 19, 1899, 8.

18. "Dramatic and Musical: May Irwin, Again on View at the Bijou, Is Both by Turns: Some New Bad Darky Songs," *New York Times*, November 8, 1898, 5. For a similar assessment, see "Home-Made Comic Plays: May Irwin in McNally's New Farce at the Bijou Theatre," *New York Times*, September 17, 1895, 5.

19. Kibler, *Rank Ladies*, 126–33; Lavitt, "First of the Red Hot Mamas," 259.

20. "Dramatic and Musical," *New York Times*, November 8, 1989, 5.

21. "Music for Flat Dwellers: Back-yard Minstrels Too Numerous for Comfort," *New York Times*, September 13, 1896, 18.

22. "Sang at Colored Home: May Irwin's Company in a Charitable Entertainment," *New York Times*, February 5, 1897, 12.

23. "Women Here and There," *New York Times*, October 6, 1901, SM15.

24. "Girls Sang Coon Songs," *Brooklyn Daily Eagle*, October 30, 1901, 20.

25. "Said She Sang Coon Songs: Colored Pastor a Witness against Alleged Annoying Tenants," *Brooklyn Daily Eagle*, October 12, 1901, 2.

26. Riis, "'Bob' Cole"; Riis, *Just before Jazz*, 26–37; Riis, *More Than Just Minstrel Shows*, 8–14; Morgan and Barlow, *From Cakewalks to Concert Halls*, 58–60. *Indianapolis Freeman*, August 22, 1891, reprinted in Abbott and Seroff, *Out of Sight*, 158; McAllister, "Bob Cole's Willie Wayside."

27. Riis, "'Bob' Cole," 138.

28. Cole understood this compromise as a necessary result of appealing to white audiences, but he also may have understood it as a product of the white control of the theater industry. He left the Black Patti Troubadours in 1897 after a wage dispute with the company's white mangers, who then blacklisted him and other defectors from appearing in New York theaters. Cole was incensed. His "Colored Actor's Declaration of Independence of 1898" insisted, "We are going to have our own shows. We are going to write them ourselves, we are going to have our own stage manager, our own orchestra leader and our own manager out front to count up. No divided houses—our race must be seated from the boxes back." See Krasner, *Resistance, Parody, and Double Consciousness*, 30.

29. Bob Cole and Billy Johnson, "Mr. Coon You're All Right in Your Place" (New York: Howley, Haviland and Co., ca. 1909). The song was written and performed during the late 1890s.

30. "An Interview of Edward H. Morris," Chicago *Inter Ocean*, July 28, 1903, in Louis R. Harlan and Raymond W. Smock, eds., *The Booker T. Washington Papers: Vol. 7, 1903–1904* (Urbana: University of Illinois Press, 1977), 227–28.

31. Bob Cole, James Weldon Johnson, J. Rosamond Johnson, "Louisiana Lize" (New York: Jos. W. Stern and Co., 1899); Bob Cole and James Weldon Johnson, "Sambo and Dinah" (New York: Joseph. W. Stern and Co., 1904).

32. Johnson, *Along This Way*, 152.

33. Johnson, *The Autobiography of an Ex-Colored Man*, 103–4, 126.

34. Johnson, *Along This Way*, 158–59 (emphasis in original). Johnson expanded on these thoughts in "The Dilemma of the Negro Author" (1928).

35. Nasaw, *Going Out*, 19–27; McLean, *American Vaudeville as Ritual*; Snyder, *The Voice of the City*; Peiss, *Cheap Amusements*, 140–45; Kibler, *Rank Ladies*; Erdman, *Blue Vaudeville*; Glenn, *Female Spectacle*.

36. Jim Walsh, "Favorite Pioneer Recording Artists: Clarice Vance," *Hobbies*, April 1963, 36.

37. Abbott and Seroff, *Ragged but Right*, 16.

38. "Some of May Irwin's Ideas," *New York Times*, November 19, 1899, 18.

39. "Dramatic and Musical," *New York Times*, October 31, 1900, 6.

40. See sheet music cover to J. W. Johnson, Bob Cole, and Rosamond Johnson, "Magdaline My Southern Queen" (New York: Joseph W. Stern and Co., 1900).

41. Johnson, *Along This Way*, 157, 178–81.

42. Woll, *Black Musical Theatre*, 19–20; Johnson, *Along This Way*, 188–89.

43. Woll, *Black Musical Theatre*, 20.

44. Will Marion Cook and William Moore, "Wid de Moon, Moon, Moon" (New York: G. Schirmer, 1907); Andrew B. Sterling and Will Marion Cook, "Whoop 'er Up" (New York: Harry Von Tilzer, 1910).

45. Woll, *Black Musical Theatre*, 19–20; Shirley, "The House of Melody," 100. On Smith, see Southern, *The Music of Black Americans*, 319, 510. On Mack, see Morgan and Barlow, *Cakewalks to Concert Halls*, 114–16. Recordings include Clarice Vance, Victor 4931 (1906); Bert Williams, Columbia 303 (3536) (1907); Bob Roberts, Edison Gold Moulded Record 9412 (1906). James Alrich Libby, of "After the Ball" fame, sang Will Marion Cook's "There's a Place in the Old Vacant Chair." The singer Nat Wills featured Alex Rogers's "Never!" Clarice Vance sang Smith and Mack's "That's Where Friendship Ends." May Kemp sang their "Down among the Sugar Cane." See Shirley, "House of Melody," 83, 81, 101. Smith's "I Want a Little Lovin', Sometimes" (New York: T. B. Harns, 1911) featured Marie Cahill on the cover. Smith and James Reese Europe, "Ballin' the Jack" (New York: Stern, 1914), featured photos of Donald Brian, Wylma Wynn,

Jean and Jeanette Warner. Johnson, Cole, and Johnson sheet music also featured pictures of a number of white singers associated with their songs. Irene Bentley sang their "When the Moon Comes Peeping O'er the Hill" (New York: Stern, 1902) in the comedy opera *A Girl from Dixie*. Peter F. Dailey sang their dialect song "Gin" (New York: Howley, Haviland and Dresser, 1901) in *Champagne Charlie*. John McVeigh and Lillian Coleman sang "Sambo and Dinah" (New York: Stern, 1904) in a Kraw and Erlanger production of London's *Humpty Dumpty*. Christie McDonald sang "A Prepossessing Little Maid" (New York: Stern, 1904) about a red-cheeked country girl. Faye Tempelton sang Johnson, Cole, and Johnson's "Lindy" (New York: Stern, 1903) in the musical review *The Evolution of Rag-Time*.

46. Grayck, *Recording Pioneers*, 68–69.

47. Recordings of songs composed by some combination of Johnson, Cole, and Johnson include Bob Roberts, "The Countess of Alagazam" (Edison Gold Moulded Record 8869, 1905); Edward Meeker, "The Sweetest Gal in Town" (Edison Standard Record 10087, 1909); Billy Murray, "Lazy Moon" (Edison Gold Moulded Record 9204, 1906); Harry MacDonough, "Mexico" (Edison Gold Moulded Record: 8936, 1905). Meeker recorded "Any Old Place in Yankee Land Is Good Enough for Me" by Cook, Smith, and Alex Rogers (Edison Standard Record 10189, 1909). Billy Murray recorded "Bon Bon Buddie" by Cook and Rogers (Indestructible Record 794, 1908). Other recordings of Chris Smith songs include Bob Roberts, "Taint de Kind o' Grub I've Been Gettin' Down Home" (Edison Gold Moulded Record: 8983, 1905); Bob Roberts, "Common Sense" (Indestructible Record 761, 1908); Edward Meeker, "If He Comes In, I'm Going Out" (Edison Standard Record 10488, 1911); Billy Murray, "Trans-mag-ni-fi-can-ban-dam-u-al-i-ty" (Edison Standard Record 10143, 1909).

48. Cecil Mack and Chris Smith, "Scaddle-de-Mooch" (New York: Joseph W. Stern and Co., 1915).

49. "Music Publishers Drawing Line," *New York Age*, February 9, 1911, 6. Reprinted in Hoffman, *Jazz Reviewed*, 5.

50. Knight, "He Paved the Way for the T.O.B.A.," 153–81, Dudley quote on 175, *Freeman* quote on 161. See also Cuney-Hare, *Negro Musicians and Their Music*, 164–165.

51. Morgan and Barlow, *Cakewalks to Concert Halls*, 114–16; Shirley, "The House of Melody."

52. Sotiropoulos, *Staging Race*, 148–62, 110–12; Shirley, "House of Melody," 82.

53. Johnson, *Black Manhattan*, 171; Sotiropoulos, *Staging Race*, 190; "New Yorkers Enjoy a Burlesque Bryan in 'The Follies of a Day,'" *Washington Post*, May 16, 1909, SM2; Riis, *Just before Jazz*, 135–41.

54. Whitfield, "Is It True What They Sing About Dixie?," 9.; Rogin, *Blackface, White Noise*. Expressing whiteness through caricatures of black culture, of course,

reaches back to the early days of minstrelsy's popularity among Irish immigrants. See Roediger, *The Wages of Whiteness*.

55. "The Playhouses," *Los Angeles Times*, May 2, 1899, 8.

56. Dumm, "Two Men," 19.

57. Haden, "Vernon Dalhart," 67–69; Vernon Dalhart, "Can't Yo' Heah Me Callin' Caroline?" (Edison Blue Amberol 3185, 1917); Caro Roma and William H. Gardner, "Can't Yo' Heah Me Callin' Caroline" (New York: M. Whitmark and Sons, 1914). See also Palmer, *Vernon Dalhart*, 12. For the details about his contract with Edison, see Palmer, *Vernon Dalhart*, 44–45. Roma was a pseudonym for the opera singer Carrie Northly, a California native born in 1866.

58. Walsh, "Favorite Pioneer Recording Artists: Vernon Dalhart," 35.

59. Vernon Dalhart to Mr. Clarence B. Hayes, September 12, 1917; quoted in Palmer, *Vernon Dalhart*, 49; my emphasis.

60. Harkins, *Hillbilly*, 29–45.

61. Bluestein, "'The Arkansas Traveler' and the Strategy of American Humor"; "From the Archives: 'The Arkansas Traveler' by H. C. Mercer," *JEMF Quarterly* 6, no. 2 (Summer 1970): 51–57; Harkins, *Hillbilly*, 26–29.

62. Eugene A. Jaudas, "Medley of Country Dances" (Edison Blue Ambersol 1716, 1913); Don Richardson, "Arkansas Traveler" (Columbia A2140, 1916). The other side of the Richardson record featured the common stock minstrel tune "Old Zip Coon."

63. "Four Records Popular in Texas," *Talking Machine World*, July 15, 1910, 6.

64. The Peerless Trio featured the well-known recording artists Steve Porter, Byron G. Harlan, and Billy Murray. Peerless Trio, "Three Rubes Seeing New York" (Indestructible 680, 1907); Byron G. Harlan and Frank C. Stanley, "Two Rubes at the Vaudeville" (Edison Concert Cylinder 8736, 1904); Cal Stewart, "Uncle Josh on a Fifth Avenue Bus" (Victor 16228, 1909); Charles Ross Taggart, "Old Country Fiddler in New York" (Victor 17700, 1914); Taggart also recorded "Old Country Fiddler in a New York Restaurant" (Victor 17737, 1915).

65. Harkins, *Hillbilly*, 51–53; Jackson, *On a Slow Train through Arkansaw*.

66. Arthur Collins and Byron G. Harlan, "When Old Silas Does the Turkey Trot (To Turkey in the Straw)" (Edison Blue Ambersol 2041, 1913); Byron G. Harlan and Frank C. Stanley, "Scene in a Country Store" (Edison Gold Moulded Record 8457, 1903); Harlan, "Merry Farmer Boy" (Standard 3651, 1907); Harlan and Stanley, "Two Rubes at the Vaudeville" (Edison Concert Cylinder 8736, 1904).

67. "The Perpetuation of a Type," *Talking Machine World*, February 15, 1920, 9.

68. Handy, *Father of the Blues*, 76–78.

69. Handy was not the first to publish blues material. His "Memphis Blues" was preceded in 1912 by the black pianist Artie Matthews's "Baby Seal Blues" and the white composer Hart A. Wand's "Dallas Blues." Yet the circulation and popularity of Handy's compositions far exceeded that of his early competitors, leav

ing many to agree with his self-appointed title "Father of the Blues." See Southern, *Music of Black Americans*, 338–39.

70. W. C. Handy, "The Blues," *Chicago Defender*, August 30, 1919. Quoted in Abbott
and Seroff, " 'They Cert'ly Sound Good to Me,' " 423.

71. Johnson, for his part, suggested that Handy missed the mark by not bringing
enough of his own originality to his compositions. In 1917, he commented, "The
name of the composer printed on the copies is Handy, who is a negro musician
of Memphis; but 'The Memphis Blues' is one of those negro songs which, like
Topsy, 'jest grew'." Quoted in Abbott and Seroff, " 'They Cert'ly Sound Good to
Me,' " 412.

72. Handy, *Father of the Blues*, 195.

73. Abbott and Seroff, " 'They Cert'ly Sound Good to Me,' " 414.

74. For excellent, detailed histories of African American vaudeville and its embrace
of the blues, see Abbott and Seroff, " 'They Cert'ly Sound Good to Me,' " and
their *Ragged But Right*.

75. Handy, *Father of the Blues*, 195.

76. George O'Connor, "Nigger Blues" (Columbia A-2064, 1916); Walsh, "Favorite
Pioneer Recording Artists: George H. O'Connor"; Abbott and Seroff, " 'They
Cert'ly Sound Good to Me,' " 409–11; Palmer, *Deep Blues*, 105–6; Charles Keil,
"People's Music Comparatively: Style and Stereotype, Class and Hegemony," in
Keil and Feld, *Music Grooves*, 198–99.

77. W. C. Handy (music) and George A. Norton (lyrics), "The Memphis Blues"
(New York: Joe Morris Music Co., 1913); Handy, *Father of the Blues*, 106–12;
Walsh, "Favorite Pioneer Recording Artists: Morton Harvey," 30–31.

78. For background on Bernard, see Gracyk, *Recording Pioneers*, 42–46; Walsh,
"Favorite Pioneer Recording Artists: Al Bernard."

79. "Enigmatic Folksongs of the Southern Underworld," *Current Opinion* 67, no. 3
(September 1919): 165.

80. Whitney Williams, "Gladsome Gilda's Gallivanting Garners Glee," *Los Angeles
Times*, April 12, 1925, 21.

81. Gilda Gray, " 'Shimmied' Her Way into Fame," *Washington Post*, March 21, 1926,
SM8. See also Bryant, "Shaking Things Up."

82. Handy and Southern, "Letters from W. C. Handy to William Grant Still," 104.

83. "The Return of Marion Harris," *New York Times*, February 20, 1927, X4; Gracyk,
Recording Pioneers, 167–78.

84. Marion Harris, "Paradise Blues" (Victor 18152, 1916).

85. Marion Harris, "When I Hear That Jazz Band Play" (Victor 18398, 1917).

86. Quoted in Gracyk, *Recording Pioneers*, 173. See also "Marion Harris," *Washington Post*, January 16, 1921, 57.

87. "Marion Harris Feature of New Hillstreet Bill," *Los Angeles Times*, January 8,
1924, A9.

88. Handy, *Father of the Blues*, 199. See also Handy, *Blues* (1926), 31: "As to the singing of the blues, it would seem necessary, first, to be a colored contralto—except for the fact that Marion Harris is white."

89. Handy, *Blues* (1926), 24.

90. "Negroes as Red Seal Buyers," *Talking Machine World*, October 15, 1920, 77.

91. "Enigmatic Folksongs," 165.

Chapter 5: Talking Machine World

1. "Selling the Talking Machines in the Foreign Markets," *Talking Machine World*, July 15, 1920, 63; "Edmond F. Sause New Columbia Export Manager," *Talking Machine World*, February 15, 1915, 55.

2. Classic studies include Gelatt, *The Fabulous Phonograph, 1877–1977*; Welch and Burt, *From Tinfoil to Stereo*. A notable exception is the work of Pekka Gronow. In addition to the articles cited below, see Gronow and Saunio, *An International History of the Recording Industry*. See also Kenney, *Recorded Music in American Life*, 65–87.

3. For an overview of the debates surrounding music and globalization, see Born and Hesmondhalgh, eds., *Western Music and Its Others*, 21–31; Radano and Bohlman, eds., *Music and the Racial Imagination*, 28–34. Some important texts on late-twentieth-century musical globalization include Steven Feld, "Notes on World Beat [1988]" and "From Schizophonia to Schismogenesis: On the Discourses and Commodification Practices of 'World Music' and World Beat," in Keil and Feld, *Music Grooves*, 238–46; 257–89; Erlmann, "The Aesthetics of the Global Imagination"; Taylor, *Global Pop*; Burnett, *The Global Jukebox*; Simon Frith, "The Discourse of World Music," in Born and Hesmondhalgh, *Western Music and Its Others*, 305–22. A notable discussion of music and globalization during the late nineteenth century is Erlmann, *Music, Modernity, and the Global Imagination*.

4. Industry sales statistics are notoriously difficult to determine for the early decades of the industry. Educated estimates suggest annual U.S. record sales in 1900 were approximately 3 million units. A steady rise occurred through 1915 when sales were approximately 55 million. The following years saw phonograph record sales rise more quickly, reaching about 140 million in the early 1920s. International figures are more difficult to determine. Yet available figures suggest that sales outside the United States in the years just after 1910 sat at around 50 million units. See Gronow and Saunio, *An International History of the Recording Industry*, 12; Gronow, "The Record Industry," 59–60.

5. "A Wonderful Invention—Speech Capable of Indefinite Repetition from Automatic Records," *Scientific American*, November 17, 1877; quoted in Welch and Burt, *From Tinfoil to Stereo*, 9

6. Quoted in Welch and Burt, *From Tinfoil to Stereo*, 32–33.

7. Gelatt, *The Fabulous Phonograph*, 73; Welch and Burt, *From Tinfoil to Stereo*, 90.

8. "Will Replace the Cheap Piano," *Talking Machine World*, March 15, 1905, 9.

9. "The Talking Machine Is Here to Stay," *Talking Machine World*, January 15, 1905, 3.

10. Katz, *Capturing Sound*, 48–71; Chanan, *Repeated Takes*, 30–31; Welch and Burt, *From Tinfoil to Stereo*, 113–14; Sanjek and Sanjek, *Pennies from Heaven*, 24.

11. Quoted in Chanan, *Repeated Takes*, 30.

12. Ibid., 30–31. For a similar assessment see Welch and Burt, *From Tinfoil to Stereo*, 113–14; Sanjek and Sanjek, *Pennies from Heaven*, 24.

13. "A Great Educational Factor," *Talking Machine World*, December 15, 1910, 4. For more information on Clark, see "How to Put Victors in the Public Schools, *Talking Machine World*, June 15, 1911, 31–32; "Mrs. Frances E. Clark's Address," *Talking Machine World*, July 15, 1912, 29–30. "Victor Educational Matter," *Talking Machine World*, September 15, 1914, 29, reports on Victor promotional material listing 1,783 cities having placed Victor machines in their public schools.

14. "Music Is Approaching its Richest Development," *Talking Machine World*, January 15, 1917, 47. See also Katz, *Capturing Sound*, 48–71.

15. Williams, *Culture and Society*; Stocking, *Race, Culture, and Evolution*, 72–74; Clifford, *The Predicament of Culture*, 234–235; Denning, *Culture in the Age of Three Worlds*, 76–81.

16. Sousa, "The Menace of Mechanical Music."

17. Denning, *Culture in the Age of Three Worlds*, 79; Sousa, "The Menace of Mechanical Music."

18. Levine, *Highbrow/Lowbrow*; quote from Leonard, *Jazz: Myth and Religion*, 12. The editorial originally appeared in the London edition of the *New York Herald*. It was reprinted in the United States by *Musical Courier*. On industry attitudes toward African American music, see also Foreman, "Jazz and Race Records," 46; Leonard, *Jazz and the White Americans*; Ogren, *The Jazz Revolution*, chap. 5 "Prudes and Primitives: White Americans Debate Jazz," 139–61.

19. In this sense, the cultural uplift campaign in the phonograph industry had parallels with the contemporaneous uplift campaign in the advertising industry. See Marchand, *Advertising the American Dream*, 87–95; Lears, *Fables of Abundance*; Ohmann, *Selling Culture*.

20. Howard Taylor, "The Prima-Donna and the Cowboy," *Talking Machine World*, May 15, 1905, 22–23.

21. "'Talker' Advertises Sousa," *Talking Machine World*, October 15, 1906, 5.

22. "Stimulates Musical Taste," *Talking Machine World*, December 15, 1905, 6. See also "Talker Succeeds Hurdy Gurdy," *Talking Machine World*, May 15, 1910, 14.

23. "Some Good Retail Sales Tips," *Talking Machine World*, June 15, 1917, 126. For a very similar argument, see "Importance of Educating Consumers," *Talking Machine World*, November 15, 1910, 3.

24. "The Talking Machine in China," *Talking Machine World*, June 15, 1905, 11.
25. "Columbia Portable Phonograph in Chilean Forests," *Talking Machine World*, October, 1927, 50; "The Talking Machine in Alaska," *Talking Machine World*, March 15, 1905, 3; " 'Talker' Among Savages," *Talking Machine World*, December 15, 1907, 4; "Carryola Master Portable in Denver-Africa Trek," *Talking Machine World*, June, 1927, 34; "Development of the Export Trade," *Talking Machine World*, October 15, 1910, 13; "Talking Machine a Civilizer," *Talking Machine World*, July 15, 1905, 7; "Jack London's Great Cruise with the Victor," *Talking Machine World*, June 15, 1908, 20.
26. Taussig, *Mimesis and Alterity*, 193.
27. "The Talking Machine in Alaska," *Talking Machine World*, March 15, 1905, 3.
28. "The Talking Machine Excites Interest among the Aleutian Islanders," *Talking Machine World*, January 15, 1905, 6.
29. Howard Taylor, "A Phonographic Legend," *Talking Machine World*, April 15, 1905, 22.
30. For a similar point, see Jones, *Yellow Music*, 10–12.
31. Deloria, *Indians in Unexpected Places*, 3–14, quote on 9.
32. "The Musical Filipinos," *Talking Machine World*, February 15, 1905, 3.
33. Kinnear, *The Gramophone Company's First Indian Recordings, 1899–1908*, 9–11, 15–17; see also Qureshi, "His Master's Voice?," 63–98; Joshi, "A Concise History of the Phonograph Industry in India"; Manuel, "Popular Music in India: 1901–86."
34. See "Talking Machines in China," *Talking Machine World*, June 15, 1906. Other early calls to record "local color" or "native bands" in foreign markets include "Great Export Trade," *Talking Machine World*, January 15, 1905, 5; "Talking Machine Prospects," *Talking Machine World*, March 15, 1905, 22, regarding Puerto Rico; "Chinese Band or Orchestra Making Records in China," *Talking Machine World*, October 15, 1905, 28; "Growth of Export Trade," *Talking Machine World*, December 15, 1905, 35, which notes the global desire for recordings of local talent; and "Cuban Trade," *Talking Machine World*, April 15, 1909, 43, calling for sensitivity to the variety of musical markets in the districts outside of Havana.
35. Heinrich Bumb, "The Great Beka 'Expedition' 1905–6," *Talking Machine Review* 41 (1976): 729–33, quoted in Gronow, "The Record Industry Comes to the Orient," 251.
36. Jones, "Gramophone," 81; Gronow, "The Record Industry Comes to the Orient," 254; Perkins, Kelly, and Ward, "On Gramophone Company Matrix Numbers 1898 to 1921," 57.
37. Gronow, "The Record Industry: Growth of a Mass Medium," 58–60. The phonograph majors' international expansion was part of a larger trend of U.S. companies looking abroad for antidotes to perceived domestic market satura-

tion. The latter part of the nineteenth century witnessed a profound increase in U.S. corporate expansion overseas, fostered by government economic policies, fear of domestic overproduction, and anxiety over the perceived closing of the American frontier. See LaFeber, *The New Empire*; Rosenberg, *Spreading the American Dream*; Carstensen, *American Enterprise in Foreign Markets*.

38. James C. Goff, "An Interesting Letter," *Talking Machine World*, July 15, 1912, 63; Gronow, "The Record Industry Comes to the Orient," 252–53; Kinnear, *The Gramophone Company's First Indian Recordings*, 22–23; Jones, "Gramophone Company," 88; Moore, *A Voice in Time*.

39. "Developing Our Export Trade," *Talking Machine World*, February 15, 1908, 18.

40. Gaisberg, *The Music Goes Round*, 62.

41. "Tells of Recording Experiences," *Talking Machine World*, December 15, 1919, 96.

42. Gaisberg, *The Music Goes Round*, 54.

43. Oscar C. Preuss, "Round the Recording Studios No. 1 Songs of Araby,' " *The Gramophone*, March 1928, 411–12; quoted in Gronow, "The Record Industry Comes to the Orient," 273.

44. Quoted in Farrell, "The Early Days of the Gramophone Industry in India," 59.

45. "India a Great Market," *Talking Machine World*, April 15, 1905, 6.

46. "Around the World with a Talker," *Talking Machine World*, December 15, 1910, 49.

47. "Developing our Export Trade," *Talking Machine World*, February 15, 1908, 18–20.

48. "Recording Artists of all Castes in India," *Talking Machine World*, April 15, 1913, 32.

49. Gaisberg, *The Music Goes Round*, 55; Gronow and Saunio, *An International History of the Recording Industry*, 11–12.

50. "Returns from Making Trip around World," *Talking Machine World*, January 15, 1913, 43–44.

51. Fewkes quoted in Spottswood, liner notes to *Folk Music in America: Volume 15*, 10.

52. Brady, *A Spiral Way*, 129; Joseph C. Hickerson, "Early Field Recordings of Ethnic Music," in American Folklife Center, *Ethnic Recordings in America*, 67–83.

53. Untitled editorial, *Talking Machine World*, May 15, 1905, 14. See also reports of anthropologists using the phonograph during fieldwork: "To Preserve Indian Songs," *Talking Machine World*, January 15, 1906, 3; "An Aid to Archeology," *Talking Machine World*, April 15, 1905, 21; "Talking Machine for Monkeys," *Talking Machine World*, August 15, 1905, 7; and "Preserving Native Languages," *Talking Machine World*, September 15, 1905, 3, which reported the praises of the phonograph at the American Anthropological Association conference.

54. Farrell, "Gramophone Industry in India," 61–62. Even as late as 1920, Victor

Talking Machine Company's catalogue maintained the category "Folk Songs" comprising selections from foreign countries. See Porterfield, *Jimmie Rodgers*, 86.

55. "Ralph Cabanas Expected," *Talking Machine World*, April 15, 1910, 34; "Successful Work in Developing Foreign Trade," *Talking Machine World*, November 15, 1912, 6; "The Talking Machine Trade in Mexico," *Talking Machine World*, October 15, 1913, 82; "New Columbia Co. Representative in Texas," *Talking Machine World*, December 15, 1913, 33; "Building Business in Texas," *Talking Machine World*, May 15, 1914, 30; "Conditions in Texas," *Talking Machine World*, June 15, 1914, 10; "Becomes Canadian Manager," *Talking Machine World*, October 15, 1915, 35.

56. "Edmond F. Sause New Columbia Export Manager," *Talking Machine World*, February 15, 1915, 55; "Developing Our Export Trade," *Talking Machine World*, February 15, 1908, 18–20; "Burns Chats of Trip to Cuba," *Talking Machine World*, July 15, 1910, 44; "Interesting Views on Mexico," *Talking Machine World*, April 15, 1911, 43; "The Old and New World Visited," *Talking Machine World*, December 15, 1911, 37–38; "To Manufacture in Germany," *Talking Machine World* (April 15, 1914), 25; "Records in Foreign Languages," *Talking Machine World*, September 15, 1917, 96.

57. *Columbia Record* 7, no. 9 (September 1909), quoted in Pekka Gronow, "Ethnic Recordings: An Introduction," in American Folklife Center, *Ethnic Recordings in America*, 3.

58. "Chinese Instead of Irish: Tunes from the Talking Machine Aroused O'Toole to Threats of Action," *Talking Machine World*, August 15, 1905, 9. For similar stories, see "Chinese Phonograph Records: Delight Chinatown Citizens in New Orleans—Grand Opera in Chinese a Great Attraction," *Talking Machine World*, January 15, 1905, 6; "The Good Old Summertime," *Talking Machine World*, October 15, 1906, 50. The latter, a veritable encyclopedia of ethnic cultural stereotypes, relates a scene on a crowded New York train featuring "a wonderful mixture of Teutons, Scandinavians, Orientals, Africans, representatives of the Latin races, an Anglo-Saxon or two, and lastly a large talking machine."

59. "New York Trade Discusses European War," *Talking Machine World*, August 15, 1914, 24; untitled editorial, *Talking Machine World*, September 15, 1914, 14–15; Howard Taylor Middleton, "Utilizing the War as an Advertising Medium," *Talking Machine World*, September 15, 1914, 28–29; untitled editorial, *Talking Machine World*, October 15, 1914, 14–15; Howard Taylor Middleton, "Fitting the Record to the Customer," *Talking Machine World*, November 15, 1914, 56–57; "Columbia Recording Laboratory Opened in Chicago," *Talking Machine World*, August 15, 1915, 67–68; "Oriental Records," *Talking Machine World*, June 15, 1917, 126; Richard K. Spottswood, "Commercial Ethnic Recordings in the United States," in American Folklife Center, *Ethnic Recordings: A Neglected Heritage*, 55–56; *Columbia Record* quoted by Spottswood, 55; Kenney, *Recorded Music in American Life*, 79–80.

60. Columbia advertisement, *Talking Machine World*, January 15, 1917, 54.

61. "Records in Foreign Languages," *Talking Machine World*, September 15, 1917, 96; "Promoting Foreign Record Business," *Talking Machine World*, September 15, 1917, 83.

62. "An Almost Untouched Record Selling Field with Millions of Prospective Customers," *Talking Machine World*, June 15, 1922, 4.

63. Pathé Frères advertisement, *Talking Machine World*, July 15, 1917, 24–25.

64. Harry A. Goldsmith, "Supplying Successfully the Needs of the Buyers of Foreign Records," *Talking Machine World*, June 15, 1918, 15.

65. Bradford, *Born with the Blues*; Titon, *Early Downhome Blues*; Barlow, *Looking Up at Down*; Malone, *Country Music USA*.

66. Gillett, *The Sound of the City*; Robert Christgau, "Rah, Rah, Sis-Boom-Bah: The Secret Relationship between College Rock and the Communist Party," in Ross and Rose, eds., *Microphone Fiends*, 221–26; Regev, "Rock Aesthetics and the Musics of the World"; Frith, "Discourse of World Music," 313–14.

67. Denning, *Culture in the Age of Three Worlds*, 79.

68. Initial accounts of late-twentieth-century globalization used the local in this way to articulate a cultural imperialism model, positing discrete, fragile local cultures smothered in a landslide of commodified, mass-mediated Western music. See Nettl, *The Western Impact on World Music*; Laing, "The Music Industry and the 'Cultural Imperialism' Thesis"; Manuel, *Popular Musics of the Non-Western World*; Goodwin and Gore, "World Beat and the Cultural Imperialism Debate"; Robinson et al., eds., *Music at the Margins*. Later formulations framed the local as a signifier of difference. Influenced by poststructuralism and postcolonialism, writers defined local music not as a distinct entity but as a position that emerged out of a historical power struggle with the West, be it characterized by its resistance to Western imperialism, its critique of Western music's canonical universalism, or its ultimate exoticism to Western listeners. See Feld, "From Schizophonia to Schmogenesis"; Lipsitz, *Time Passages*; Guilbault, *Zouk*; Stokes, ed., *Ethnicity, Identity and Music*; Erlmann, "Aesthetics of the Global Imagination"; Erlmann, *Music, Modernity, and the Global Imagination*; Hayward, ed., *Widening the Horizon*. A final conception identified the local as a historically specific articulation of the global, a site in which global flows of media, money, people, and power intercut and interacted in unique ways. This school of scholars explored, to paraphrase Stuart Hall, the musical aesthetics of the hybrid, the crossover, the diaspora, and creolization. Hybrid musical forms could speak of being a global and local citizen simultaneously, complete with the contradictions such twoness implied. See Appadurai, *Modernity at Large*; Hall, "The Local and the Global," 38–39; Du Bois, *The Souls of Black Folk*, 3; Robinson, *Black Marxism*; Gilroy, *The Black Atlantic*; Lipsitz, *Dangerous Crossroads*; Taylor, *Global Pop*.

1. Bradford, *Born with the Blues*, 19.

2. Ibid., 117.

3. Ibid, 118.

4. Hagar may have had a special appreciation for expanding the music available on record. He is understood to be the first violinist to make commercial recordings in the 1890s. For background on Hager, see Gracyk, *Popular American Recording Pioneers*, 150–56. Hager's assistant director Ralph Peer later explained, "Okeh was in a rather tough spot. They were competing with Victor [and] Columbia; and Edison was then important. They were selling maybe three or four million records a year, which was nothing. Something like this was needed because it was really difficult in those days to compete." Quoted in Porterfield, *Jimmie Rodgers*, 92.

5. Gussow, *Seems Like Murder Here*, 161–63.

6. Foreman, "Jazz and Race Records," 158.

7. Interview with Ralph Peer, 1959, Hollywood, California, by Lillian Borgeson, Southern Folklife Collection, tape #FT2772c.

8. Foreman, "Jazz and Race Records," 57, 61.

9. "Records for the Okeh Library," *Talking Machine World*, October 15, 1920, 220.

10. Okeh advertisment, *Talking Machine World*, November 15, 1920, .n.p. As coverage of Mamie Smith continued, the journal and Okeh began portraying her as a "colored" artist but continued to market her toward white consumers. A December ad featured a large photograph of Smith with the headline "Biggest Vocal Seller, You All Know It," implying a wide customer base. A March advertisement portrayed Smith and her African American band performing for formally attired white dancers. See Okeh advertisement, *Talking Machine World*, December 15, 1920, n.p.; Okeh advertisement, *Talking Machine World*, March 15, 1921, 113.

11. "Songwriter Faces Two Suits," *Talking Machine World*, May 15, 1921, 149.

12. Waters, *His Eye on the Sparrow*, 175.

13. Foreman, "Jazz and Race Records," 61.

14. "Down Home Blues" was by Tom Delaney, an African American songwriter who would become one of the most prolific blues composers of the decade.

15. Anton Lada and Spencer Williams, "Arkansas Blues (A Down Home Chant)" (Chicago: Francis Clifford Music Co., 1921).

16. Foreman, "Jazz and Race Records," 70.

17. Okeh advertisement, *Talking Machine World*, August 15, 1921, 35.

18. Norfolk Jazz Quartette, "Strut Miss Lizzie/My Mammy" (Okeh 8007, 1921); Mary Stafford and Her Jazz Band, "Strut Miss Lizzie" (Columbia A-3418, 1921); Al Bernard, "Strut Miss Lizzie" (Edison Blue Amberol 4248, 1921).

19. Waters, *His Eye Is on the Sparrow*, 151, 183–84. See also Cherry, "Ethel Waters."

20. Ethel Waters, Alberta Hunter, and Fletcher Henderson, "Down South Blues" (New York: Down South Music Publishing Co., 1923).

21. "Down South Blues" recordings include Clara Smith (Columbia A-3961, 1923) on their general list; Alberta Hunter (Paramount 12036, 1923); Hannah Sylvester (with Fletcher Henderson) (Pathe 32007, 1923). The Virginians (a satellite band of the Paul Whiteman Orchestra) recorded an instrumental jazz version (Victor 19175-B, 1923).

22. Interview with Ralph Peer.

23. Howard Taylor Middleton, "Records of the Old Songs," *Talking Machine World*, January 15, 1907, 11. Other articles strategizing about rural marketing include Howard Taylor Middleton, "The Country in Autumn," *Talking Machine World*, October 15, 1906, 5; "Timely Talks," *Talking Machine World*, November 15, 1909, 34; "In the Olden Times," *Talking Machine World*, April 15, 1910, 54; Howard Taylor, "Call of the Country," *Talking Machine World*, August 15, 1911, 14; "To Keep the Farm Hands Content," *Talking Machine World*, January 15, 1911, 7; Howard Taylor, "About That Holiday Campaign," *Talking Machine World*, December 15, 1911, 34.

24. Howard Taylor Middleton, "Concerning the Black Race and Blue Records," *Talking Machine World*, September 15, 1913, 26. "Blue" here refers to Edison Blue Ambersol Records and has nothing to do with the blues.

25. Howard Taylor Middleton, "The Talking Machine Store in the Small Village," *Talking Machine World*, April 15, 1916, 53–54; "Working the Rural Field," *Talking Machine World*, September 15, 1917, 1; George B. Hewitt, "How Exhibits at State and County Fairs Help to Boost Your Business," *Talking Machine World*, September 15, 1917, 11; Warfield Webb, "Reaching the Country Customer through the Agency of the Automobile," *Talking Machine World*, November 15, 1917, 11; "Helpful Suggestions on Getting Farmer Business," *Talking Machine World*, April 15, 1920, 40; "Influence of the Talking Machine 'On the Farm,'" *Talking Machine World*, August 15, 1920, 55; "Rural Residents Average Well as Music Lovers," *Talking Machine World*, December 15, 1920, 66; "40% of Farmers Possess Talkers," *Talking Machine World*, January 15, 1921, 79; W. B. Stoddard, "Developing Business in the Small Town," *Talking Machine World*, May 15, 1923, 21; "Radio Opportunities in the Rural Sections," *Talking Machine World*, November 15, 1923, 30.

26. For two typical examples, see Howard Taylor, "Sunshine and Shadow: A Tale of a Southern Hunting Trip," *Talking Machine World*, July 15, 1905, 19–21; and "Across the Continent," *Talking Machine World*, December 15, 1907, 55–56.

27. "Excellent Conditions in the South," *Talking Machine World*, June 15, 1917, 55.

28. "Trade Possibilities in the South," *Talking Machine World*, June 15, 1920, 32.

29. Quote from "Atlanta Continues to Be a Very Busy Trade Center," *Talking Ma-*

chine World, April 15, 1918, 6. See also "Better Feeling in the South," *Talking Machine World*, November 15, 1915, 78; "Virginia Trade Unusually Active," *Talking Machine World*, March 15, 1916, 38; "Conditions Good in Texas," *Talking Machine World*, June 15, 1917, 73; "Brisk Business in Nashville," *Talking Machine World*, March 15, 1919, 22; "Sales Are Imposing in Atlanta," *Talking Machine World*, April 15, 1919, 89; "Visit of Opera Co. Helps Expand Sales in Atlanta," *Talking Machine World*, May 15, 1919, 126; "Southern States Make Encouraging Business Showing," *Talking Machine World*, June 15, 1919, 72; "Demand Keeping Up in the South," *Talking Machine World*, October 15, 1920, 65.

30. Bradford, *Born with the Blues*, 117.
31. Foreman, "Jazz and Race Records," 58–61.
32. "Atlanta," *Talking Machine World*, June 15, 1922, 155.
33. Green, "Hillbilly Music," 208; "James K. Polk, Inc., Has Won High Rank in Seven Years," *Talking Machine World*, December 1928, 36; "James K. Polk, Inc., Holds Its Annual Staff Dinner," *Talking Machine World*, January 15, 1926, 116.
34. Green, "Hillbilly Music," 208.
35. Interview with Ralph Peer. Most accounts determine that the initial order was for five hundred, not one thousand records. See Green, "Hillbilly Music," 209; Wiggins, *Fiddlin' Georgia Crazy*, 75. Brockman recalled, "Well those people in New York there, they thought so little of it actually the lady didn't even want to put a number on the record. They wanted to stick it out as more or less a specialty to satisfy my yearning for it. That's actually the truth. They didn't want to put a number on it. They didn't even want to put it in the catalog." Interview with Polk Brockman August 11, 1961, by Archie Green, Southern Folklife Collection, tape S#FT 3274c.
36. Interview with Polk Brockman.
37. Peterson, *Creating Country Music*, 28.
38. Roger S. Brown, "Recording Pioneer Polk Brockman," *Living Blues* 23 (September/October 1975): 31; "James K. Polk, Inc., Holds Its Annual Staff Dinner," *Talking Machine World*, January 15, 1926, 116.
39. Wolfe, *Devil's Box*, 16; Norman Cohen, "Early Pioneers," in Malone and McCulloh, eds., *Stars of Country Music*, 11–13.
40. Green, "Hillbilly Music," 210–16.
41. Wiggins, *Fiddlin' Georgia Crazy*, 1–20.
42. Hall et al., *Like a Family*, 174–75.
43. Quoted in Wiggins, *Fiddlin' Georgia Crazy*, 24.
44. Wiggins alludes to this possibility; ibid., 25.
45. Ibid., 45–56; Linton K. Starr, "Georgia's Unwritten Airs Played by Old 'Fiddlers' for Atlanta Prizes," *Musical America*, March 21, 1914, 23. See also Campbell, *Music and the Making of a New South*.
46. Dixon and Godrich, *Recording the Blues*, 283, 289–90.

47. Okeh advertisement, *Talking Machine World*, November 15, 1920, 190. See also "Okeh Foreign Language Records," *Talking Machine World*, April 15, 1922, 21.

48. "Emerson Co. Adds 'Race' Records to Its Catalog," *Talking Machine World*, May 15, 1924, 106.

49. "Will Radio Craze Affect Our Industry?," *Talking Machine World*, March 15, 1922, 8; "Why Music Broadcasting by Radio Should Not Hurt Sales of Talking Machines and Records," *Talking Machine World*, March 15, 1922, 25; "Makes Survey of Rural Field," *Talking Machine World*, July 15, 1923, 66; "Talking Machines Dealers Discuss Effect of Radio," *Talking Machine World*, September 15, 1923, 158.

50. "Radio and the Foreign Records," *Talking Machine World*, April 15, 1924, 66.

51. "Officers and Directors Elected at Annual Meeting of the General Phonograph Corp.," *Talking Machine World*, April 15, 1925, 48. Those in the radio trade were soon proving Heineman wrong, yet they also viewed the future of the medium in terms of the same separate niche markets. In 1926, *Talking Machine World* reported that the market for radio had tripled since radio dealers discovered "Negroes," "farmers," and "the foreign born." See "New Field for Radio Sales Open to Trade," *Talking Machine World*, January 15, 1926, 28.

52. Interview with Ralph Peer.

53. Such euphemisms for white consumption were even promoted by Harry Pace, the African American owner of Black Swan Records. See "Demand for Ethel Waters Record," *Talking Machine World*, August 15, 1921, 89.

54. "Okeh Window Display Service," *Talking Machine World*, January 15, 1922, 48.

55. Records were far from the only product advertised with minstrel imagery. In general stores, African American patrons confronted the derogatory images of blackness that increasingly graced nationally advertised brands of consumer goods, from Aunt Jemima cornmeal to Gold Dust Washing Power. Evidence suggests that black consumers avoided brands featuring blackface images in their advertising. However, soap or pancake mix rarely announced their own authenticity in the way the recordings of black music did. See Hale, *Making Whiteness*, 168–79, 193; Morgan, "Mammy the Huckster."

56. "Okeh Window Display Service," *Talking Machine World*, January 15, 1922, 48. On Sullivan, see Foreman, "Jazz and Race Records," 217. For discussion of the use of minstrel imagery in race record advertisements, see Foreman, "Jazz and Race Records," 211–64; Titon, *Early Downhome Blues*, 218–60.

57. "Widening the Breach," *Half-Century Magazine*, January–February 1925, 3, 21. Also see Foreman, "Jazz and Race Records," 211.

58. The Vocalion label, for example, entered the trade in 1926 touting "Better and Cleaner Race Records." It ran benign advertisements until 1928 when it gave up its slogan and began featuring stereotypical images. See Dixon and Godrich, *Recording the Blues*, 39; Foreman, "Jazz and Race Records," 227.

59. Black Swan Records advertisement, *Chicago Defender*, June 2, 1923, 7.

60. *Chicago Defender*, October 10, 1925, 7.

61. Ibid., November 22, 1924, 7.

62. Ibid., September 6, 1924, 8; Ibid., August 25, 1928, 9; Ibid., January 11, 1930, 9.

63. Ibid., April 27, 1929, 10.

64. "Two New Columbia Artists from Carolina," *Talking Machine World*, June 15, 1924, 26.

65. "Increased Demand for All Products in Atlanta Indicates Healthy Condition," *Talking Machine World*, September 15, 1924, 176.

66. "Columbia Co. Advertising Commended by Publication," *Talking Machine World*, March 15, 1925, 176.

67. Ulysses J. Walsh, "Selling Records in a Mountain Town," *Talking Machine World*, September 15, 1929, 17.

68. Interview with Maybelle Carter, August 31, 1961, by Ed Khan and Archie Green, Southern Folklife Collection, FT #4069.

69. Porterfield, *Jimmie Rodgers*, 42.

70. Mendoza, *Lydia Mendoza*, 18.

71. Scarborough, *On the Trail of Negro Folk-Songs*, 3.

72. Columbia Records advertisement, *Talking Machine World*, May 15, 1924, 153.

73. Ibid., June 15, 1924, 17. See also Green, "Hillbilly Music," 216.

74. Okeh Records advertisement, *Talking Machine World*, June 15, 1924, n.p. Another ad elaborated, "Daily we receive hundreds of requests from Carson's admirers asking for lists of his records and even for his photograph. The most surprising and important part of it is that many of these requests come from territories which ordinarily are supposed to have no market for 'Fiddlin'' records." See Okeh Records advertisement, *Talking Machine World*, September 15, 1924, n.p.

75. Okeh Records advertisement, *Talking Machine World*, June 15, 1924, n.p.; Titon, *Early Downhome Blues*, 240.

76. "Fiddlin' John Carson Records Widely Popular," *Talking Machine World*, August 15, 1925, 81.

77. Interview with Tony Alderman, April 26, 1975, on WAMU-FM, Tony Alderman Papers, Ralph Rinzler Folklife Archive, Smithsonian Center for Folklife and Cultural Heritage.

78. Tony Alderman to Archie Green, May 6, 1961, Tony Alderman Papers. See also Harkin, *Hillbilly*, 78–81.

79. Walsh, "Selling Records in a Mountain Town," *Talking Machine World*, September 15, 1929, 17.

80. Malone, *Don't Get Above Your Raisin'*, 172–73; Harkins, *Hillbilly*, 76; Grundy, " 'We Always Tried to Be Good People,' " 1600–1601; Seeger, "Who Chose These

Records?"; Blue Ridge Corn Shuckers, "Old Time Corn Shucking #1" (Victor 20835, 1927).

81. Cohen, "The Skillet Lickers," 242; Clayton McMichen's Melody Men, "Taking the Census Part 1" (Columbia 15549D, 1930). The band was a side project of the Skillet Lickers' fiddler.

82. Allegheny Highlanders, "A Trip to New York #1–#4" (Brunswick 324/325, 1929).

Chapter 7: Black Folk and Hillbilly Pop

1. Crawford, *America's Musical Life*, 546–50.

2. Ernest Thompson, "Alexander's Ragtime Band" (Columbia 15000-D, 1924); Carlin and Terill, *String Bands in the North Carolina Piedmont*, 131–40, quote on 133.

3. Carlin and Terill, *String Bands*, 135; Russell and Pinson, *Country Music Records*, 902. Francis Byrne and Frank McIntyre, "How Are You Goin' to Wet Your Whistle?" (New York: Leo Feist, 1919); George L. Cobb and Jack Yellen, "Are You From Dixie?" (New York: M. Witmark and Sons, 1915); Percy Wenrich and Jack Mahoney, "Snow Deer" (New York: Wenrich-Howard Co., 1913); Jack Yellen and Milton Ager, "Don't Put a Tax on the Beautiful Girls" (New York: Leo Feist, 1919); Charles Cartwell and John Queen, "I Got Mine" (New York: Howley, Haviland and Dresser, 1901).

4. Carlin and Terill, *String Bands*, 135; "Ernest Thompson Signed as a Columbia Artist," *Talking Machine World*, June 15, 1924, 58–59.

5. Seeger, "Who Chose These Records?," 15–16.

6. Ibid., 17. The week the American Record Corporation recorded the African American blues singer Robert Johnson in a San Antonio hotel room they also captured tunes by W. Lee O'Daniels and his Hillbilly Boys, the Hermanas Barraza, and the Chuck Wagon Gang. See "Columbia San Antonio Series" List, Columbia Phonograph Company V-File, American Folklife Center.

7. Peg Leg Howell, "Turkey Buzzard Blues" (Columbia 14382-D, 1928); Mississippi John Hurt, "Frankie" (Okeh 8560, 1928); Julius Daniels, "Can't Put the Bridle on the Mule This Morning" (Victor 21359, 1927). These are but a few examples for the purpose of illustration. For a much more exhaustive list, see Russell, *Blacks, Whites, and Blues*.

8. Wolfe, "Rural Black String Band Music"; Zwigoff, "Black Country String Bands"; Wald, *Escaping the Delta*, 48.

9. Cohn, liner notes to *Maple Leaf Rag*. The compilation album is split along racial lines. The first side features black ragtime string bands, the second side white.

10. Frank Stokes, "I Got Mine" (Victor 38512, 1928); Fiddlin' John Carson, "I Got Mine" (Okeh 40119, 1924); Gid Tanner's Skillet Lickers, "I Got Mine," (Columbia 15134D, 1926).

11. Ernest Thompson, "Chicken Roost behind the Moon" (Columbia 206-D, 1924); Henry Whitter, "Chicken, You Better Go behind the Barn" (Okeh 40077, 1924); Carlisle Brothers, "Chicken Roost Blues" (Champion 45132, 1931); Beale Street Sheiks, "Chicken You Can't Roost behind the Moon" (Paramount 12576, 1927). See also Oliver, *Songster and Saints*, 99–100.

12. Korma, ed., *Encyclopedia of the Blues*, vol. 1, 423–24.

13. Oliver, *Songsters and Saints*, 89–93.

14. Charters, *The Blues Makers*, part 2, 15–64.

15. Seeger, "Who Chose These Records?," 16.

16. Austin and Lee Allen, "Laughing and Crying Blues" (Columbia 14266-D, 1927).

17. Columbia advertisement, *Chicago Defender*, January 7, 1928, 9.

18. Cohn, liner notes to *Roots and Blues*; Wolfe, "The White Man's Blues, 1922–40"; Nelson, "The Allen Brothers"; Seeger, "Who Chose These Records," 16–17.

19. Black Swan Records advertisement, *Chicago Defender*, June 2, 1923, 7.

20. Calt, "Anatomy of a 'Race' Label," 95.

21. Interview with Samuel Chatman, November 14, 1973, by Margaret McKee and Fred Chisenhall, "Beale Street Black and Blue," oral history transcripts; Wald, *Escaping the Delta*, 52.

22. *Columbia Records*, June 1920, 3. Warshaw Collection, National Museum of American History, Smithsonian Institution.

23. "'Negro Spirituals' Are Classics," *Talking Machine World*, September 15, 1926, 28.

24. "New Okeh Record Artists," *Talking Machine World*, November 15, 1921, 142.

25. These examples from the phonograph industry press actually touted black creativity more than many folklorists. By the time of their publication, there had been a long and still-vigorous debate regarding the origins of the African American spirituals. As some white writers defined African Americans as un-creative primitives, they insisted that the sophisticated artistry and emotion of the black spirituals must have resulted from black imitation of white sources. Black people could not have created them on their own. The battle over origins was deeply entangled with languages of race and culture that transformed evidence of interracial culture into an argument for black inferiority. A useful overview of the black spiritual origins debate can be found in Wilgus, *Anglo-American Folksong Scholarship since 1898*, 344–64. See also Levine, *Black Culture and Black Consciousness*, 19–25; Radano, "Denoting Difference"; Cruz, *Culture on the Margins*. Some major contributors to the debate include Allen, Ware, and Garrison, *Slave Songs of the United States*; Du Bois, *The Souls of Black Folk*; Jackson, *White and Negro Spirituals*; Johnson, *The Book of American Negro Spirituals*; Johnson, *Folk Culture on St. Helena Island, South Carolina*.

26. "The Evolution of the "Blues," *Talking Machine World*, December 15, 1921, 136.

27. "Bessie Smith Renews Contract," *Talking Machine World*, January 15, 1924, 158.

28. "Bessie Smith Scores Success," *Talking Machine World*, August 15, 1923, 116.

29. "Aeolian Co. Announces First List of Race Records," *Talking Machine World*, July 15, 1923, 137; "Revival in 'Blues' Numbers," *Talking Machine World*, August 15, 1923, 132.

30. Okeh advertisement, *Talking Machine World*, May 15, 1925, n.p.

31. Evans, *Big Road Blues*, 75. The quote comes from a *Chicago Defender* ad that ran on April 3, 1926, touting Jefferson's "old-time tunes." See Samuel Charters, *The Blues Makers*, part 1, 177.

32. Charters, liner notes to *The Country Blues, Vol. 2*.

33. Charters, *The Country Blues*, 52–53; Charlie Jackson, "Papa Charlie and Blind Blake Talk about It (Part I and II)" (Paramount 12911, 1929); Charlie Jackson, "Salty Dog Blues" (Paramount 12236, 1924); Freddie Keppard Jazz Cardinals, "Salty Dog" (Paramount 12399, 1926); Allen Brothers, "Salty Dog Blues" (Columbia 15174D, 1927).

34. Wald, *Escaping the Delta*, 43–69; quote on 65.

35. Wolfe, "Columbia Records and Old-Time Music."

36. This is just a small sampling of the popular songs Carson recorded. See Norm Cohen, "Fiddlin' John Carson Discography," in Wiggins, *Fiddlin' Georgia Crazy*, 273–84. Archie Gottler and Howard Johnson and Coleman Goetz, "I'm Glad My Wife's in Europe" (New York: Leo Feist, 1914); Wendell W. Hall, "It Ain't Gonna Rain no Mo' " (Chicago: Wendell Wood Hall, 1923). On the Wendell Hall hit, see Russell, *Blacks, Whites, and Blues*, 28–29.

37. Cohen, "The Skillet Lickers," 233–34. Charles K. Harris, "Hello Central, Give Me Heaven" (New York: Charles K. Harris, 1901); Egbert Van Alstyne and Harry Williams, "In the Shade of the Old Apple Tree" (New York: Shapiro, Remick and Co. 1905); Florence Charlesworth, Charles Harrison, and Jacak Sadler, "I'm Drifting back to Dreamland" (Chicago: Ted Browne Music Co., 1922); John Kellette and Jaan Kenbrovin, "I'm Forever Blowing Bubbles" (New York: Jerome H. Remick and Co., 1919); Ernest Ball and J. Keirn Brennan, "Let the Rest of the World Go By" (New York: M. Witmark and Sons, 1919); Will Rossiter and W. R. Williams, "Don't You Remember the Time?" (Chicago: Will Rossiter, 1919).

38. Rorrer, *Rambling Blues*; Sapoznik, liner notes to *"You Ain't Talkin' to Me"*; Shepard N. Edmonds, "I'm Goin' to Live Anyhow, 'Till I Die" (New York: Joseph W. Stern, ca. 1901).

39. "You're as Welcome as the Flowers in May" was recorded by Byron Harlan and Frank Stanley (Edison Gold Moulded 8767, 1904); Richard Whiting, "They Made It Twice as Nice as Paradise (And They Called it Dixieland)" (New York: Jerome H. Remick, 1916); Ernest Heck and Floyd Whitmore, "Underneath the Southern Moon" (Scranton: Whitmore, 1905); Raymond Egan and Richard Whiting, "Mammy's Little Coal Black Rose" (New York: Jerome H. Remick, 1916). For Sides's discography, see, Russell and Pinson, *Country Music Records*, 834.

40. Kerry Mills, "At a Georgia Camp Meeting" (New York: F. A. Mills, 1897).

41. Tribe, *Mountaineer Jamboree*, 28–29; Russell and Pinson, *Country Music Records*, 200, 529–30. Jack Judge and Harry Williams, "It's a Long Way to Tipperary" (London: Feldman and Co., 1912); see also " 'It's A Long, Long Way to Tipperary.'—An Army Marching-Song," *Musical Times*, December 1, 1914, 696–97. On "Chicken," see Oliver, *Songsters and Saints*, 99–100. George L. Cobb and Jack Yellen, "Alabama Jubilee" (New York: Jerome Remick, ca. 1914); Percy Wenrich and Jack Mahoney, "When You Wore a Tulip and I Wore a Big Red Rose" (New York: Leo Feist, 1914).

42. Ernest Thompson, "Are You From Dixie?" (Columbia 130D, 1924).

43. The story of this record has been retold numerous times. A good early source remains Cohen, "Commercial Music Documents."

44. See the amazing Dalhart discography by Robert Olson appended to Palmer, *Vernon Dalhart*, 273–387.

45. Wolfe, liner notes to *White Country Blues*; Doc Boggs, *Country Blues* (Revenant 205, 1997); Doc Boggs, "Down South Blues" (Brunswick 118, 1927); Larry Hensley, "Match Box Blues" (Vocalion 02678, 1934); Slim Jim, "Soap Box Blues" (Bluebird B-6603, 1936); Herschel Brown, "Talking Nigger Blues" (Okeh 45247, 1928); Riley Puckett, "A Darkey's Wail" (Columbia 15163-D, 1927).

46. Cohen, "The Skillet Lickers," 240.

47. Nolan Porterfield offers a landmark description of Peer's process in *Jimmie Rodgers*, 96–99.

48. Interview with Polk Brockman, August 11, 1961, by Archie Green, Southern Folklife Collection, tape S#FT 3274c.

49. Interview with Ralph Peer, 1959, Hollywood, California, by Lillian Borgeson, Southern Folklife Collection, tape #FT 2772c.

50. Ibid.

51. Quoted in Porterfield, *Jimmie Rodgers*, 96. Peer recalled a similar process resulting in Jimmie Rodgers's popular recording of "Waiting for a Train": "Somebody sent the words to Jimmie, and he looked at them. And he said, 'Oh, I remember that.' So he picks up his guitar and he starts to do this thing. Well, Jimmie only knew I think two chords on the guitar. So he couldn't fit the words you see. And anyway he changed the words . . . He wouldn't like the way the words went. He said, 'The way I know it is so and so.' So we end up with what has never been challenged as a completely new song because both the music and the words changed." Interview with Ralph Peer.

52. Interview with Ralph Peer.

53. Cohen, "Robert W. Gordon and the Second Wreck of 'Old 97,' " 17–18. Gordon eventually did testify on behalf of Victor in the infamous suit over the authorship of "The Wreck of the Old 97." Challenged by a man claiming to have

written the tune, Victor employed the folklorist to demonstrate that the song was in the public domain. See also Boos, "The Wreck of the Old 97," 3–18.

54. Interview with Ralph Peer. Peer clarified, "If it's legendary, it's in the public domain. They don't know who wrote it."

55. Porterfield, *Jimmie Rodgers*, 80.

56. *Meridian Star*; quoted in Porterfield, *Jimmie Rodgers*, 110.

57. It is unclear why the split between the musicians occurred. Grant recalls that the group had a falling out over who would get top billing. Peer remembers that Rodgers recorded solo on his suggestion. See Porterfield, *Jimmie Rodgers*, 107–11.

58. Russell, *Blacks, Whites, and Blues*, 69; Wolfe, liner notes to *White Country Blues*; Abbott and Seroff, "America's Blue Yodel"; Wald, *Escaping the Delta*, 56, 69, 80, 118,

59. Jimmie Rodgers, "Sleep, Baby Sleep" (Victor 20864, 1927); J. Churchill, "Sleep, Baby, Sleep" (Paramount 12091, 1923); Charles Anderson, "Sleep, Baby, Sleep" (Okeh 4980, 1923); George P. Watson, "Sleep, Baby, Sleep" (Monarch [Victor] 673, 1901). Abbott and Seroff, "America's Blue Yodel." See also Gac, *Singing for Freedom*.

Chapter 8: Reimagining Pop Tunes as Folk Songs

1. John Lomax to Ruby Terrill, June 29, 1933, Lomax Family Papers, box 3D149, folder 3; Lomax, "Half-Million Dollar Song"; Mechem, "Home on the Range."

2. John Lomax to Ruby Terrill, July 21, 1933, Lomax Family Papers, box 3D149, folder 3.

3. "Sweet Singer of the Swamplands Here to Do a Few Tunes between Homicides," *New York Herald Tribune*, January 3, 1935, quoted in Carby, *Race Men*, 104.

4. Herskovits, "Negro Art," 295.

5. White, *American Negro Folk-Songs*, 16–17.

6. John Lomax to Ruby Terrill Lomax, January 21, 1935, Lomax Family Papers, box 3D150, folder 6.

7. Wolfe and Lornell, *The Life and Legend of Leadbelly*; Filene, *Romancing the Folk*; Porterfield, *Last Cavalier*; Carby, *Race Men*.

8. John A. Lomax, "Notes on the Songs of Huddie Ledbetter (Leadbelly)," National Folksong Archive, 103–4.

9. It should be noted that the title of the Leadbelly collection was the result of a compromise between the authors and the ethnomusicologist George Herzog, who provided the musical transcriptions. Herzog objected to the original title of the book, *Negro Sinful Songs*, thinking the word "sinful" was not appropriate to the book's contents. See Wolfe and Lornell, *Life and Legend of Leadbelly*, 183, 195.

10. Lomax and Lomax, *American Ballads and Folk Songs*, xxvi–xxvii.

11. Wolfe and Lornell, *Life and Legend of Leadbelly*, 144–45. Ledbetter was not alone

among black musicians influenced by the yodeling of Jimmie Rodgers. Mississippi John Hurt and Skip James also included songs written by the white singer in their repertoire. See Russell, *Blacks, Whites, and Blues*, 69.

12. Lomax and Lomax, *Negro Folk Songs as Sung by Lead Belly*, 52.

13. Ibid., 52.

14. White, *American Negro Folk-Songs*, xxi–xxii.

15. L. W. E., "*Folk Songs from the South*," *Music and Letters* 6, no. 3 (1925): 282–83. "The Dying Californian" with words by Kate Harris, was first published in 1850 and enjoyed distribution through nineteenth-century shape-note hymnals. See Cazden, Haufrecht, and Studer, eds., *Folk Songs of the Catskills*, 321. "Just before the Battle, Mother" was based on a Civil War poem by George Frederick Root. The song was recorded for commercial phonograph companies by artists including J. W. Myers, Will Oakland, and the duo of Frank Stanley and Henry Burr.

16. Guy B. Johnson, "Recent Contributions to the Study of American Negro Songs," *Social Forces* 4, no. 4 (1926): 791. Johnson referred to Scarborough, *On the Trail of Negro Folk-Songs*.

17. Lowry Charles Wimberly, "On the Trail of Negro Folk-Songs," *American Speech* 1, no. 5 (1926): 286–87.

18. Isabel Gordon Carter, review of *On the Trail of Negro Folk-Songs* by Dorothy Scarborough and *The Negro and His Songs* by Howard W. Odum and Guy B. Johnson, *Journal of American Folklore* 38, no. 150 (1925): 623.

19. White, *American Negro Folk-Songs*, 28.

20. Scarborough, *On the Trail of Negro Folk-Songs*, 37.

21. Ibid., 287.

22. Charles K. Wolfe, "Introduction to the New Edition," in Talley and Wolfe, *Thomas W. Talley's Negro Folk Rhymes*, vii–xxv.

23. Talley and Wolfe, *Negro Folk Rhymes*, 233.

24. Ibid., 245.

25. Johnson, ed., *The Book of American Negro Poetry*, vii, x–xi. It is notable that some passages of the essay that dealt with the spirituals and ragtime were revisions of similar passages Johnson published in *The Autobiography of an Ex-Colored Man* in 1912. In the first book, Johnson did not term black music and creativity as folklore while in the 1922 revisions he did. See *Autobiography*, 63–64, 72–73, and *American Negro Poetry*, vii–xi.

26. Johnson, ed., *Book of American Negro Poetry*, xi–xii.

27. Johnson, "James W. Johnson Replies to Criticism of His Preface," *New York Tribune*, April 9, 1922, sec, 4, 5.

28. Krehbiel, *Afro-American Folksongs*, 4.

29. H. E. Krehbiel, "James W. Johnson's Comments on American Negro Music," *New York Tribune*, April 1, 1922, sec. 4, 5.

30. Johnson, *Book of American Negro Poetry*, x.

31. Robert E. Park, review of *Negro Folk Rhymes* by Thomas W. Talley, *American Journal of Sociology* 28, no. 4 (1923): 486–87.

32. Anderson, *Deep River*, 119, 123, 159, quote on 154.

33. Ibid., 91, 101–2.

34. Exceptions include "Enigmatic Folksongs of the Southern Underworld," *Current Opinion* 67, no. 3 (September 1919): 165; Lomax, "Self-Pity in Negro Folk-Songs."

35. Perrow, "Songs and Rhymes from the South," 190.

36. Odum, "Folk-Song and Folk-Poetry as Found in the Secular Songs of Southern Negroes," 272; Odum, "Folk-Song and Folk-Poetry as Found in the Secular Songs of the Southern Negroes (Concluded)," 363.

37. Webb, "Notes on the Folk-Lore of Texas," 292.

38. Abbott and Seroff, " 'They Cert'ly Sound Good to Me,' " 408–9.

39. W. C. Handy, "How I Came to Write the 'Memphis Blues,' " *New York Age*, December 7, 1916, 6; reprinted in Hoffman, ed., *Jazz Reviewed*, 22. W. C. Handy, "The Blues," *Chicago Defender*, August 30, 1919, quoted in Abbott and Seroff, " 'They Cert'ly Sound Good to Me,' " 423–24.

40. Handy, ed., *Blues* (1926), 1.

41. Guy B. Johnson, review of *Blues: An Anthology*, *Social Forces* 5, no. 3 (1927): 539–40.

42. "Gouge to Supplant Blues, as Popular Music, Says Handy," *Pittsburgh Courier*, April, 26, 1924, 10; reprinted in Hoffmann, *Jazz Reviewed*, 52. Handy's compositions "The Chicago Gouge" and "Gouge of Amour Avenue" were featured in Handy, ed., *Blues* (1926), 142–47.

43. Scarborough, "The 'Blues' as Folk-Songs."

44. Scarborough, *On the Trail of Negro Folk-Songs*, 264–65.

45. Carl Van Vechten, "The Black Blues," *Vanity Fair*, August 1925, reprinted in Van Vechten, *"Keep A-Inchin' Along,"* 43. In the same collection, see also Van Vechten, "Folksongs of the American Negro" (*Vanity Fair*, July 1925), and "Prescription for the Negro Theatre" (*Vanity Fair*, October 1925).

46. Odum and Johnson, *The Negro and His Songs*, 149–50.

47. Odum and Johnson, *Negro Workaday Songs*, 6–7, 22–23, 25–34.

48. For a somewhat similar argument regarding the relationship between geographical separation and folklorists' racial/musical categories, see McNutt, "Mapping the Terrain with Folk Songs," 19–20.

49. Scarborough, *On the Trail of Negro Folk-Songs*, 10–18.

50. Ibid., 9.

51. Ibid., 238–40.

52. Webb, "Notes on the Folk-Lore of Texas," 291–92.

53. Ibid., 292.

54. Quoted in Porterfield, *The Last Cavalier*, 523, n. 29.

55. John Lomax, "'Sinful Songs' of the Southern Negro," *Musical Quarterly* 20 (1934): 182; quoted in Hirsch, "Modernity, Nostalgia, and Southern Folklore Studies," 193.

56. John Lomax to Ruby Terrill, June 29, 1933, Lomax Family Papers, box 3D149, folder 3.

57. John Lomax to Ruby Terrill, August 1, 1933, Lomax Family Papers, box 3D149, folder 3.

58. Ibid.

59. Hirsch, "Modernity, Nostalgia," 195; Porterfield, *Last Cavalier*, 298.

60. John A. Lomax to Henry G. Alsberg, undated, Lomax Family Papers, box 3D171, folder 1.

61. Ibid.

62. R. E. Thurston to George Leadbetter, December 9, 1934, Lomax Family Papers, box 3D171, folder 1.

63. Thomas J. Hanlon to John Lomax, December 7, 1934, Lomax Family Papers, box 3D171, folder 1.

64. Miss Ray M. Hanchett to John Lomax, December 7, 1934, Lomax Family Papers, box 3D171, folder 1.

65. E. McFate to John Lomax, December 10, 1934, Lomax Family Papers, box 3D171, folder 1.

66. M. F. Amrine to Bureau of Prisons, Department of Justice, July 6, 1935, Lomax Family Papers, box 3D171, folder 1.

67. Lomax, "'Sinful Songs' of the Southern Negro," 185, quoted in Hirsch "Modernity, Nostalgia," 192.

68. Hirsch, "Modernity, Nostalgia," 195.

69. John Lomax to Ruby Terrill, August 10, 1933, Lomax Family Papers, box 3D149, folder 3.

70. Ibid.

71. John Lomax, "Self-Pity in Negro Folk-Songs," 141–45.

72. Lomax and Lomax, *American Ballads and Folk Songs*, xxxii.

73. John A. Lomax to Henry G. Alsberg, undated, Lomax Family Papers, box 3D171, folder 1.

74. Lomax did appeal to authorities on behalf of a number of imprisoned informants. His letter to Alsberg is but one example.

75. Lomax, *The Land Where the Blues Began*, 10.

76. Mrs. M. B. Wright to John Lomax, April 24, 1910, Lomax Family Papers, box 3D169, folder 7.

77. A. P. Welchman to John Lomax, May 15, 1907, Lomax Family Papers, box 3D169, folder 7.

78. O. S. Miller to John Lomax, February 8, 1911, Lomax Family Papers, box 3D169, folder 8.

79. Cox, *Folk Songs of the South*, xxi.

80. Odum, "Folk-Song and Folk-Poetry as Found in the Secular Songs of the Southern Negroes," 262.

81. Charters, *The Blues Makers*, 66.

82. Spottswood, liner notes to *Folk Music in America, Vol. 10: Songs of War and History*, 9; Lomax, *Land Where the Blues Began*, 5.

83. Lomax, "Self-Pity in Negro Folk-Songs," 143.

84. Scarborough, *On the Trail of Negro Folk-Songs*, 10–11.

85. Elizabeth Gordon, "Narrative Report for September 1936," Folk Music Project, box 34, folder: Mississippi Folk Music. For a similar example, see White and White, *The Sounds of Slavery*, 96.

86. Huddie Ledbetter to John Lomax, July 20, 1934 and August 10, 1934, Lomax Family Papers, box 3D157, folder 11.

87. Huddie Ledbetter to John Lomax, September 6, 1934, Lomax Family Papers, box 3D157, folder 11.

88. John Lomax to Ruby Terrill Lomax, February 11, 1935, Lomax Family Papers, box 3D150, folder 6.

89. John Lomax to Ruby Terrill, September 26, 1934, Lomax Family Papers, box 3D150, folder 3.

90. Wolfe and Lornell, *Life and Legend of Leadbelly*, 128–29.

91. John Lomax to Ruby Terrill Lomax, October 2, 1934, Lomax Family Papers, box 3D150, folder 3.

92. Ibid.

93. Lomax and Lomax, *Negro Folk Songs*, 52.

94. Ibid., 52.

95. Porterfield, *Last Cavalier*, 342–43, 530.

96. John Lomax to Ruby Terrill Lomax, January 7, 1935, Lomax Family Papers, box 3D150, folder 5.

97. Porterfield, *Last Cavalier*, 347–56, 364–67; Wolfe and Lornell, *Life and Legend of Leadbelly*, 168.

98. John Lomax to Ruby Terrill Lomax, March 6, 1935, Lomax Family Papers, box 3D150, folder 7.

99. John Lomax to Ruby Terrill Lomax, March 17, 1935, Lomax Family Papers, box 3D150, folder 7.

100. Quoted in Oakley, *The Devil's Music*, 153.

101. Palmer, *Vernon Dalhart*, 183, 129.

102. Lomax, "Half-Million Dollar Song"; Mechem, "Home on the Range"; Davidson, "'Home on the Range' Again."

103. John Lomax to George S. Jeffers, May 24, 1933, Lomax Family Papers, box 3D174, folder 2.

104. See Lomax Family Papers, box 3D174, folder 2.

105. "$500,000 Suit Hinges on Shifting of Nouns," *New York Times*, June 15, 1934, 3; "Plagiarism Suits Name Two Popular Songs; One Is about Arizona, Other about the Moon," *New York Times*, October 31, 1934, 20.

106. Porterfield, *Last Cavalier*, 327.

107. Mechem, "Home on the Range," 313–39, quote on 333. Mechem's article includes a complete version of Moanfeldt's report to the Music Publishers Protection Association.

Afterword

1. "Folk Singing," *Time*, November 23, 1962, 54–60, quote on 60; "Mississippi: Laughable, but Not Funny," *Time*, November 23, 1962, 14.

2. A sample of works quoting Broonzy includes "Best of the Blues," *Time*, September 1, 1958, 39; Keil, *Urban Blues*, 37; Levine, *Black Culture and Black Consciousness*, 202–3; Jones and Rahn, "Definitions of Popular Music," 86; Ross, *No Respect*, 65; Middleton, *Studying Popular Music*, 3; Kelley, "Notes on Deconstructing 'The Folk,'" 1403; Bayles, *Hole in Our Soul*, 164; Murray, *Boogie Man*, 28; Bertrand, *Race, Rock, and Elvis*, 134; Lawson, "The First Century of Blues," 56.

3. "Folk Singing," 54–60.

4. Keil, *Urban Blues*, 37; Charters, *The Country Blues*, vii–xvi.

5. Keil, *Urban Blues*, 8–10, 95; Kelley, *Yo' Mama's Disfunktional!*, 22–24.

6. Levine, *Black Culture and Black Consciousness*, 202–3.

7. Ross, *No Respect*, 65–71; Kelley, "Notes on Deconstructing 'The Folk,'" 1403.

8. Middleton, *Studying Popular Music*, 3.

9. Big Bill Broonzy, *Amsterdam Live Concerts 1953* (Holland: Munich Records MRCD 275, 2006).

10. Broonzy, *Big Bill Blues*, 34–35; Lawrence Cohn, liner notes to Big Bill Broonzy, *Good Time Tonight* (CBS Records, Columbia CK 46219, 1990).

11. Ellison, *Shadow and Act*, 123–24.

BIBLIOGRAPHY

Archives

American Folklife Center, Library of Congress, Washington, D.C.

"Beale Street Black and Blue." Oral history transcripts by Margaret McKee and Fred Chisenhall. Oral History Collection, Memphis Public Library, Memphis, Tennessee.

Folk Music Project. Works Progress Administration Papers. National Archives, Washington, D.C.

Klaw and Erlanger Papers, Squires (Art and Barbara) Papers. Center for American History, University of Texas, Austin.

Lomax Family Papers. Center for American History, University of Texas, Austin.

National Folksong Archive. Library of Congress, Washington, D.C.

Smithsonian Center for Folklife and Cultural Heritage, Washington, D.C.

Southern Folklife Collection, Manuscript Department. University of North Carolina, Chapel Hill.

Digital Archives

African American Sheet Music, 1850–1920, selected from the Collections of Brown University. American Memory, Library of Congress, Washington, D.C. http://memory.loc.gov/ammem/collections/sheetmusic/brown.

Archive of Popular American Music. University of California, Los Angeles. http://digital.library.ucla.edu/apam/index.html.

Cylinder Preservation and Digitization Project. Department of Special Collections, Donald D. Davidson Library, University of California, Santa Barbara. http://cylinders.library.ucsb.edu/index.php.

Historic American Sheet Music, 1850–1920. American Memory, Library of Congress, Washington, D.C. http://memory.loc.gov/ammem/award97/ncdhtml/hasmhome.html.

Internet Archive. www.archive.org.

New York Public Library Digital Gallery. New York Public Library, New York. http://
digitalgallery.nypl.org/nypldigital/index.cfm.
Online Discographical Project. http://settlet.fateback.com.

Newspapers and Periodicals

Atlanta Constitution
Billboard
Brooklyn Daily Eagle
Chicago Defender
Current Opinion
Downbeat
Farm and Fireside Magazine
Galveston Daily News
Los Angeles Times
The Nation
New York Journal
New York Times
San Antonio Light
Talking Machine World
Washington Post

Books and Articles

Abbott, Lynn. " 'Play That Barber Shop Chord': A Case for the African-American
Origin of Barbershop Harmony." *American Music* 10 (fall 1992): 289–325.
Abbott, Lynn, and Doug Seroff. "America's Blue Yodel." *Music Traditions* (1993).
Reprinted on www.mustrad.org.uk/articles/b_yodel.htm (visited October 30,
2008).
———. *Out of Sight: The Rise of African American Popular Music, 1889–1895*. Jackson:
University of Mississippi Press, 2002.
———. *Ragged but Right: Black Traveling Shows, "Coon Songs," and the Dark Pathway
to Blues and Jazz*. Jackson: University Press of Mississippi, 2007.
———. " 'They Cert'ly Sound Good to Me': Sheet Music, Southern Vaudeville, and the
Commercial Ascendancy of the Blues." *American Music* 14, no. 4 (winter 1996):
402–54.
Abrahams, Roger. "Phantoms of Romantic Nationalism in Folkloristics." *Journal of
American Folklore* 106, no. 419 (1993): 3–37.
———. *Singing the Master: The Emergence of African American Culture in the Planta-
tion South*. New York: Pantheon, 1992.
Agan, John A. "The Voice of the Southland: Louisiana's Gene Austin." *North Loui-
siana Historical Association Journal* 28, no. 4 (fall 1997): 123–37.
Agawu, Kofi. *Representing African Music: Postcolonial Notes, Queries, Positions*. New
York: Routledge, 2003.

Allen, William Francis, Charles Pickard Ware, and Lucy McKim Garrison. *Slave Songs of the United States*. Bedford: Applewood Books, 1867.

Alter, Stephen G. *Darwinism and the Linguistic Image: Language, Race, and Natural Theology in the Nineteenth Century*. Baltimore: Johns Hopkins University Press, 1999.

American Folklife Center. *Ethnic Recordings in America: A Neglected Heritage*. Washington: Library of Congress, 1982.

Ammon, Elizabeth, and Valerie Rohy, eds. *American Local Color Writing, 1880–1920*. New York: Penguin, 1998.

Anderson, Paul Allen. *Deep River: Music and Memory and Harlem Renaissance Thought*. Chapel Hill: Duke University Press, 2001.

Appadurai, Arjun. *Modernity at Large: Cultural Dimensions of Globalization*. Minneapolis: University of Minnesota Press, 1996.

Armstrong, George. Liner notes to *Hobart Smith*. Folk-Legacy Records FSA-17, 1964.

Ayers, Edward. *The Promise of the New South: Life after Reconstruction*. New York: Oxford University Press, 1992.

——. *What Caused the Civil War? Reflections on the South and Southern History*. New York: W. W. Norton, 2005.

Bacon, Alice Mabel. "Work and Methods of the Hampton Folk-Lore Society." *Journal of American Folklore* 11, no. 40 (1898): 17–21.

Baker, Lee. *From Savage to Negro: Anthropology and the Construction of Race, 1896–1954*. Berkeley: University of California Press, 1998.

Barlow, William. *Looking Up at Down: The Emergence of Blues Culture*. Philadelphia: Temple University Press, 1989.

Bascom, Louise Rand. "Ballads and Songs of Western North Carolina." *Journal of American Folklore* 22, no. 84 (1909): 238–50.

Bayles, Martha. *Hole in Our Soul: The Loss of Beauty and Meaning in American Popular Music*. Chicago: University of Chicago Press, 1996.

Bean, Anna, James V. Hatch, and Brooks McNamara, eds. *Inside the Blackface Mask*. Middletown, Conn.: Wesleyan University Press, 1996.

Becker, Jane S. *Selling Tradition: Appalachia and the Construction of an American Folk, 1930–1940*. Chapel Hill: University of North Carolina Press, 1998.

Beckerman, Michael B. *New Worlds of Dvořák: Searching in America for the Composer's Inner Life*. New York: W. W. Norton, 2003.

Bell, Bernard. "Folk Art and the Harlem Renaissance." *Phylon* 36, no. 2 (1960): 155–63.

Bell, Michael J. " 'No Borders to the Ballad Maker's Art': Francis James Child and the Politics of the People." *Western Folklore* 47, no. 4 (1988): 285–307.

Bendix, Regina. *In Search of Authenticity: The Formation of Folklore Studies*. Madison: University of Wisconsin Press, 1997.

Bernal, Martin. *Black Athena: The Afroasiatic Roots of Classical Civilization*, Volume

1: *The Fabrication of Ancient Greece 1785–1985*. New Brunswick, N.J.: Rutgers University Press, 1987.

Bernheim, Alfred L. *The Business of the Theatre: An Economic History of the American Theatre, 1750–1932. Prepared on behalf of the Actors' Equity Association by Alfred L. Bernheim, assisted by Sara Harding and the staff of the Labor Bureau, Inc.* New York: Benjamin Bloom, 1932.

Bertrand, Michael T. *Race, Rock, and Elvis*. Urbana: University of Illinois Press, 2000.

Beveridge, David R., ed. *Rethinking Dvořák: Views from Five Countries*. Oxford: Clarendon Press, 1996.

Bledstein, Burton J. *The Culture of Professionalism: The Middle Class and the Development of Higher Education in America*. New York: W. W. Norton, 1976.

Blue, Carroll Parrott. *The Dawn at My Back: Memoir of a Black Texas Upbringing*. Austin: University of Texas Press, 2003.

Bluestein, Gene. " 'The Arkansas Traveler' and the Strategy of American Humor." *Western Folklore* 21, no. 3 (July 1962): 153–60.

Boas, Franz. "The Limitations of the Comparative Method of Anthropology." *Science* 4, no. 103 (December 16, 1896): 901–8.

Boos, Gregory D. "The Wreck of the Old 97: A Study in Copyright Protection of Folksongs for Lawyers, Folklorists and Songwriters." *Seattle Folklore Society Journal* 9, no. 11 (1977): 3–18.

Born, Georgina, and David Hesmondhalgh, eds. *Western Music and Its Others: Difference, Representation, and Appropriation in Music*. Berkeley: University of California Press, 2000.

Bradford, Perry. *Born with the Blues*. New York: Oak Publications, 1965.

Brady, Erika. *A Spiral Way: How the Phonograph Changed Ethnography*. Jackson: University Press of Mississippi, 1999.

Brinton, Daniel. "The Aims of Anthropology." *Proceedings of th American Association for the Advancement of Science* 44 (1895): 1–17.

——. *Races and Peoples: Lectures on the Science of Ethnography*. New York: Hodges, 1890.

Bronner, Simon J. *American Folklore Studies: An Intellectual History*. Lawrence: University Press of Kansas, 1986.

Brooks, Tim. *Lost Sounds: Blacks and the Birth of the Recording Industry, 1890–1919*. Urbana: University of Illinois Press, 2004.

Broonzy, Big Bill, as told to Yannick Bruynoghe. *Big Bill Blues*. New York: Oak Publications, 1955.

Brown, Jayna. *Babylon Girls: Black Women Performers and the Shaping of the Modern*. Durham: Duke University Press, 2008.

Brundage, W. Fitzhugh. *The Southern Past: A Clash of Race and Memory*. Cambridge, Mass.: Belknap Press of Harvard University Press, 2005.

Bryant, Rebecca A. "Shaking Things Up: Popularizing the Shimmy in America."
    American Music 20, no. 2 (summer 2002): 168–87.

Buettner-Janusch, John. "Boas and Mason: Particularism versus Generalization."
    American Anthropologist 59 (1957): 318–24.

Burnett, Robert. *The Global Jukebox: The International Music Industry*. London:
    Rutledge, 1996.

Calt, Stephen. "Anatomy of a 'Race' Label." *Rhythm and Business: The Political Econ-
    omy of Black Music*, edited by Norman Kelley, 86–111. New York: Akashic Books,
    2002.

——. Liner notes to Henry Thomas, *Texas Worried Blues*. Yazoo Records, 1989.

Calt, Stephen, Don Kent, and Michael Stewart. Liner notes to Mississippi Sheiks,
    Stop and Listen. Yazoo 2006, 1992.

Campbell, Gavin James. *Music and the Making of a New South*. Chapel Hill: Univer-
    sity of North Carolina Press, 2004.

Cantwell, Robert. *When We Were Good: The Folk Revival*. Cambridge, Mass.:
    Harvard University Press, 1996.

Carby, Hazel. "It Just Be's Dat Way Sometime: The Sexual Politics of Women's
    Blues." *Radical America* 20, no. 4 (1986): 9–24.

——. *Race Men*. Cambridge, Mass.: Harvard University Press, 2000.

Carlin, Bob, and Steve Terill. *String Bands in the North Carolina Piedmont*. Jefferson,
    N.C.: McFarland, 2004.

Carstensen, Fred V. *American Enterprise in Foreign Markets: Studies of Singer and
    International Harvester in Imperial Russia*. Chapel Hill: University of North
    Carolina Press, 1984.

Cazden, Norman, Herbert Haufrecht, and Norman Studer, eds. *Folk Songs of the
    Catskills*. Albany: State University of New York Press, 1982.

Chanan, Michael. *Repeated Takes: A Short History of Recording and Its Effects on
    Music*. London: Verso, 1995.

Charosh, Paul. "Studying Nineteenth-Century Popular Song." *American Music* 15,
    no. 4 (1997): 459–92.

Charters, Samuel. *The Blues Makers*. New York: Da Capo, 1991.

——. *The Country Blues*. New York: Da Capo, 1975 [1959].

——. Liner notes to *The Country Blues, Vol. 2*. Folkways RFB 9, 1964.

Cherry, Randal. "Ethel Waters: The Voice of an Era." *Temples for Tomorrow: Looking
    Back at the Harlem Renaissance*, edited by Geneviève Fabre and Michael Feith,
    99–124 (Bloomington: Indiana University Press, 2001).

Chestnutt, Charles W. *The Colonel's Dream*. New York: Doubleday, Page and
    Company, 1905.

Child, James Francis. *The English and Scottish Popular Ballads*, volumes 1–5. New
    York: Dover, 1965 [1882–98].

Chude-Sokei, Louis. *The Last "Darkey": Bert Williams, Black-on-Black Minstrelsy
    and the African Diaspora*. Durham, N.C.: Duke University Press, 2006.

Clifford, James. *The Predicament of Culture: Twentieth-Century Ethnography, Literature, and Art*. Cambridge, Mass.: Harvard University Press, 1988.

Cobb, James C. *Away Down South: A History of Southern Identity*. New York: Oxford, 2005.

Cohen, Anne, and Norm Cohen. "Folk and Hillbilly Music: Further Notes on their Relation." *JEMF Quarterly* 13, no. 46 (summer 1977): 50–57.

Cohen, John. "The Folk Music Interchange: Negro and White," *Sing Out!* 14, no. 6 (December 1964–January 1965): 42–49.

Cohen, Norman. "Commercial Music Documents: Number Six." *JEMF Quarterly* 6, no. 4 (winter 1970): 171–73.

——. "Riley Puckett: 'King of the Hillbillies.'" *JEMF Quarterly* 12, no. 44 (winter 1976): 175–84.

——. "Robert W. Gordon and the Second Wreck of 'Old 97.'" *Journal of American Folklore* 87, no. 343 (1974): 12–38.

——. "The Skillet Lickers: A Study of a Hillbilly String Band and its Repertoire." *Journal of American Folklore* 78, no. 309 (July–September 1965): 229–44.

——. "Tin Pan Alley's Contribution to Folk Music." *Western Folklore* 29, no. 1 (January 1970): 9–20.

Cohn, Lawrence. Liner notes to Big Bill Broonzy, *Good Time Tonight*. Columbia CK 46219, CBS Records, 1990.

——. Liner notes to *Maple Leaf Rag: Ragtime in Rural America*. New World Records 235, 1976.

——. Liner notes to *Roots and Blues: The Retrospective, 1925–1950*. Columbia/Legacy 47911, 1992.

Coleman, Leon. "Carl Van Vechten Presents the New Negro." *Studies in the Literary Imagination* 7, no. 2 (fall 1974): 85–104.

Conrad, Alfred F. "The Privilege of Forcibly Ejecting an Amusement Patron." *University of Pennsylvania Law Review and American Law Register* 90, no. 7 (May 1942): 809–23.

Cox, John Harrington. *Folk Songs of the South*. Cambridge, Mass.: Harvard University Press, 1925.

Crafts, Susan D., Daniel Cavicchi, Charles Keil, and the Music in Daily Life Project. *My Music*. Hanover, N.H.: Wesleyan University Press, 1993.

Crawford, Richard. *America's Musical Life: A History*. New York: W. W. Norton, 2001.

Cruz, Jon. *Culture on the Margins: The Black Spiritual and the Rise of American Cultural Interpretation*. Princeton, N.J.: Princeton University Press, 1999.

Cuney-Hare, Maud. *Negro Musicians and Their Music*. Washington, D.C.: Associated Publishers, 1936.

Dailey, Jane, Glenda Elizabeth Gilmore, and Bryant Simon, eds. *Jumpin' Jim Crow: Southern Politics from Civil War to Civil Rights*. Princeton, N.J.: Princeton University Press, 2000.

Daniel, Pete. *Lost Revolutions: The South in the 1950s*. Chapel Hill: University of North Carolina Press, 2000.

Darnell, Regena. "American Anthropology and the Development of Folklore Scholarship, 1890–1920." *Journal of the Folklore Institute* 10, no. 1–2 (1973): 23–39.

———. *And Along Came Boas: Continuity and Revolution in Americanist Anthropology.* Amsterdam: John Benjamins Publishing Company, 1998.

———. "Daniel Garrison Brinton: An Intellectual Biography." Ph.D. dissertation, University of Pennsylvania, 1967.

Davidson, Levette Jay. " 'Home on the Range' Again." *California Folklore Quarterly* 3, no. 3 (1944): 208–11.

Davis, Gussie Lord, Josephine R. B. Wright, and Sam Lucas. "Gussie Lord Davis (1863–1899): Tin Pan Alley Tunesmith." *Black Perspective in Music* 6, no. 2 (autumn 1978): 189–230.

Deloria, Philip J. *Indians in Unexpected Places*. Lawrence: University Press of Kansas, 2004.

Denison, Sam. *Scandalize My Name: Black Imagery in American Popular Music*. New York: Garland, 1982.

Denning, Michael. *Culture in the Age of Three Worlds*. London: Verso, 2004.

di Leonardo, Micaela. *Exotics at Home: Anthropologies, Others, American Modernity*. Chicago: University of Chicago Press, 1998.

Dixon, Robert, and John Goodrich. *Recording the Blues*. New York: Stein and Day, 1970.

Dormon, James H. "Shaping the Popular Image of Post-Reconstruction American Blacks: The 'Coon Song' Phenomenon of the Gilded Age." *American Quarterly* 40, no. 4 (December 1988): 450–71.

Du Bois, W. E. B. *Black Reconstruction in America, 1860–1880*. Cleveland: Meridian, 1964 [1935].

———. *The Souls of Black Folk*. New York Bantam, 1989 [1903].

Durham, Weldon B. "The Tightening Rein: Relations between the Federal Government and the American Theatre Industry during World War One." *Educational Theatre Journal* 30, no. 3 (October 1978): 387–97.

Ellison, Ralph. *Shadow and Act*. New York: Quality Paperback Book Club, 1994 [1964].

Emerson, Ralph Waldo. *Essays and Lectures*. New York: Library of America, 1983.

———. *The Harvard Classics*, Volume 5, *Essays and English Traits*. Edited by Charles W. Eliot. New York: P. F. Collier and Son, 1909.

Epstein, Dena J. *Sinful Tunes and Spirituals: Black Folk Music to the Civil War*. Urbana: University of Illinois Press, 1977.

———. "A White Origin for the Black Spiritual? An Invalid Theory and How It Grew." *American Music* (1983): 53–59.

Erdman, Andrew L. *Blue Vaudeville: Sex, Morals, and the Mass Marketing of Amusement, 1895–1915*. Jefferson, N.C.: McFarland, 2004.

Erlmann, Veit. "The Aesthetics of the Global Imagination: Reflections on World Music in the 1990s." *Public Culture* 8 (1996): 467–88.

———. *Music, Modernity, and the Global Imagination: South Africa and the West*. New York: Oxford University Press, 1999.

Evans, David. *Big Road Blues: Tradition and Creativity in the Folk Blues*. New York: Da Capo Press, 1982.

Fabian, Johannes. *Time and the Other: How Anthropology Makes Its Object*. New York: Columbia University Press, 1983.

Farrell, Gerry. "The Early Days of the Gramophone Industry in India: Historical, Social, and Musical Perspectives." *The Place of Music*, edited by Andrew Leyshon, David Matless, and George Revill, 57–82. New York: Guilford Press, 1998.

Favor, J. Martin. *Authentic Blackness: The Folk in the New Negro Renaissance*. Durham, N.C.: Duke University Press, 1999.

Ferris, William. *Blues from the Delta*. New York: Da Capo Press, 1978.

———. "Racial Repertoires among Blues Performers." *Ethnomusicology* 14, no. 3 (September 1970): 439–49.

Fields, Barbara Jean. "Slavery, Race and Ideology in the United States of America." *New Left Review* 181 (1990): 95–118.

Filene, Benjamin. *Romancing the Folk: Public Memory and American Roots Music*. Chapel Hill: University of North Carolina Press, 2000.

Finnegan, Ruth. *The Hidden Musicians: Music-Making in an English Town*. Cambridge: Cambridge University Press, 1989.

Fletcher, Tom. *One Hundred Years of the Negro in Show Business: The Tom Fletcher Story*. New York: Burdge and Company, 1954.

Floyd Jr., Samuel A. *The Power of Black Music: Interpreting Its History from Africa to the United States*. New York: Oxford, 1995.

Foreman, Ronald Clifford Jr. "Jazz and Race Records, 1920–1932: Their Origins and Their Significance for the Record Industry and Society." Ph.D. dissertation, University of Illinois, 1968.

Fortier, Alcée. "Customs and Superstitions in Louisiana." *Journal of American Folklore* 1, no. 2 (1888): 136–40.

Fredrickson, George M. *The Black Image in the White Mind: The Debate on Afro-American Character and Destiny, 1817–1914*. Hanover, N.H.: Wesleyan University Press, 1987 [1971].

Frith, Simon. *Performing Rites: On the Value of Popular Music*. Cambridge, Mass.: Harvard University Press, 1996.

Frost, William Goodell. "Our Contemporary Ancestors in the Southern Mountains." *Atlantic Monthly* 83 (March 1899). Reprinted in *Appalachian Images in Folk and Popular Culture*, edited by W. K. McNeil, 91–106. Ann Arbor: UMI Research Press, 1989.

Gac, Scott. *Singing for Freedom: The Hutchinson Family Singers and the Nineteenth-*

Century Culture of Antebellum Reform. New Haven, Conn.: Yale University Press, 2007.

Gaisberg, Fred. *The Music Goes Round*. New York: Macmillan, 1943.

Gelatt, Roland. *The Fabulous Phonograph, 1877–1977*. 2nd rev. ed. New York: Macmillan, 1977.

Gennari, John. *Blowin' Hot and Cool: Jazz and Its Critics*. Chicago: University of Chicago Press, 2006.

Genovese, Eugene. *Roll, Jordan, Roll: The World the Slaves Made*. New York: Pantheon, 1974.

George, Nelson. *Hip Hop America*. New York: Penguin, 1998.

Gillett, Charlie. *The Sound of the City: The Rise of Rock and Roll*. New York: Outerbridge and Dienstfrey, 1970.

Gilroy, Paul. *The Black Atlantic: Modernity and Double Consciousness*. Cambridge, Mass.: Harvard University Press, 1993.

Gioia, Ted. *Work Songs*. Durham, N.C.: Duke University Press, 2006.

Glenn, Susan A. *Female Spectacle: The Theatrical Roots of Modern Feminism*. Cambridge, Mass.: Harvard University Press, 2000.

Goehr, Lydia. *The Imaginary Museum of Musical Works: An Essay on the Philosophy of Music*. Oxford: Clarendon Press, 1992.

Goertzen, Chris. "Mrs. Joe Person's Popular Aires: Early Blackface Minstrel Tunes in Oral Tradition." *Ethnomusicology* 35, no. 1 (winter 1991): 31–53.

Goodwin, Andrew, and Joe Gore. "World Beat and the Cultural Imperialism Debate." *Socialist Review* 20 (1990): 174–90.

Govenar, Alan B., and Jay F. Brakefield. *Deep Ellum and Central Track: Where the Black and White Worlds of Dallas Converged*. Denton: University of North Texas, 1998.

Gracyk, Tim, with Frank Hoffmann. *Popular American Recording Pioneers, 1895–1925*. New York: Haworth Press, 2000.

Graff, Gerald. *Professing Literature: An Institutional History*. Chicago: University of Chicago Press, 1987.

Grau, Robert. *The Business Man in the Amusement World: A Volume of Progress in the Field of Theatre*. New York: Broadway Publishing Co., 1910.

Graziano, John. "Music in William Randolph Hearst's New York Journal." *Notes*, 2nd series, 48, no. 2 (December 1991): 383–424.

Green, Archie. "Hillbilly Music: Source and Symbol." *Journal of American Folklore* 78, no. 309 (July–September 1965): 204–28.

Green, Laurie B. *Battling the Plantation Mentality: Memphis and the Black Freedom Struggle*. Chapel Hill: University of North Carolina Press, 2007.

Greene, Victor. *A Passion for Polka: Old-Time Ethnic Music in America*. Berkeley: University of California Press, 1992.

Gregory, James N. *The Southern Diaspora: How the Great Migrations of Black and*

White Southerners Transformed America. Chapel Hill: University of North Carolina Press, 2005.

Griffin, Farah Jasmine. *"Who Set You Flowin'?" The African-American Migration Narrative*. New York: Oxford University Press, 1996.

Gronow, Pekka. "The Record Industry Comes to the Orient." *Ethnomusicology* 25, no. 2 (1981): 251–84.

——. "The Record Industry: The Growth of a Mass Medium." *Popular Music* 3 (1981): 53–75.

Gronow, Pekka, and Ilpo Saunio. *An International History of the Recording Industry*. Translated by Christopher Moseley. London: Cassell, 1998.

Grundy, Pamela. " 'We Always Tried to Be Good People': Respectability, Crazy Water Crystals, and Hillbilly Music on the Air, 1933–1935." *Journal of American History* 81, no. 4 (March 1995): 1591–1620.

Guilbault, Jocelyne. *Zouk: World Music in the West Indies*. Chicago: University of Chicago Press, 1993.

Gummere, Francis B. *The Popular Ballad*. New York: Dover, 1959 [1907].

Gussow, Adam. *Seems Like Murder Here: Southern Violence and the Blues Tradition*. Chicago: University of Chicago Press, 2002.

Hale, Grace Elizabeth. *Making Whiteness: The Culture of Segregation in the South*. New York: Pantheon Books, 1998.

Hall, Jacquelyn Dowd. *Revolt against Chivalry: Jessie Daniel Ames and the Women's Campaign against Lynching*. New York: Columbia University Press, 1993.

Hall, Jacquelyn Dowd, James Leloudis, Robert Korstad, Mary Murphy, Lu Ann Jones, and Christopher B. Daly. *Like a Family: The Making of a Southern Cotton Mill World*. New York: W. W. Norton, 1987.

Hall, Roger Allan. " 'Black America': Nate Salsbury's 'Afro-American Exhibition.' " *Educational Theatre Journal* 29, no. 1 (March 1977): 49–60.

Hall, Stuart. "The Local and the Global: Globalization and Ethnicity." *Culture, Globalization and the World-System*, edited by Anthony D. King, 19–40. Binghamton: Department of Art and Art History, State University of New York at Binghamton, 1991.

——. "What Is This 'Black' in Black Popular Culture?" *Black Popular Culture: A Project by Michele Wallace*, edited by Gina Dent, 21–33. Seattle: Bay Press, 1992.

Haller, John S. *Outcasts from Evolution: Scientific Attitudes of Racial Inferiority, 1859–1900*. Urbana-Champaign: University of Illinois Press, 1971.

Hamm, Charles. *Yesterdays: Popular Song in America*. New York: W. W. Norton, 1979.

Handler, Richard. "Boasian Anthropology and the Critique of American Culture." *American Quarterly* 42, no. 2 (June 1990): 252–73.

Handy, W. C., *Father of the Blues: An Autobiography*. New York, Da Capo Press, 1990 [1941].

——, ed. *Blues: An Anthology*. New York: Albert and Charles Boni, 1926.

——, ed. *Blues: An Anthology* [revised, with an introduction from 1949]. New York: Da Capo Press, 1990.

Handy, W. C., and Eileen Southern. "Letters from W. C. Handy to William Grant Still." *Black Perspective in Music* 8, no. 1 (spring 1980): 65–119.

Harkins, Anthony. *Hillbilly: A Cultural History of an American Icon*. New York: Oxford University Press, 2005.

Harris, Charles K. *After the Ball: Forty Years of Melody*. New York: Frank-Maurice, 1926.

Harris, Joel Chandler. *Uncle Remus: His Songs and His Sayings*. New York: D. Appleton and Company, 1928 [1880].

Hartley, Florence. *The Ladies' Book of Etiquette and Manual of Politeness; Being a Complete Hand-book for the Use of a Lady in Polite Society*. Boston: DeWolfe, Fiske and Co., ca. 1879.

Hawkins, John. "An Old Mauma's Folk-Lore." *Journal of American Folklore* 9, no. 33 (1896): 129–31.

Hayward, Philip, ed. *Widening the Horizon: Exoticism in Post-War Popular Music*. Sydney: J. Libbey, 1999.

Herring, Scott. "Du Bois and the Minstrels." *MELUS* 22, no. 2 (1997): 3–17.

Herskovits, Melville J. *The Myth of the Negro Past*. Boston: Beacon Press, 1990 [1941].

——. "Negro Art: African and American." *Social Forces* 5, no. 2 (December 1926): 291–98.

Hirsch, Foster. *The Boys from Syracuse: The Shuberts' Theatrical Empire*. Carbondale: Southern Illinois University Press, 1998.

Hirsch, Jerrold. "Modernity, Nostalgia, and Southern Folklore Studies: The Case of John Lomax." *Journal of American Folklore* 105 (1992): 183–207.

Hoffman, Franz, ed. *Jazz Reviewed: Working Book to Jazz Advertised in the Negro Press of New England, 1910–1949*. Berlin: F. Hoffmann, 1995.

Hofstadter, Richard. *Social Darwinism in American Thought*. Boston: Beacon Press, 1955.

Jackson, George Pullen. *White and Negro Spirituals: Their Life Span and Kinship*. New York: J. J. Augustin, 1944.

Jackson, Thomas W. *On a Slow Train through Arkansaw*. Edited with an introduction by W. K. McNeil. Lexington: University Press of Kentucky, 1985.

Johnson, Guy B. "Double Meaning in the Popular Negro Blues." *Journal of Abnormal and Social Psychology* 22, no. 1 (April 1927): 12–20.

——. *Folk Culture on St. Helena Island, South Carolina*. Chapel Hill: University of North Carolina Press, 1930.

Johnson, James Weldon. *Along This Way: The Autobiography of James Weldon Johnson*. New York: Da Capo Press, 2000 [1933].

——. *The Autobiography of an Ex-Colored Man*. New York: Penguin, 1990 [1912].

——. *Black Manhattan*. New York: Da Capo, 1991 [1930].

——. *The Book of American Negro Spirituals*. Binghamton, N.Y.: Viking, 1925.

——, ed. *The Book of American Negro Poetry*. New York: Harcourt, Brace and Company, 1922.

——. "The Dilemma of the Negro Author." *American Mercury* 15 (December 1928): 477–81.

Johnston, Winifred. "Medicine Show." *Southwest Review* 21, no. 4 (summer 1936): 390–99.

Jones, Andrew F. *Yellow Music: Media Culture and Colonial Modernity in the Chinese Jazz Age*. Durham, N.C.: Duke University Press, 2001.

Jones, Gaynor, and Jay Rahn. "Definitions of Popular Music: Recycled." *Journal of Aesthetic Education* 11, no. 4 (October, 1977): 79–92.

Jones, Geoffrey. "The Gramophone Company: An Anglo-American Multinational, 1898–1931." *Business History Review* 59 (spring 1985): 76–100.

Jones, LeRoi [Amiri Baraka]. *Blues People*. New York: William Morrow, 1963.

Joshi, G. N. "A Concise History of the Phonograph Industry in India." *Popular Music* 7, no. 2 (1988): 147–56.

Joyner, Charles. *Shared Traditions: Southern History and Folk Culture*. Urbana: University of Illinois Press, 1999.

Kapchan, Deborah A. "Performance." *Journal of American Folklore* 108, no. 430, "Common Ground: Keywords for the Study of Expressive Culture" (1995): 479–508.

Kaplan, Amy. "Nation, Region, and Empire." *The Columbia History of the American Novel*, edited by Emory Elliott, 240–66. New York: Columbia University Press, 1991.

Katz, Mark. *Capturing Sound: How Technology Changed Music*. Berkeley: University of California Press, 2004.

Keil, Charles. *Urban Blues*. Chicago: University of Chicago Press, 1966.

Keil, Charles, and Steven Feld. *Music Grooves*. Chicago: University of Chicago Press, 1994.

Kelley, Robin D. G. *Hammer and Hoe: Alabama Communists during the Great Depression*. Chapel Hill: University of North Carolina Press, 1990.

——. "Notes on Deconstructing 'The Folk.'" *American Historical Review* 97, no. 5 (1992): 1400–1408.

——. *Race Rebels: Culture, Politics and the Black Working Class*. New York: Free Press, 1994.

——. *Yo' Mama's Disfunktional! Fighting the Culture Wars in Urban America*. Boston: Beacon Press, 1997.

Kenney, William Howland. *Recorded Music in American Life: The Phonograph and Popular Memory, 1890–1945*. New York: Oxford University Press, 1999.

Kibler, Alison. *Rank Ladies: Gender and Cultural Hierarchy in American Vaudeville*. Chapel Hill: University of North Carolina Press, 1999.

Kinnear, Michael S. *The Gramophone Company's First Indian Recordings, 1899–1908.* Bombay: Popular Prakashan, 1994.

Kirshenblatt-Gimblett, Barbara. "Folklore's Crisis." *Journal of American Folklore* 111, no. 441 (1998): 281–327.

Knight, Athelia. "He Paved the Way for the T.O.B.A." *Black Perspective in Music* (autumn 1987): 153–81.

Korma, Edward M., ed. *Encyclopedia of the Blues*, volume 1. New York: Routledge, 2006.

Krasner, David. *Resistance, Parody, and Double Consciousness in African American Theatre, 1895–1910.* New York: St. Martin's Press, 1997.

Krehbiel, Henry Edward. *Afro-American Folksongs: A Study in Racial and National Music.* New York: G. Schirmer, 1914.

Krummel, D. W. "Counting Every Star; or, Historical Statistics on Music Publishing in the United States (American Music Bibliography, IV)." *Anuario Interamericano de Investigacion Musical* 10 (1974): 175–93.

LaFeber, Walter. *The New Empire: An Interpretation of American Expansion, 1860–1898.* Ithaca, N.Y.: Cornell University Press, 1963.

Laing, Dave. "The Music Industry and the 'Cultural Imperialism' Thesis." *Media, Culture and Society* 8 (July 1986): 331–41.

Lavitt, Pamela Brown. "First of the Red Hot Mamas: 'Coon Shouting' and the Jewish Ziegfeld Girl." *American Jewish History* 87, no. 4 (1999): 253–90.

Lawson, R. A. "The First Century of Blues: One Hundred Years of Hearing and Interpreting the Musicians." *Southern Cultures* 13, no. 3 (2007): 39–61.

Lears, Jackson. *Fables of Abundance: A Cultural History of Advertising in America.* New York: Basic Books, 1994.

——. *No Place of Grace: Antimodernism and the Transformation of American Culture, 1880–1920.* New York: Pantheon Books, 1981.

Leonard, Neil. *Jazz: Myth and Religion.* New York: Oxford, 1987.

——. *Jazz and the White Americans: The Acceptance of a New Art Form.* Chicago: University of Chicago, 1962.

Leonard, Susan. "An Introduction to Black Participation in the Early Recording Industry, 1890–1920." *Annual Review of Jazz Studies* 4 (1988): 31–44.

Levine, Lawrence W. *Black Culture and Black Consciousness: Afro-American Folk Thought from Slavery to Freedom.* Oxford: Oxford University Press, 1977.

——. "The Folklore of Industrial Society: Popular Culture and Its Audiences." *American Historical Review* 97, no. 5 (1992): 1369–99.

——. *Highbrow/Lowbrow: The Emergence of Cultural Hierarchy in America.* Cambridge, Mass.: Harvard University Press, 1988.

Leyshon, Andrew, David Matless, and George Revill, eds. *The Place of Music.* New York: Guilford Press, 1998.

Lhamon, W. T. Jr. *Raising Cain: Blackface Performance from Jim Crow to Hip Hop*. Cambridge, Mass.: Harvard University Press, 1998.

Lieb, Sandra R. *Mother of the Blues: A Study of Ma Rainey*. Amherst: University of Massachusetts Press, 1981.

Lindfors, Bernth, ed. *Africans on Stage: Studies in Ethnological Show Business*. Bloomington: Indiana University Press, 1999.

——. "Ethnological Show Business: Footlighting the Dark Continent." *Freakery: Cultural Spectacles of the Extraordinary Body*, edited by Rosemarie Garland Thomson, 207–18. New York: New York University Press, 1996.

Lippman, Monroe. "Battle for Bookings: Independents Challenge the Trust." *Tulane Drama Review* 2, no. 2 (February 1958): 38–45.

Lipsitz, George. *Dangerous Crossroads: Popular Music, Postmodernism and the Poetics of Place*. London: Routledge, 1994.

——. *Footsteps in the Dark: The Hidden History of Popular Music*. Minneapolis: University of Minnesota Press, 2007.

——. *The Possessive Investment in Whiteness: How White People Profit from Identity Politics*. Philadelphia: Temple University Press, 1998.

——. *Time Passages: Collective Memory and American Popular Culture*. Minneapolis: University of Minnesota Press, 1990.

Litwack, Leon F. *Trouble in Mind: Black Southerners in the Age of Jim Crow*. New York: Vintage, 1999.

Loesser, Arthur. *Men, Women and Pianos: A Social History*. New York: Simon and Schuster, 1954.

Lomax, Alan. *The Land Where the Blues Began*. New York: Bantam Dell, 1993.

Lomax, John A. *Adventures of a Ballad Hunter*. New York: Macmillan, 1947.

——. *Cowboy Songs and Other Frontier Ballads*. New York: Sturgis and Walton, 1910.

——. *Cowboy Songs and Other Frontier Ballads*. New York: Macmillan, 1918.

——. "Half-Million Dollar Song: Origin of 'Home on the Range.'" *Southwest Review* 31, no. 1 (fall 1945): 1–8.

——. "Self-Pity in Negro Folk-Songs." *The Nation* 105 (August 9, 1917): 141–45.

Lomax, John A., and Alan Lomax. *American Ballads and Folk Songs*. New York: Macmillan, 1934.

——. *Negro Folk Songs as Sung by Lead Belly*. New York: Macmillan, 1936.

Lott, Eric. *Love and Theft: Blackface Minstrelsy and the American Working Class*. Oxford: Oxford University Press, 1995.

Mahar, William J. *Behind the Burnt Cork Mask: Early Blackface Minstrelsy and Antebellum American Popular Culture*. Champaign: University of Illinois Press, 1998.

Malone, Bill C. "Blacks and Whites and the Music of the Old South." *Black and White Cultural Interaction in the Antebellum South*, edited by Ted Ownby, 149–70. Jackson: University Press of Mississippi, 1993.

——. *Country Music USA*. Revised ed. Austin: University of Texas Press, 1985.

——. *Don't Get Above Your Raisin': Country Music and the Southern Working Class*. Urbana: University of Illinois Press, 2002.

——. *Southern Music/American Music*. Lexington: University of Kentucky Press, 1979.

Malone, Bill C., and Judith McCulloh, eds. *Stars of Country Music: Uncle Dave Macon to Johnny Rodriguez*. New York: Da Capo, 1975.

Manuel, Peter. "Popular Music in India: 1901–86." *Popular Music* 7, no. 2 (1988): 157–76.

——. *Popular Musics of the Non-Western World*. New York: Oxford University Press, 1988.

Marchand, Roland. *Advertising the American Dream: Making Way for Modernity, 1920–1940*. Berkeley: University of California Press, 1985.

Marcus, Greil. *Invisible Republic: Bob Dylan's Basement Tapes*. New York: Henry Holt, 1997.

Mason, Otis. "The Natural History of Folk-Lore." *Journal of American Folklore* 4, no. 13 (1891): 97–105.

Matthiessen, F. O. *American Renaissance: Art and Expression in the Age of Emerson and Whitman*. New York: Oxford University Press, 1941.

McAllister, Marvin. "Bob Cole's Willie Wayside: Whiteface Hobo, Middle-Class Farmer, White Trash Hero." *Journal of American Drama and Theatre* 14 (winter 2002): 64–77.

McCracken, Allison. " 'God's Gift to Us Girls': Crooning, Gender, and the Re-Creation of American Popular Song, 1928–1933." *American Music* 17, no. 4 (winter 1999): 365–95.

McKay, Robert B. "Segregation and Public Recreation." *Virginia Law Review* 40, no. 6 (October 1954): 697–731.

McKee, Margaret, and Fred Chisenhall. *Beale Black and Blue: Life and Music on Black America's Main Street*. Baton Rouge: Louisiana State University Press, 1981.

McLean, Albert F. *American Vaudeville as Ritual*. Lexington: University of Kentucky Press, 1965.

McMillen, Neil R. *Dark Journey: Black Mississippians in the Age of Jim Crow*. Urbana: University of Illinois Press, 1990.

McNamara, Brooks. *Step Right Up*. Revised ed. Jackson: University Press of Mississippi, 1995.

McNutt, James. "Mapping the Terrain with Folk Songs." *Texas Humanist* 7, no. 6 (July–August 1985): 19–20.

Mechem, Kirke. "Home on the Range." *Kansas Historical Quarterly* 17, no. 4 (1949): 313–39.

Mendoza, Lydia. *Lydia Mendoza: A Family Autobiography*. Compiled and introduced by Chris Strachwitz with James Nicolopulos. Houston: Arte Público Press, 1993.

Menefee, Larry T. "A New Hypothesis for Dating the Decline of the 'Road.'" *Educational Theatre Journal* 30, no. 3 (October 1978): 343–56.

Merwin, Henry Childs. "On Being Civilized Too Much." *Atlantic Monthly* 79 (1897): 838–46.

Middleton, Richard. *Studying Popular Music*. Buckingham: Open University Press, 1990.

Miller, Karl Hagstrom. "Mexican Past and Mexican Presence: Capital, Tourism, and the Creation of the Local in San Antonio's Market Square." *City and Nation: Rethinking Place and Identity*, 206–42. Comparative Urban and Community Research 7. New Brunswick: Transaction, 2001.

Mizejewski, Linda. *Ziegfeld Girl: Image and Icon in Culture and Cinema*. Durham, N.C.: Duke University Press, 1999.

Moffat, Adelene. "The Mountaineers of Middle Tennessee." *Journal of American Folklore* 4, no. 15 (1891): 314–20.

Mooney, James. "Folk-Lore of the Carolina Mountains." *Journal of American Folklore* 2, no. 5 (1889): 95–104.

Moore, Jerrold Northrop. *A Voice in Time: The Gramophone of Fred Gaisberg, 1873–1951*. London: Hamish Hamilton, 1976.

Moore, MacDonald Smith. *Yankee Blues: Musical Culture and American Identity*. Bloomington: Indiana University Press, 1985.

Morgan, Jo-Ann. "Mammy the Huckster: Selling the Old South for the New Century." *American Art* 9, no. 1 (1995): 86–109.

Morgan, Thomas L., and William Barlow. *From Cakewalks to Concert Halls: An Illustrated History of African American Popular Music from 1895 to 1930*. Washington, D. C.: Elliot and Clark, 1992.

Morton David C., with Charles K. Wolfe. *DeFord Bailey: A Black Star in Early Country Music*. Knoxville: University of Tennessee Press, 1991.

Mott, Margaret M. "A Bibliography of Song Sheets: Sports and Recreations in American Popular Songs: Part I." *Notes*, 2nd series, 6, no. 3 (June 1949): 379–418.

Murray, Charles Shaar. *Boogie Man: The Adventures of John Lee Hooker in the American Twentieth Century*. New York: St. Martin's Press, 2000.

Murray, Pauli. *States' Laws on Race and Color*. Cincinnati: Women's Division of Christian Service, 1950.

Nasaw, David. *Going Out: The Rise and Fall of Public Amusements*. New York: Basic Books, 1993.

Nathan, Hans. *Dan Emmett and the Rise of Early Negro Minstrelsy*. Norman: University of Oklahoma Press, 1962.

Navárez, Peter. "Afro-American and Mexican Street Singers: An Ethnohistorical Hypothesis." *Southern Folklore Quarterly* 42 (1978): 73–84.

——. "The Influences of Hispanic Music Cultures on African-American Blues Musicians." *Black Music Research Journal* 14, no. 2 (1994): 203–24.

Nelson, Donald Lee. "The Allen Brothers." *JEMF Quarterly* 7 (winter 1971): 147–50.

Nettl, Bruno. *The Study of Ethnomusicology: Twenty-Nine Issues and Concepts.* Urbana: University of Illinois Press, 1982.

———. *The Western Impact on World Music: Change, Adaptation, and Survival.* New York: Schirmer Books, 1985.

Newell, William Wells. "Early American Ballads." *Journal of American Folklore* 12, no. 46 (1899): 241–54.

———. "Myths of Voodoo Worship and Child Sacrifice in Hayti." *Journal of American Folklore* 1, no. 1 (1888): 16–30.

———. "On the Field and Work of a Journal of American Folk-Lore." *Journal of American Folklore* 1, no. 1 (1888): 3–7.

———. "Reports of Voodoo Worship in Hayti and Louisiana." *Journal of American Folklore* 2, no. 4 (1889): 41–47.

Nicholls, David G. *Conjuring the Folk: Forms of Modernity in Africa America.* Ann Arbor: University of Michigan Press, 2000.

Niles, John Jacob. "Shout, Coon, Shout." *Musical Quarterly* 16, no. 4 (1930): 516–30.

Oakley, Giles. *The Devil's Music: A History of the Blues.* New York: Harcourt Brace Jovanovich, 1976.

Odum, Howard W. "Folk-Song and Folk-Poetry as Found in the Secular Songs of the Southern Negroes." *Journal of American Folklore* 24, no. 93 (1911): 255–94.

———. "Folk-Song and Folk-Poetry as Found in the Secular Songs of the Southern Negroes (Concluded)." *Journal of American Folklore* 24, no. 94 (1911): 351–96.

———. "Religious Folk-Songs of the Southern Negroes." *American Journal of Religious Psychology and Education* 3, no. 3 (July 1909): 265–365.

Odum, Howard W., and Guy B. Johnson. *The Negro and His Songs: A Study of Typical Negro Songs in the South.* Chapel Hill: University of North Carolina Press, 1925.

———. *Negro Workaday Songs.* Chapel Hill: University of North Carolina Press, 1926.

Ogren, Kathy J. *The Jazz Revolution: Twenties America and the Meaning of Jazz.* New York: Oxford University Press, 1989.

Ohmann, Richard. *Selling Culture: Magazines, Markets, and Class at the Turn of the Century.* London: Verso, 1996.

Oliver, N. T., as told to Wesley Stout. "Alagazam: The Story of Pitchmen, High and Low." *Saturday Evening Post* 202 (October 19, 1929), 26–28, 76, 79–80.

———. "Med Show." *Saturday Evening Post* 202 (September 14, 1929), 12–13, 166, 169, 173–74.

Oliver, Paul. *Songsters and Saints: Vocal Traditions on Race Records.* New York: Cambridge University Press, 1984.

O'Meally, Robert G. " 'Game to the Heart': Sterling Brown and the Badman." *Callaloo* 14, no. 15 (1982): 43–54.

Otto, John S., and Augustus M. Burns. "Black and White Cultural Interaction in the Early Twentieth Century South: Race and Hillbilly Music." *Phylon* 35, no. 4 (December 1974): 407–17.

——. "John 'Knocky' Parker—A Case Study of White and Black Musical Interaction." *JEMF Quarterly* 10, no. 1 (spring 1974): 23–26.

Painter, Nell Irvin. *Exodusters: Black Migration to Kansas after Reconstruction*. New York: Alfred A. Knopf, 1976.

Palmer, Jack. *Vernon Dalhart: First Star of Country Music*. Denver: Mainspring Press, 2005.

Palmer, Robert. *Deep Blues*. New York: Penguin, 1981.

Parker, Haywood. "Folk-Lore of the North Carolina Mountaineers." *Journal of American Folklore* 20, no. 79 (1907): 241–50.

Patterson, Daniel W., and Allen Tullos. *Born for Hard Luck: Background, Transcription, and Commentary*. Chapel Hill: Curriculum in Folklore at the University of North Carolina at Chapel Hill, 1981.

——. *Southern History across the Color Line*. Chapel Hill: University of North Carolina Press, 2002.

Peabody, Charles. "Notes on Negro Music." *Journal of American Folklore* 16, no. 62 (July 1903): 148–52.

Pecknold, Diane. *The Selling Sound: The Rise of the Country Music Industry*. Durham, N.C.: Duke University Press, 2007.

Peiss, Kathy. *Cheap Amusements: Working Women and Leisure in Turn-of-the-Century New York*. Philadelphia: Temple University Press, 1986.

Peña, Manuel. *The Texas-Mexican Conjunto: History of a Working-Class People*. Austin: University of Texas Press, 1985.

Perkins, John, Alan Kelly, and John Ward, "On Gramophone Company Matrix Numbers 1898 to 1921." *Record Collector* 23, nos. 3–4 (May 1976): 51–90.

Perrow, E. C. "Songs and Rhymes from the South." *Journal of American Folklore* 25, no. 96 (1912): 137–55. The collection continues under the same title in 26, no. 100 (1913): 123–73; and 28, no. 108 (1915): 129–90.

Person, Alice. "The Chivalry of Man, as Exemplified in the Life of Mrs. Joe Person." Typescript edited and compiled by Louise Stephenson, Raleigh, 1971. Reproduced in *Southern Women and their Families in the Nineteenth Century: Papers and Diaries: Series A, Holdings of the Southern Historical Collection, University of North Carolina, Chapel Hill. Part 8: North Carolina: Papers of Alice Morgan Person*, consulting ed. Anne Firor. Bethesda, Md.: University Publications of America, ca. 1991.

Peterson, Richard A. *Creating Country Music: Fabricating Authenticity*. Chicago: University of Chicago Press, 1997.

Place, Jeff. "Supplemental Notes on the Selections." *A Booklet of Essays, Appreciations, and Annotations pertaining to the Anthology of American Folk Music*. Washington, D.C.: Smithsonian Folkways Recordings, 1997.

Poggi, Jack. "The Beginnings of Decline." *Tulane Drama Review* 10, no. 1 (autumn 1965): 88–94.

———. *Theater in America: The Impact of Economic Forces, 1870–1967.* Ithaca, N.Y.: Cornell University Press, 1968.

Porter, J. Hampden. "Notes on the Folk-Lore of the Mountain Whites of the Alleghanies." *Journal of American Folklore* 7, no. 25 (1894): 105–17.

Porterfield, Nolan. *Jimmie Rodgers: The Life and Times of America's Blue Yodeler.* Urbana: University of Illinois Press, 1992.

———. *The Last Cavalier: The Life and Times of John A. Lomax.* Urbana: University of Illinois Press, 1996.

Potter, David M. *The South and the Sectional Conflict.* Baton Rouge: Louisiana State University Press, 1968.

Pound, Louise. "The Southwestern Cowboy and the English and Scottish Popular Ballads." *Modern Philology* 11, no. 2 (October 1913): 195–207.

Qureshi, Regula Burckhardt. "His Master's Voice? Exploring Qawwali and 'Gramophone Culture' in South Asia." *Popular Music* 18, no. 1 (1999): 63–98.

Radano, Ronald. "Denoting Difference: The Writing of the Slave Spirituals." *Critical Inquiry* 22, no. 3 (spring 1996): 506–44.

———. *Lying Up a Nation: Race and Black Music.* Chicago: University of Chicago, 2003.

Radano, Ronald, and Philip V. Bohlman, eds. *Music and the Racial Imagination.* Chicago: University of Chicago Press, 2000.

Ramsey, Guthrie P. "Cosmopolitan or Provincial? Ideology in Early Black Music Historiography, 1867–1940." *Black Music Research Journal* 16, no. 1 (spring 1996): 11–42.

———. "The Pot Liquor Principle: Developing a Black Music Criticism in American Music Studies." *American Music* 22, no. 2 (2004): 284–95.

———. *Race Music: Black Cultures from Bebop to Hip-Hop.* Berkeley: University of California Press, 2003.

Randle, William. "Payola." *American Speech* 36, no. 2 (May 1961): 104–16.

Regester, Charlene. "From the Buzzard's Roost: Black Movie-Going in Durham and Other North Carolina Cities during the Early Period of American Cinema." *Film History* 17 (2005): 113–24.

Regev, Motti. "Rock Aesthetics and the Musics of the World." *Theory, Culture and Society* 14 (1997): 125–42.

Rehding, Alexander. "The Quest for the Origins of Music in Germany circa 1900." *Journal of the American Musicological Society* 53, no. 2 (2000): 345–85.

Rice, Edward Le Roy. *Monarchs of Minstrelsy.* New York: Kenny Publishing Company, ca.1911.

Riis, Thomas L. " 'Bob' Cole: His Life and His Legacy to Black Musical Theater." *Black Perspective in Music* 13 (1985): 135–50.

——. *Just before Jazz: Black Musical Theater in New York, 1890–1915*. Washington, D.C.: Smithsonian Institution Press, 1989.

——. *More than Just Minstrel Shows: The Rise of Black Musical Theatre at the Turn of the Century*. ISAM Monographs: Number 33. Brooklyn: Institute for Studies in American Music, Brooklyn College, 1992.

——. "The Music and Musicians in Nineteenth-Century Productions of *Uncle Tom's Cabin*." *American Music* 4, no. 3 (autumn 1986): 268–86.

Roberts, John Storm. *The Latin Tinge: The Impact of Latin American Music on the United States*. Tivoli, N.Y.: Original Music, 1985.

Roberts, John W. *From Trickster to Badman: The Black Folk Hero in Slavery and Freedom*. Philadelphia: University of Pennsylvania Press, 1989.

Robinson, Cedric J. *Black Marxism: The Making of the Black Radical Tradition*. Chapel Hill: University of North Carolina Press, 2000 [1983].

Robinson, Deanna Campbell, Elizabeth Buck, and Marlene Cutbert, eds. *Music at the Margins: Popular Music and Cultural Diversity*. London: Sage Publications, 1991.

Roediger, David R. *The Wages of Whiteness: Race and the Making of the American Working Class*. New York: Verso, 1991.

Roell, Craig H. *The Piano in America, 1890–1940*. Chapel Hill: University of North Carolina Press, 2000.

Rogin, Michael P. *Blackface, White Noise: Jewish Immigrants in the Hollywood Melting Pot*. Berkeley: University of California Press, 1996.

Rorrer, Kinney. *Rambling Blues: The Life and Songs of Charlie Poole*. London: Old Time Music, 1982.

Rosaldo, Renato. *Culture and Truth: The Remaking of Social Analysis*. Boston: Beacon Press, 1993 [1989].

Rose, Tricia. *Black Noise: Rap Music and Black Culture in Contemporary America*. Hanover, N.H.: Wesleyan University Press, 1994.

Rosenberg, Emily. *Spreading the American Dream: American Economic and Cultural Expansion, 1890–1945*. New York: Hill and Wang, 1982.

Rosenberg, Neil V., ed. *Transforming Tradition: Folk Music Revivals Examined*. Urbana: University of Illinois Press, 1993.

Ross, Andrew. *No Respect: Intellectuals and Popular Culture*. New York: Routledge, 1989.

Ross, Andrew, and Tricia Rose, eds. *Microphone Fiends: Youth Music and Youth Culture*. New York: Routledge, 1994.

Royster, Jacqueline Jones, ed. *Southern Horrors and Other Writings: The Anti-Lynching Campaign of Ida B. Wells, 1982–1900*. New York: Bedford, 1997.

Rudy, Jill Terry. "Toward an Assessment of Verbal Art as Performance: A Cross-Disciplinary Citation Study with Rhetorical Analysis." *Journal of American Folklore* 115, no. 455, "Toward New Perspectives on Verbal Art as Performance" (2002): 5–27.

Russell, Tony. *Blacks, Whites, and Blues*. New York: Stein and Day, 1970.

Russell, Tony, and Bob Pinson. *Country Music Records: A Discography, 1921–1942*. New York: Oxford University Press, 2004.

Rydell, Robert W. *All the World's a Fair: Visions of Empire at American International Expositions, 1876–1916*. Chicago: University of Chicago Press, 1984.

Rydell, Robert W., and Rob Kroes. *Buffalo Bill in Bologna: The Americanization of the World, 1869–1922*. Chicago: University of Chicago Press, 2005.

Sanjek, Russell. *American Popular Music and Its Business: The First Four Hundred Years*, volume 2. New York: Oxford University Press, 1988.

Sanjek, Russell, and David Sanjek. *Pennies from Heaven: The American Popular Music Business in the Twentieth Century*. New York: Da Capo Press, 1996.

Sapoznik, Henry. Liner notes to *"You Ain't Talkin' to Me": Charlie Poole and the Roots of Country Music*. Columbia Legacy 92780, 2005.

Saxton, Alexander. *The Rise and Fall of the White Republic: Class Politics and Mass Culture in Nineteenth-Century America*. London: Verso, 1990.

Scarborough, Dorothy. "The 'Blues' as Folk-Songs." *Texas Folklore Society Publications* 2 (1923): 52–66.

———. *On the Trail of Negro Folk-Songs*. Cambridge, Mass.: Harvard University Press, 1925.

———. *A Song Catcher in the Southern Mountains: American Folk Songs of British Ancestry*. New York: Columbia University Press, 1937.

Seeger, Charles. "Professionalism and Amateurism in the Study of Folk Music." *Journal of American Folklore* 62, no. 243 (1949): 107–13.

Seeger, Mike. "Who Chose These Records? A Look into the Life, Tastes, and Procedures of Frank Walker." *Anthology of American Folk Music*, edited by Josh Duncan, 8–17. New York: Oak Publications, 1973.

Shapiro, Henry D. *Appalachia on Our Mind: The Southern Mountains and Mountaineers in the American Consciousness, 1870–1920*. Chapel Hill: University of North Carolina Press, 1978.

Shirley, Wayne D. "The House of Melody: A List of Publications of the Gotham-Attucks Music Company at the Library of Congress." *Black Perspective in Music* 15, no. 1 (spring 1987): 79–112.

Shufeldt, Robert W. *The Negro, a Menace to American Civilization*. Boston: Gorham Press, 1907.

Silber, Nina. *The Romance of Reunion: Northerners and the South, 1865–1900*. Chapel Hill: University of North Carolina Press, 1993.

Small, Christopher. *Music of the Common Tongue: Survival and Celebration in Afro-American Music*. New York: Riverrun Press, 1987.

Snyder, Robert W. *The Voice of the City: Vaudeville and Popular Culture in New York*. New York: Oxford University Press, 1989.

Sobel, Mechal. *The World They Made Together: Black and White Values in Eighteenth-Century Virginia.* Princeton, N.J.: Princeton University Press, 1987.

Sotiropoulos, Karen. *Staging Race: Black Performers in Turn of the Century America.* Cambridge, Mass.: Harvard University Press, 2006.

Sousa, John Philip. "The Menace of Mechanical Music." *Appleton's Magazine* 8 (1906): 278–84.

Southern, Eileen. *The Music of Black Americans.* New York: W. W. Norton, 1997 [1971].

——, ed. *Readings in Black American Music.* 2nd ed. New York: W. W. Norton, 1983.

Spottswood, Richard. Liner notes to *Folk Music in America.* Washington, D.C.: Library of Congress, 1978.

Stagg, Jerry. *The Brothers Shubert.* New York: Random House, 1968.

Stevenson, Robert. "America's First Black Music Historian." *Journal of the American Musicological Society* 26, no. 3 (1973): 383–404.

Stocking, George W. *Race, Culture, and Evolution: Essays in the History of Anthropology.* Chicago: University of Chicago Press, 1968.

Stokes, Martin, ed. *Ethnicity, Identity and Music: The Musical Construction of Place.* Oxford: Berg, 1994.

Sumner, William Graham. *Folkways.* New York: Mentor, 1940 [1906].

Szwed, John F. "Race and the Embodiment of Culture." *Ethnicity* 2, no. 1 (1975): 19–33.

Talley, Thomas W., and Charles K. Wolfe. *Thomas W. Talley's Negro Folk Rhymes: A New Expanded Edition, with Music.* Knoxville: University of Tennessee Press, 1991.

Taussig, Michael. *Mimesis and Alterity: A Particular History of the Senses.* New York: Routledge, 1993.

Taylor, Timothy. *Global Pop: World Music, World Markets.* New York: Routledge, 1997.

Terry, William E. "The Negro Music Journal: An Appraisal." *Black Perspectives in Music* 5, no. 2 (1977): 140–60.

Tindall, George. *The Emergence of the New South, 1913–1945.* Baton Rouge: Louisiana State University Press, 1967.

Titon, Jeff Todd. *Early Downhome Blues: A Musical and Cultural Analysis.* Chapel Hill: University of North Carolina Press, 1994 [1977].

Toll, Robert C. *Blacking Up: The Minstrel Show in Nineteenth-Century America.* New York: Oxford University Press, 1974.

Torgovnick, Marianna. *Gone Primitive: Savage Intellects, Modern Lives.* Chicago: University of Chicago Press, 1991.

Travis, Steve. "The Rise and Fall of the Theatrical Syndicate." *Educational Theatre Journal* 10, no. 1 (March 1958): 35–40.

Tribe, Ivan M. *Mountaineer Jamboree: Country Music in West Virginia.* Lexington: University Press of Kentucky, 1996.

Trietler, Leo. "Toward a Desegregated Music Historiography." *Black Music Research Journal* 16, no. 1 (spring 1996): 3–10.

Trotter, James Monroe. *Music and Some Highly Musical People*. New York: Charles Dillingham, 1881 [1878].

Tullos, Allen. "Born for Hard Luck." *Southern Exposure* 3 (winter 1976): 40–45.

Tyson, Timothy B. *Radio Free Dixie: Robert F. Williams and the Roots of Black Power*. Chapel Hill: University of North Carolina Press, 1999.

Van Vechten, Carl. *"Keep A-Inchin' Along": Selected Writings of Carl Van Vechten about Black Art and Letters*. Edited by Bruce Kellner. Newport: Greenwood Press, 1979.

Vincent, Ted. *Keep Cool: The Black Activists Who Built the Jazz Age*. London: Pluto Press, 1995.

Wald, Elijah. *Escaping the Delta: Robert Johnson and the Invention of the Blues*. New York: Amistad, 2004.

Waller, Gregory A. *Main Street Amusements: Movies and Commercial Entertainment in a Southern City, 1896–1930*. Washington, D.C.: Smithsonian Institution Press, 1995.

Walser, Robert. "Rhythm, Rhyme, and Rhetoric in the Music of Public Enemy." *Ethnomusicology* 39, no. 2 (1995): 193–218.

Walsh, Jim. "Favorite Pioneer Recording Artists: Al Bernard." *Hobbies* (serialized March 1974–February 1975).

——. "Favorite Pioneer Recording Artists: George H. O'Connor." *Hobbies* (serialized January–March 1955).

——."Favorite Pioneer Recording Artists: Morton Harvey." *Hobbies* (December 1955).

——. "Favorite Pioneer Recording Artists: Vernon Dalhart." *Hobbies* (serialized May–December 1960).

Waters, Ethel, with Charles Samuels. *His Eye Is on the Sparrow: An Autobiography*. Garden City, N.Y.: Doubleday, 1951.

Webb, Barbara L. "Authentic Possibilities: Plantation Performance of the 1890s." *Theatre Journal* 56 (2004): 63–82.

Webb, W. Prescott. "Notes on the Folk-Lore of Texas." *Journal of American Folklore* 28, no.109 (1915): 290–99.

Welch, Walter L., and Leah Brodbeck Stenzel Burt. *From Tinfoil to Stereo: The Acoustic Years of the Recording Industry, 1877–1929*. Gainesville: University Press of Florida, 1994.

Wells, Richard A. *Manners, Culture and Dress of the Best American Society*. Springfield, Mass.: King, Richardson, 1894.

Whisnant, David E. *All That Is Native and Fine: The Politics of Culture in an American Region*. Chapel Hill: University of North Carolina Press, 1983.

White, Deborah Gray. *Ar'N't I a Woman? Female Slaves in the Plantation South*. New York: W. W. Norton, 1999.

White, Newman Ivey. *American Negro Folk-Songs*. Cambridge, Mass.: Harvard University Press, 1928.

White, Shane, and Graham J. White. *The Sounds of Slavery: Discovering African American History through Songs, Sermons, and Speech*. Boston: Beacon Press, 2005.

Whitfield, Stephen J. "Is It True What They Sing about Dixie?" *Southern Cultures* 8, no. 2 (summer 2002): 8–37.

Wiggins, Gene. *Fiddlin' Georgia Crazy: Fiddlin' John Carson, His Real World, and the World of His Songs*. Urbana: University of Illinois Press, 1987.

Wilgus, D. K. *Anglo-American Folksong Scholarship since 1898*. New Brunswick, N.J.: Rutgers University Press, 1959.

Williams, John Alexander. "Radicalism and Professionalism in Folklore Studies: A Comparative Perspective." *Journal of the Folklore Institute* 11, no. 3 (1974): 211–34.

Williams, Raymond. *Culture and Society*. New York: Harper and Row, 1958.

Willis, William S. Jr. "Franz Boas and the Study of Black Folklore." *The New Ethnicity: Perspectives from Ethnology*, edited by John W. Bennett, 307–34. St. Paul: West Publishing, 1975.

Wilson, Olly. "Black Music as an Art Form." *The Jazz Cadence of American Culture*, edited by Robert O'Meally, 82–101. New York: Columbia University Press, 1998.

Wolfe, Charles K. "Columbia Records and Old-Time Music." *JEMF Quarterly* (autumn 1978): 118–26.

——. *The Devil's Box: Masters of Southern Fiddling*. Nashville: Country Music Foundation Press, 1997.

——. "Rural Black String Band Music." *Black Music Research Journal* 10, no. 1 (spring 1990): 32–35.

——. *Tennessee Strings: The Story of Country Music in Tennessee*. Knoxville: University of Tennessee Press, 1977.

——. Liner notes to *White Country Blues: 1928–1938, A Lighter Shade of Blues*. Columbia Legacy C2K 47466, 1993.

——. "The White Man's Blues, 1922–40." *Journal of Country Music* 17, no. 3 (1993): 38–44.

Wolfe, Charles K., and Kip Lornell. *The Life and Legend of Leadbelly*. New York: Harper Perennial, 1992.

Woll, Alan. *Black Musical Theatre: From Coontown to Dreamgirls*. New York: Da Capo, 1991.

Woodward, C. Vann. *Origins of the New South, 1877–1913*. Baton Rouge: Louisiana State University Press, 1951.

——. *The Strange Career of Jim Crow*. 2nd rev. ed. London: Oxford University Press, 1966.

Zumwalt, Rosemary Lévy. *American Folklore Scholarship: A Dialogue of Dissent*. Bloomington: Indiana University Press, 1988.

Zwigoff, Terry. "Black Country String Bands." *American Visions* (February 1991): 50–52.

African culture and music (*continued*)
223–27, 318n.25; Western scholarship
on, 292n.65
"After the Ball" (song), 15, 27, 35–37, 50,
127, 136, 233
"After You've Gone" (song), 153
Agawu, Kofi, 292n.65
Ager, Milton, 140
A. G. Field Minstrels, 35–36
"Aggravatin' Papa" (song), 59
"Ain't It Hard to Be a Nigger" (song),
293n.85
Ajax Record Company, 207
Akst, Harry, 60
Alderman, Tony, 211
"Alexander's Ragtime Band" (song),
140, 215, 229, 232
"All Coons Look Alike to Me" (song),
41, 123–25, 136
Allegheny Highlanders, 214
Allen, James Lane, 102
Allen, Lee and Austin, 220–21, 226, 233
American Folklore Society, 114; forma-
tion of, 2–3; isolation paradigm and,
87–97; race and culture debates
within, 19, 242–45; racial stereotyp-
ing by, 107–8; scientific mandate of,
107. See also *Journal of American
Folklore*
American Record Corporation, 317n.6
American Theatrical Exchange, 30
Amrine, M. F., 263
Anderson, Charles, 239
Anderson, Paul Allen, 252
Anderson, Pink, 47
"And Her Golden Hair Was Hanging
Down Her Back" (song), 177
Anthony, Eddie, 218
anthropology: in folklore studies, 93–
97; globalization of recording indus-
try and, 178–80; justification of segre-

gation through, 110–12, 296n.27;
primitivism and globalization of
recording industry and, 168–80
"Any Old Place in Yankee Land Is Good
Enough for Me" (song), 303n.47
Appalachia: identification of, 102–5; in
hillbilly music, 143–47
"Are You from Dixie?" (song), 216
"Arkansas" (song), 71
"Arkansas Blues" (song), 194–95, 231
"Arkansas Traveler, The" (song and
comedy sketch), 103, 143–47, 213,
297n.50
Armstrong, Howard, 75–79
Arnold, Matthew, 162–63, 186
art music, cultural concept of, 55–57,
112–13; the New Negro Renaissance
and, 252–53; recording industry's
promotion of, 158–67
Arto company, 193
Ashley, Clarence, 291n.46
Askt, Harry, 196, 209
"At a Georgia Camp Meeting" (Mills
song), 230
Attila (Verdi opera), 130
Austin, Gene, 60, 300n.23
authenticity: in African American folklore, 113–15; African American musicians and, 4–6, 74–84, 130–31, 142,
191, 225, 243, 250–53, 322.n25; in blues
music, 147–55, 224; in coon songs,
45–50, 132–42; folkloric paradigm of,
6, 19, 98–99, 217, 241–53, 263–65; isolation paradigm as cornerstone for,
251–53, 263–65; minstrelsy and concepts of, 4–6, 141–42; in popular
music, 276–82; romantic context for,
277–82; technological innovation
and, 278–79; white southern musicians' claim of, 6, 140–42, 146–47, 153,
155, 197, 216–17, 228, 242–46, 258–65

Autobiography of an Ex-Colored Man
(Johnson), 133–34, 149, 322n.25
Autry, Gene, 230, 238, 246
Ayers, Edward, 8

Baartman, Saarjie, 99
"Baby Face" (song), 60
"Baby Seal Blues" (song), 304n.69
Bacon, Alice Mabel, 113–15
Bailey, Deford, 57
Baker, Lee, 111
ballads: early blues interpreted as, 254;
folkloric studies of, 88–93, 248. *See
also* sentimental ballad
Bandana Land (musical), 138
Barlow, William, 73
Barnum, P. T., 5
Bascom, Louise Rand, 103–4
Bauman, Richard, 14
Baxter, Andrew, 218
Bayes, Nora, 137, 194
"Beale Street Blues" (song), 148, 151–52,
154
Beale Street Sheiks, 218–19
Beka-Record Company, 171–72
Bentley, Irene, 136, 302n.45
Bergen, Flora Batson, 49
Berlin, Irving, 140, 215–16
Bernard, Al, 151, 194, 196
Bernheim, Alfred L., 33
Bigeou, Esther, 219
Black America (stage production), 98–
101, 119–20, 130, 195, 300n.96
blackface minstrelsy. *See* minstrelsy
Black Patti Troubadours, 130, 301n.28
Black Swan Records, 113, 193, 196, 207
Blackwell, Henry M., 167–70, 181
Blackwell, Willie, 265, 267
Blake, Blind, 218–20, 226
Blake, James, 214
Bland, James, 34

Blue Ridge Cornshuckers (band), 212–13
blues: African American musicians confined to recording, 221–27, 232–40;
African and African American
origins of, 2, 6–7; commercial negotiations over, 267–74; early composers of, 304n.69; folkloric paradigm
applied to, 224–26, 232–40, 253–75,
277–82; musical training and, 58–61;
in New York City, 147–55; Peabody's
research on, 23; performance process
and, 73–84; pop music influence on,
9, 232–40; sexuality in, 78–79; slide
guitar and, 71; southern recordings
of, 196–97; stereotypes about, 208–14,
232–40, 252; white performances of,
150–51, 233–40; yodeling and, 238–40
Boas, Franz, 95–97, 100, 110, 113–15,
296n.30, 298n.65
"Bob McKinney" (song), 71
Boggs, Doc, 62, 233
Bohee, May, 120
"Bon Bon Buddie" (song), 303n.47
Booker, Jim, 218
booking agencies, formation of, 28–34
Book of American Negro Poetry, The
(Johnson), 249, 251, 253, 322n.25
Boykin, Edwin, 199
Bradford, Perry, 190–91, 194, 200, 224
Brian, Donald, 136, 302n.45
Brinton, Daniel, 94–95, 108, 110–11
British Gramophone Company, 170–73
Broadway music, 9, 138, 302n.45
Brockman, Polk C., 200–204, 222,
314n.35
Brooks, Tim, 310n.7
Brooks, Shelton, 229
Broonzy, Bill, 57, 62, 275–82
Brown, Herschel, 234
Brown, Sterling, 252
Brunswick recording company, 231

Collins, Arthur, 125, 136–37, 145, 151, 210, 234

Collins, Sam, 219

Colonialism, 167–69, 311n.68

Colored Vaudeville and Benevolent Association (CVBA), 190

Columbia Graphophone Company: blues recordings by, 151, 190, 193; "Familiar Tunes" series of, 233; foreign music sales in U.S. by, 180, 182; globalization of music and, 157–60, 181–83; Harris's defection to, 153; old-time music recordings by, 202, 208–16, 227; race records by, 220; southern musicians' recordings of popular songs and, 229; spirituals recordings by, 223

commercial revolution, 25–26, 37, 42

commercial expansion of popular music: African American music and, 23–25, 245–53; authenticity and, 276–82; blues music and, 148–55, 253–57; coon songs' and, 45–50; folkloric participation in, 265–74; folklorists' rejection of, 241–53; piano sales increases and, 38–41; recording industry's cultural uplift campaign and, 157–67; southern musicians and, 3–4, 7, 25–34, 216–17, 228–40. *See also* marketing and economics

"Common Sense" (Smith song), 303n.47

communalist theory, in folklore studies, 92–97, 117, 244–45, 248, 251, 278–82

Compania Fonografica Mexicana, 180

comparative ethnology, folkloric studies and, 94–97, 296n.30

"Congo Love Song" (Cole-Johnson song), 136

Conner, Babe, 46

consumption patterns for music and recordings: of African Americans, 198–99, 224–25; marketing of southern music and, 198–206; for old-time music, 209–14, 315n.53; for race and old-time records, 188–214; recording industry's cultural uplift campaign and, 162–67. *See also* marketing and economics

Cook, William Marion, 45, 123, 136–38, 302n.45

"Coon Crap Game" (song), 216

"Coon from Tennessee" (song), 230

coon shouters, 125–28, 135

coon songs: African American modifications to, 130–42, 219; popularity in New York of, 123–29; racial politics in, 24–25, 41–50; ragtime and, 218, 250–53; southern popularity of, 34–35, 71; white performances of, 124–29, 228–29; yodeling and, 239

copyright issues: for folk music, 241–42, 273–74; for old-time recordings, 235–40. *See also* royalty issues

"Corn Licker Still in Georgia, A" (recording), 213–14

Cotten, Elizabeth, 15

"Countess of Alagazam, The" (song), 303n.47

country music: origins of, 6–7; as rural white southern music, 2. *See also* old-time music

Courlander, Harold, 277

Cowboy Songs and Other Frontier Ballads (Lomax), 56, 85–86, 89, 117–18, 241–42, 272

Cox, Ida, 226

Cox, John Harrington, 246–47, 266

Cox, Quince, 63

"Crazy Blues" (song), 153, 184, 187, 191–94, 200, 204, 224–25, 232

Creamer, Henry, 153, 193, 195–96

Crim, Will, 44

industry, 160–62, 166–67, 179–80, 307n.13

Ellison, Ralph, 74, 282

Emerson, Ralph Waldo, 90, 101

Emmett, Dan, 34, 40

English and Scottish Popular Ballads, The (Child), 91–92

E. P. Christy's Minstrels, 287n.29

Erlanger, Abraham, 29, 135

ethnic recordings, sale in U.S. of, 181–83, 310n.58

Europe, James Reese, 219, 302n.45

Evans, George, 151

"Everybody's Crazy 'Bout the Doggone Blues but I'm Happy" (song), 153

"Everything Is Peaches Down in Georgia" (song), 140

evolutionary anthropology: in folklore studies, 93–97; segregation justification with, 110–12

Evolution of Rag-Time, The (stage production), 302n.45

Fagan, Barney, 125

Farber, H. C., 165

Farrell, Billy, 120

"Fatal Wedding, The" (song), 36–37

Feld, Steven, 16–17

Fewkes, J. Walter, 178

"Fiddler's Convention in Georgia, A" (recording), 213

fiddling contests, 203–4

Fisk Jubilee Singers, 116, 223

Fletcher, Alice, 100

Fletcher, Tom, 32, 119–20

Flowers, Madame, 49, 120

folk music: by African Americans, 1, 109–10, 113, 249–53; blues music and, 152; commercial aspects of, 241–45, 265–74; copyright and royalties on, 235–40; functional role of, 55–57;

local music stereotyped as, 178–80, 309n.54; mid-twentieth century revival of, 275–76

folkloric paradigm: African American music and, 1, 109–10, 113–15, 149–50, 245–53; authenticity as cornerstone of, 242–45; blues music and, 224–26, 232–40, 253–57; commercial aspects of, 265–74; communalist theory in, 92–97, 117, 244–45, 248, 251, 278–82; coon song collections and, 47; copyright and royalty issues and, 236–40, 319n.53; history of, 6, 21; influence on southern music of, 3; isolation concept in, 86–87; local music paradigm parallel with, 178–80; marketing strategies based on, 222–27; minstrelsy and, 9–11, 19–20, 152, 242; old-time music popularity and, 210–14, 216–17, 232–40; performance *vs.* repertoire in, 14–16; popular music and, 228–40, 243–53; in popular press, 244–45; race records' marketing and, 232–40; segregation defended by, 110–12, 118–19, 257–65, 276–82; southern culture and, 8–9; spirituals in context of, 223–24, 318n.25

foreign music, marketing in America of, 180–83

Fortier, Alcée, 107

Foster, Stephen, 34–35, 40, 132, 146, 215, 228, 230, 287n.29, 300n.23

Fox, John Jr., 102

"Frankie and Johnny" (song), 218

Fruit Jar Guzzlers (band), 212

functionalist view of music, 55–57

Gaieties of 1919, The, 151

Gaisberg, Fred, 124, 171, 173, 176–77, 179–81

General Phonograph, 172, 205

Gennett Company, 193

immigrants: blackface performances by, 140, 303n.54; sales of foreign music in U.S. to, 180–83, 310n.58

India, recording industry in, 170–71, 174–76

industrialization: commercial expansion of popular music and, 25–34; impact on mountain culture of, 104–5

interracial music culture: blue yodel recordings and, 238–39; coon song recordings and, 124–26; folklorist paradigm and, 245–53; hillbilly-minstrel roots of, 142–47; historical aspects of, 12; marketing of African American music and, 66–71; musical training and, 60–61; old-time music and, 217–27, 233–40; race records and, 189–97; white performers and African American composers, 136–42, 302n.45

"In the Baggage Coach Ahead" (Davis song), 36–37, 228, 233

"In the Jailhouse Now" (song), 219, 239

"In the Shade of the Old Apple Tree" (song), 229

"In the Shadow of the Pine" (song), 230

Irwin, May, 23–24, 27, 46, 71, 127–28, 135, 192, 194, 247, 250

isolation paradigm: authenticity defined by, 251–53, 263–65; as basis for segregation, 110–11, 118–19; for blues music marketing, 224–27; in folklore studies, 86–87, 100–104, 244–53; globalization of recording industry and, 176–80; prison songs in context of, 262–65; segregation supported with, 257–65; in southern music, 87–97. See also folkloric paradigm

"It Ain't Gonna Rain No Mo'" (song), 228, 233

"It's a Long Way to Tipperary" (song), 231

"I Want a Little Lovin,' Sometimes" (Smith song), 136, 302n.45

"I Want Dem Presents Back" (song), 125–26

Jackson, Arthur, 69–71

Jackson, Jim, 227

Jackson, Papa Charlie, 220, 226, 291n.46

Jackson, Thomas, 145

Jagger, Mick, 10–11

James, Skip, 238, 321n.11

Jaudas, Eugene A., 144

jazz, 12, 13; black cultural stereotypes in, 252; Ledbetter's performances of, 246; southern musicians discouraged from performance of, 234–35

Jefferson, Blind Lemon, 60–63, 78, 82–83, 197, 225, 227, 233

Jewish songwriters, dialect songs by, 140

Jim Crow segregation. See segregation

"Jinny Put the Kettle On" (song), 60

"John Henry" (song), 71, 234

Johnson, Billy, 130–31

Johnson, George W., 124, 220

Johnson, Guy B., 79, 255–56

Johnson, James P., 77–78

Johnson, James Weldon, 302n.45, 303n.47, 305n.71; on African American musical traditions, 249–53, 322n.25; coon song collaborations by, 124, 131–37; dialect love songs by, 135–37, 139, 147, 249; migration to New York City, 123, 129, 197; minstrel dialect in songs of, 149; popular music embraced by, 231; white performances of music by, 142, 154, 230

Johnson, J. Rosamond, 302n.45, 303n.47; Bradford and, 190; coon song collaborations by, 131–37; dialect love songs by, 135–37, 139, 147; migration to New York City, 123, 129, 197; popular music embraced by, 231; white performances of music by, 142, 154, 230

Johnson, Jube, 120

Johnson, Robert, 1–2, 197, 227, 238, 317n.6

Johnson, Tommy, 238

Jolson, Al, 140, 228, 230

Jones, Coley, 218

Jones, Irving, 71

Jones, Sisteretta, 49, 130

Joseph W. Stern and Company, 135–36

Journal of American Folklore: African American work songs discussed in, 23; Appalachia discussed in, 102–4; black folklore discussed in, 114; blues discussed in, 253; promotion of phonograph by, 178–79; racial stereotypes in, 107–8; scientific scholarship standards discussed in, 87; segregation discussed in, 259

Jug Stompers, 219

Junior Brass Band, 49–50

"Just Because She Made Dem Goo Goo Eyes" (song), 23–24, 125

"Just Before the Battle, Mother" (song), 246–47, 322n.15

Kazee, Buell, 291n.46

Keil, Charles, 277–78

Kelley, Robin D. G., 278–79

Kelly, Daniel, 274

Kemp, May, 302n.45

Keppard, Freddie, 226

"kerosene circuit," 202

"Kickapoo Medicine Show" (recording), 213

Kittredge, George Lyman, 92, 117

Klavier Schule, 54

Klaw, Marc, 29, 135

Klaw and Erlanger (booking agency), 29, 130

Krehbiel, Henry Edward, 93, 251, 253

Krummel, D. W., 33

Lada, Anton, 195

Lara, Augustin, 206

"Laughing and Crying Blues" (song), 220

"Laughing Song, The" (song), 124, 220

Lawlor, Charles, 214

Lawson, Sherman, 82

Layton, J. Turner, 153, 193, 195–96

"Lazy Moon" (song), 303n.47

Leadbelly. *See* Ledbetter, Huddie

Leake County Revelers, 218, 238

Lebert, Siegmund, 54

Ledbetter, Huddie, 59–60, 62, 238, 241–42, 244–46, 265, 269–72, 300n.32, 321nn.9, 11

Lenberg, Samuel, 182–83

"Let Me Bring My Clothes Back Home" (song), 71

"Let the Rest of the World Go By" (song), 229

Levine, Lawrence, 163–67, 278

Lewis, Furry, 291n.46

Libby, James Aldrich, 27, 136, 302n.45

Light Crust Doughboys, The, 61

Lighthall, Jim, 68

"Light House by the Sea, The" (Davis song), 37

"Lil' Gal" (Dunbar-Johnson song), 142

Lindfors, Bernth, 99

"Lindy" (Cole-Johnson song), 302n.45

Lipscomb, Mance, 63

"Little Brown Jug" (song), 144

"Little Log Cabin in the Lane" (Hays song), 34

"Little Old Log Cabin in the Lane" (Hays' song), 228

McFate, E., 263

McGee, Sam, 64–65

McKee, Margaret, 293n.85

McMichen, Clayton, 213, 234

McPherson, Richard C. *See* Mack, Cecil

McTell, Blind Willie, 79–80, 227

McVeigh, John, 136, 302n.45

medicine shows: impact of recording technology on, 165–67; performance economics and, 68–71, 291nn.46, 49, 292n.55

"Medley of Country Dances" (record), 144

Meeker, Edward, 137, 303n.47

Melville, Rose, 143

"Memphis Blues" (song), 148–51, 254, 304n.69, 305n.71

Memphis Jug Band, 219

Mendoza, Lydia, 63–64, 209–10

Meredith, James, 275

"Merry Farmer Boy" (song), 147

Merwin, Henry Childs, 101–2

"Mexico" (Cole-Johnson song), 303n.47

Middleton, Howard Taylor. *See* Taylor, Howard

Middleton, Richard, 279–81

Middleton, Scott, 219

Miller, Emmett, 234

Miller, O. S., 266

Mills, Kerry, 230

"Miner's Blues" (song), 83–84

minstrelsy: advertising imagery using, 207–14, 315n.55; African American performances of, 4–6, 23–24, 30–36, 130–42, 195–97; *Black America* and, 97–101; blues music and, 151–52, 193–96, 225; commercial expansion of popular music through, 27, 287n.29; Dvořák's support of, 109; emergence of, 4–6, 34; by European immigrant performers, 140, 303n.54; folk music and, 9–11, 19–20, 152, 242, 248–53; folkoric paradigm and, 107–8, 242–43, 258–65; hillbilly music and, 142–47; marketing using, 207–8, 315n.55; mixed-race audiences for, 31–34; political and racial implications of, 34–35; in patent medicine shows, 69–71; popularity in New York of, 123–29, 215; race records and images of, 224–27; racial stereotypes based on, 34–35, 105–8, 141–42; white musicians' performance in, 124–29, 140–42, 233; yodeling and, 239

Mississippi Possum Hunters (band), 212

Mississippi Sheiks (band), 222, 238

Moanfeldt, Samuel, 274

Moffat, Adelene, 103

Montgomery, Little Brother, 227

Mooney, James, 102

Morgan, Lewis Henry, 94

Morris, Edward H., 131

mountain life and culture: folklorist interpretations of, 102–5; minstrelsy and music in, 142–47; old-time music marketing and, 208–14; recording technology and, 165–67

Moynihan, Daniel Patrick, 13

"Mr. Coon You're All Right in Your Place" (song), 130–31, 139

Mseleku, William, 238

Murfree, Mary Noailles, 102

Murray, Billy, 125, 137, 210, 216, 303n.47

musical training: cultural role of, 54–57; musicians' efforts to gain, 58–61

Music Publishers Protective Association (MPPA), 274

Myers, J. W., 125, 322n.15

"My Gal Is a High Born Lady" (song), 124–25

"My Mammy" (song), 196

"Paradise Blues" (song), 153

Paramount Records, 204, 207, 221, 225–26, 231, 239

Paredes, Américo, 14

Park, Robert E., 251–52

Parker, Haywood, 103

Parker, "Knocky," 61, 82, 300n.26

Parks, William, 215

Patton, Charley, 197, 227

Peabody, Charles, 23–24, 42, 49–50, 71

Peer, Ralph, 220, 312n.4, 314n.35, 320n.51; copyright and royalty issues and, 235–40, 263; "Crazy Blues" recording and, 192; creation of race and hillbilly categories by, 198, 211; Fiddlin' John Carson recordings and, 200–202; Mexican music scouted by, 205–6; popular music lamented by, 1–4, 18, 24

Peerless Trio, The (band), 144

Pené, Xavier, 100

Perrow, E. C., 104–5, 253

Person, Alice, 39–41

philology, 19, 89–91, 94

phonograph: early technology of, 157–59; impact on local music of, 165–67; influence on southern music of, 3; international exposure of, 167–68. *See also* phonograph industry

phonograph industry: African American artists and, 19–21, 124, 300n.7; blues music and, 151; commercial negotiations by southern artists with, 267–74; coon songs and evolution of, 124–29; copyrights and royalty costs of, 235–40; cultural uplift campaign of, 159–67, 307n.19; first-contact narratives as promotional tool for, 167–80; hillbilly music and, 143–47; international expansion of, 157–58; native southern singers, campaign for, 197–206; old-time records produced by,

187–88; race records by, 187–88, 190–97; sales statistics for, 158, 306n.4; southern musicians' dealings with, 235–40; Southern recording sessions by, 197; white performers–African American composers collaboration and, 136–42, 302n.45

phrenology, 163

piano: economic and cultural importance of, 37–38, 54–57

"Play that Barbershop Chord" (song), 190

Plessy v. Ferguson, 2, 36

"polite vaudeville," 135

Polk, Inc., 201

polygenist theory, in anthropology, 296n.27

Poole, Charlie, 214, 219, 229–31

popular (commercial) music: African American music and, 23–25; authenticity of, 278–82; black prisoners' love for, 262–65; blues as, 233–40, 253–57; coon songs' and, 45–50; coon songs as segment of, 45–50; copyright and royalty costs for, 235–40; cultural uplift campaign and, 159–67; folklorists' view of, 98–99, 241–53; folk music and, 8–9; globalization of recording industry and, 157–59, 184–86; local music as, 179–80; Lomax's *Cowboy Songs* and, 117–18; Lomax's cowboy studies and influence of, 86–87; piano sales increases and, 38–41; race and old-time records and, 187–214, 218–29; southern culture and, 3–4, 7, 25–34, 242–45; southern musicians' participation in, 122–55; white southern artists' recordings of, 227–40. *See also* commercial expansion of popular music

Porter, S., 174

Potter, David, 8

Pound, Louise, 117–18

Powell, J. W., 106

"Prepossessing Little Maid, A" (song), 302n.45

primitivism: blues music and, 148–55; folklorists embrace of, 94–98, 100–105, 261–65; globalization of phonograph industry and rhetoric of, 167–80; in hillbilly music, 144–47; in Lomax's *Cowboy Songs*, 118; southern music and concepts of, 55–57. *See also* folkloric paradigm; isolation paradigm

Primrose and West Minstrels, 27, 36

"Prisoner Song, The," 232–33

prison songs, 260–65

Proctor, Jenny, 12

professionalism: of southern musicians, 52–54, 56–57, 70–71, 74–84, 267–68; in folklore studies, 88–97

Prosser, Rees, 35–36

Puckett, Riley, 63, 202, 213, 229–31, 233–34

Pure Food and Drug Law, 68

Putman, Frederic, 99–100

Queen, John, 24, 46–47

Rabbit Foot Minstrels, 254

race records: advertising and marketing of, 206–14, 224–27, 232–33, 235; blues music and, 255–57; emergence of, 184, 187–214; international marketing and, 198–206; interracial music culture and, 217–27, 233–40

racial difference: civil rights politics and, 11; coon songs' expression of, 41–50, 127–42; folkloric paradigm and, 241–47, 261–65; folk music and, 275–82; foreign music sales and U.S.

and, 181–83; globalization of recording industry and images of, 168–80; language and, 88–90; minstrelsy and paradigm of, 34–35, 105–8, 141–42, 242–45; old-time music categorization and, 216–17; recording industry's cultural uplift campaign and, 159–67; research on, 12; southern music and, 2–4. 24

radio, impact on recording industry of, 205, 315n.51

ragtime, 13, 41, 45–46, 133, 218–19, 239, 250–53

"Railroad Blues, The" (song), 253–54

"Railroadin' Some" (song), 51–53

railroad, expansion, 25–34

Rainey, Ma, 226

Rainier Family, 239

"Rastus Johnson Brown" (song), 44–45

Reaves White Country Ramblers (band), 219

recording industry. *See* phonograph industry

Rector, John, 211

Red Moon, The (stage show), 139

Reneau, George, 202

repertoire, methodological focus on, 14–16

Richardson, Carrie, 268

Richardson, Don, 144

Roberts, Bob, 136–37, 302n.45, 303n.47

Roberts, Fiddlin' Doc, 230

Roberts, John, 46

Robertson, Eck, 202

Robeson, Paul, 223

Robison, Carson G., 273

"Rock-a-Bye Your Baby with a Dixie Melody" (song), 196

Rodgers, Jimmie, 57, 205, 209, 219, 234, 237–40, 245–46, 291n.46, 320n.51, 321n.57, 321n.11

Rogers, Alex, 302n.45, 303n.47

Roosevelt, Franklin Delano, 273

Roosevelt, Theodore, 85–86

Root, George Frederick, 322n.15

Ross, Andrew, 278–79

royalty issues: folk music and, 241–42, 273–74; southern recording artists and, 222, 235–40. See also copyright issues

Ruby, Harry, 140

"Rumblin' and Ramblin' Boa Constrictor Blues" (song), 208

rural communities: impact of recording industry on, 165–67, 184–86; marketing to, 198–99; minstrelsy and music of, 142–47. See also southern identity and culture

Russell, Tony, 12, 284n.23

"St. Louis Blues" (Handy song), 148, 151, 153, 254

Sales, Doc, 120

"Salty Dog Blues" (song), 226

"Sambo and Dinah" (song), 132–34, 139, 302n.45

Sam T. Jack Creole Show, 130

Sanders, Wallis, 266

Sause, Edmond, 157–59, 180, 184

"Scaddle-De-Mooch" (song), 137

Scarborough, Dorothy: on blues music, 256–60; criticism of research by, 246–48; folk music research by, 1–4; nostalgia expressed by, 264; popular music disparaged by, 18, 24, 210; research interviews recalled by, 267–68

"Scene in a Country Store" (recording), 145

segregation: advertising and marketing to African Americans and, 206–7; biological basis alleged for, 110–11;

coon songs' critique of, 45–50, 130–42; cultural uplift campaign and, 163–67; folklorists and, 110–12, 118–19, 257–65, 275–82; influence on Southern music of, 2–3, 7–9; music as escape from, 280–82; in New York music industry, 123–55; performances by African American musicians and, 78–84; of public performance spaces, 31–34, 287n.23; race records and enforcement of, 217–27; racial categorization of music and, 218–27; on railroad cars, 36–37; in recording industry, 190–95; southern music and, 2–3, 8–9, 54, 66–84; touring theater companies and, 31–34

Selkia, Madame, 31–32

sentimental ballad: evolution and commercial success of, 34–41, 187, southern musicians' recordings of, 229

"separate but equal" doctrine, 2, 36

Seroff, Doug, 239

sexuality: in African American music, 79; in blues music, 151–52; coon songs and coon shouters expression of, 125–28, 139–40; interracial love in African American productions and, 139–40

Shade, Will, 219

"Shanty Blues" (song), 71

Sharp, Cecil, 154

sheet music publishing: African American musicians' success in, 132–42; piano sales increases and, 38–41; popularity of, 26–34; southern musicians' awareness of, 267–74. See also commercial expansion of popular music, Tin Pan Alley

Shepard, Burt, 124

"Shew! Fly, Don't Bother Me" (song), 145

Shines, Johnny, 1–2, 227, 238

white southern musicians (*continued*)
hillbilly-minstrel common culture
and, 142–47, 243–45; old-time rec-
ords by, 187–216; in local perfor-
mance, 61–71; popular music
recorded by, 227–40
Whitney, Annie, 27
Whitter, Henry, 202, 210, 218, 232–33,
236
"Who Do You Love" (song), 136
Williams, Bert, 45, 123, 136–38, 190, 194,
302n.45
Williams, J. Mayo, 221, 235
Williams, Joe, 70–71, 291n.46
Williams, Nathaniel D., 66
Williams, Spencer, 153, 193, 195
Wills, Nat, 302n.45
Windom, William, 27, 36
Winslow, Max, 137
Wolfe, Charles, 72, 227–28, 233, 249
women musicians and performers:
blues music and, 151–53; coon shout-
ing by, 125–29; amateur piano playing
by, 37–41

work songs, 56–58, 82–84, 262
Works Progress Administration (wpa),
268
"Wreck of the Southern Old 97" or
"The Wreck of the Old 97" (song),
232–33, 320n.53
Wright, Louis, 32–33
Wynn, Wylma, 136, 302n.45

Yellen, Jack, 231
yodeling, 234, 245–46, 237–40, 321n.11
"Yodeling Blues" (song), 238
"Yodeling Fiddling Blues" (song), 238
"You Ain't Talkin' to Me"(song), 229
"You Can't Keep a Good Man Down"
(song), 191
Young, Joe, 196, 209
"You're as Welcome as the Flowers in
May" (song), 230
"You're in the Right Church, but the
Wrong Pew" (song), 136

Ziegfeld, Florenz, 125, 135

Karl Hagstrom Miller is an assistant professor at the University of Texas, Austin, where he teaches courses in history and musicology.

Library of Congress Cataloging-in-Publication Data
Miller, Karl Hagstrom, 1968–
Segregating sound : inventing folk and pop music in the age of Jim Crow /
Karl Hagstrom Miller.
p. cm.—(Refiguring American music)
Includes bibliographical references and index.
ISBN 978-0-8223-4689-0 (cloth : alk. paper)
ISBN 978-0-8223-4700-2 (pbk. : alk. paper)
1. Music and race—Southern States—History—19th century. 2. Music and race—Southern States—History—20th century. 3. Folk music—Southern States—History—19th century. 4. Folk music—Southern States—History—20th century. 5. Popular music—Southern States—History—19th century. 6. Popular music—Southern States—History—20th century. 7. African Americans—Segregation. I. Title. II. Series: Refiguring American music.
ML3551.H198 2010
781.64089'00973—dc22   2009019108